Chile: the Carretera Austral

A guide to one of the v
most scenic road trips

D0770083

the Bradt Travel Guide

Hugh Sinclair
Warren Houlbrooke

edition
I

www.bradtguides.com

Bradt Travel Guides Ltd, UK
The Globe Pequot Press Inc, USA

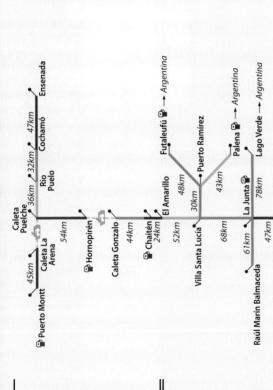

Bradt

KEY

Paved road
Gravel road
Poor gravel road
Non-vehicular access
Entry/exit points
(page 28)

**NORTHERN
SECTION**
map, page 62

**CLASSIC
SECTION**

Puerto Montt

45km

Caleta La
Arena

**Caleta
Puelche**

54km

Hornopirén

44km

Caleta Gonzalo

36km

Río
Puelo

32km

Cochamó

47km

Ensenada

Chaitén

24km

El Amarillo

Futaleufú ⟶ *Argentina*

52km

48km

Villa Santa Lucía

30km

Puerto Ramírez

68km

43km

Palena ⟶ *Argentina*

Raúl Marín Balmaceda

61km

La Junta

78km

Lago Verde ⟶ *Argentina*

47km

Puyuhuapi

56km

Puerto Cisnes

35km

Cisnes Junction
34km

Villa Amengual

45km

106km

Paso Río Frías ⟶ *Argentina*

Mañihuales

12km

70km

25km

Nirehuao

Paso Puesto Viejo ⟶ *Argentina*

Puerto Aysén

57km

76km

14km

63km

45km

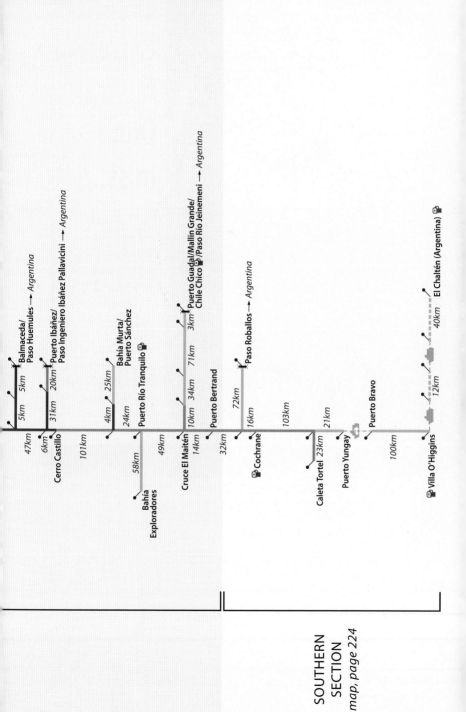

Balmaceda/
Paso Huemules → *Argentina*

Puerto Ibáñez/
Paso Ingeniero Ibáñez Pallavicini → *Argentina*

5km 5km
47km
6km
Cerro Castillo
31km 20km
101km

Bahía Murta/
Puerto Sánchez

Puerto Río Tranquilo

4km 25km
24km

58km
Bahía
Exploradores
49km

Puerto Guadal/Mallín Grande/
Chile Chico /Paso Río Jeinemeni → *Argentina*

Cruce El Maitén
10km 34km 71km
3km
14km

Puerto Bertrand

32km

Paso Roballos → *Argentina*

72km

Cochrane
16km

103km

Caleta Tortel 23km
21km

Puerto Yungay

Puerto Bravo

100km

Villa O'Higgins
12km

El Chaltén (Argentina)
40km

SOUTHERN
SECTION
map, page 224

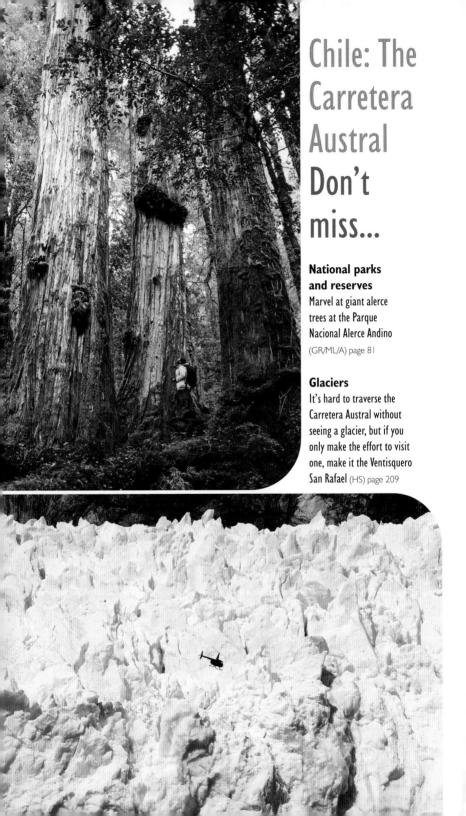

Chile: The Carretera Austral
Don't miss...

National parks and reserves
Marvel at giant alerce trees at the Parque Nacional Alerce Andino
(GR/ML/A) page 81

Glaciers
It's hard to traverse the Carretera Austral without seeing a glacier, but if you only make the effort to visit one, make it the Ventisquero San Rafael (HS) page 209

Trekking

Cerro Castillo is one of the key trekking areas in southern Chile, with options for gentle hikes and challenging climbs (PR/A) pages 198–200

History

The history of the Carretera Austral is fascinating but relatively undocumented – pictured here are the Puyuhuapi pioneers, whose legacy is still visible in the town today (LL) pages 132–6

Caleta Tortel

Meander along wooden boardwalks and visit the mysterious graveyard at this magical car-free village (JH) pages 242–51

above The ferry ride from Hornopirén to Caleta Gonzalo through the Fiordo Comau is a dramatic introduction to what lies in store further south (HS) pages 96–7

left The pretty cemetery of the San Miguel de Aulen chapel, along the coastal road towards Hornopirén (HS) pages 88–9

below The quaint church in Villa Santa Lucía (PP) pages 108–9

above & below **A private initiative pioneered by conservationist Doug Tompkins, Parque Pumalín has two volcanoes and plenty of well-marked waking tails** (HS) and (PaP) pages 107–8

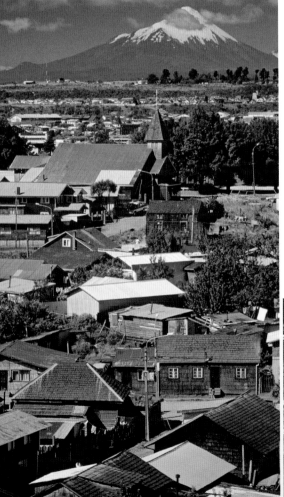

above & left Set between Volcán Osorno and the Reloncaví Sound, Puerto Montt is the last major city before heading south on the Carretera Austral — and it is certainly worth exploring
(IBH/S) and (WB/AWL) pages 63–78

below The characterful suburb of Angelmó, built in the traditional *palafito* style of Chiloé, has a wonderful market with plenty of excellent seafood
(WB/AWL) page 76

AUTHORS

Hugh Sinclair lives in Bariloche (Argentina) with his Dutch wife and two daughters. He is an author, economist, former investment banker, and Chief Operating Officer of Mission Alliance, a Norwegian social-impact fund that owns and manages four microfinance institutions around the world. In 2001 he successfully established the Guinness World Record for the fastest traverse of the Americas (Prudhoe Bay, Alaska to Ushuaia, Argentina) by motorbike, fully sponsored and raising money for UK charity Action  Aid. He has traversed the entire Carretera Austral six times, by car and motorbike, including with a three-year-old child and his heavily pregnant wife.

Warren Houlbrooke is originally from New Zealand, where he worked predominantly in agriculture, both on farms and as a sales rep for international agricultural companies. He has lived in Bariloche for six years with his wife and daughter, working in agriculture, property development and real estate. He has travelled extensively in Latin America, in particular across both Chilean and Argentine Patagonia. Warren is a stand-by tour guide for Compass Motorbike Tours, and has worked with  Bariloche Moto Tours, who also offer trips along the CA. He is a highly proficient motorcyclist, scuba-diver, skier, equestrian, cyclist and sailor. He has traversed the entire Carretera Austral seven times – this is his first book.

PUBLISHER'S FOREWORD · Adrian Phillips, Managing Director

The introduction to this book leaves me thoroughly depressed. Hugh and Warren describe a road that takes in wild rivers and subtropical jungles, a drive beneath soaring condors and looming alerce trees. My commute home this evening past concrete housing blocks and flattened foxes seems even less appealing than usual. But the truth is that any journey would struggle to compete with the Carretera Austral, a road trip with a just claim to being the world's best. And we've the best authors to write about it, a pair who couple enthusiasm for motoring with an appreciation of the beauty and fragility of the environment in this region of the world.

First edition published January 2016

Bradt Travel Guides Ltd
IDC House, The Vale, Chalfont St Peter, Bucks SL9 9RZ, England
www.bradtguides.com
Print edition published in the USA by The Globe Pequot Press Inc,
PO Box 480, Guilford, Connecticut 06437–0480

Text copyright © 2016 Hugh Sinclair & Warren Houlbrooke
Maps copyright © 2016 Bradt Travel Guides Ltd
Photographs copyright © 2016 Individual photographers (see below)
Project Managers: Laura Pidgley & Anna Moores
Cover research: Pepi Bluck, Perfect Picture

ISBN: 978 1 78477 003 7 (print)
e-ISBN: 978 1 78477 143 0 (e-pub)
e-ISBN: 978 1 78477 243 7 (mobi)

British Library Cataloguing in Publication Data
A catalogue record for this book is available from the British Library

Photographs Alamy: Galen Rowell/Mountain Light (GR/ML/A), Pep Roig (PR/A); AWL: Walter Bibicow (WB/AWL); Daniel Martínez Pereira (DMP); Edison Zanatto (EZ); Hugh Sinclair (HS); Luisa Ludwig (LL); Petra Patitucci (PP); Shutterstock: Ammit Jack (AJ/S), Eduardo Rivero (ER/S), Idan Ben Haim (IBH/S), Rich Lindie (RL/S); SuperStock (SS); Warren Houlbrooke (WH)
Front cover Ventisquero Leones (HS)
Back cover Ventisquero San Rafael (HS); Lago General Carrera (HS)
Title page Alerce tiles on the San Nicolas de Tolentino chapel, near La Poza (HS); Lago Bertrand (HS); guanacos (ER/S)
Part openers Page 61: The road from Hornopirén, with Volcán Osorno in the background (HS); Page 111: The road on the Levicán Peninsula, with Lago General Carrera and Cerro Castillo in the background (HS); Page 225: Parque Patagonia (HS)

Maps David McCutcheon FBCart.S; maps include data © OpenStreetMaps contributors (under Open Database License)

Typeset by BBR, Sheffield and Ian Spick, Bradt Travel Guides
Production managed by Jellyfish Print Solutions; printed in Turkey
Digital conversion by www.dataworks.co.in

Foreword

by Douglas Tompkins

The Carretera Austral is perhaps the most spectacular road in the world. If there is another that provides access to nearly 20 national parks (with as many as five new ones in the making), several national reserves, two of the world's largest private parks with full public access (Pumalín and Patagonia), as well as wild and wide open landscapes, soaring mountains, lakes, glaciers, forests and fjords, then I would like to know where it is. Having travelled to many parts of the world, I have yet to find anything comparable. It is nothing short of a wonder.

So, if you are not yet on this Southern Highway 'Route of Parks', then don't hesitate to make plans for a trip that you will remember forever. The landscapes are unrivalled in their beauty, and the people are friendly and will welcome you with open arms. In short, the Carretera Austral is a trip of a lifetime, and although my wife Kris and I have been living in this fantastic place for the last 25 years, we never tire of travelling up and down this magnificent road. It is a guaranteed adventure of scenic beauty.

What you are about to read in the subsequent pages is a guidebook, but of a different calibre than almost any you will find elsewhere. Besides providing practical information, it considers the 'development model' with which Chile, as a country, evolves its economy. The story along this road is familiar – one of human colonisation that is common throughout history across the world. You see, roads are many-edged swords, and if we start with the old adage that 'it is hard to destroy wilderness without roads', we promptly arrive at the grain of the argument. As beautiful and awesome as the Carretera Austral may be, it has been pivotal in human development. Overgrazing, burned forests, mining, and industrial fish farming are all present as a result of the roads built.

Yet saying all that, we are really bemoaning the state of the world: and Chile is just another country caught up in the 'Myth of Progress'. Yet, no matter where we may be from, we are now united in the challenge to reverse this massive environmental crisis in which we find ourselves and the world embroiled. We are now in what is the 6th Mass Extinction Event, the worst environmental crisis in the last 65 million years. Additionally we have, as a civilisation, had a negative impact on the climate as well – what could be worse than that? So, as we traverse the Carretera Austral, let's pause to reflect about these sobering issues, and when we return home begin the work, as socially responsible citizens of the world, to start paying our rent for living on the planet. There is a place for everyone along the long front of environmental and conservation activism to lend a hand in directing humanity towards harmony with nature.

Douglas Tompkins is a conservationist working on the large national park project in Chile and Argentina (see box, pages 104–5).

AUTHOR'S STORY   *Hugh Sinclair*

It always puzzled me why other children forgot to mention South America in geography classes. For as long as I can remember this was the mysterious continent I had to visit. Straight after university I packed my bags and headed south, and never quite left. During a year-long assignment in Mongolia my wife and I discovered we were expecting a baby, and for all the joys of life in Ulaanbaatar, raising a family there did not appeal. Instead of endlessly moving to where work dictated, we opened the map to decide where we wanted to go to start a new chapter in life. One place sprung to mind – Patagonia.

I had motorbiked through Patagonia in 2001 as part of a Guinness World Record expedition to establish the fastest passage through the Americas by motorbike, and we had visited the region numerous times since. But it was not until 2011 that I realised I had not actually visited the true gem of this region. I drove down from Bariloche to Cochrane along the Carreterra Austral and discovered a region of verdant jungle, eye-popping glaciers, stunning lakes, and rivers of colours I did not know existed. Thus began my love affair with the Carretera Austral.

I began to receive endless emails from friends, bikers, backpackers, cyclists, etc, asking for information about this mysterious region. Instead of replying to each, perhaps it would be easier to write a summary to send to people? As I thought about the size of such a summary I realised 'book' was a fairer description, and thus I approached Bradt, who leapt at the chance, and supported the project from a crazy idea to the book you now hold in your hands. Patagonia is now open. Enjoy it, and protect it.

AUTHOR'S STORY   *Warren Houlbrooke*

One of my great passions is to jump on my trusted motorbike and explore the vast Patagonia region. I like to cross the Andes and go on the 4x4 tracks and do the river crossings to discover absolutely pristine lakes and rivers where most don't dare venture. I first explored part of the Carretera Austral in 2010. This spectacular road trip is like a magnet to me, and I have returned multiple times since to further explore this region. I have backpacked through 27 different countries and yet I rate the Carretera Austral as the most spectacular road trip by a wide margin. Where else can you see 1,200km of pristine trout-filled lakes and rivers, rugged snow-capped mountain ranges, glaciers, ice fields, volcanoes, fjords and temperate rainforests? This is truly one of the last great largely unexplored frontiers left on our planet and long may it remain that way for future generations to appreciate.

I met Hugh Sinclair in Bariloche in 2011 and quickly discovered that he also is a motorbike fanatic and shares my passion for the Carretera Austral. One night, over an ale or two in our local, we were discussing our adventures on the Carretera Austral and our frustrations over the lack of quality information available. We both agreed this road trip is worthy of its own dedicated quality guidebook to help promote sustainable tourism, and the idea evolved from there. A year later and I can proudly say that I feel very privileged to be a co-author of the first international guidebook to this region.

Acknowledgements

A special thanks to the staff in the various parks. Their work, often in relative isolation for months at a time, is essential to protect this region, and their patience in answering our endless questions is warmly appreciated. In particular, Carolina Morgado helped us hugely in gathering information for some of the most important parks, and also with proofreading. Eliana Oyarzún in Puerto Montt has been an invaluable support over the years, providing great accommodation, insightful local information, and even helping with ferry bookings. Idanna Pucci's efforts to document the history of the region have been very helpful, and set an example for others to follow. Likewise, Luisa Ludwig was infinitely patient with us as we investigated the history of Puyuhuapi. As descendants of the original settlers to the region it was an honour to be able to speak so extensively with them.

Danka Ivanoff's historical books of the region are some of the definitive texts spanning the pre-settlement through to the current day, and Danka's help in proofreading our Caleta Tortel discussion, as well as spending hours chatting with Hugh, was most informative.

Many guides went beyond the normal 'tour-of-duty' to explain to us such extensive information about the regions they have come to love and know so well. In particular, Pascual Díaz in Puerto Guadal, Christian Bore in Puerto Río Tranquilo, Jonathan Hechenleitner in Raúl Marín Balmaceda, and Manuel and Hugo in Coyhaique. A number of travellers, hitchhikers and explorers became inadvertent members of the team as we explored regions of the Carretera. In particular a special thanks to Charlie Russell for his literary expertise, Lars Langsrud for his unparalleled trekking abilities, and David Sparkman for his advanced trekking suggestions, Oliver Page for his wisdom on ancient mythology and Idi Zveibil for his cultural insights.

We were highly fortunate to be able to drag fellow-Barilochense Randy Clouse along with us for parts of our road trips. Few guidebook writers can enjoy their own dedicated fishing, trekking and beer-drinking expert as part of the team. Randy helped with some of the longer treks, as well as successfully convincing us that drinking exotic local beers in the evenings was 'work-related'.

Kris and Doug Tompkins, as well as many of the staff of Patagonia and Pumalín, have taken time out of their hugely important work to explain so many aspects of the region to us, from how to regenerate overgrazed grassland to the lesser-known habits of puma. They have single-handedly contributed to the conservation of this region to an extent rarely found anywhere on the planet, for the benefit of generations to come. As praiseworthy as their work is, it is also a call for further action, and we urge every visitor to this region to not merely appreciate their contribution, but to learn about what each and every one of us can do. We cannot all be 'Ecobarons', but collectively we can have a profound impact for the good of our fragile world. Also, a big thanks to James Lowen for his help on the natural history section.

Above all, we would like to thank the countless people who shared their stories with us, who told us about the arrival of their ancestors to the region, who opened their houses to us, and who form an integral component in the splendour of this land. Many have fought to overcome the over-grazing and environment damage inflicted in the early years of settlement, and continue to fight to this day to protect the region, with movements such as Patagonia Sin Represas.

SPECIAL THANKS *Hugh Sinclair*

A special thanks to my astonishingly patient wife, Jessica, who accompanied me on one trip down the Carretera while pregnant and with our four-year-old daughter, unwittingly contributing to the *Travelling with children* section! She also put up with my endless absences as I researched unusual lakes and climbed active volcanoes, tolerated my late nights researching Carretera facts, and also helped with some of the history sections.

SPECIAL THANKS *Warren Houlbrooke*

A special thanks to Carina, my wife, and Nina, my daughter, for their patience and understanding in helping Hugh and me make this book possible.

FEEDBACK REQUEST AND UPDATES WEBSITE

We have gone to lengths to confirm the accuracy of data in this book – a serious challenge in a region where bus drivers themselves might not know where they will be in a week's time! Part of the charm of the Carretera Austral is the informality, but this comes at a price, and all we can urge readers is to be patient, plan ahead, and have a few spare days in hand. That said, any factual errors beyond erratic timetables are our own responsibility, and we encourage readers to send any such observations to e info@bradtguides. com. You'll find out before us when a fine new family-run hotel opens or a favourite restaurant changes hands and goes downhill – you can share those experiences with us such that future editions of this book will constantly improve. Updates may be posted to www.bradtupdates.com/schile.

Contents

HOW TO USE THIS GUIDE

QUICK-REFERENCE GUIDE

MAPS

Keys and symbols Maps include alphabetical keys covering the locations of those places to stay, eat or drink that are featured in the book.

Grids and grid references Two maps use gridlines to allow easy location of sites. Map grid references are listed in square brackets after the name of the place or sight of interest in the text, with page number followed by grid number, eg: [103 C3].

AS THE CONDOR FLIES Throughout the guide we have included boxes to indicate where a town is in relation to the start and end points of the Carretera Austral (by the definition of this guide, Puerto Montt in the north and the border crossing at Villa O'Higgins in the south).

LIST OF MAPS

Introduction

'The best road-trip in the world' is an oft-heard claim, but in the case of the Carretera Austral it is well and truly justified. This book describes a road trip through one of the most magnificently scenic and diverse regions on earth. From the subtropical jungles south of Puerto Montt to glaciers of dimensions that defy belief, a new vista emerges with almost every bend along the road. Wild rivers connect the Andes with the Pacific Ocean, carving through the narrow strip of land that forms Chile, pausing only to fill lakes with every shade of blue imaginable. Alerce trees have stood guard over the region for thousands of years, towering high above the Carretera Austral. Wild guanacos serve as traffic lights, pumas are considered a pest, Andean condors glide majestically through the valleys in search of carcasses, and beyond the confines of the road itself evidence of mankind's impact is the exception rather than the rule. And yet within this wilderness it is possible to find excellent accommodation, eat fine food, and interrupt the driving with an ever-expanding range of activities. The Carretera is rapidly gaining recognition for being up there with the finest road trips in the Americas, if not worldwide. That being said, it is a challenging region to visit, and even as additional sections of the road are paved each season, it provides access to a mere sliver of Chile, albeit one that runs the length of an area the size of Greece.

Bruce Chatwin's 1977 book *In Patagonia* and Paul Theroux's 1979 *The Old Patagonian Express* both fired the public's imagination for Patagonia – the end of the earth. However, upon closer inspection we find that much of the literature over the last century has focused on *Argentine* Patagonia. Chilean Patagonia's time has surely come. This expansive region is so unique as to awe even those who have spent substantial time there. Along the Carretera Austral it is possible to see the ice fields behind vast glaciers, which elsewhere show only their snouts. Apart from Antarctica and Greenland, which are hugely expensive to visit and offer limited variety in terms of terrain and the range of activities possible, the Carretera Austral is the only place where travellers can see such ice fields.

The variety of flora and fauna along the Carretera Austral warrants its own encyclopaedia, and this book merely scratches the surface of the wildlife encountered. For those interested in nature and conservation, this stretch of Chile competes with some of the flagship regions of the continent, such as the Amazon and Darién, yet it is surrounded by snow-capped mountains rather than wild, tropical forest.

In addition to its scenic beauty, the stretch of land alongside the Carretera Austral is becoming an adventure activity hub. The trekking and climbing opportunities are already sufficient to keep the most avid hiker busy for multiple seasons. Horseriding, meanwhile, is so commonplace that it is considered a standard form of transport. The kayaking and rafting is world class. Keen to capitalise on the nascent tourism sector, new guides and routes spring up each season. Whenever a new road is blasted, this opens up access to climbs, lakes, mountains, glaciers and usually reaches isolated villages. The entire region is essentially a work in progress.

For those with a little more time, the history of this region is fascinating. The first settlers were true pioneers, building villages in places that even a century later could hardly be described as accessible. Some of these settlers and their ancestors live in the same villages to this day. Alas, their tale is not well documented, so you should make the most of any opportunity to hear it from those who lived it while you still can!

No trip to South America is complete without visiting Patagonia, and no trip to Patagonia is complete without traversing the Carretera Austral. Northern Patagonia is a well-established and increasingly developed tourist destination – for better or worse. Southern Patagonia, less so. Regions such as Ushuaia, El Chaltén and Calafate in Argentina, and Torres del Paine and Punta Arenas in Chile, are popular destinations in the extreme south. The Carretera Austral forms a natural bridge between the two, and a route that is far more interesting than a 2-hour flight or a 50-hour bus ride across the arid Argentine steppe.

The main challenge facing visitors to the Carretera Austral is simply the lack of information. Tourism is in its infancy here. Many villages are isolated and lack internet access, while cellphone coverage renders communication with the outside world more limited than in other regions of South America. Natural obstacles, most obviously volcanic eruptions, occasional floods, landslides, fallen trees, relentless rain and highly changeable weather require a greater degree of flexibility among residents and visitors alike. Plan ahead as much as possible, especially ferries and accommodation in peak season, and always have a back-up plan when travelling the Carretera.

The Carretera Austral is magical partly as a consequence of its isolation and lack of outside influences. But times are changing, and any trip along this route throws into sharp relief the tensions between the fast-paced, growing tourism industry and the local culture. The original settlers are being rapidly replaced by a younger generation, who have access to airplanes and internet and television. Migration to the region, from abroad and within Chile, is fundamentally altering the social fabric and culture of the area. Whether this will be to the long-term benefit or harm of the region and its local communities remains to be seen.

The region is changing so rapidly that even from one summer to the next the transformation is visible to the untrained eye. Castro (Chiloé) has a new airport, as does Chaitén in the northern section of the Carretera. Protected by extensive national parks and natural barriers, and indeed its very location at the tip of the continent, the Carretera Austral has thus far been somewhat shielded from the trappings of economic development. Chatwin wrote of Patagonia, 'It is the farthest place to which man walked from his place of origins. It is therefore a symbol of his restlessness.' That restlessness is reflected in the curiosity, the desire for adventure and the eagerness to get off the beaten track of visitors exploring the Carretera Austral. But let's not forget Jan Lundberg's warning: 'It's hard to destroy wilderness without roads'. Visitors to this region have a responsibility to preserve it.

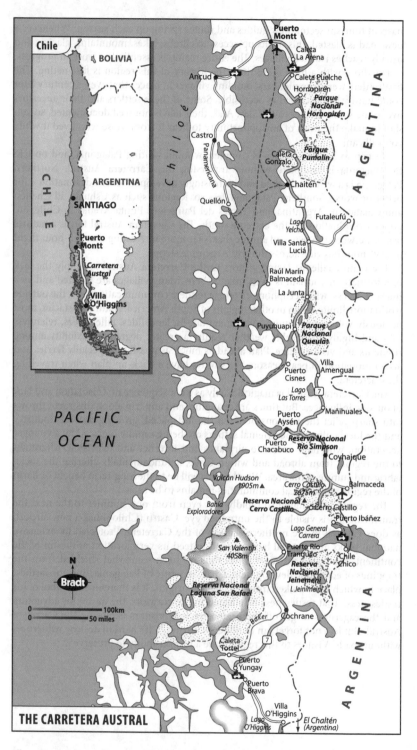

THE CARRETERA AUSTRAL

Part One

GENERAL INFORMATION

CHILE AT A GLANCE

Location The Carretera Austral stretches 1,270km through Southern Chile, from Puerto Montt in the north to Villa O'Higgins in the south. Chile is located in the southwest of South America.

Size The total area covered by the region, provinces and communes encompassed by the Carretera Austral is 128,000km^2. The total surface area of Chile is 756,000km^2.

Climate Spanning 38° of latitude it is hard to generalise about the climate of Chile. Along the Carretera Austral the climate is mostly temperate oceanic to sub-Polar oceanic, with sections of semi-arid (Patagonian steppe, along the border with Argentina).

Time Chile Standard Time (GMT – 3 hours) – no daylight saving time since 2015

International telephone code +56

Currency Chilean pesos ($), US$/ARG$ denotes United States dollars/ Argentine pesos where appropriate

Electricity 220–240V (50Hz AC), European two-pin plugs

Exchange rate £1 = $1,069, US$1 = $703, €1 = $755 (November 2015)

Population Within region encompassed by the Carretera Austral: 115,000. Chile: 18 million.

Capital Aysén's capital is Coyhaique; Chile's is Santiago de Chile

Language Spanish

Religion Roman Catholic (60%), Protestant (15%), agnostic/atheists (22%), other (3%)

Flag Plain red lower half, upper half has white section to right, white star on blue background to left

Economy Mining (driven largely by copper), agriculture (including salmon, forestry and wine) and services (finance and tourism)

SEND US YOUR SNAPS!

We'd love to follow your adventures using our *Chile: the Carretera Austral* guide – why not send us your photos and stories via Twitter (@BradtGuides) and Instagram (@bradtguides) using the hashtag #schile. Alternatively, you can upload your photos directly to the gallery on the Carretera Austral destination page via our website (*www.bradtguides.com*).

1

Background Information

GEOGRAPHY

The Carretera Austral, Chile's Ruta 7, stretches for over 1,270km through rural Patagonia in southern Chile, from Puerto Montt in the north to Villa O'Higgins in the south. It encompasses an area of 128,000km^2 – about the size of Greece, or the US state of Mississippi – and covers a wide range of geographical features including ice fields, rainforest, high snow-capped mountain ranges, hissing volcanoes, arid steppe and pristine rivers and lakes.

Covering a coastal strip between the Pacific Ocean to the west and the southern Andes Mountains to the east, the Valdivian temperate rainforest extends from Villarrica, north of the Carretera Austral, down to Parque Nacional Queulat, Puerto Cisnes and south (and further west) beyond Coyhaique, as far as Caleta Tortel and the Reserva Nacional Katalalixar, where the Magellanic sub-polar forest begins. Further to the west of the Carretera Austral the rainforest spreads from the Reserva Nacional Guaitecas, part of the Chonos archipelago, south of the island of Chiloé, to islands west of the Northern Ice Field in the Parque Nacional Laguna San Rafael. These islands are largely inaccessible and uninhabited.

The region also contains the entire Northern Ice Field, as well as the northernmost 100km or so of the Southern Ice Field. To the east lie the Andes and the border with Argentina. Here, relatively high mountain ranges, with border crossings typically located at historic passes, give way to desert-like areas south of Lago Verde, particularly on the border east of Coyhaique, along the road towards Paso Río Frias-Apeleg, and to the east of Reserva Nacional Jeinemeni, which straddles the Patagonian steppe. Chile is divided into **15 regions**. Each region is divided into provinces, and each province into communes. The Carretera Austral traverses Aysén del General Carlos Ibáñez del Campo (abbreviated to Aysén, Region XI), and parts of Los Lagos, Region X. Depending on the precise definition used, the most southern extremity of the Carretera Austral is at the border between Aysén and Magallanes y La Antártica Chilena (known as Magallanes), Region XII. To define the area around the Carretera Austral more precisely, and assuming that Puerto Montt is *not* included in the definition of the Carretera Austral (see box, page 4), it includes three components: the entire **region of Aysén**, plus the **province of Palena** (one of the four provinces of Los Lagos, consisting of four communes: Chaitén, Futaleufú, Hualaihué and Palena), and the single **commune of Cochamó** (one of two communes in the province of Llanquihue, itself one of the four provinces of Region X).

This latter addition is debatable – the traditional definition of the Carretera Austral may not include Cochamó, and the official Ruta 7 does not traverse the south of the Reloncaví Estuary but heads directly north to Puerto Montt. However,

3

due to the importance of Cochamó as a key entry point to the Carretera, and with respect to the residents of this commune who refer to their main road as 'the Northern Carretera Austral', it shall be included in our definition of the territory. Prior to the ferry connection between Caleta Puelche and Caleta La Arena this was the only access point to the Carretera.

Most definitions of Patagonia include the regions of Aysén and Magallanes, as well as the province of Palena. The commune of Cochamó is therefore the only region considered (by the authors) as part of the Carretera Austral to lie outside the formal definition of Patagonia.

Aysén is divided into the following provinces and communes:
- Aysén (capital: Puerto Aysén; communes: Aysén, Guaitecas and Cisnes)
- Capitan Prat (capital: Cochrane; communes: Cochrane, O'Higgins and Tortel)
- Coyhaique (capital: Coyhaique, also regional capital; communes: Coyhaique and Lago Verde)
- General Carrera (capital: Chile Chico; communes: Chile Chico and Río Ibáñez)

The entire **population** of these three combined areas is approximately 115,000 according to the 2012 census.

The inhabitants of the Carretera Austral represent a mere 0.6% of the total population of Chile (approximately 18m), and yet the area covers 17% of the surface area of the country. Indeed, the population of the Carretera Austral is slightly under one person/km2, on a par with Alaska (across Chile as a whole, the average population density is 22 people/km2). In terms of global rankings, only Svalbard, Greenland and the Falkland Islands have lower population densities. Mongolia is approximately twice as densely populated as the Carretera Austral.

Of the 128,000km^2 encompassing the region, approximately 87,000km^2 is protected, ie: just over two-thirds. Of the remaining third, much of it is uninhabitable thanks to mountains, swamps, lakes, etc, and large parts of non-protected territory is dedicated to farming. Thus, although this population density appears astonishingly low, the reality is that only a slither of the Carretera Austral is actually inhabitable.

According to the definition used in this book the Carretera Austral stretches from 41°30'S at Puerto Montt and Cochamó to 49°00'S at Candelario Mancilla, just south of Villa O'Higgins. The **most easterly point** is Paso Río Frias-Apeleg, which is 71°06'W. The most westerly accessible point is either Bahía Exploradores or Caleta Tortel, at 73°30'W. However, the **most westerly point** of mainland Chile is within the province of Aysén, although not easily accessible: the Taitao Peninsula is 75°39'W, at approximately the same latitude as Puerto Río Tranquilo.

CLIMATE

The Carretera Austral has four distinct seasons. The **summer** begins in December and extends into March, although January and February are the most popular months to visit, coinciding with Chilean school holidays. Temperatures exceed 20°C in summer, and very rarely 30°C. The **winter** extends from June to September, and temperatures routinely fall below freezing. The lowest recorded temperature in Coyhaique is −15°C. **Rainfall** is abundant across most of this region, with the wettest months generally being April to August, particularly on the western coast. Puerto Cisnes and Puyuhuapi receive inordinate amounts of rain, contributing in part to the lush vegetation of the region. However, there is no month in the year where a waterproof jacket is not useful. Southern Chile is one of the rainiest regions on the planet. Annual rainfall in Puerto Cisnes, often considered one of the wettest regions, can reach 4,000mm compared with a mere 600mm/year in London. The driest month of the year in Puerto Cisnes, February, typically receives 120mm of rain, raining every other day.

As a general rule, rainfall is lowest in February, and further to the east: Lago Verde receives an average of only 6mm of rain (three days of rain), Coyhaique perhaps double this, and Futaleufú 42mm (five days of rain). Snowfall is actually limited in the region. The 2014 ski season was a disaster due to lack of snow.

See the *When to visit* section (page 22) for more information.

NATURAL HISTORY AND CONSERVATION

FLORA AND FAUNA ALONG THE CARRETERA AUSTRAL   with James Lowen

Chilean poet Pablo Neruda once argued that 'who doesn't know the Chilean forest, doesn't know the planet'. In traversing a vast swathe of Chile dominated by wooded eco-regions, the Carretera Austral offers visitors the opportunity to gain insights into planet earth.

Much of the region lies in the floristic zone known as **Magellanic rainforest**. This comprises boggy forest dominated by evergreen broadleaf trees. Between Puerto Montt and Ventisquero San Rafael, the evergreen **Siempreverde forest** is common and contains tracts of cypress trees. East of the Carretera towards the national border lie **forests of the Patagonian Andes**. There are broadleaf trees and conifers here too, but also dwarf shrubs at the treeline. In a few areas are areas of **Patagonian steppe**, where chilly plains are dominated by grasses and stunted shrubs.

Even without deviating from the Carretera, you should see a modicum of the commoner and larger wildlife, particularly birds. But to respond properly to

Neruda's encouragement, detours are advisable, mainly to protected areas scattered off-route. Helpfully for the non-expert, printed materials provided at the reserve entrances generally list the site wildlife.

In Los Lagos (Region X), try Parque Nacional Alerce Andino (a rugged montane, wooded wilderness) and Parque Pumalín (established by conservationist Doug Tompkins, where pristine forests nudge Andean glaciers). In Aysén (Region XI), key national parks and reserves include: Queulat (montane forest), Río Simpson (evergreen and deciduous forest), Lago Jeinemeni (Patagonian steppe and deciduous forest), Lago Cochrane (lakeside forest), Laguna San Rafael (fjords, snowfields and mountains) and Bernardo O'Higgins (fjords, rainforests and glaciers).

Three introductory thoughts about Carretera flora and fauna. First, bear in mind that some species are unique to the region, and one conservation concern is that undiscovered species may be eradicated before they have been documented – a result of deforestation, water contamination and global warming. Second, vast sections of the region have barely been explored. There has been minimal underwater research, and some regions are barely accessible. It is possible that an entirely new species could be discovered at any bend in the road! Third, enjoy. For naturalists, travelling the Carretera Austral is an opportunity to observe wildlife that may be unique to this region, and even if the amateur cannot name the genus of the Andean condor, it is impressive when one flies overhead. Take decent boots, a pair of good binoculars, and plenty of patience. Pablo Neruda would be proud.

Land mammals Native Chilean mammals tend to be difficult to see, a legacy of nocturnal habits, scarcity and hunting-induced timidity. The Carretera's most iconic mammal is **huemul** (*Hippocamelus bisulcus*), a globally threatened Andean deer. Just 2,000 remain overall (some in Argentina), most in the region's protected areas. Your best chance of seeing it is to join a guided trek at Lago Cochrane or Reserva Nacional Tamango. You would need even greater luck to see **pudú** (*Pudu pudu*), a dwarf deer that lurks in dense forests. One of South America's four camelids, **guanaco** (*Lama guanicoe*), is a leggy, elegant inhabitant of steppe plains including those at Lago Jeinemeni or Cerro Castillo national reserves.

Two omnivorous canids occur: **South American grey fox** (*Lycalopex griseus*) and the larger, scarcer **culpeo** (*L. culpaeus*). You could bump into either anywhere, as their habitat preferences range from arid plains to montane forests. Two felines at opposite ends of the size spectrum are only occasionally observed. **Puma** (*Felis concolor*) is widespread but rare, while the tiny, arboreal **kodkod** (*Leopardus guigna*) skulks in bamboo thickets. Two species of **hog-nosed skunk** (*Conepatus* spp.) and **lesser grison** (*Galictis cuja*) – black, white and/or grey relatives of the weasel – inhabit open or lightly wooded terrain.

Rodents scrape into double figures, and come in many forms. The largest and easiest to see is **coypu** (*Myocastor coypus*), a beaver-like animal that munches aquatic vegetation. The most striking rodent is the rabbit-like mountain **viscacha** (*Lagidium viscacia*), which inhabits rocky uplands. Should a bubbling call emanate from under your feet, it will be a **Magellanic tuco-tuco** (*Ctenomys magellanicus*), a toothy burrowing rodent of Patagonian steppes. A clear sign of their presence is holes surrounded by recently excavated soil. Two further subterranean mammals of open grasslands are big hairy **armadillo** (*Chaetophractus villosus*) and its smaller relative, the **pichi** (*Zaedyus pichiy*).

Finally, introduced mammals include **red deer** (*Cervus elephus*), **American mink** (*Neovison vison*), **European rabbit** (*Oryctolagus cuniculus*), **brown hare** (*Lepus europaeus*) and **wild boar** (*Sus scrofa*).

Marine mammals Only the northernmost section of the Carretera Austral winds around coastal waters, so you will need to maximise opportunities for seeing marine mammals or make a dedicated detour – for example, to Chiloé, where **blue whale** (*Balaenoptera musculus*) breeds from February to April. Closer to the Carretera, your best chance of seeing cetaceans is to take a ferry within Parque Pumalín, where **Peale's dolphin** (*Lagenorhynchus australis*) has been recorded.

South American sea lion (*Otaria flavescens*) and **South American fur seal** (*Arctocephalus australis*) both occur in Bernardo O'Higgins, although seeing them probably involves a boat trip along the Canal Baker. To distinguish the superficially similar duo, look for the latter's long pointed snout. Both sea lions and fur seals belong to the Otariidae (eared seals) and are descended from a bear-like animal – as oppose to members of the Phocidae (true seals), whose ancestors were otter-like carnivores. Talking of which… there are **marine otters** (*Lutra felina*) at Bernardo O'Higgins as well as at Laguna San Rafael (which, along with Queulat, also hosts southern sea lion). Do not assume that every otter swimming in salty water is marine otter, however, as **southern river otter** (*L. provocax*) also occurs along rocky coastal shores.

Birds Of all wildlife along and around the Carretera Austral, birds are the easiest to spot. Each habitat – forest, wetland or coast – has its own distinctive suite of species. Fortunately for the novice birdwatcher, there are not too many types to try to recognise. Propitiously for the expert, several are sought-after species whose world range is concentrated on southern South America. So there's something for everyone.

Wetland birds tend to be easy to find – and identify. On freshwater lakes, look for three attractive species of **grebe**: white-tufted (*Rollandia rolland*), silvery (*Podiceps occipatilis*) and great (*P. major*). Common ducks on waterbodies include **speckled teal** (*Anas flavirostris*), **Chiloé wigeon** (*A. sibilatrix*) and **Andean duck** (*Oxyura ferruginea*), the last with its distinctive electric-blue bill and cocked tail. Two species of **steamerduck** occur: flightless (*Tachyeres pteneres*) exclusively on rocky coasts and flying (*T. patachonicus*) on both fresh and marine waters.

Larger, more elegant wildfowl comprise **coscoroba** (*Coscoroba coscoroba*) and **black-necked swans** (*Cygnus melancoryphus*). The former has a rosy, plastic-looking bill, whilst the last has knobbly red caruncles adjoining its black bill. On damp fields, **black-faced ibis** (*Theristicus melanopis*) deploys its long decurved bill to rootle for insects in the soil alongside **ashy-headed** (*Chloephaga poliocephala*) and **upland geese** (*C. picta*). Nearby may be southern lapwings (*Vanellus chilensis*), a noisy, strikingly patterned and ubiquitous wader that often hangs out in trios during the breeding season. In boggy moorlands in particular, look for two small birds bobbing around: **dark-bellied** (*Cinclodes patagonicus*) and **bar-winged cinclodes** (*C. fuscus*).

Birds of prey vary in size from the titchy **American kestrel** (*Falco sparverius*) to the massive **Andean condor** (*Vultur gryphus*). Both are easy to recognise: the former hovers readily whilst the condor has enormously long, evenly broad wings that end in 'fingered' tips. Common **raptors** in between these two size extremes are southern caracara (*Caracara plancus*), chimango caracara (*Milvago chimango*), variable hawk (*Buteo polysoma*) and turkey vulture (*Cathartes aura*), whilst cinereous harriers (*Circus cinereus*) ghost gracefully over marshy grasslands.

If you visit rocky coastlines, look for four species of **cormorant**, each with distinctively coloured areas of bare facial skin: red-legged (*Phalacrocorax gaimardi*), Magellan (*P. magellanicus*), guanay (*P. bougainvillii*) and imperial (*P. atriceps*). If you see a cormorant away from the coast, it will be a fifth species: Neotropic (*P. brasilianus*). Along the coast look also for **kelp gull** (*Larus dominicanus*) and the attractive **dolphin gull** (*L. scoresbii*). Should your vista include fjords or open sea at any point, perhaps in Bernardo O'Higgins, you may chance upon maritime wanderers such as **black-browed albatross** (*Thalassarche melanophrys*), **Chilean skua** (*Stercorarius chilensis*) or **Magellanic penguin** (*Spheniscus magellanicus*).

Keen birdwatchers may want to spend time tracking down avian specialities in the Magellanic forests. Fine sites include Alerce Andino, Pumalín and San Rafael. Several species are easier to hear than see, so either patience or luck is essential to get views. Tapaculos are particularly notorious for their skulking nature. **Chucao tapaculo** (*Scelorchilus rubecula*) and **black-throated huet-huet** (*Pteroptochus albicollis*) are both ventriloquists with a musical chuckle. When seen well, the former's red face and breast are uncannily reminiscent of a robin! Surprisingly tricky to locate, given its large size and bold coloration, is the **Magellanic woodpecker** (*Campephilus magellanicus*). Once located, however, these can be confiding birds. The same is true of **austral pygmy-owl** (*Glaucidium nanum*), which is usually heard before being spotted.

Forest residents that are somewhat easier to see include **striped woodpecker** (*Picoides lignarius*) and **Patagonian sierra-finch** (*Phrygilus patagonicus*). The **thorn-tailed rayadito** (*Aphrastura spinicauda*) is a smart treecreeper-like bird with a spiky tail, often seen hanging upside-down. Always heading upwards is the **white-throated treerunner** (*Pygarrhichas albogularis*). Other forest residents are the world's southernmost hummingbird, **green-backed firecrown** (*Sephanoides sephanoides*) and parrot, **austral parakeet** (*Enicognathus ferrugineus*).

While woodpeckers are traditionally associated with trees, **Chilean flickers** (*Colaptes pitius*) feed on the ground in sparsely wooded countryside. Other birds of open habitats include **austral thrush** (*Turdus falcklandii*), **southern house wren** (*Troglodytes musculus*), **austral blackbird** (*Curaeus curaeus*), **fire-eyed diucon** (*Xolmis pyrope*) and **black-chinned siskin** (*Carduelis barbatus*). A personal favourite is **tufted tit-tyrant** (*Anairetes parulus*), with its punky crest and staring eye, whilst one bird that is hard to miss is **rufous-collared sparrow** (*Zonotrichia capensis*).

Reptiles and amphibians
About 15 species of reptile occur either side of the Carretera. Two-thirds are Neotropical ground **lizards** occupying the genus *Liolaemus*. These are typically 10–15cm long, cryptically patterned and covered in coarse scales. All bar two are terrestrial: painted tree lizard (*L. pictus*) and thin tree lizard (*L. tenuis*) are strikingly coloured tree-climbers that can be seen at Pumalín. The greatest diversity of *Liolaemus* is at Jeinemeni and Bernardo O'Higgins reserves. The spiny-backed Magellanic lizard (*L. magellanicus*) is the world's most southerly reptile: look for it at Río Simpson, Jeinemeni and Bernardo O'Higgins. If you spot a lizard with a large, triangular head in any Aysén reserves, it will be either Darwin's (*Diplolaemus darwinii*) or the similar-looking Bibron's grumbler (*D. bibronii*). The distantly related southern grumbler (*Pristidactylus torquatus*) has a distinctive wrinkled neck-collar; it occurs at Alerce Andino. This site also marks the southernmost location for the region's sole **serpent**, Chilean slender snake (*Tachymenis chilensis*).

Of Chile's 60-odd species of **frogs and toads**, one-quarter reside in the region's damp forests. The star is Darwin's frog (*Rhinoderma darwinii*), named after the great man. Male frogs guard their eggs, then incubate them inside their vocal sac before giving birth through their mouth! Although endangered, you have a fair chance of seeing this frog at Alerce Andino, Laguna San Rafael, Queulat or Río Simpson. The amphibian's scientific name means 'rhinocerus-nosed' and refers to the distinctive, long snout protruding from the forehead. Among other oddities, any frog that appears to have two pairs of eyes will be either Chile four-eyed frog (*Pleurodema thaul*) or grey four-eyed frog (*P. bufoninum*). Look for the former at Alerce Andino and the latter at Aysén's reserves. Bumps on the hips explain the extra set of 'eyes'.

A quartet of wood frogs (*Batrachyla*) occur, none larger than 5cm. Males utter their territorial call during autumn (January–May) from secluded spots in the forest. The similar-sized Chiloé ground frog (*Eupsophus calcaratus*) inhabits wet areas in southern beech forests, including at Pumalín. Emerald forest frog (*Hylorina sylvatica*) – a verdant jewel with a vertical pupil – occurs at Alerce Andino. The five species of spiny-chest frogs (*Alsodes* spp.) favour scrubby ravines with fresh water, and are most readily encountered in Aysén. You need a close view to spot the spiny underside. The sole toad, Patagonian toad (*Chaunus variegatus*), has distinctive pale stripes on its back and flanks. Although rare, it has been recorded at Alerce Andino and Pumalín.

Plants The Carretera Austral provides easy access to the great temperate rainforests of southern Chile: Magellanic forest (as at Alerce Andino, Laguna San Rafael and Queulat) and Patagonian Andean forest (Río Simpson and Jeinemeni).

The boggy Magellanic forest is dominated by the **Magellanic coigüe** (*Nothofagus betuloides*), one of three evergreen species of southern beech trees in Chile. Trees are often covered with lichens, filmy ferns and **mistletoe** (*Misedendrum* spp.). Near the treeline, stunted versions of this species grow alongside ferns, **barberry** (*Berberis* spp.) and **red crowberry** (*Empetrum rubrum*). Along the coast, Magellanic coigüe may grow with **canelo** (*Drimys winterii*). In well-drained soils, companion species include **Magellanic maitén** (*Maytenus magellanica*).

One of Chile's seven deciduous beeches, **lenga** (*Nothofagus pumilio*), predominates in the forests of the Patagonian Andes. This beautiful tree has copper-tinged leaves and can reach 40m in height. It often grows alongside another deciduous beech, **ñirre** (*N. antarctica*), a small tree with crinkled leaves that grows further south than any other tree. The scrubby forest edge can have colourful flowers such as notro (*Embothrium coccineum*), **calafate** (*Berberis buxifolia*) and the stately **dog orchid** (*Codonorchis lessonii*).

Two particular trees are worth making the effort to see. The first is **Patagonian cypress** (alerce; *Fitzroya cupressoides*) at Alerce Andino and Pumalín. This is the world's second-oldest living tree species and is protected wherever it grows in Chile as a 'natural monument'. The second is **Guaitecas cypress** (*Pilgerodendron uviferum*), which provides aromatic, gold-coloured timber prized by furniture-makers. It grows at San Rafael and Pumalín.

The Patagonian steppe is the realm of grasses waving in the incessant wind. Occasional bushes manage to grow, and wildflowers lend colour during spring and summer. Their number include the startlingly yellow **sisi iris** (*Sisyrinchium patagonicum*). Plants can of course grow anywhere. By far the most striking plant for many visitors, however, flourishes by the asphalt of the Carretera itself: **giant rhubarb** (*Gunnera tinctoria*). It is well named: leaves stretching more than 2m wide even obscure roadside signposts.

MAIN GLACIERS ALONG THE CARRETERA AUSTRAL While it is hard to traverse the Carretera Austral without seeing a glacier (*ventisquero*), it is a pity to visit the region and not do a specific trip to see these magnificent natural phenomena. The Ventisquero Queulat is one of the most accessible. Caleta Tortel lies between the Campos de Hielo Norte y Sur (the Northern and Southern ice fields), an obvious location for glacier-spotting, but entering the ice fields tends to be a specialised dedicated expedition. Local tour operators can arrange trips to the glaciers. Some are accessible directly from the Carretera Austral, often without a fee. The following list covers only those glaciers that can be readily accessed or seen from the Carretera itself (from north to south):

1

THE ALERCE TREE

The legendary alerce tree (*Fitzroya cupressoides*), cut almost to extinction, has attained celebrity status, and can be seen in a number of isolated spots, most easily in Parque Pumalín. It is called larch, or the Patagonian cypress in English, or lahuán in Mapuche. It is the unique species within this genus of tree, and also the largest tree in South America, reaching up to 70m with a diameter of 5m although Darwin recorded an alerce with a 12.6m diameter. In 1993 a Chilean alerce was found to be 3,622 years old. Alerces have been found in Tasmania, dated to some 35 million years old, demonstrating the connectivity between Australasia and South America. The symbiotic community formed around, and on, the alerce tree is testimony to its ecological value. In addition to its extraordinary girth, the mature alerce is notable for its vertical trunk with the first branches at great height. It grows in cooler regions and in soil of elevated acidity due to ash from volcanic eruptions.

The wood, especially when cut into small tiles, is hard-wearing, waterproof, lightweight and resistant to insects, and is a highly popular building material as a consequence. To the detriment of the survival of the species it thus became unusually valuable and was heavily harvested to the point of becoming a quasi-currency in Chiloé. Logging alerce was banned in 1976 and the tree was elevated to the status of National Monument. It is only possible to extract dead alerce trees, and only with the permission of CONAF. The value of secondhand alerce has risen accordingly, and it is still most clearly visible on Chiloé, and on churches throughout the region. The Alerce trail in Parque Pumalín (page 107) is one of the best places to observe living alerces, looming over the other trees in the forest.

El Amarillo Parque Pumalín Sud, El Amarillo; pages 107–8

Yelcho Between El Amarillo & Villa Santa Lucía; page 109

Queulat South of Puyuhuapi; pages 141–2

Chico Visible from the sea by kayak in Puyuhuapi; page 142

San Rafael By scheduled boat from Bahía Exploradores, near Puerto Río Tranquilo, or from Puerto Aysén; pages 163 & 208

Exploradores Short trek to lookout point along the route to Bahía Exploradores; pages 207–8

Leones Visible across the lake, detour to Lago Leones south of Puerto Río Tranquilo; page 214

Calluqueo Accessible from Cochrane; pages 241–2

Montt and Steffen By charter boat from Caleta Tortel; page 251

O'Higgins By scheduled boat from Villa O'Higgins, also by charter to the Chico & Bravo glaciers; pages 259 & 262

PARKS ALONG THE CARRETERA AUSTRAL Chile has four main types of 'park': national parks, national reserves, national monuments, and private parks. The first three categories are managed by the state-run La Corporación Nacional Forestal (CONAF); private parks, on the other hand, are run by either private companies or, most usually, private foundations. For all practical purposes there is no major difference between these categories. **National parks** (*parques nacionales*) are generally larger, and the flora, fauna and geological formations within them do not require immediate conservation efforts but rather are protected regions. **National reserves** (*reservas nacionales*) are regions requiring special care for their susceptibility to degradation and explicit conservation efforts such as protecting the soil and threatened species are under way. **National monuments** are smaller areas with native species of flora and fauna and used for research, recreational and educational purposes. **Private parks** have their own distinct characteristics depending on the purpose of the park. Entrance fees to parks vary: some are free, including some private parks. No park costs over US$10 per person (for entrance, camping may incur an additional charge).

Forests cover 17.3 million hectares of Chile, approximately 23% of the country. According to the World Bank data on terrestrial protected areas (2012), 18.6% of Chile is protected, compared with only 6.9% in neighbouring Argentina, and slightly below the average for Latin America (21.1%). However, within the region covered by the Carretera Austral this percentage is substantially higher, and most estimates suggest approximately 60% of the territory as protected.

The following parks, reserves and monuments are accessible from the Carretera Austral (from north to south).

Note: * indicates no public access; ** indicates that the park is not directly accessible from the Carretera Austral, but requires a boat or trekking.

Reserva Nacional Llanquihue (340km²) Access point to the Volcán Calbuco (erupted on 22 Apr 2015; at time of writing entry to the park was prohibited).
Parque Nacional Alerce (393km²) Drive & treks to lakes, endangered alerce trees.
Parque Nacional Hornopirén (482km²) Trek to Lago Concha & on to Río Puelo.
Parque Pumalín (private) (3,250km²) Varied park with a wide range of treks. 2 volcanoes, abundant wildlife, alerce forests, lakes & camping.
Parque Nacional Corcovado* (2,096km²)
Reserva Nacional Futaleufú (121km²) Endangered wildlife, treks & camping.
Reserva Nacional Lago Palena** (405km²) On Lago Palena, start/end point for Sendero de Chile trek to Lago Verde.
Reserva Nacional Lago Rosselot (127km²) Main attraction is fishing.
Parque Nacional Queulat (1,541km²) Access point for treks to Ventisquero Queulat viewpoint, various shorter treks.
Parque Nacional Isla Magdalena** (1,576km²)
Reserva Nacional Lago Carlota** (181km²)
Reserva Nacional Lago Las Torres (165km²) Main attraction is fishing.
Mañihuales National Reserve (12km²) Of limited interest.
Reserva Nacional Trapananda (23km²) Small park close to Coyhaique, treks through protected lenga forest.
Reserva Nacional Río Simpson (405km²) Riverside treks & camping, close to Coyhaique.
Parque Aikén (private) (3km²) Small park close to Puerto Aysén, short treks & birdwatching.
Cinco Hermanas National Monument** (2km²)

Reserva Nacional Coyhaique (22km²) Treks of various lengths, close to Coyhaique.
Two Lakes Natural Monument (2km²) A small park containing short treks, lakes & ample birdwatching opportunities, close to Coyhaique.
Reserva Nacional Cerro Castillo (1,797km²) Some of the finest trekking along the Carretera Austral.
Parque Nacional Lago San Rafael (17,420km²) A vast park containing the entire Northern Ice Field; main access points are Puerto Río Tranquilo or Puerto Aysén for Ventisquero San Rafael, or further south to Ventisquero Leones.
Reserva Nacional Las Guaitecas** (10,980km²)
Reserva Nacional Lago General Carrera (1,784km²) The main lake along the Carretera Austral, & the largest in Chile.
Reserva Nacional Lago Jeinemeni (1,611km²) Start/end point for the 3-day trek to Parque Patagonia.
Parque Patagonia (private) (809km²) Hub for the future union of this park with Jeinemeni & Tamango national reserves, start/end point for the trek to Reserva Nacional Jeinemeni, other treks in the region, extensive wildlife & birdwatching.
Reserva Nacional Tamango (69km²) Small park close to Cochrane, lakes, trekking & wildlife.
Reserva Nacional Katalalixar** (6,245km²) A large, rarely visited park accessible by boat from Caleta Tortel, evergreen forest & abundant flora & fauna.
Parque Nacional Bernardo O'Higgins (35,259km²) Home of the Ventisquero O'Higgins, challenging treks, entry/exit point to El Chaltén (Argentina).

Mankind's inevitable impact on the natural environment is often facilitated by the construction of roads as a principal means of access, and the Carretera Austral is no exception. While pristine untouched nature abounds along the Carretera, the impression of man is equally visible. Obvious examples include roads and buildings, land cleared for farming, electricity pylons, and pollution (limited mostly to Coyhaique in winter). Less obvious threats also exist, often with far-reaching implications.

One such threat is **fish farming**. After Norway, Chile is the second-largest trout and salmon farmer in the world and, from Puerto Montt to the deep south, these farms are prevalent. Aesthetically alone, the floating cages, farming structures and associated debris of the industry disfigure many a view across the region. However, more importantly, the chemicals (pesticides, antibiotics, disinfectants) used in fish farming pollute rivers and lakes, rendering water unfit for consumption and damaging precious aquatic and marine habitats. The government body responsible for regulating the industry, Sernapesca, has been largely ineffective in preventing this contamination over the last three decades. Fines for violating regulations are trivially small and zoning laws have proved ineffective.

The international NGO Oceana (*www.oceana.org*) is active in campaigning against chemical-led industrialised salmon farming, but you can do your bit: if you're eating salmon along the Carretera Austral, be sure to ask if it is natural/river caught or bred artificially before deciding what to order. It is worth tasting both simply to compare the difference.

Forestry is also big business. It has been estimated that two-thirds of native forest in southern Chile have been lost through logging. Deforestation began with the arrival of settlers in the early 19th century, often utilising slash and burn policies to clear land for agriculture, the evidence of which can be seen to this day, particularly around Coyhaique. However, the **National Forest Corporation** or **CONAF** (*Corporación Nacional Forestal; www.conaf. cl*) – a Chilean non-profit organisation funded and overseen by the Ministry of Agriculture – has worked hard since 1972 to develop and sustain the country's forest resources. Reforestation initiatives have seen exotic pine species rather than local species planted across the region because they are fast growing and can more quickly protect the land from soil erosion. CONAF is also responsible for Chile's national parks and for fire control within the parks and reserves.

A final contentious issue in the region is the proposed **damming of the rivers Baker and Pascua** which has sparked passionate protests and debates from interested parties and remains unresolved at the time of writing – see box, pages 172–4 for more on this.

Beyond CONAF and the work of NGOs, the care of southern Chile's precious eco-system has so far been left to dedicated individuals such as Doug and Kris Tompkins who have, at times, provoked negative reactions locally, although there is no denying the vast potential of their ambitious conservation projects in the protection of one of the world's last great wildernesses (see pages 104–5 for full details).

The most basic conservation axiom is applicable to all visitors to the region: Take only photos, leave only footprints.

HISTORY OF THE CARRETERA AUSTRAL – AN OVERVIEW

The history of the Carretera Austral can be divided into four distinct periods: pre the 1973 coup, when the region was isolated, undeveloped and disconnected from mainland Chile; during the Pinochet regime, when the majority of the Carretera Austral was constructed; the years following the dictatorship when work continued (though at a more leisurely pace); and the current day, perhaps the most important and challenging stage in the evolution of the Carretera Austral.

PRE-PINOCHET The first record of a European visiting southern Chile was in 1520, when Ferdinand Magellan christened the region Patagonia, referring to the indigenous residents as Patagones (meaning 'large-footed'). Evidence of these inhabitants is abundant in various archaeological sites dotted along the Carretera, principally the Tehuelches, Aónikenk and Kawesqar. Evidence of these inhabitants is abundant in various archaeological sites dotted along the Carretera, principally the Tehuelches, Aónikenk and Kawesqar. The first wave of German settlers to southern Chile (around Lago Llanquihue) arrived in 1848, and monuments to these pioneers are visible in Puerto Montt, Frutillar and Puerto Varas. In 1899 Hans Steffen explored the region of Aysén, documenting the potential opportunities for settlement as well as naming the Río Baker. He also described the Valle Chacabuco (now Parque Patagonia), a rare east–west valley that had been used by the indigenous population for millennia, and would become a key access point to the region for Argentine settlers, explorers and livestock. William Norris used this corridor in the development of what is now Caleta Tortel (see box, pages 246–7).

In 1927 President Carlos Ibáñez del Campo initiated a formal settling process in Aysén, and throughout the early 20th century a number of concessions and lands were granted to private individuals. However, potential land reforms threatened the ruling elite, eventually leading to a coup d'état.

In the early 1900s, progress on the Carretera Austral occurred at a glacial pace and the region was better connected to Argentina than to Chile. One of the first documented accounts of road construction in the region took place as early as 1904. The SIA (Aysén Industrial Company, page 164) built a road from Puerto Aysén to Coyhaique by hand and required 100,000 coigüe tree-trunks cut in half to traverse the swampy sections. It could take weeks to travel this section, which nowadays takes less than an hour.

As early as the 1940s it was possible to drive from Coyhaique to Balmaceda, and by the 1950s this stretch of road had been extended to Puerto Ibáñez and Villa Cerro Castillo. In the 1960s the section between El Maitén to Cochrane was completed, and the trail to Argentina through the Valle Chacabuco (now Parque Patagonia, to Paso Roballos) had been used since the early 20th century.

By 1968, the construction of the President Ibáñez Bridge in Puerto Aysén vastly improved travel between Puerto Aysén and Coyhaique. The road north of Coyhaique extended as far north as Mañihuales. Puyuhuapi had built sections of what was to become the Carretera Austral to facilitate the transport of animals. A ferry connection between Puerto Ibáñez and Puerto Guadal, close to Cruce El Maitén, facilitated transport across the lake prior to the road around the north of the lake via Puerto Río Tranquilo. Prior to 1973 Chilean governments had made half-hearted attempts to complete sections of the Carretera, but in practice these were isolated sections of road.

PINOCHET (1973–90) Pinochet seized power from Salvador Allende in a military coup on 11 September 1973, and embarked on the project to complete the Carretera Austral three years later. Quite what motivated the president is uncertain. Connecting

ALLENDE AND PINOCHET

Salvador Allende became president in 1970 and was the first ever freely elected Marxist, arousing concerns not only amongst the Chilean elite but also in the USA. In addition to land reforms, he nationalised a number of companies and re-established communication and trade with Cuba and China. However, by 1972 the economy was in crisis, partly as a result of socialist reforms which had slowed production and frozen prices while increasing wages. The banking sector was gradually nationalised, as was access to natural resources. As the economy stagnated the CIA began inserting secret operatives into Chile, and the Supreme Court denounced Allende for the havoc he had caused. In a failed military coup in June 1973, former army commander Carlos Prats was forced to resign as Interior Minister, and Allende installed Augusto Pinochet as army commander on 23 August that year.

A month later a successful coup ousted Allende. It is still not known whether Allende killed himself or was murdered, but Pinochet seized power. Henry Kissinger eventually admitted that the USA had assisted the coup. Pinochet changed his title to president in December 1974, and ruled until 1989. In what was likely a rigged election, Pinochet won a plebiscite in 1980 and launched a new constitution. However, the next plebiscite, in 1989, was less successful. According to the Mayor of Puerto Cisnes, Eugenia Pirzio Biroli, this was due to Pinochet selecting a date poorly aligned with the stars. Pinochet was a firm believer in astrology, but failed to consult Eugenia on this occasion (see box, page 145).

remote regions of Chile to the 'mainland' was important, and was used as the principal justification for the massive investment. However, concern over encroachments from Argentina in ongoing territorial disputes was also a factor. In 1982 Argentina invaded the Falklands and Pinochet was quick to support the British, and in particular his personal friend Margaret Thatcher, irritating his neighbour enormously. There was a valid reason to construct a road capable of supporting troop deployments in the case of an Argentine invasion, and this no doubt influenced Pinochet.

Over the next decade and a half, employing 10,000 members of Cuerpo Militar de Trabajo (Military Workforce, abbreviated as CMT) and a similar number of civilians, Pinochet embarked on one of the most ambitious infrastructure projects in South America. His critics mocked the idea, suggesting it was of no use to the people, was economically unviable, and that the Aysén Province was bankrupt.

Between 1979 and 1982 the road from Puerto Cisnes to Mañihuales was completed, facilitated in part by the close friendship between Pinochet and the Mayor of Puerto Cisnes, Eugenia Pirzio Biroli (see box, page 145). Futaleufú was finally connected to the Carretera Austral in 1980, up until which point its only terrestrial connection was with Argentina. By 1982 the Carretera extended from Chaitén to Coyhaique, some 420km.

Between 1980 and 1988 the section from Villa Cerro Castillo to Bahía Murta, Puerto Río Tranquilo and to Cruce El Maitén was completed, and by late 1988 it had extended as far south as Cochrane. This was of fundamental strategic importance, reducing dependence upon the ferry between Puerto Ibáñez and Puerto Guadal, and also offering uninterrupted terrestrial access between Chaitén and Cochrane. By some definitions the Carretera Austral, as we know it today, was largely completed by 1988. Meanwhile, further north, from 1982 to 1992 the trunk road from La Junta to Lago Verde was constructed, presumably to provide a connection to Argentina. Chile is still waiting for Argentina to construct a bridge over the Río Pico, until then this border remains largely useless.

Villa Santa Lucía was an important camp, as this junction acted as a hub for construction north towards Chaitén, south towards La Junta, and east towards Futaleufú, Palena and the Argentine border. It was named after Pinochet's wife, Lucía Hiriart. To encourage workers to develop a small village they were entitled to buy land at one Chilean peso per square metre. Some of the original settlers continue to live in the village – the Illampu guesthouse, for example, is run by one of the original employees of the CMT (page 109).

A project of this scale came at a cost. In financial terms, this has been estimated at US$300m – some 3km of bridges were constructed, over four million cubic metres of rubble were removed, and eight million cubic metres of rock was blasted, using half a million kilos of explosives. This was a vast sum for a relatively poor nation in the 1970s and 80s; by comparison, this was a third as much as the cost of constructing the Santiago subway. However, there were costs beyond the financial. Conditions for the labourers bordered on slavery: workers were entitled to ten days of rest for every three months worked, camps were primitive with mud floors and no services despite freezing temperatures. Construction was largely completed with minimal machinery, mostly by hand, and at least 25 lives were lost. In February 1995, five members of the CMT were killed when 60,000m^3 of rock and mud fell on them in the sector Vagabundo just north of Puerto Yungay.

It's perhaps curious to note that despite the widely held belief that the Carretera Austral begins (or ends) in Puerto Montt, Ralún was included in Pinochet's initial plans for the road, supporting the case that this northeastern section of the Carretera, even now referred to as 'the Northern Carretera Austral', should indeed be considered the road's starting point equally alongside Puerto Montt.

Criticism of the Pinochet years is rife, and there is no excusing the brutal actions taken by the military dictatorship (see box, page 17). However, such atrocities were rare in the south, and pro-Pinochet sentiment echoes to this day. Consider the words of one of the founders of Puyuhuapi, Walter Hopperdietzel, with relation to the arrival of the Carretera Austral (*Ercilla* Magazine, 11 October 1989, page 28):

We used to travel by boat to get anywhere. This change has brought tremendous development for agriculture. Then came electricity, allowing us to have refrigerators to store perishable foods. This affects the welfare and health of the population. And now this [referring to the telephone], which has allowed us to speak and with our family in Santiago and Germany. I had not seen any deputy or senator here. However, during this time President Pinochet visited four times. We know each other, and when he comes, he greets me by name. I consider myself as his friend and that's a very nice thing.

The Bishop of Aysén, Monsignor Bernardo Cazzaro, wrote on 5 March 1988:

Mr. President, I should like to thank you in my capacity as a Chilean for the contribution that you and your Government have given this land. We have seen tangible progress. As a foreign priest we have lived here for many years and seen many hardships, isolation and neglect. We are grateful first to God and then to the instruments that He has used to promote progress in the region.

Thus, the Carretera Austral was largely built by Pinochet, and was initially named after him. Only two monuments reflect his accomplishment: one in La Junta and another in Puerto Yungay. Chile may attempt to rewrite its history (and the road has been renamed as the Carretera Austral, or Ruta 7), but to some of the more elderly residents of the region, it will always be Pinochet's Highway. For those interested in learning more, *The Dictator's Highway* by Justin Walker (page 271) is well worth a read.

POST-PINOCHET (1991 TO CURRENT DAY) The road south of Cochrane started in 1990, reaching Puerto Yungay in 1996. Initially it was hoped to connect Villa O'Higgins without recourse to a ferry, but this proved impossible. The last 100km to the current end of the Carretera Austral opened in September 2000, with the use of a 13km ferry connection between Puerto Yungay and Río Bravo (the ferry is named after Father Ronchi; see box, page 125).

The road along the south of Lago General Carrera to Chile Chico was completed in 1991. The following year bridges were completed over the rivers Palena and Rosselot, near La Junta.

The offshoot to Caleta Tortel was finished in 2003, shortly after Prince William completed his voluntary project in the village (page 245). In 2007 the Ministry of Public Works decided to pave Chaitén to Coyhaique, aiming to complete this by 2015 or 2016. Raúl Marín Balmaceda was connected to the Carretera Austral in 2009, 120 years after the village was founded, and would provide access from the Pacific to Argentina, were Argentina to complete the crucial bridge required to enter the country at Lago Verde.

Certainly it was important, and no trivial task, to connect Villa O'Higgins with the Carretera Austral. It is now possible to drive from Puerto Montt to Villa O'Higgins in perhaps three days, requiring the use of four ferries, a feat that would have seemed unimaginable prior to Pinochet, and has had a profound impact on the region. Those who were once isolated, who perhaps had stronger ties with Argentina than to their own national capital, are now part of a larger country. Public services have arrived, although there have been problems, and the civil unrest in 2012 (pages 172–4) demonstrates that there are still fundamental tensions between Aysén and the Metropolitan region. One should not exaggerate the work that Pinochet accomplished – sections of the Carretera were already in place prior to 1973, and his methods were not necessarily in strict accordance with 21st-century health and safety standards. But to deny that progress occurred as a result of Pinochet's bold vision is a myopic view shared by few who actually live in the region.

FUTURE PLANS This brings us to the current day, and perhaps the most important and challenging stage in the evolution of the Carretera Austral lies ahead. Logistically (and literally) two major 'gaps' still require bridging. The first is between Hornopirén and Caleta Gonzalo, where the land in-between is largely owned by Fundación Pumalín, a foundation established by US conservationist Doug Tompkins (pages 104–5). The 10km road between Fiordo Largo and Leptepú is already complete, as is the 35km section south of Hornopirén, up to Pichanco, just north of Fiordo Quintupeu. The 22km, stretches between Leptepú and Huinay, and between Fiordo Largo and Caleta Gonzalo, are feasible but incomplete.

The problem is how to cross the Cahuelmó and Quintupeu fjords between Huinay and Pichanco. As the condor flies, this is only a 25km stretch, but completing this section in an environmentally sustainable way – the only constraints placed by the two foundations that own the intervening territory – will be expensive and complicated. A viable alternative is to improve the ferry service that currently traverses this section, which would be far quicker and cheaper to implement, and have a reduced environmental impact (see box, pages 98–9).

PINOCHET'S FINAL YEARS

Pinochet was accused of employing a number of oppressive and barbaric tactics during his 16-year rule, perhaps the most notorious of which was the Caravan of Death – a Chilean army death squad that tortured and executed at least 75 people shortly after the coup in September 1973. Precise numbers are unknown, but it is estimated that during the dictatorship, up to 3,000 were executed, 30,000 were tortured and 80,000 were interned.

Pinochet was also a central player in Operation Condor, a campaign carried out by right-wing dictatorships of South America (and backed by the US) for political repression against claimed communists and those willing to oppose governments. Under this operation a number of critics of the Pinochet dictatorship were assassinated, including in Argentina, Italy and the US.

The first attempt to arrest Pinochet for human rights violations came in 1994 by Amnesty International, but this was unsuccessful. In 1998 Pinochet retired from the army, and was arrested in the UK on 16 October while seeking medical treatment. He had been indicted by Spanish magistrate Baltasar Garzón on the grounds of torture of Spanish citizens, the assassination of a Spanish diplomat, and conspiracy to commit torture. The Pope, Margaret Thatcher and the Archbishop of Canterbury leapt to his defence. Pinochet had powerful friends in the UK having supported the British in the Falklands War: he had allowed British planes to fly under the Chilean flag, and provided military intelligence and radar surveillance to the British, enabling them to anticipate pending attacks from Argentina's military base in Comodoro Rivadavia. Pinochet claimed immunity as a former head of state but this was eventually overturned by the House of Lords on the basis that crimes such as torture were beyond immunity and that Pinochet should be extradited to Spain. Then Home Secretary Jack Straw disagreed, and allowed Pinochet to return to Chile on the grounds of ill-health.

In Chile, Pinochet was initially granted immunity from prosecution, but this was subsequently lifted. He was indicted in late 2000, but evaded prosecution on health grounds. In 2004 he was placed under house arrest and indicted once again, only to see his immunity from prosecution restored by the Supreme Court. He was eventually charged with kidnapping, torture and one murder, but died of heart failure on 10 December 2006 having never faced a conviction. He had also been accused of tax fraud, bribery and illegal arms trades.

Many of the ageing perpetrators of the atrocities are taking their secrets to the grave. It is unlikely that the full magnitude of the murky occurrences of the 1970s will ever come to light, and the extent to which Pinochet ordered specific assassinations may never be known. Many Chileans prefer to consider this a closed chapter, particularly in southern Chile, which was relatively spared of the human rights abuses carried out during this period.

Perhaps optimistically, it is hoped that the entire Carretera Austral will be paved by 2018, and Subtel recently agreed to lay a fibre-optic cable from Puerto Montt to Punta Arenas at a cost of US$100m. This would leave just one remaining gap: there is no means to reach Magallanes Province by land from mainland Chile – the only options are to fly, or to travel via Argentina. The three southernmost border crossings around Villa O'Higgins are impassable by vehicle, thus the only vehicular access is via Paso Roballos close to Cochrane, then heading south to the Don Guillermo crossing just north of Puerto Natales (700km by road). A ferry connection is the most likely solution, and according to media reports a ferry between Caleta Tortel and Puerto Natales could be in operation as soon as late 2015. Two road construction projects are under way, in all likelihood to facilitate and shorten such a ferry crossing. The first is from Puerto Natales to Fiordo Staines, some 80km west-northwest of Puerto Natales. The second is the slightly mysterious detour just south of Río Bravo on the way to Villa O'Higgins, towards Puerto Pisagua, very close to the Ventisquero Montt. This seems counter-intuitive, however, as it makes more logistical sense to build the port north of Río Bravo, either at Puerto Yungay or at Caleta Tortel. But if this road is not for a potential ferry port, it is unclear why it was built, as there is almost no population along this stretch.

The biggest challenge of all is, of course, how to truly complete the Carretera Austral while preserving the unique nature and culture of this region and improved ferry services seem the obvious choice.

GOVERNMENT AND POLITICS

Chile is a representative democratic republic. The president is both head of state and head of government. The two predominant political parties are the Christian Democrats and the Independent Democratic Union, followed by the National Renewal Party, Party for Democracy and Socialist Party. The current and former President Michelle Bachelet is from the Socialist Party.

Legislative power is exercised by the government and two chambers of the National Congress: the Senate, with 38 elected members serving eight-year terms; and the Chamber of Deputies, with 120 members serving four-year terms). The judiciary is independent. The Constitution was approved in the 1980 plebiscite under Pinochet, with minor amendments since.

Presidents may not serve consecutive terms, but non-consecutive terms are not limited. The president is selected by direct public vote, with a runoff election if no candidate obtains an absolute majority. Each political party presents one candidate for president. Elections take place on the third Sunday of November of the year prior to the current presidential term. Municipal elections occur every four years and elect a mayor and a number of councillors.

Universal suffrage was instigated in 1970. From 1949 to 1970 only literate men and women over 21 years of age could vote. From 1934 to 1949 literate women over the age of 25 were allowed to vote, but only in local elections.

Chile had compulsory voting until 2009. Voter turnout in the 2013 election was approximately half that of previous elections since World War II.

ECONOMY

NATIONAL ECONOMY Chile's economy is healthy – its main challenge is a chronic inequality in the distribution of income and wealth. GDP in 2014 was US$277 billion, making it the fifth-largest economy in Latin America after Argentina, Brazil, Colombia and Mexico. GDP growth is currently 4%. In terms of GDP per head Chile competes only with Uruguay for the number-one slot. Historically Chile has been the 'poor-brother' of Argentina, but fortunes reversed in the early 21st century and it appears unlikely that Argentina will overtake Chile anytime soon, fundamentally altering the attitudes between the two nationalities. Inflation is under 5%, while Argentina enjoys one of the highest inflation rates on earth. Unemployment is

6% and fairly stable. According to Transparency International Chile is ranked 21 in the world, one place behind the USA. Meanwhile its neighbour, Argentina, is ranked 107, one place behind Niger. In terms of absolute poverty, according to the *CIA Factbook* 11.5% of Chile's population lived below the poverty line in 2012, the lowest in Latin America. However, according to the World Bank the percentage is slightly higher, and Uruguay and Brazil are at similar if not lower levels. The Human Development Index is perhaps a more all-encompassing measure of national welfare, and data for 2013 suggests that Chile is the most developed Latin American nation, on a par with Portugal and ahead of its neighbour, Argentina. However, the inequality-adjusted Human Development Index places Argentina one spot above Chile, reflecting the unequal nature of Chilean society.

Copper is by far the largest driver of the economy, accounting for 20% of GDP and 60% of exports. Chile is also the second-largest **salmon farmer** in the world after Norway, producing approximately one-third of world demand, and accounting for 3.7% of national exports. Salmon farms are prolific in the south, often at the expense of a pleasant view out to the fjords, and with a detrimental impact upon the environment. Restaurants will boast of non-farmed salmon – the difference in flavour is immediately obvious. See box, page 12, for more on this.

In South America, only Brazil and Argentina exceed Chile in terms of visitor numbers, and Chile has consistently been ranked in the top five adventure tourism destinations worldwide (for developing countries) since 2008, coming #1 in 2011.

However, not all is rosy in the Chilean economy. Copper production is energy-hungry, and Chile is energy-poor (pages 172–4). This has sparked some of the greatest civil unrest in recent years, as some political and business sectors view the southern region as ripe picking for hydro-electric development and extractive industries, often with scant regard for the environmental impact or the views of local residents.

REGIONAL ECONOMY The **principal economic activities** in this region are raising livestock, forestry, mining, fishing, tourism and a small amount of agriculture. Owing to the adverse weather conditions for much of the year only a relatively small share of the region is suitable for growing crops, mainly around Coyhaique, Chile Chico and Puerto Ibáñez. GDP per head is approximately US$10,000 in nominal terms, slightly below the Chilean average of nearly US$14,000 but certainly not the poorest region in Chile. However, such statistics are likely to be biased in a region where much production is used for local domestic consumption and not necessarily captured in national statistics. Living costs are also higher along the Carretera Austral compared with better-connected regions of Chile to the north.

According to statistics from the Central Bank of Chile (2013), the largest single contributor to regional GDP was the public sector, at 22.2% of total output. Mining accounted for 16.8%, construction for 14%, and 'education, health and other services' for 12.5%. Fishing accounted for only 8.2% despite accounting for nearly 80% of all salmon produced in Chile, while 'commercial, restaurants and hotels' – a proxy for tourism, accounted for 6.1%. The principal commodities mined include zinc, gold and silver. **Tourism** is growing in importance in Chile, and with the recent completion of the Carretera Austral this is likely to continue, particularly in the far south. Tensions run extremely high regarding the exploitation of natural resources in Aysén, and this came to a head in 2012 with the protests over damming the Baker and Pascua rivers (pages 172–4). Tourism is seen as both an alternative source of revenue and an opportunity to persuade the Chilean government not to flood vast sections of this pristine landscape in order to produce electricity.

1

The **inhabitants** of Aysén fall into four broad groups. Firstly, those that have never lived elsewhere, including some that trace their ancestry to the indigenous populations, now largely vanished. Secondly, well-established families who migrated to the region between the mid 19th century and mid 20th century, including a large number of Germans, but also Belgians (around Chile Chico) and lesser numbers from other European countries. Thirdly, in part for the endless bickering over the precise border dividing Chile and Argentina, migration between the countries particularly in the south has blurred the distinction between the two nationalities. There is less animosity between the nationalities here – many people have families on both sides of the border, and customs are shared. For example, drinking *maté* and use of certain Argentine colloquialisms is common around the Aysén border regions.

Finally, a number of relatively recent immigrants, both from other parts of Chile and further afield, have arrived in the region around the Carretera Austral – a trend that is likely to increase. Many new hotels and businesses emerge each year largely owned by people not originally from the region seeking to escape the rat race and take advantage of the potential for tourism in this area. In addition, the recent economic crisis in Argentina has prompted a number of Argentines to look for employment opportunities across the border.

Chile is generally considered a **conservative** country. Some 59% of the population are Catholic, 16% are Protestant, 22% are atheist or agnostic, and 3% are other. Abortion laws are considered some of the most restrictive in the world, with abortion being entirely illegal without exception, including when the mother's life is in danger. Divorce was legalised only in 2004. However, things are changing, and Chile is one of few Latin American countries to permit same-sex marriages (April 2015). Women were permitted to vote in municipal elections in 1931, and in national elections in 1949. Female participation rates in the workforce are low by Latin American standards. However, according to the UN Gender Inequality Index Chile is the least unequal country in Latin America after Cuba, ranked 68th in the world. This places Chile somewhere between Barbados and Thailand. Chile is one of relatively few countries in the world with a female president (Michelle Bachelet), and one of even fewer countries to have had two female presidents (Bachelet winning a second term in March 2014).

Despite Chile blurring the distinction between developed and developing nation, **education** remains a serious weakness within the country, prompting the civil unrest of recent years. Many of the riots in Coyhaique that began with the Patagonia Sin Represas movement (pages 172–4) were subsumed by broader social concerns, and in particular education. Chile's education is considered one of the most commoditised in the world (only 4% of the country's GDP is spent on education putting it only marginally behind Rwanda), and in terms of purchasing power, the cost of tertiary education in Chile is the highest in the world. Pinochet began to dismantle free universal education in the 1970s, and the trend continued with subsequent governments, and has only been partially reversed by the recent Bachelet government. Less than two-fifths of children attend increasingly impoverished state schools, which accounted for 80% of all education in 1980. Private schools dominate at all levels. In no other country in Latin America do students receive the education their parents can afford, as in Chile. More than two-fifths of students, mainly from poorer neighbourhoods, do not complete high school. Even public universities charge substantial tuition fees, although accounting for only one-fifth of tertiary education. The best universities in Chile are basically inaccessible to all but the elite. The Pontificia University, University of Chile,

University of Santiago and University of Concepcion consistently score within the top ten best universities in all of Latin America, for those who can afford it.

Chile has, by far and away, the most unequal distribution of income within the OECD. The richest 1% earn 30.5% of the income (compared with 21% in the USA). Critics of the education sector claim that this inequality is enshrined in an elitist education system, and suggest Bachelet's recent reforms merely scratch the surface of this societal problem. They call for a complete renationalisation of the education sector. Meanwhile, conservatives are content with the current system, which ensures a smooth transition into top jobs for their children.

Chile has a rich culture, particularly in the **arts**. Famous authors include Pablo Neruda and Gabriela Mistral (both Nobel Laureates), Isabel Allende and Luis Sepúlveda. World-class artists include Roberto Matta, Carlos Sotomayor, Claudio Bravo and Camilo Mori. Only one Chilean film (*No*, 2012) has ever been nominated for an Academy Award.

LANGUAGE

With the exception of a dozen Kawésqar speakers and one Yagán speaker, Spanish dominates southern Chile. In Puerto Montt and some isolated spots further south such as Puyuhuapi, German is fairly common. English is now mandatory in high school, and thus younger inhabitants are likely to have a basic grasp of English. Otherwise, unless working in upmarket hotels or with tour operators, assume that most people will not speak English. For a description of linguistic etiquette, see page 59. For some unique Chilean words encountered in this region, see page 268.

2

Practical Information

WHEN TO VISIT

The Carretera Austral extends from approximately 41°S to 48°S, and as such suffers cold and extended winters (June–September) and surprisingly warm summers (December–March). Hours of daylight in Coyhaique, approximately midway along the Carretera, range from nine hours in June to 15 hours in December. Snow is less common on the western side of the Andes, but precipitation is notably higher in winter. However, the coastal region of the Carretera is notoriously wet throughout the year. Puerto Cisnes suffers approximately 4,000mm of annual rain.

The **peak summer** season, when most tourists visit, is January and February, when most of the festivals take place. It can be hard to book ferries in these months, and hotels also fill up, so it is worth booking in advance. The ideal time to visit is possibly from mid-November until the end of the year, or in March when the Chilean school holidays end, as during this time there are fewer tourists and traffic, lower prices and decent weather. November and April are the earliest and latest times when the Carretera is readily accessible. In the low season, transport connections, including ferries, are fewer and many businesses simply close.

HIGHLIGHTS

Spanning more than 1,000km from north to south, the Carretera Austral contains a bewildering array of scenery, from sub-tropical rainforests to glaciers. The range of

HIGH SEASON TEMPERATURE AND RAINFALL ALONG THE CARRETERA AUSTRAL					
	Nov	**Dec**	**Jan**	**Feb**	**Mar**
Chaitén (north)					
Temp (°C min/max)	7–14	5–14	6–14	4–12	1–10
Rainfall	147mm	216mm	96mm	21mm	33mm
Coyhaique (central)					
Temp (°C min/max)	4–15	6–16	7–18	7–20	5–16
Rainfall	22mm	27mm	21mm	16mm	33mm
Cochrane (south)					
Temp (°C min/max)	5–15	5–16	6–17	6–16	3–14
Rainfall	18mm	21mm	39mm	12mm	9mm

activities possible is extensive, including rafting, climbing, diving, trekking, cycling, fishing and horseriding, to name but a few. Two-thirds of the territory is protected, thus human interference is invisible most of the time. In addition to being sparsely populated, it is rarely visited (although more so each passing year) and offers a more spectacular alternative route from northern to southern Patagonia than the arid terrain of the Argentine steppe. Highlights include:

COCHAMÓ (Pages 83–7) One of the lesser-known entry points to the Carretera Austral, Cochamó is a delightful village perched on the edge of the Reloncaví Sound. Trekking options abound to the extent that it is colloquially referred to as the 'Yosemite of South America'. Longer treks extend across the border to the Argentine towns of El Bolson and Bariloche.

PARQUE PUMALÍN (Pages 103–8) One of the first entirely private initiatives to restore exploited land to its former glory, pioneered by US conservationist Doug Tompkins (pages 104–5). The park is free to enter and has a number of well-marked treks, camp grounds, two volcanoes, and is easily accessed from Chaitén.

FUTALEUFÚ (Pages 112–19) The village of 'Futa' is home to some of the best rafting and kayaking on the planet, as well as boasting a number of other activities for those less interested in watersports. It is also a main entry/exit point to the Carretera Austral, being located close to the Argentine border near Esquel and El Bolson.

RAÚL MARÍN BALMACEDA TO LAGO VERDE (Pages 127–31) The only road directly connecting Argentina to the Pacific in this region, the road traverses a variety of terrains, following the Figueroa and Palena rivers and terminating at Raúl Marín – a paradise for those keen on bird and other wildlife watching.

CERRO CASTILLO AND THE BACK ROAD TO IBÁÑEZ (Pages 193–200) The Cerro Castillo mountain range is fast becoming one of the key treks in southern Chile, with options for those seeking a gentle stroll to the most experienced climbers. To the southwest lie some of the most beautiful stretches of road in the region.

VENTISQUERO SAN RAFAEL (Page 209) It is almost impossible to visit this region and not see a glacier, but the San Rafael is one of the more impressive and easily accessed. The sheer size and remoteness of the white mass before you is simply breathtaking.

SOUTHERN ROAD ALONG LAGO GENERAL CARRERA (Pages 211–23) From Chile Chico to the main Carretera Austral the road hugs South America's second-largest lake, the turquoise colour of which seems to defy belief.

PARQUE PATAGONIA (Pages 229–34) With the pending merger of this park with Tamango and Jeinemeni national reserves, this will become one of South America's leading parks. Abundant wildlife, countless lakes, excellent short and multi-day hikes, and stunning scenery.

CALETA TORTEL (Pages 242–51) Perched on a series of boardwalks between the Northern and Southern ice fields, Caleta Tortel is a magical village with a mysterious history. The complete absence of cars, with all houses built along the cliffs, make this village unique in Chile.

VILLA O'HIGGINS (Pages 252–60) The end, or beginning, of the Carretera Austral. Sandwiched between lakes, glaciers and mountains, the border crossing to El Chaltén in Argentina is one of the lesser-known and yet iconic crossings on the continent. The Ventisquero O'Higgins is one of the largest in the region.

SUGGESTED ITINERARIES

The optimal itinerary depends on four factors: distance, time available, means of transport and budget. It is important to plan a journey along the Carretera Austral carefully, as there are relatively few entry/exit points, and ferries in particular need to be booked in advance.

Chile is more expensive than neighbouring countries, and more so in the south, and this may be a deciding factor on how thoroughly to explore the region. Visiting the Carretera Austral is often part of a broader circuit around southern South America, particularly as the road connects the popular northern and southern regions of Patagonia (pages 27–9). It should be noted that travelling on public transport is slower than private transport, and hitchhiking is possible although not completely reliable. Below are some suggested one-way journeys along parts, or all, of the Carretera Austral.

THE CLASSIC ROUTE: FUTALEUFÚ TO CHILE CHICO (*774km; 8 days*) This route is something of a 'classic'. It encompasses many of the highlights of the region and uses the easiest entry and exit points. Ignoring all the detours off the Carretera Austral, it can be covered comfortably in eight days, but it can also take up to three weeks. This route encompasses many of the highlights of the region, from jungle to glaciers, coastline to high mountains, large towns to minuscule villages, stunning lakes, fascinating history, and endless activities and opportunities to observe wildlife. However, for those with more time, including the northern and southern extremes of the Carretera Austral is well worth considering.

The route A suggested route (in this case from north to south) may be as follows:

- **Day one** Arrive at Futaleufú; spend a complete day in the town rafting, kayaking, etc.
- **Day two** (*193km; 1 day; mostly gravel*) Travel to Puyuhuapi.
- **Day three** A day exploring Puyuhuapi and the surrounding area including Ventisquero Queulat.
- **Day four** (*223km; ½ day; mostly paved*) A leisurely drive to Coyhaique over the Queulat Pass, via Villa Amengual and Mañihuales.
- **Day five** A day in and around Coyhaique visiting Parque Nacional Coyhaique, the Río Simpson or the various lakes in the immediate vicinity. For those willing to get up at 05.00 it is possible to view Andean condors departing from their nests on the cliffs.
- **Day six** (*93km; 1½hrs; paved*) A short drive to Villa Cerro Castillo and a half-day hike or horseback ride around the Cerro Castillo mountain.
- **Day seven** (*125km; 2hrs; gravel*) Travel to Puerto Río Tranquilo to visit the marble caves.
- **Day eight** (*165km; 4hrs; gravel*) Travel to Chile Chico via Puerto Guadal for lunch, along the south side of Lago General Carrera.

Suggested detours A more thorough journey along this 'classic' route would include some detours, and add up to two additional weeks. The following suggestions are listed from north to south:

- **From La Junta to Raúl Marín Balmaceda** (*140km round-trip; 2 days; gravel*) One of the best detours in the region. Enjoy an overnight stay in the village, plus a boat trip to the islands, extensive wildlife, a visit to the hot springs and a short hike.
- **From La Junta to Lago Verde** (*156km round-trip; 2 days; gravel*) For fishing and trekking.
- **Horseriding from Lago Verde to Villa La Tapera** (*59km; 3 days*) Become entirely disconnected from the modern world in one of the most remote regions of Patagonia.
- **Puerto Cisnes** (*70km round-trip from the Carretera Austral; 1 day; paved*) This town has a fascinating history and hikes of various lengths.
- **Puerto Aysén and the surrounding area** *en route* to **Coyhaique** (*63km from Coyhaique, 57km from Mañihuales; 1 day; paved*) Lakes and parks accessible within an hour of the town.
- **Around Coyhaique** You can also spend an additional day here exploring the national parks and observing Andean condors.
- **Glaciers and lakes of Cerro Castillo** (*3 days*) This is one of the most spectacular and accessible treks along the Carretera Austral.
- **Ventisquero San Rafael or Ventisquero Leones** (*1 day; Ventisquero San Rafael 1hr drive/bus each way & 5hrs on boat; Ventisquero Leones 30km south of Puerto Río Tranquilo, 2hr trek & 1hr boat ride each way*) Two impressive glaciers accessible from the Carretera Austral.

THE NORTHERN CARRETERA AUSTRAL (*219km; 3 days*) The Futaleufú (or Palena) access point joins the Carretera Austral at Villa Santa Lucía, where most visitors head south on the 'classic' route as detailed above. North of this point are three fascinating regions, and this extension to the classic itinerary connects the Carretera Austral to Puerto Montt in mainland Chile. The road extends north to Chaitén, which can be visited in one day, at which point the only northbound connection is via a ferry connection to Hornopirén. From here, it is possible to reach Puerto Montt in a single day. Budget for at least three days' travel. We have described the route from north to south to correspond with the coverage in *Part Two* of this guide.

The route A suggested route, from Puerto Montt to Villa Santa Lucía (or vice versa if you're joining the road at Futaleufú/Palena and choose to head north):

- **Day one** (*99km or 135km; gravel & paved*) Drive to Hornopirén, ideally via the coastal route, taking the short ferry from Caleta La Arena to Caleta Puelche.
- **Day two** (*44km; gravel, last 5km paved*) Take the ferry to Caleta Gonzalo and do one or two of the shorter treks in Pumalín before reaching Chaitén.
- **Day three** (*33km poor gravel, 43km paved*) Drive to Villa Santa Lucía, visiting (and maybe staying at) the El Amarillo hot springs, and possibly visiting the southern region of Parque Pumalín.

Suggested detours Those listed below (from north to south) can take as little as three additional days, but also as long as two weeks to do this region thoroughly, especially if trekking over to Argentina via Cochamó.

- **Valle Cochamó** Rather than heading from Puerto Montt directly to Hornopirén, head towards Ensenada via this valley, with some spectacular trekking options ranging from one day to over a week, including the possibility to trek into Argentina.

2

- **Explore Hornopirén** (*at least 2 days*) Take time to explore this village and treks in a wonderful national park nearby which include a volcano hike (*trek to volcano takes 2 days, other shorter treks*). Also consider taking the slightly slower coastal route down from Puerto Montt to Hornopirén (*1 additional day; around 20km extra; mostly gravel*).
- **Parque Pumalín** (*at least 2 days*) For multiple treks including one to the Volcán Chaitén.
- **Lago Yelcho and Ventisquero Yelcho Chico** (*1 day;* en route) The first of the 'great lakes' with ample opportunities for fishing, and the most northern glacier.

THE SOUTHERN CARRETERA AUSTRAL (*332km to Villa O'Higgins (inc detour to Caleta Tortel), gravel; 12km hike to Argentina; 40km to El Chaltén; 7 days; gravel*)
In some respects this is the most spectacular region of the entire Carretera Austral, but it is often overlooked by those who opt to combine their journey instead with a visit to southern Argentine Patagonia and thus exiting the Carretera Austral at Cruce El Maitén, heading to Chile Chico in order to cross into Argentina. However, there are in fact three border crossings south of Chile Chico and the border crossing at Villa O'Higgins offers foot or bicycle passengers the opportunity to connect directly from the southernmost part of the Carretera Austral with El Chaltén in Argentina, a common destination for southbound travellers. Do keep in mind that this is one of the least travelled parts of the Carretera Austral; it is entirely unpaved, and relies on two ferries, one of which is relatively expensive. Note that for those with a vehicle it is not possible to cross into Argentina – the most southern vehicular border crossing is at Cochrane, so those with vehicles will either have to return to Cochrane to cross into Argentina, or leave the car in Villa O'Higgins and return at a later date. Estimates of the time involved are approximate.

The route The southern route adds at least six days, but it is safer to assume a week for delays with boat connections. Considering the Cruce El Maitén as the beginning point for this section (where the detour to Chile Chico commences), the route may be as follows:

- **Day one** (*62km; gravel*) Drive to Cochrane – the road itself is spectacular, and around the town are various lakes and an accessible glacier.
- **Days two and three** (*126km; gravel*) Drive the spectacular road from Cochrane to Caleta Tortel, weaving alongside the Río Baker. Caleta Tortel is one of the highlights of the entire Carretera Austral, with a boat trip to the Isla de los Muertos or to one of the glaciers.
- **Days four to six** (*144km & 12km hike (Chile); 40km (Argentina); gravel*) Depart from Caleta Tortel to Villa O'Higgins, and on to El Chaltén in Argentina – a spectacular journey to the extreme south of the Carretera Austral. From here the only route (currently) to Magallanes (Torres del Paine, Punta Arenas and Puerto Natales) is via Argentina. The border crossing is only possible without a vehicle. The nearest vehicular border crossing is at Cochrane.

Suggested detours For a more thorough exploration of the southern region of the Carretera Austral, consider adding the following:

- **Puerto Bertrand and surrounding area** (*1 day*) For fishing and rafting.
- **Parque Patagonia** (*2 days*) For trekking, including the multi-day trek to Reserva Nacional Jeinemeni.

NAVIMAG FERRY ROUTE: PUERTO MONTT TO/FROM PUERTO NATALES

In addition to saving the inconvenience of a return trip, this is a spectacular journey through fjords and channels, surrounded by raw nature and marine/birdlife, with almost no visible sign of human habitation along the entire route. Accommodation is comfortable and prices include all food, which is fine. Wine and beer is expensive, but you can bring your own. For sunny days there is a large deck, and a dedicated area inside for children. The shared bathrooms are adequate.

Price per person ranges from US$450 (bunk bed, shared bathroom) to US$1,050 for a double cabin with private bathroom and window. Cars cost approximately US$500 southbound and US$300 northbound, motorbikes cost US$150 in either direction, and bicycles cost US$50 in either direction. Prices fall in low season. It is possible to book online (credit cards are accepted), otherwise there are offices at the following:

Santiago Av El Bosque Norte 0440, oficina 1103, Las Condes; ☎(2) 24423120
Puerto Montt Angelmó 1735; ☎(65) 2432360

Coyhaique Paseo Horn 47; ☎(67) 2233306
Puerto Natales Av España 1455; ☎(61) 2412554

The ferry from Puerto Montt to Puerto Natales departs Fridays at 16.00 (check-in before noon), and arrives Monday morning around noon. The reverse journey from Puerto Natales to Puerto Montt departs Tuesdays at 06.00 (check-in before 19.00 Monday), and arrives Friday morning. Note that although Navimag have an office in Coyhaique, the boat does not stop along the Carretera Austral. Navimag also have a ferry between Puerto Chacabuco and Puerto Montt – see page 45 for details.

For further information, e sales@navimag.cl, or visit www.navimag.com.

- **Exploring the lakes and hiking routes around Cochrane** (*1 day*)
- **Montt or Steffen glaciers from Caleta Tortel** (*1 day each*)
- **Horseriding/trekking from Cochrane to Villa O'Higgins** (*at least 1 week*)
  For an alternative means to reach the southernmost point of the Carretera Austral, the old trail used by the pioneers is passable by horse, or on foot. A long, remote and spectacular alternative to driving, for those without a car and wishing to cross into Argentina, this is ideal.
- **Visiting the glaciers and treks around Villa O'Higgins** (*at least 1 day*)
  Ranging from short, easy treks to multi-day treks only for qualified professional mountaineers.

TIME REQUIRED TO TRAVEL THE COMPLETE CARRETERA AUSTRAL Omitting most detours (including Caleta Tortel), it is possible to travel the complete length of the Carretera Austral in two weeks; a more thorough trip would take four weeks. A complete trip including all the key detours, Caleta Tortel, the glaciers, an extended hike in Cerro Castillo and a day or two of rest may take approximately six weeks.

COMBINING THE CARRETERA AUSTRAL WITH OTHER DESTINATIONS The Carretera Austral is a natural bridge between northern and southern Patagonia,

From/to	From/to	Border	Transport
Puerto Montt	Caleta Gonzalo		🚌🚐🛥
Ensenada	Caleta Gonzalo		🚗
Quellón (Chiloé)	Chaitén		🛥
Puerto Montt	Chaitén		🛥✈
Cochamó	El Bolsón (Arg)	Paso Río Manso	🚶
Cochamó/Puelo	Lago Puelo (Arg)	Paso Río Puelo	🚶
Futaleufú	Trevelin (Arg)	Paso Futaleufú	🚌🚐
Palena	Corcovado (Arg)	Paso Río Encuentro	🚌
Raúl Marín Balmaceda	Quellón/Melinka (Chiloé)		🛥
Lago Verde	Las Pampas (Arg)	Paso Las Pampas	🚜🚶
Cisnes junction	Aldea Apeleg	Paso Río Frias-Apeleg	🚌
Puerto Cisnes	Quellón (Chiloé)		🛥
Puerto Montt	Chacabuco		🛥
Ñirehuao	El Coyte (Arg)	Paso Puesto Viejo	🚌
Coyhaique	Río Mayo (Arg)	Paso Coyhaique/Triana	🚐🚌
Balmaceda	Río Mayo (Arg)	Paso Huemules	🚌
Puerto Ibáñez	Perito Moreno (Arg)	Paso Ingeniero Ibáñez Pallavicini	🚌
Puerto Montt	Balmaceda		✈
Chile Chico	Los Antiguos/Perito Moreno (Arg)	Paso Río Jeinemeni	🚌
Cochrane	Argentina	Paso Roballos	🚜🚶
Villa O'Higgins	El Chaltén (Arg)		🚶🚲

meaning that many visitors to the region also intend to visit San Carlos de Bariloche (Argentina) and the Chilean Lake District north of Puerto Montt. In the far south, popular destinations include El Chaltén (directly accessible from Villa O'Higgins), El Calafate (in particular the Ventisquero Perito Moreno) and Tierra del Fuego in Argentina; and Torres del Paine in Chile. An attractive option to avoid repeating parts of the journey is to take the Navimag ferry (see box, page 27) from Puerto Natales (entry point to Torres del Paine) to or from Puerto Montt; it makes no stops along the spectacular and relaxing four-day journey.

The basic route An ideal journey (north to south, easily reversed) could be to traverse the length of the Carretera Austral in perhaps two to six weeks, ending in El Chaltén. You could spend a week or so trekking around Fitz Roy and visiting El Calafate (if you have a desire to see more glaciers), and then continue to Torres del Paine, inevitably taking an additional week to enjoy the multi-day treks around the park. Those wishing to take a detour to Tierra del Fuego and Ushuaia would head over from Puerto Natales, before returning to Puerto Natales to take the Navimag ferry north. This journey could be completed in five to 12 weeks in total, including the entire Carretera Austral.

The ultimate Patagonia experience To complete this entire itinerary, encompassing the entirety of Andean Patagonia on both sides of the border, could easily take an entire season (December to February inclusive). This could be considered the ultimate Patagonia trip, and could run as follows:

- One week in the Chilean Lake District
- One week in and around San Carlos de Bariloche (Argentina)
- Six weeks thoroughly exploring the Carretera Austral, starting with a trek from El Bolsón (Argentina) to Cochamó (Chile), and departing via Villa O'Higgins to El Chaltén
- One week trekking in El Chaltén and El Calafate (Argentina)
- One week trekking in Torres del Paine (Chile)
- One week visiting Ushuaia and Tierra del Fuego (Argentina)
- One week to return to Puerto Montt on the Navimag ferry from Puerto Natales (Chile)

TOUR OPERATORS

The Carretera Austral is not yet part of either the 'Gringo Trail' (the stretch of South America most visited by foreigners) or the standard itineraries offered by tour companies. Patagonia remains dominated by trips to Bariloche and the Chilean Lake District in the north, and El Chaltén, Tierra del Fuego, Torres del Paine and Punta Arenas in the south. There are more 'off-the-shelf' tours to Antarctica than to the Carretera Austral. However, a few operators do offer packages to the region, and this is likely to increase as the Carretera Austral increasingly becomes the natural bridge between northern and southern Patagonia.

BikeTours.com US; \+1 877 4622423, + 1 423 7568907; e info@biketours.com; www.biketours. com. Offers a 14-day guided cycle tour from Coyhaique to El Chaltén in Argentina. Guide, food, accommodation & support vehicle included.

Dittmar Adventures Puerto Natales, Chile; \+56 61614201; US; \+ 1 281 2130115; e info@ dittmaradventures.com; www.dittmaradventures. com. Offer 3 different cycle tours along the Carretera Austral. Their 40-day 'Lifetime Tour' starts at Bariloche, Argentina, crosses into Chile at Futaleufú & heads south along the Carretera Austral to Villa O'Higgins, finishing at El Chaltén in Argentina. Support vehicle, food & accommodation provided. There is also a 10-day northern Carretera Austral trip from Puerto Montt to Coyhaique & a 14-day southern Carretera Austral trip from Coyhaique to El Chaltén. Rental mountain bikes are available. This company also offers kayak excursions in the Chilean fjords just south of the Carretera Austral.

Dragoman UK; \+44 1728 861133; www. dragoman.com. This international overland tour company has several options that pass through parts of the Carretera Austral. The 23-day Santiago to Ushuaia trip has 4 days in the Carretera Austral, entering at Puerto Rio Tranquilo & leaving at Futaleufú.

Journey Latin America UK; \+44 20 8747 8315; e groups@journeylatinamerica.co.uk; www.journeylatinamerica.co.uk. Offer a 2-week 'Untouched Aisen: Little-known Patagonia' trip, which originates in Buenos Aires & ends in Santiago. The journey enters the Carretera Austral at Futaleufú, & goes as far south as Puerto Bertrand. They are also a full travel agency able to arrange international & domestic flights.

PROTOURS Chile Puerto Varas, Chile; \(65) 2772900; e contact@protourschile.com; www. protoursdestination.com/en. Offer guided & self-drive tours along the northern, central or southern Carretera Austral, with accommodation & car-hire/drop-off arranged. The main guided tour is focused upon Lago General Carrera; tailor-made tours including fishing options. The one-way self-drive 'Grand Patagonia' tour starts in Puerto Montt, leaving the Carretera at Paso Roballos north of Cochrane, & continues down the Ruta 40 in Argentina, visiting El Chaltén & Calafate before crossing back into Chile at Torres del Paine. Ends in Punta Arenas (19 days).

Pura Aventura UK; ☏ +44 1273 676712; e info@pura-aventura.com; www.pura-aventura.com; see ad, 2nd colour section. Good local knowledge, & since 2000 have tailored trips to any budget & specific interests (trekking, glaciers, fishing, wildlife, etc) & visit the more remote regions. Their self-drive 'Southern Highway' trip is dedicated to the stretch south of Coyhaique as far as Caleta Tortel with guided days & activities for various highlights along the way. They also offer a more comprehensive trip from Puerto Montt to Villa O'Higgins, including cross-border car hire, flights, accommodation & guided activities.

Ride Adventures Lincoyan 361A, Pucon, Chile; US; ☏ +1 305 6000611; e ulli@rideadv.com; www.rideadv.com. This motorbike tour company specialise in custom & group tours. The 13-day 'Patagonia Experience Tour' from Osorno to Punta Arenas enters the Carretera Austral at Futaleufú & leaves 5 days later at Chile Chico. The base price includes a Kawasaki KLR 650 but there is the option to upgrade to a BMW. There is also a budget option for the lone wolf motor biker who wants to do it independently without a support vehicle or pre-booked accommodation. Ride notes are available with suggested places to stay & eat.

Swoop Patagonia UK; ☏ + 44 117 369 0196; e advice@swooptravel.co.uk; www.swoop-patagonia.co.uk. These specialise in custom-made tours & group tours of Patagonia. The 21-day 'Pioneers of Patagonia, Southern highway & Cape Horn' tour heads down the Carretera Austral in a 4x4, crossing over to El Chaltén in Argentina & finishing with an optional 7-day sailing adventure to Cape Horn.

TOURIST INFORMATION

Most towns and villages along the Carretera Austral have a small information booth handing out free maps and fliers listing hotels and restaurants. Asking for more specific information is often, alas, a pointless exercise. While there are notable exceptions (Puerto Ibáñez boasts the most informative tourist information centre along the Carretera Austral; page 191), most of these booths offer little more than a map. The information centre at Chile Chico is probably the worst in the region, unable to even confirm the year of founding of the town. The two most common complaints amongst travellers tend to be the lack of information and the apparent impossibility of booking ferries.

Generally speaking, a backpacker hostel will have more information available than a tourist information centre. The police are usually oblivious to such matters, and the border guards tend to rotate between posts quite frequently and have relatively little information about the surrounding area. Even the local tour operators don't know much about regions beyond their immediate vicinity. One should bear in mind that this is an area that has only recently become 'known' by the outside world; even Chileans from further north or south barely know this region, so much so that it often fails to appear on the national weather!

RED TAPE

You don't have to jump through many bureaucratic hoops to enter Chile. No vaccination certificates are required. The USA recently allowed Chile to enter the Visa Waiver Program and as a result Chile has completely dropped the reciprocity fee for US citizens entering Chile (previously US$160). However, Australian citizens must pay $117 and the fee is valid for only 90 days. Mexicans must pay $23 and Canadians $132, but the fee is valid for the life of the passport. Australians, New Zealanders, most European and Latin American citizens do not require a visa and will be granted a tourist visa for up to 90 days. Do not exceed the 90 days as this will be registered and incurs a fine. However, hopping across the border to

Argentina and returning a day or two later is acceptable if not done too often. Visas are required for most Asian nations except Japan, Hong Kong, Mongolia, Macau, Malaysia, Singapore, South Korea and Thailand. Visas are not required for citizens of Russia or Israel.

Chile takes the illegal import of restricted goods very seriously, including various agricultural or food stuffs. Fruit, dairy products, honey, etc, are all prohibited and strictly enforced at all airports and to varying extents at land borders. If in doubt, openly ask the border guards – they are generally very relaxed if you are honest, and will allow you to eat any apples or sandwiches in their office before entering Chile.

EMBASSIES

There are 68 embassies in Santiago. Of the countries without a full embassy, Bolivia has a Consulate-General, the European Union has a Delegation, the Sahrawi Arab Democratic Republic has a Mission, and Taiwan has a Trade Office. Argentina has a Consulate in Puerto Montt and Punta Arenas. For a full list of embassies see: www. wikipedia.org/wiki/List_of_diplomatic_missions_in_Chile.

PRINCIPAL EMBASSIES IN SANTIAGO

Australia Isidora Goyenechea 3621, Torre B 13th Floor; (2) 25503500; e consular.santiago@ dfat.gov.au; www.chile.embassy.gov.au

Canada World Trade Center, 12th Floor Torre Norte, Tajamar 481; (2) 26523800; e stago@ international.gc.ca; www.canadainternational. gc.ca/chile-chili/

France Av Condell 65; (2) 24708000; e ambassade@ambafrance-cl.org; www. ambafrance-cl.org

Germany Las Hualtatas 5677, Vitacura; (2) 24632500; e info@santiago-de-chile.diplo. de; www.santiago.diplo.de

Israel San Sebastián 2812, 5th Floor, Las Condes; (2) 27500500; e ambassador-sec@ santiago.mfa.gov.il; www.embassies.gov.il/ santiago

UK Av El Bosque Norte 0125; (2) 23704100; e embsan@britemb.cl; www.gov.uk/government/ world/chile

US 2800 Av Andrés Bello, Las Condes; (2) 23303000; www.santiago.usembassy.gov

GETTING THERE AND AWAY

BY AIR

International flights Santiago has one international airport – Aeropuerto Internacional Arturo Merino Benítez. International airlines flying to/from Santiago include: Aerolineas Argentinas, Austral, Aeromexico, Air Canada, United, Air Europa, American Airlines, Air France, KLM, Avianca, Copa, Delta, Gol, Iberia, LAN, Sky Airline, Taca, Tam and Quant.

From the **UK**, British Airways flies direct to Buenos Aires, but there are no direct flights between the UK and Chile. Flights from London to Santiago typically go via Paris, São Paulo, Madrid, Toronto or via the USA. From the **US**, there are daily direct flights from Dallas, Houston, JFK and Miami.

Elsewhere, there are **direct** flights to Santiago from Australia (Sydney), Bolivia (La Paz and Santa Cruz), Brazil (São Paulo and Rio de Janeiro), Canada (Toronto), Colombia (Bogotá), Costa Rica (San José), Dominican Republic (Punta Cana), Ecuador (Guayaquil and Quito), France (Paris), Mexico (Mexico City and Cancun), New Zealand (Auckland), Panama (Panama City), Paraguay (Asuncion), Peru (Lima), Spain (Madrid), Uruguay (Montevideo) and Venezuela (Caracas). Lufthansa and KLM fly via Argentina. From the Falkland Islands flights go via Punta Arenas, from where it is possible to fly to Balmaceda, Puerto Montt or Santiago.

From **Africa**, the only connections possible are South African Airways (Johannesburg to São Paulo); Ethiopian Airlines (Addis Ababa to São Paulo via Lomé); TAAG Angola Airlines (Luanda to Rio de Janeiro and São Paulo).

From **Asia**, almost all flights go via either the USA or Europe. Emirates flies from Dubai to São Paulo and Rio de Janeiro and on to Buenos Aires; Turkish Airlines flies from Istanbul to São Paulo and on to Buenos Aires; Qatar Airways has a flight from Doha to São Paulo; and Ethiad Airways flies from Abu Dhabi to São Paulo.

Air New Zealand, Qantas and LAN operate flights between Australasia and Santiago and/or Buenos Aires.

The relevant **Argentine airports for accessing the Carretera Austral** are Bariloche and El Calafate, both of which are served by LAN and Aerolineas Argentinas from Buenos Aires. Aerolineas Argentinas also has a flight between Bariloche and El Calafate in high season, and regular flights from Buenos Aires to Esquel. Aerolineas Argentinas is a member of Sky Team; LAN is a member of OneWorld.

Domestic flights The two principal domestic airlines are LAN and Sky Airline. Connections with the Carretera Austral are generally via the commercial airports of Puerto Montt, Osorno or Valdivia (to access the northern region of the Carretera); via Castro (the only airport on the island of Chiloé); via Coyhaique/Balmaceda (the only commercial airport on the Carretera Austral); or via the deep south of Chile (Punta Arenas – flights to Puerto Natales are currently on hold).

✈ **LAN** ✆ 600 526 2000; www.lan.com. They fly to Puerto Montt, Osorno, Valdivia, Chiloé (via Puerto Montt), Punta Arenas (direct or via Puerto Montt) & Coyhaique/Balmaceda (direct or via Puerto Montt). LAN & TAM (same group) have extensive international flights to Europe, the Americas & direct flights to both Auckland (New Zealand) & Sydney (Australia). They have offices in Aysén (*Sargento Aldea 701*), Castro (*O'Higgins 412*), Coyhaique (*Moraleda 402*), Osorno (*Eleuterio Ramírez 802*) & Puerto Montt (*O'Higgins 167*). LAN is also a member of One World.

✈ **Sky Airline** ✆ 600 600 2828; www. skyairline.cl. These fly to Puerto Montt, Valdivia, Punta Arenas, Coyhaique/Balmaceda (via Puerto Montt or Punta Arenas), & also to Osorno in high season. They have international flights to Buenos Aires (Argentina), La Paz (Bolivia), Lima (Peru) & São Paulo (Brazil), & codeshare agreements with Avianca (Colombia) & Taca (Peru). They have offices in Aysén (*Teniente Merino 660*), Castro (*Blanco 388 local 2*), Coyhaique (*Arturo Prat 203*), Osorno (*Mackenna 1100*), & Puerto Montt (*Benavente 405*).

Private airlines A number of smaller airlines with propeller planes fly to, from and within the region, and are described in each relevant section. These are mostly charter. Scheduled flights on these smaller airlines connect Melinka and Chaitén with Puerto Montt, and Villa O'Higgins with Coyhaique. All other destinations are charter only.

BY ROAD The various border crossings are described in more detail in the respective sections, as these are critical for planning a successful trip along the Carretera Austral. The box on page 28 gives an idea of the various options for entering/leaving Chile. The main road border crossings to/from Argentina accessible by a regular private vehicle (in north to south order, Chile town/Argentine town) are: Futaleufú/Trevelin; Palena/Corcovado; Río Frías/Aldea Apeleg; Ñirehuao/El Coyte; Coyhaique/Río Mayo (two border crossings); Balmaceda/Río Mayo; Puerto Ibáñez/Perito Moreno; and Chile Chico/Los Antiguos.

The Paso Roballos border crossing is possible only in a 4x4 or on foot, but is a challenging border crossing as there is relatively little infrastructure or traffic on the Argentine side. Paso Las Pampas is not possible most of the year due to an incomplete bridge on the Argentine side. Very occasionally trucks and 4x4s can cross this border. The Río Mayer crossing northeast of Villa O'Higgins is not passable.

BY FERRY Ferry connections with the Carretera Austral run between Puerto Montt and Caleta Gonzalo, Puerto Chacabuco and Chaitén; and between Quellón (Chiloé) and Chaitén, Raúl Marín Balmaceda and Puerto Cisnes (also highlighted on the map, page 62). The only means to cross from Hornopirén to Caleta Gonzalo is by ferry, and this needs to be booked well in advance (see box, pages 46–7). The two main companies are Naviera Austral and Navimag (see page 45 for details). Ferries are generally no slower than travelling by land; for example, the direct ferry from Puerto Montt to Puerto Chacabuco takes 24 hours (without delays), and it is a challenge to beat this travelling overland, even via Argentina. Unless opting for a private cabin, prices tend to be reasonable for passengers; cars and motorbikes incur an additional fee, very roughly approximate to the cost of a person.

BY BUS International buses run between Futaleufú (Chile) and Trevelin (Argentina; change bus at border, synchronised), and between Coyhaique (Chile) and Río Mayo (Argentina; the bus continues to Comodoro Rivadavia). Direct buses from Coyhaique to Puerto Montt and Osorno travel via Argentina and are not permitted to pick up or drop off passengers in Argentina. There are no direct buses between Bariloche and the Carretera Austral, nor are there buses from Tecka, in Argentina, to Chile, despite this being an obvious route to consider.

As it is impossible to fly directly from Argentina to any point along the Carretera Austral, it is cheaper and quicker to take the bus. Within Chile it is certainly convenient to fly to Puerto Montt, and flights are not substantially more expensive than buses if booked in advance, while being far quicker. The key decision is whether to fly to/from Balmaceda; although it is quicker, it often means missing a large section of the Carretera Austral. Ultimately this is more likely to be determined by the chosen itinerary. Overnight buses from Santiago to Puerto Montt are cheaper than flying, also save on a hotel night, and for taking larger items such as bicycles it may be easier, and certainly cheaper, by bus.

Long-distance buses in Chile range in price/comfort. Bus connections between anywhere along the Carretera Austral and Argentina tend to be shorter distances and less comfortable, but far more convenient that attempting the same route by air. One common route to the Carretera Austral from Argentina is to fly to Esquel and take the shuttle bus to the border and on to Futaleufú.

BY FOOT The crossing from Villa O'Higgins to El Chaltén is possible only on foot or by bicycle, and the crossings from El Bolsón and Lago Puelo in Argentina to Cochamó or Puelo in Chile (via Paso Río Manso and Río Puelo) are only possible by foot.

HEALTH *with Dr Felicity Nicholson*

Medical facilities are limited in the Carretera – any serious accident or illness will involve evacuation to Puerto Montt or Santiago. Every village has a *posta de salud*, which is a minimal medical centre for minor problems. Certainly outside of Coyhaique it is unlikely that doctors will speak English.

Tap water is drinkable across Chile, although mineral water is almost always available. **Food poisoning and cholera** are not a great problem, but uncooked *ceviche* (shellfish) should be avoided (see below). Depletion of the ozone layer, coupled with dry, unpolluted air, has led to increased levels of ultraviolet radiation in southern Chile, causing **sunburn** and increasing the risk of cataracts and **skin cancer**. Be sure to wear good sunglasses and plenty of sunscreen.

Whilst on the road, it is a good idea to carry a personal **first-aid kit**. Contents might include a good drying antiseptic (eg: iodine or potassium permanganate), Band-Aids, suncream, insect repellent, aspirin or paracetamol, antifungal cream (eg: Canesten), ciprofloxacin or norfloxacin (for severe diarrhoea), antibiotic eye drops, tweezers, condoms, a digital thermometer and a needle and thread.

INOCULATIONS No vaccinations are legally required, but make sure you're up to date with **tetanus** and **diphtheria** – which these days comes with polio as the all-in-one Revaxis – and **hepatitis A**. **Typhoid** may also be recommended for most trips unless you're going for a week or less and there is no time for immunity to develop. **Hepatitis B** may be recommended for those working in hospitals or with children. Three doses of vaccine should be given ideally over a minimum of three weeks for those aged 16 or over. Longer is needed for younger travellers. A **rabies** vaccine is advised for people working with animals, but ideally all travellers should be offered a course of three pre-exposure vaccines. Although Chile is considered a low-risk rabies country treatment is not always readily available. The last case of human rabies was reported in 2013 but sporadic cases of dog and cat rabies occur when they are in contact with bats. **Yellow fever** is not present in Chile and there is no requirement for proof of vaccination even if you are entering the country from yellow fever-infected areas.

LONG-HAUL FLIGHTS, CLOTS AND DVT Any prolonged immobility, including travel by land or air, can result in deep-vein thrombosis (DVT), which can be dangerous if the clot travels to the lungs to cause pulmonary embolus. The risk increases with age, and is higher in obese or pregnant travellers, heavy smokers, those taller than 6ft/1.8m or shorter than 5ft/1.5m, and anybody with a history of clots, recent major operation or varicose vein surgery, cancer, a stroke or heart disease. If you think you are at increased risk of a clot, ask your doctor if it is safe to travel.

ANIMAL/INSECT BITES There are **no poisonous snakes**, although the **recluse spider** (*araña de rincón*), found in many homes, has a venomous bite which can kill. There are **biting insects** in summer in the south (and sometimes around Arica) but they don't carry disease. *Tabanos* (horseflies) are a nuisance but not life-threatening. They attack humans, particularly short-sleeved, short-wearing trekkers, often in swarms, and do give a nasty bite. However, they are slow and easily swatted once they have landed on exposed skin. They are prevalent across Patagonia in the summer. Motorcyclists should keep their visors closed if there is any danger of *tabanos*.

SHELLFISH The Marea Roja or 'Red Tide' is an accumulation of **toxic algae** which concentrate in shellfish and can cause death in humans; it occurs in southern Chile in hot weather. Shellfish is very closely monitored in markets and restaurants, but you should be extremely careful about any you gather yourself.

HANTA VIRUS The **hanta fever** virus (or hanta virus pulmonary syndrome) does best in dark unventilated areas, so there's a higher risk in huts and *cabañas* that have been shut up over the winter. It's transmitted mainly by the long-tailed mouse, so don't touch food that's been chewed or defecated on by a rodent, and don't leave it where this might happen. The symptoms are flu-like fever, muscle pains, headache and fainting, followed by breathing difficulties and possible heart failure. Hanta fever is not responsive to drugs but with good care the body usually fights it off.

TRAVELLERS' DIARRHOEA Travelling in Chile carries a moderate risk of getting a dose of travellers' diarrhoea. It is estimated that around half of all visitors will suffer and the newer you are to exotic travel, the more likely you will be to succumb. By taking precautions against travellers' diarrhoea you will also avoid other infections such as typhoid, etc. Travellers' diarrhoea and the other faecal-oral diseases come from getting other people's faeces in your mouth. This results most often from cooks not washing their hands after a trip to the toilet, but even if the restaurant cook does not understand basic hygiene you will be safe if your food has been properly cooked and arrives piping hot. The most important prevention strategy is to wash your hands before eating anything. The maxim to remind you what you can safely eat is: PEEL IT, BOIL IT, COOK IT OR FORGET IT.

Fruit you have washed and peeled yourself, and hot foods, should be safe but be careful with raw foods and foods kept lukewarm in hotel buffets, as they can be dangerous. Dairy products such as yoghurt and ice cream are best avoided unless they come in proper packaging. That said, most good hotels and restaurants have good standards of hygiene and travellers should be able to enjoy a variety of foods.

HIV/AIDS The risks of sexually transmitted infection are moderately high in Chile whether you sleep with fellow travellers or locals. In 2012, 0.4% of the adult population were HIV positive but this is probably an underestimate. Be safe and use condoms or femidoms, which help reduce the risk of transmission. If you notice any genital ulcers or discharge, get treatment promptly since these increase the risk of acquiring HIV. If you do have unprotected sex, visit a clinic as soon as possible – this should be within 24 hours or no later than 72 hours – for post-exposure prophylaxis.

TRAVEL CLINICS AND HEALTH INFORMATION A full list of current travel clinic websites worldwide is available on www.istm.org. For other journey preparation information, consult www.nathnac.org/ds/map_world.aspx (UK) or http://wwwnc.cdc.gov/travel/ (US). Information about various medications may be found on www.netdoctor.co.uk/travel. All advice found online should be used in conjunction with expert advice received prior to or during travel.

SAFETY AND HASSLES

The entire region of the Carretera Austral is astonishingly safe. The greatest threats are road accidents, or accidents relating to outdoor activities. Consider that communications are often poor, ambulances may have to travel extended distances on poor-quality roads, and medical facilities are limited. The best means to avoid **road accidents** are: drive slowly; avoid driving at night; always use headlights (even during the day); use a vehicle suitable for the road conditions (see page 41); ensure you can see through the rear-view mirror (especially if packing extensive luggage); assume there will be an on-coming truck in the middle of the road on every blind corner and brow of a hill; do not stop on a corner; and pull off to the side of the road when snapping a photograph.

Outdoor activities such as climbing, rafting, diving and horseriding carry inherent risks. Ensure the guide is qualified, has insurance, and participate according to your abilities. Use reputable operators, and if in doubt ask to see the SERNATUR qualification. Companies offering water activities require a licence, although informal and unlicensed companies also operate. Trekking, particularly in mountains, can be lethal for the ill-prepared. Although not as high as other parts of the Andes, weather can deteriorate rapidly.

Glaciers are potentially dangerous. Large chunks of ice fall at random intervals, often emitting small shards of ice in the process. When ice falls into lakes the subsequent wave can be sufficient to topple a boat. Trekking on glaciers should only be done with guides, as crevices are not always visible to the untrained eye. Do not touch a glacier, or approach the snout of a glacier, unless you know it is specifically safe.

Particularly for those coming from other countries in Latin America it is worth remembering that **Chilean police** and **border guards** do not take bribes, and to offer one is a serious offence.

While **same-sex unions** were legalised in Chile in April 2015, keep in mind that this is still a very conservative country and gay couples would be best advised to avoid public displays of affection. The only gay bar along the Carretera Austral is Club Angels in Puerto Montt (page 74).

TRAFFIC VIOLATIONS The only encounter a traveller on the Carretera Austral is likely to have with the authorities is for traffic violations. Traffic regulations are more tightly enforced than in Argentina, but not with the vigour of central and northern Chile. Speed cameras or radar guns are almost unheard of, and where there are speed limits the road condition itself generally limits maximum speed. The main offences foreigners are commonly guilty of are:

- Driving without adequate road insurance – this is obligatory and usually verified at the border upon arrival.
- Drink driving – Chile has a zero tolerance policy, ie: no alcohol whatsoever, and no negotiating if caught. Random breathalyser tests are common in Coyhaique, less so elsewhere.
- Seat belt usage – all passengers, including in the back seats, must have seat belts secured, and children must use booster seats when required.
- Driving without headlights on – it is obligatory 24 hours a day to drive with headlights on, for cars and motorbikes alike.
- Parking offences – it is illegal to park facing oncoming traffic, ie: always park in the direction of traffic.

WOMEN TRAVELLERS Women travellers are equally safe. Care must be taken in certain rougher areas of Puerto Montt largely due to the prevalence of drunks. Taxis are the best means to travel at night. South of Puerto Montt there are very few safety issues. Around the mining areas it is possible to encounter the occasional drunk miner, but the same common-sense rules apply here as at home. Bars with suspicious red curtains are generally not the safest places in town, as they offer a range of 'services' not found in standard bars, and are perhaps best avoided by women travellers.

TRAVELLERS WITH DISABILITIES Where possible this book lists hotels and restaurants with facilities for those with disabilities; unfortunately, these are few and far between. For example, it is impossible to drive a car down to Caleta Tortel, let alone a wheelchair, as access is via steep steps made all the more challenging by frequent rain, and having to carry luggage. Large sections of the Carretera Austral are not paved and, although this is slowly changing, the reality is simply that disabilities have not been considered in the construction of the vast majority of towns, buildings, restaurants, hotels, public transport options, roads or tourism facilities, and nor are the inhabitants of this region accustomed to assisting those with disabilities. It is rare to see people with disabilities, whether visitors or residents, along the Carretera Austral.

TRAVELLING WITH KIDS Although the Carretera Austral cannot be compared to Disneyworld, it is a surpassingly child-friendly region. The author travelled the length of the Carretera Austral in January 2014 with a four-year-old daughter and a seven-month-pregnant wife. Most villages have a central plaza with a playground, although dedicated amusement parks for children are largely absent. Hitchhiking or travelling by public transport may not be ideal with children, but with a private vehicle, and not travelling for extended distances each day, the region offers excellent and unusual activities for children such as horseriding, swimming, moderate trekking, camping, boat trips, hot springs and limited cycling routes. There are very few museums, nor is there a cinema in the entire region, meaning that entertaining children on a rainy day can be a challenge. If driving it might be wise to have toys available to keep kids amused on long stretches of road.

There are usually child discounts for entry to parks, activities and hotels. Some restaurants have dedicated children's menus, and those that do not will usually rustle up a suitable dish, or serve a smaller portion. However, note that most restaurants do not open before 20.00 for dinner.

For those with very young children, or wishing to do extended treks, a baby-carrier might be a wise purchase. Buggies are not really suitable outside of the towns due to the generally poor road quality. Baby/child seats in cars are obligatory, and the traffic regulations are enforced. It is rare, but not impossible, to find hotels with baby cribs, particularly amongst the budget options. For any outdoor activities, ensure that children have decent boots and waterproofs for some mild trekking.

WHAT TO TAKE

Self-sufficiency is the guiding principle when travelling on the Carretera Austral. Shops are few and far between, and generally overpriced.

GENERAL In addition to the usual items, be sure to take the following:

- Hats: for cold weather and blistering sunshine.
- Suncream and sunglasses: the sunshine can be relentless in this region, particularly on lakes and when trekking on snow or glaciers.
- Torches with plenty of batteries: many campsites do not have electricity.
- Basic medical kit (page 34).
- Binoculars: the scenery is spectacular, the distances vast, and the wildlife extensive.
- For those travelling by car, a cooler is a welcome treat, and a spare fuel tank may be advisable for some sections.
- Walking poles are useful.
- Adapter: electricity is 220–240V, standard two-pin European sockets.

CLOTHES Regardless of the time of year, it rains and is windy in Patagonia. One quip about the changeability of the weather reassures, 'if you don't like the weather, just wait five minutes'. A waterproof jacket is essential, and if planning to do extensive or multi-day trekking, consider suitable trousers also. There are a few outdoor clothing shops in Coyhaique, Puerto Natales, Bariloche and Puerto Montt, but along most of the Carretera Austral there are none. Make sure that hiking boots are in good condition – even a simple repair can be hard to arrange and a loose sole could spell the end of some spectacular trekking. Likewise with tents – be prepared for all weather. In Cerro Castillo the weather can change alarmingly quickly; in January 2014 Israeli Noam Rubenstein froze to death on the mountain following a minor accident. If hiking in the high mountains take the required gloves, base layers, thermal socks, gaiters, crampons, etc. Laundry facilities are not always close to hand, so it is useful to have clothes for perhaps a week, and biodegradable soap for the occasional hand wash. Be sure to take swim gear.

CAMPING All standard camping equipment is required, white fuel (*bencina blanca*) is hard to obtain and most Chilean hikers use gas canister stoves, available in most towns. Where possible take repair kits for stoves, inflatable mattresses, tents, etc. Which sleeping bag to take is a tough decision, as temperatures can range dramatically according to the region, altitude and time of year. Stock up on essential food in large towns.

CLIMBERS Stock up on supplies in Puerto Montt, otherwise Coyhaique is the next place with a range of stores. It may be possible to borrow or buy equipment from local guides, but they tend to guard their equipment jealously given the difficulty of replacing it. At the very minimum take your own harness and climbing boots.

(FREE) DIVERS For those wishing to dive, there is currently only one registered dive centre in the entire region, in Cochrane (page 238). The divers working on the salmon farms are generally unwilling, or not permitted, to fill tanks. Wetsuits and weights are available in Puerto Montt, and Coyhaique sells basic equipment. In practice it is generally easier to take the bare minimum (7mm hooded wetsuit, mask, snorkel, fins, weights and neoprene socks and gloves) and rely on snorkelling and apnea.

CYCLISTS Welding is generally possible at most towns, but there are few specialist cycle shops along the entire Carretera Austral outside of Coyhaique, and even here spare parts are limited. If buying a bike in Puerto Montt it may be wise to buy a brand widely available in Chile, such as Trek or Oxford. Be entirely prepared for almost any conceivable repair: spare chain, inner tubes, puncture repair kit, pump, lubricant, basic tools, etc. Also consider a face mask, particularly in January and February when traffic is at its highest and rain is limited. The gravel roads become very dusty and passing cars produce a dust cloud that can linger for minutes. Bicycle helmets are not obligatory, but highly advisable. Cycle racks and panniers should be of high quality and purchased in advance.

MOTORCYCLISTS The simpler the motorbike the better. BMWs will struggle to find parts south of Osorno. On-board computers are a challenge, although Coyhaique and Futaleufú have fairly well-equipped mechanics. It is useful to have a 12v tyre pump. Off-road or dual-purpose tyres can be bought in Puerto Montt, Osorno or Punta Arenas, and possibly in Coyhaique. The golden rule for motorcyclists is simply to know your bike, and to know and anticipate its weaknesses. Essential spares or accessories to carry at all times include a chain link, chain lube, wet-weather clothing and good panniers. It is highly recommended to have a sump guard, engine guard, headlight protector and handlebar protectors (to protect the brake and clutch levers as well as hands). Optional accessories would include spare levers, cables and possibly tyres. Most motorcyclists carry a spare fuel tank, but this might not be necessary: the longest stretches between petrol stations are detailed on page 43.

MONEY AND BUDGETING

MONEY
Banks and ATMs Only the larger towns have banks or ATMs (Puerto Montt, Futaleufú, Puerto Aysén, Coyhaique, Chile Chico and Cochrane). Coyhaique has the widest range, and it is wise to stock up on pesos, as many places simply do not accept cards. Interestingly the only airport in the region, Balmaceda, does not have an ATM. Depending on the card, daily withdrawal limits are generally US$200, although sometimes it is possible to do multiple withdrawals in a single day from different banks.

Currency The national currency of Chile is the peso ($). The current exchange rate (November 2015) is US$1=$703, £1=$1,069 and €1=$755. Security is generally not a problem along the Carretera Austral, so travelling with substantial sums of cash is not as risky as it would be in other regions, with a little common sense. One option is to buy a small car safe that secures around a metal fixture in the car (typically under the seat), and can also be secured inside a hotel room if required.

US dollars can be used fairly extensively, and are worth having as a backup. Argentine pesos are begrudgingly accepted in some places, but at an ever deteriorating exchange rate. PayPal is becoming increasingly popular, but do not rely on it. Tips are occasionally included on the bill in a restaurant; if not, they are not expected, and rounding up the amount is appreciated and sufficient.

Credit cards MasterCard works at the most prolific bank in the region – Banco del Estado. Other debit/credit cards are more challenging for cash withdrawals, although paying in shops and petrol stations is usually possible with most major cards. As a general rule, most places are **cash only** – establishments that accept credit cards are listed as such. Also note that some hotels, shops and tour operators will accept foreign credit cards in-store, but not by telephone. Some hotels insist on a deposit to secure a booking, and if they are unable to take a credit card by phone or a written authorisation to charge the card in the case of a no-show, the only alternative is to deposit funds in a local bank account, which is common amongst Chileans. However, most Chileans working in tourism understand the difficulty this presents to foreigners and are flexible, particularly in the case of Argentines who simply cannot do international transfers. For the benefit of all concerned, do not make reservations that you are not 99% sure to satisfy, as this will merely encourage operators to stop accepting reservations made in good faith. Most report that they have not had problems with taking reservations from foreigners *en confianza* (ie: based on trust), and long may this remain the case.

BUDGETING Chile is not the cheapest country in South America, and the Carretera Austral is not the cheapest region within Chile. Petrol is relatively expensive, approaching as much as $1,000 (US$1.50) per litre in the most remote regions. In most places it is possible to sleep for under US$20 per person per night with a simple breakfast, although there are numerous places where wild camping is possible without cost. It is equally possible to eat a decent meal for under US$10 in most places; buying and cooking food is even cheaper. Public transport is generally quite reasonably priced considering the distances involved, but ferry connections can vary dramatically in cost depending on whether the route is subsidised or not. For example, the ferry from Caleta Gonzalo to Hornopirén is approximately one-third of the price of the ferry from Chaitén (slightly further south) to Puerto Montt (a couple of hours' drive north of Hornopirén). The ferries from Villa O'Higgins to El Chaltén are notoriously expensive, but one has to consider the alternative cost of heading north, crossing the border at Paso Roballos or Paso Río Jeinemeni and travelling down to El Chaltén. The mode of transport and number of people sharing a vehicle can alter the travel cost substantially. Needless to say, chartering private aircraft is not a budget option, but details of landing strips are covered in the relevant guide chapters.

Activities range in price dramatically, particularly when visiting Ventisquero San Rafael (*US$250pp*) or the glaciers around Caleta Tortel (*US$150pp*). The Ventisquero San Rafael is more economically visited from Puerto Río Tranquilo than from Puerto Chacabuco. Some of the more exclusive fishing lodges can be surprisingly expensive.

Travelling on a budget A budget traveller should consider US$50 per person per day as reasonable, with some flexibility to reduce this slightly by camping, hitching and cooking. A more comfortable budget, including the occasional tour to one of the more expensive locations, could approach US$100 per person per day, staying in decent accommodation with a private bathroom and generally eating out, slightly less per person if travelling as a couple and splitting accommodation costs. For a couple travelling the Carretera Austral on a tight budget for 20 days it is likely they would spend between US$1,500 and US$2,000 in total.

Travelling without budget constraints At the other end of the spectrum, there are relatively few accommodation options costing more than US$150 per couple per night, and it is a challenge for a couple to spend more than US$100 per day on food, although fancy wines could stretch this. The few options to fly within the Carretera Austral generally involve missing key sections of the route. For example, to fly from Puerto Montt to Chaitén omits entirely the region around Hornopirén, and then requires renting a car with fewer options. Altogether, a couple travelling the Carretera 'in style' and returning on the finest cabin of the Navimag would be hard-pressed to spend more than US$10,000 for a thorough one-month trip (note that this excludes the cost of international flights).

GETTING AROUND

There is public transport to almost every inhabited community, but the frequency and reliability of such offerings is subject to wide variation. Public transport between Coyhaique and Puerto Aysén is abundant, Puerto Cisnes and Balmaceda airport are well served, while Lago Verde and Villa La Tapera are probably the hardest places to reach by public transport. Less frequent are buses to/from Chile Chico and Raúl Marín Balmaceda, and there is currently no public transport to Paso Roballos or Paso Puesto Viejo, the Levicán Peninsula or Bahía Exploradores. For a list of the various entry and exit points along the Carretera Austral, see page 28.

BY PRIVATE VEHICLE Private vehicle is by far the most common form of transport. Renting a car is a viable option, and as the road conditions improve it is not necessary to hire a 4x4 to reach most parts of the Carretera Austral. International car-hire companies operate in Puerto Montt, with small concessions in Balmaceda airport affiliated to main offices in Coyhaique and are listed in the relevant sections.

Selecting a vehicle Foreign travellers visiting the Carretera Austral for a month or less are unlikely to bring their own vehicle or motorbike over, as it is too expensive to warrant the cost of shipping. Renting a vehicle or motorbike locally is the obvious alternative. However, an ever increasing number of travellers ship their vehicles to South America to do an extended tour around the continent, in which case the Carretera Austral is a great option, and unlikely to be the most challenging terrain encountered on such a trip. The Atacama Desert, the sand dunes of Bolivia and Peru, the salt flats of Bolivia, and the mud tracks through the Amazon are more demanding on a vehicle than the roads of this region.

Popular choices for extended South American overland trips are long, wheelbase 4x4s easily serviced in most regions, such as a Land Rover, Toyota Land Cruiser or Hilux. Any of these vehicles would be more than capable of traversing the Carretera Austral.

Is a 4x4 necessary? This depends on the route followed and the time of year. Certainly for the paved sections a 4x4 is not needed. Roadworks continue along the Carretera Austral as part of the broader road-paving project; ironically in the short term this might actually increase the usefulness of a 4x4, as the road quality generally deteriorates before improving with the arrival of the eventual tarmac. The worst section for roadworks is currently from Cisnes Junction to approximately halfway between La Junta and Puyuhuapi. The longest uninterrupted section of paved road is currently from Cisnes Junction to Villa Cerro Castillo or Puerto Ibáñez, from where it is possible to cross the lake to Chile Chico (also paved) and cross into Argentina and join the (paved) Ruta 40 north or south.

There are relatively few places where a 4x4 is absolutely obligatory. Two notable exceptions would be Paso Roballos when wet and the westwards back road between Puerto Ibáñez and Cerro Castillo. As a rule, the major advantage of a 4x4 vehicle is the extra traction, the higher clearance and the heavier suspension more suitable for steep, heavily corrugated gravel roads with pot-holes. For the very few people who visit the Carretera Austral in winter, a 4x4 would be advisable.

Outside of winter a high ground clearance (>20cm) car is highly recommended to clear the ridge in the centre of gravel roads formed by tyre ruts and road graders; to cross the occasional river crossing; and for protection of larger rocks and potholes. A steel sump guard protector is useful, and all-terrain tyres help to reduce wheel slip and increase traction on gravel roads. Overloading a front-wheel drive reduces traction precisely when it is most needed: ascending steep gravel sections.

We used a standard Renault Duster (1.6-litre petrol, two-wheel drive with 210mm clearance). Such a vehicle will reach all sections of the Carretera Austral in all but extreme cases (snow storms in winter, landslides, floods, etc), and 95% of the detours. Many people living in this region do not have such a car, let alone a fancy 4x4. In the rare cases where such a vehicle cannot reach a certain destination, alternative transport is generally possible for a reasonable fee.

Car hire Most car-hire companies require a minimum age of 22–24 years, a valid driver's licence in the country of origin or a valid international driver's licence, valid passport and a credit-card guarantee of between US$500 and US$1,000. If renting a car in the Carretera Austral it is important to

2

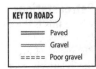

KEY TO ROADS
=== Paved
=== Gravel
===== Poor gravel

RULES AND REGULATIONS

- Drive on the right-hand side.
- Driving with headlights turned on is mandatory.
- Seat belts are obligatory for all.
- The alcohol limit is 0.05%. There are heavy fines or possible imprisonment for exceeding the blood alcohol limit.
- The use of a mobile phone whilst driving without a hands-free kit is prohibited.
- Smoking or listening to a personal music player with headphones whilst driving is illegal.
- Speed limits: 100–120km/h on two-lane highways, 60km/h in urban areas.

SAFE-DRIVING PRACTICES

- Care should be exercised when changing lanes or merging as many drivers do not signal lane changes and rarely give way to merging traffic.
- Always drive slowly when approaching a road junction and be prepared to give way even if you have the right of way or the green light (especially relevant for motorbikes and cyclists).
- Give way to pedestrians at all times.
- Take extra care when driving in the mountains because of tight switchbacks without guardrails, and watch out for large pot-holes, rocks and loose gravel.

WHAT TO TAKE

- International driver's licence permit.
- Passport – in case you get stopped by the police.
- Road map of the area you are driving in (pages 43 and 271).

consider the following factors. Firstly, much of the Carretera Austral is unpaved, meaning that a small car with low clearance will not traverse some sections, particularly when wet, and most vehicles have an excess for damages. If considering the more remote sections of the Carretera Austral, get a car that is suitable for the terrain. Secondly, one-way rentals tend to be expensive, so it is generally wise to plan a loop or round trip, or to return to Puerto Montt on the Navimag (page 27). Thirdly, you will need the vehicle registration to book a ferry ticket; this can be provided at a later date (ie: collection date), but be sure to inform the ferry company via phone or in person of the registration as soon as it is known. Finally, if intending to pass through Argentina ensure the car is able to be taken out of the country and that you have the required paperwork, including insurance – there is a delay of up to ten days to obtain such documentation, so make sure you plan ahead. Wicked Campers (see box, page 44) offer car and van hire specifically along the Carretera Austral and one-way fees are not prohibitive.

Petrol stations Petrol is available in most towns along the Carretera Austral – where this is the case, it is listed. The dominant petrol companies are COPEC and Petrobras; COPEC petrol stations list other stations in the region with approximate distances. However, as of early 2015 these signs had not been updated to reflect the relatively recent additions to their network, namely at Futaleufú and Villa

O'Higgins. There are, however, certain areas where petrol is unavailable, such as the 270km route from Cochrane to Villa O'Higgins (with a detour to and from Caleta Tortel).Towns without a petrol station are as follows:

- Raúl Marín Balmaceda and Lago Verde (140km/156km round-trip from La Junta)
- Alto Río Cisnes and the Río Frias Apeleg border (104km one-way along the detour to La Tapera)
- Balmaceda (55km from Coyhaique, 169km from Puerto Río Tranquilo)
- Cerro Castillo (93k from Coyhaique, 125km from Puerto Río Tranquilo), Puerto Ibáñez (118km from Coyhaique, 138km from Puerto Río Tranquilo) and Caleta Tortel (126km from Cochrane, 144km from Villa O'Higgins)
- The longest single stretch without a formal petrol station is currently Coyhaique to Puerto Río Tranquilo going via Puerto Ibáñez and Puerto Sánchez, which is approximately 330km.

Informal vendors of petrol do exist, but their availability and the quality of the petrol are uncertain. We have bought petrol from informal vendors in Cerro Castillo and Puerto Ibáñez of reasonable quality, but wouldn't advise relying on this. It is almost unheard of for petrol stations to run out of petrol, unlike in Argentina where the problem is frequent. **Note** that it is not permitted to cross the border with a spare fuel tank, in either direction.

Maps The easiest map for most travellers on the Carretera Austral to obtain is COPEC's **Chiletur Zona Sur** (*http://chiletur.eoslibros.cl/index.php*). This is a small book that is updated annually and includes town and regional maps. This is not the most detailed map on the market, but for most travellers it is sufficient. The COPEC guide can be purchased at any COPEC service station throughout Chile. Other maps are available for purchase at kiosks and bookstores throughout the region. **Local tourist information centres** are a great place to pick up a free street map of the town and surrounding areas. Some tourist information centres have an excellent free foldout map of the entire Carretera Austral – it's well worth getting hold of one of these. All national parks and reserves provide maps for the trails within their boundaries.

Downloadable maps are available from www.maps.com and www.pdf-maps. com. See page 271 for further information.

BY BUS In high season buses fill up quickly (particularly the international bus from Coyhaique to Río Mayo in Argentina), and in low season the frequency diminishes yet further; departure and arrival times are 'flexible'. Some buses deliberately synchronise with connecting boats or buses from other regions, adding an inevitable element of volatility into the timetables. It is wise to arrange public transport in advance wherever possible, arrive early and be prepared to wait – when staying in a village for a few days consider buying your departing bus ticket as soon as you arrive. Often it is possible to make a change for a small fee, or cancel with relatively little penalty if done in advance. However, many routes are served only once per day by public transport. Note that a major advantage of travelling by public transport between Chaitén and Hornopirén/ Puerto Montt is that the ferry crossing is included in the price, and the bus has an assured place on the ferry. There are buses between Puerto Montt and Hornopirén (direct or via Cochamó/Puelo), with connections to Chaitén. From Chaitén there are frequent buses to La Junta – a relative transport hub in the region – and there are also less frequent buses to both Futaleufú and Palena. La Junta is well connected

CAMPERVANS: FEELING WICKED?

Another valid option is to hire a van through **Wicked Campers** ✆ *(9) 42073790;* e *info@wickedsouthamerica.com; www.wickedsouthamerica.com, www.wickedcampers.cl),* a franchise of the Australian company. Vans range in size and quality, and a typical one-way rental for three weeks is approximately US$2,400, although cheaper options and special offers exist. The company offers roadside assistance along the entire length of the Carretera Austral, it is possible to cross into Argentina, the vehicles come with insurance, and include a basic cooking stove and beds. Sleep quality is reportedly quite good. Standard vehicle rental terms apply (valid driving licence, etc) and there is a daily 250km limit with a fee for exceeding this. Surprisingly there are no restrictions on where the vans can go, although visiting Raúl Marín Balmaceda, Lago Verde or attempting Paso Río Frias-Apeleg or Roballos might be unwise. The company has offices (also pickup/drop-off points) in Puerto Varas (just north of Puerto Montt; the ideal start/end point for the Carretera Austral), Punta Arenas (close to Puerto Natales for Torres del Paine and the Navimag ferry), as well as Santiago and San Pedro de Atacama in the extreme north. One-way rentals incur an additional fee but it is not prohibitive. Currently there is no office along the Carretera Austral.

An alternative is **Holiday Rent** ✆ *(2) 22582000;* e *reservas@holidayrent.cl;* www. holidayrent.cl), a Santiago-based rental agency offering eight different designs of campervan, seven of which are 4x4, suitable for traversing the Carretera Austral. Staff speak Spanish, English and German, and offer 24-hour emergency support. Permits for entering Argentina need to be arranged in advance. Pickup and drop-off points include Puerto Montt, Coyhaique, Balmaceda, Puerto Natales and Punta Arenas. One-way rentals can be arranged for a reasonable fee.

to Coyhaique, with stops at all main towns and villages along the Carretera Austral. Likewise, Coyhaique is well connected with Cochrane, further south. From Cochrane there are buses to Caleta Tortel and to Villa O'Higgins, but with reduced frequency.

Bus times from Puerto Montt are fairly reliable, but thereafter less so. Scheduled bus times not only change frequently, but even when fixed are subject to the vagaries of weather conditions and traffic. Some buses synchronise with others, injecting an additional element of chaos to the equation.

In this guide, we have given as much information as is available on those companies operating the routes along the various stages of the Carretera Austral within the relevant sections of the book. Note that bus times, companies, telephone numbers, routes, prices, frequencies and times are subject to constant, apparently random, changes. Most companies do not have a functioning website, those that do are often not accessible, and those that are accessible are often inaccurate. Telephone is the only reliable method to confirm a bus time and to discover how to buy a ticket, but most do not take credit cards so making a reservation can be a challenge. Services are broadly becoming more frequent and reliable each summer, albeit from a low starting point. Many buses can only be booked locally, in particular those serving the various detours off the Carretera. If travelling by local transport, it is often a case of sticking your thumb out on the side of the road and getting on the first thing that stops.

ON FOOT Hitchhiking is a viable alternative to public transport. Certain stretches are reportedly harder than others, in particular from Chile Chico to the main

Carretera. Security concerns associated with hitchhiking seem non-existent along the Carretera.

BY SEA The ferry crossings are the single biggest logistical hurdle in the entire region. After long-haul flights this is probably the most important element to arrange in advance. Once organised, be sure to get to the ferry on time, and check the updated time at least one day before departure. A missed ferry can have dire consequences: detours via Argentina can add hundreds of kilometres to the journey and days of additional travel. Chaitén to Puerto Montt takes 9 hours by ferry. Driving south to Futaleufú, crossing into Argentina, crossing back into Chile at Paso Cardenal Samoré and getting to Puerto Montt is an entire day's drive.

Ferry companies

Naviera Austral www.navieraustral.cl. Main office Puerto Montt ✆ (65) 2270430/1/2; Castro ✆ (65) 2635254; Quellón ✆ (65) 2682207; Hornopirén ✆ (65) 2217266; Chaitén ✆ (65) 2731011; Futaleufú ✆ (65) 2721412; Puerto Aguirre ✆ (67) 2361357; Puerto Cisnes ✆ (9) 84482837; Coyhaique ✆ (67) 2210727; Chacabuco ✆ (67) 2351493. See pages 46–7 for warning.

Navimag e sales@navimag.cl; www. navimag.com. Offices in Puerto Montt, Angelmó 1735; ✆ (65) 2432360; & Coyhaique, Paseo Horn 47; ✆ (67) 2233306. See also page 27.

Sotramin Terminal Portuario, Chile Chico; ✆ (67) 2411003; e chilechico@sotramin.cl; www. sotramin.cl. Services the route between Puerto Ibáñez & Chile Chico on Lago General Carrera (page 190).

Transportes Austral www.taustral.cl. Walk-in client service operated through the Naviera Austral offices. Transportes Austral is notably better, does take foreign credit cards, & does display availability, but only offers the Hornopirén–Caleta Gonzalo route (below).

Ferry services The following ferry services are currently in operation across the region. Beware that times are subject to change due to tides/weather.

Puerto Montt to Chaitén (via Ayacara) Late evening Mon, Thu, Fri, returns midnight Sun, 10.00 on Thu & 11.00 on Fri (*9hrs; $16,000pp, $88,000/car, 1 passenger travels free with car*).

Puerto Montt to Chacabuco 23.59 Wed & Sat (boarding 22.00, check-in 09.00–13.00 & 14.30–20.00 on Wed, 15.00–19.00 on Sat), returns 18.00 Tue & Fri (boarding at 16.00, check-in 13.00–14.00). Subject to delays due to weather (*24hrs; $48,000pp, $168,000/car, $76,000/motorbike*).

Caleta La Arena to Caleta Puelche Every 45mins in either direction starting at 06.45 from Caleta Puelche (last ferry at 23.45) & 07.15 from Caleta La Arena (last ferry at 00.30); prior reservations not necessary (*30mins; $600pp, $2,700/ bicycle, $6,900/motorbike & $9,500/car one-way*).

Hornopirén to Caleta Gonzalo (via Leptepú & Fiordo Largo) Once daily in low season at 11.00, twice daily in high season at 10.00 & noon, returns at 13.45 in low season, or noon & 15.00 in high season. Note this ferry is actually operated by Transportes Austral & tickets can be (more easily) purchased direct from them (see above). Tickets also sold in Naviera Austral offices. The journey actually involves 2 separate ferries, but sold as a single ticket this costs $30,000/car or $7,500/motorbike, 1 passenger travels free with car/motorbike, $5,000 each additional passenger. The northern section takes approximately 3½hrs, the southern section only 40mins. The ferries are synchronised with one another, but assume this entire journey will take between 5 & 6hrs.

Chaitén to Quellón 10.00 Tue, returns 03.00 Thu (*5hrs; $12,000pp, $82,000/car*).

Raúl Marín Balmaceda to Quellón 20.00 Tue & 08.00 Sat, returns 23.00 Wed & Sat (*9hrs; $6,900pp, $51,100/car*).

Puerto Cisnes to Quellón noon Wed, returns 19.00 Tue (*11hrs; $13,000pp, $70,000/car*).

Chacabuco to Quellón 23.00 Mon, returns 23.00 Wed & Sat (*28hrs, slow indirect service visiting various islands* en route), or at noon Fri (*9hrs, semi-direct service heading south; $15,000pp, $120,000/car*).

Visitors to the northern Carretera Austral face a difficult trade-off, as there is no means to travel from Hornopirén to Caleta Gonzalo without taking a ferry, albeit along a stunning fjord. It is possible to enter/leave the Carretera Austral further south at the Futaleufú border crossing, but this means missing Parque Pumalín, Chaitén and Hornopirén. Flying to/from Chaitén is a reasonably priced alternative, but flying still means you'll miss Hornopirén and is not an option for those with cars, motorbikes or bicycles. The boat is the ideal solution, but there is one unavoidable obstacle: Naviera Austral (see details, page 45).

Naviera Austral is a private monopoly. The owners of the boats are not necessarily the operators of the service, and a number of companies work together, or independently, on the various routes in the region. Concessions are offered by the Chilean government with varying subsidies depending on the route, in order to encourage these companies to service remote regions that would otherwise be insufficiently profitable for private companies to offer. This is a form of public–private partnership, and to some extent the actual clients of the ferry companies are not the individuals on the boats, but the Chilean government. Navimag and Skorpios are purely private companies, with price tags and service quality to match. Naviera Austral, and the medley of companies surrounding it, rely on these subsidies; although, in a final twist, Navimag is one of the principal shareholders of Naviera Austral.

The boats themselves are fine, although capacity constraints in high season are a problem. Installed capacity has not kept up with the rapid growth in demand for these services, and ageing port facilities further hinder the ability of ferry operators to offer good services. The more pressing problem, however, is that it is awkward for foreigners to purchase tickets for ferry crossings offered by Naviera Austral. The website is confusing, and it is challenging to buy a ticket online, despite claims to the contrary. Their three dedicated phone lines in Puerto Montt are often left unanswered or are busy (calling the regional offices is often better); emails are often ignored. Attempting to pay with a foreign credit card creates all manner of problems, particularly if not physically in an office of theirs (when it generally is possible). Wiring payments to them is apparently possible, but there is no documented case of this ever having worked. Needless to say any contact with Naviera Austral requires both patience and fluent Spanish.

🛥 **Puerto Ibáñez to Chile Chico** 19.00 Mon, Tue, Wed, Fri & Sun, with a 2nd departure on Wed at 10.00, 20.00 Thu & noon Sat, returns at 08.00 Mon, Tue & Thu, 10.00 Wed, 16.00 Fri & Sun, 09.00 Sat (2½hrs; $2,100pp one-way, $18,650 for a vehicle). The main route is across the lake to Chile Chico, but it also services Puerto Avellanos

& Puerto Cristal. Book weeks in advance in high season, particularly if travelling with a car. Foot passengers can usually get a seat within a day or 2.

🛥 **Puerto Yungay to Puerto Bravo** Dec–Mar 10.00, noon & 18.00 daily, returns 11.00, 13.00 & 19.00; Apr–Nov noon & 15.00 daily, returns 13.00 & 16.00 (free).

BY AIR Charter flights are expensive, although if travelling with sufficient people to fill the plane the price becomes more accessible. Currently the only scheduled flights within the Carretera Austral are Villa O'Higgins to/from Coyhaique and Chaitén to/from Puerto Montt, each costing at least US$100 one-way per person,

This does not lend itself to forward planning, and in peak season these boats may fill up for weeks in advance. This bottleneck encourages visitors to fly to Chaitén or Balmaceda (Coyhaique) or use the Futaleufú border crossing instead, missing the northern section of the Carretera Austral. The residents of the northern region obviously suffer as a result of the poor ferry service and the relative absence of tourists in their region. Naviera Austral receives the subsidy regardless, and as long as it operates the minimal service, the boats are sufficiently full with local passengers to warrant little effort to secure additional sales from foreigners. Local residents also moan about the ferries, but they have the luxury of being able to stroll down to a local office to buy a ticket, and may not have international flight connections to consider.

Naviera Austral claim to be working to improve their website, and to incorporate WebPay functionality permitting foreign credit cards. However, with the threat of a possible road connection across this section of the Carretera Austral (see box, pages 98–9), Naviera Austral have little incentive to invest further money in a route that may eventually become obsolete.

One alternative, something of a last resort if all efforts to buy directly from Naviera Austral fail, is to find a tour operator or make a reservation at a hotel that also offers tours and offer to pay them a premium if they will physically go and buy the ticket for you. But get your plans crystal clear beforehand, as changes are equally complex. Although one date change to a ticket is possible for free, it depends on availability, which becomes increasingly scarce each passing minute.

Beware that if planning to use a rental car you will not have the number plate at the time of booking, which you will need to book these ferries in advance, especially in high season. Turning up at Caleta Gonzalo hoping to hop on the next ferry, particularly with a car, is not just likely to cause disappointment, but the alternative drive back down to Villa Santa Lucía, up to Futaleufú, into Argentina, up through Bariloche and back over to Chile via Osorno is a long journey.

Our advice: plan your trip carefully beforehand; be patient; get the ferry connections sorted out first; avoid having to make changes; if travelling without a vehicle simply buy a bus ticket for the ferry sections as the buses are guaranteed spaces; and consider that there are flights to/from Chaitén and ferries from Cisnes to Quellón.

if seats are available. Commercial flights between Coyhaique/Balmaceda and Puerto Montt/Santiago are reasonably priced.

ACCOMMODATION

Options abound along most sections of the Carretera Austral. Wherever people live there is a hostel or a *casa familiar*, but in peak season these can fill up quickly, particularly in towns such as Lago Verde, Puyuhuapi, Raúl Marín Balmaceda, Puerto Río Tranquilo, Villa Santa Lucía and Caleta Tortel. There is a bewildering range of names for accommodation in Chile, each referring to a specific legal structure. Budget accommodation tends to be referred to as *hostal*, *residencial* or *hospedaje*; *cabañas* (cabins) can range from cheap to positively pricey options; lodges and hotels tend to be mid price and upwards. Confusingly the term *spa* can refer to a spa (sauna, pool, massages, etc) or to a legal structure of a company in Chile. Camping is possible in every town, and if not, wild camping is usually tolerated.

The Carretera Austral lends itself to the adventure traveller, as typified by the younger backpacker armed with a tent and flexible accommodation requirements but comparatively modest budget. Mid-price-range accommodation and food options are increasingly common, but at the higher end of the spectrum those with fewer budget constraints seeking adventurous alternatives to the standard luxury options within South America have a surprising array of options. High-end accommodation along the Carretera Austral was arguably pioneered by the Puyuhuapi Lodge and Spa (page 138), and some upmarket fishing lodges, but there are now a number of positively comfortable, even luxurious, hotels (and to a lesser extent, restaurants) for those not necessarily interested in fishing. Indeed, at the time of writing, the only principal destinations lacking an upper-end place to sleep are Hornopirén, downtown Chaitén, Palena, Puerto Cisnes, Chile Chico, Puerto Río Tranquilo, Cerro Castillo and Puerto Ibáñez.

Hot water can generally be taken for granted. Some hostels rely on one central wood stove to heat the building, which is not ideal in winter, but increasingly central heating is becoming an economical and convenient alternative. In all but the most basic accommodation a towel and soap are provided. Wi-Fi is prolific, laundry less so; it is really only upper-end accommodation options that offer a laundry service. Off-road parking is abundant, but not strictly necessary as car theft is rare. Motorcyclists typically prefer not to leave their bikes parked on the street if only to enable them to leave non-urgent accessories attached to the bike and avoid kids playing with them.

All accommodation listed is open during high season (mid-November to mid-March), but this is extending each year. Places which close during this period, or are open outside of high season, are listed as such.

ACCOMMODATION PRICE CODES

The following accommodation price codes are very approximate and refer to a typical double room with a private bathroom (where a private bathroom is available) in peak season. Many hotels/hostels in this region have a wide range of options within a single property, so we have also included prices within listings to cover anomalies to the double room price.

Luxury	$$$$$	over $100,000	over US$170
Upper range	$$$$	$50,000–100,000	US$85–170
Mid range	$$$	$30,000–50,000	US$50–85
Budget	$$	$20,000–30,000	US$35–50
Low end	$	up to $20,000	up to US$35

Some hotels, typically more formally registered companies, are able to offer discounts to foreigners paying in US dollars or on a foreign credit card, with proof that they are non-resident in Chile (passport with stamp suffices). This is because the sale is classified as an 'export' and thus exempt from sales tax (19%).

LUXURY ACCOMMODATION ALONG THE CARRETERA AUSTRAL

For those looking to splash the cash, a number of options exist from north to south along the Carretera Austral (all **$$$$-$$$$$**).

Hotel Manquehue Puerto Montt. Modern, hip hotel, debatably the finest in town but for surprisingly reasonable rates, & a great restaurant/bar; page 70.

Caleta Gonzalo Cabins Caleta Gonzalo. Delightful, rustic cabins at the edge of Parque Pumalín, with a stunning view over the fjord & the only restaurant for miles; pages 106–7.

Termas Río Amarillo Lodge 5km from El Amarillo. Excellent location for visiting Parque Pumalín & wonderful hot springs at the property; page 107.

Yelcho en la Patagonia 51km south of Chaitén, this upmarket dedicated fishing lodge on the lake is close to the glacier & has a fine restaurant; page 109.

Hotel El Barranco Futaleufú. The finest accommodation in town with pool & quality restaurant; pages 115–6.

Uman Lodge Just outside Futaleufú. Possibly the best hotel on the entire Carretera; pages 116–17.

Hotel Espacio y Tiempo La Junta. Fine hotel, excellent service & the best restaurant in town; page 124.

Fundo Los Leones Raúl Marín Balmaceda. Private beach & landing strip; page 128.

El Pangue Lodge Between La Junta & Puyuhuapi. Top-quality adventure lodge; pages 138–9.

Puyuhuapi Lodge & Spa 20km south of Puyuhuapi. Refurbished, classic, top-end lodge with idyllic remote location & hot springs; page 138.

Los Loberías del Sur Puerto Chacabuco. Standard 5-star option, but offers a catamaran trip to Ventisquero San Rafael; page 161.

Nómades Coyhaique. A definitive boutique hotel & oasis in the relative hustle of Coyhaique, with fantastic views over the valley, & yet within walking distance of the centre; page 175.

Patagonia Bay Lodge 25km north of Puerto Río Tranquilo. Decent lodge for those with a private vehicle, in a large property bordering the lake; pages 201–2.

Hacienda Tres Lagos &/or Mallin Colorado EcoLodge 50km south of Puerto Río Tranquilo, close to Puerto Bertrand & the detour towards Chile Chico. Top-end adventure lodges with good restaurants; pages 210 & 211.

Hotel El Mirador de Guadal &/or Patagonia Acres Lodge On the road from Chile Chico – probably the finest accommodations on Lago General Carrera; page 213. Top-end cabins with spectacular views over the lake.

The Lodge at Chacabuco Valley 15km north of Cochrane. Magnificent lodge within the spectacular Parque Patagonia, wildlife visible from almost every window; page 232.

Ultimo Paraíso Cochrane. The only upper–mid-range option in Cochrane, hub of activities, owner is a fanatical fishing guide; pages 238–9.

Entre Hielos Lodge Caleta Tortel. The only boutique option in town, with a well-run, homely feel. Can arrange incredible glacial tours; page 248.

Robinson Crusoe Deep Patagonia Lodge Villa O'Higgins. Excellent accommodation but no restaurant, operates the boat to Argentina via Ventisquero O'Higgins; page 256.

As a general rule, in early 2015 most villages have basic accommodation with a simple breakfast for under $15,000 per person (US$20). It is rare to find accommodation for under $10,000 per person (or US$15) without camping.

Practical Information ACCOMMODATION

2

EATING AND DRINKING

Every village, however small, has a place to eat and a shop. Whether these are open or not is another issue. In smaller villages businesses tend to close around 20.00 or 21.00 if there are no customers, and restaurants will not have formal opening hours. It is wise to eat early. Lunch is generally available from 13.00 to 15.00. In the larger towns it is possible to find somewhere to eat all day and up to midnight. Coyhaique is the only place with all-night restaurants.

Chilean fare can become rather repetitive particularly along the Carretera Austral, where culinary creativity seems scarce. Expect to find *merluza* (hake), *congrio* (eel), *mariscos* (shellfish), *puye* (small, whitebait-like fish), a meat dish, perhaps *cazuela* (meat or fish stew), chips, potatoes, a basic salad, deep fried bread and a range of nondescript puddings. Meat described as *mechada* is shredded, and *milanesa* is in thin strips; *a lo pobre* contains salad, a fried egg and chips. *Curanto* is a particular delicacy originating in Chiloé, and is certainly worth trying. It generally contains two plates – one of shellfish and fish, and one of meat, a sausage, potatoes and a potato dumpling, all cooked together in the same pot. Strictly speaking a proper curanto should be cooked in a hole in the ground covered with leaves and mud, but this is generally only available on the island of Chiloé.

Although limited, there are some variations from Chilean cuisine: Coyhaique has sushi, Peruvian food and some excellent high-end restaurants. The German settlers of the region in the early 20th century secured an ongoing supply of decent bread, cakes and savoury snacks (*kuchen*). Lamb (*cordero*), where available, is excellent; beef is abundant but rarely cooked to the standard found on the Argentine side of the Andes. Seafood is common and vegetarians, even vegans, may actually find this region to be more compatible with their food tastes than Argentina. A number of restaurants offer a vegetarian option.

Many restaurants offer a *menu del dia* (set menu with limited choice), which are generally very good value and popular amongst the locals. Many cabins, and some hostels or hotels offer self-catering barbecue facilities (*parrilla/asado*), and often these are included in a separate outhouse, called a *quincho*. Ideal for groups, this is basically a building available for rent with tables, plates, cutlery, etc, where guests can prepare their own food, usually lamb or steak, bought privately or arranged through the hotel/hostel.

Wine is available in mid-range restaurants but tends to be overpriced and offers limited variety; a finer range is available in upper-end restaurants, albeit at a price. Local **beers** are more abundant and cheaper. Chileans debate with Peruvians as to the true inventor of **Pisco**, but it is fair to say that almost anywhere along the Carretera Austral it is possible to find a decent Pisco Sour, including flavoured with local berries and fruits. The water is generally fine to drink straight from the tap.

RESTAURANT PRICE CODES

Given the common tendency to offer set menus (*menú del día*), the following restaurant price codes refer to a typical meal, per person, excluding drinks.

Luxury	$$$$	over $12,000	over US$20
Upper range	$$$	$8,000–12,000	US$13–20
Mid range	$$	$5,000–8,000	US$8–13
Budget	$	up to $5,000	up to US$8

A growing passion in the region is the production of fine craft beer (*cerveza artesanal*). What better way to utilise the abundant pure water of southern Chile than to make great beer? Most restaurants and bars will have at least one regional beer (usually bottled, sometimes on tap). After a long day on the dusty road, it's always a pleasure to enjoy a cool and refreshing beverage.

If you tire of the hearty Carretera Austral microbrews try the traditional popular beers common throughout Chile such as Cristal and Escudo, or the now semi-national beers from medium-sized breweries like Kunstmann and Austral.

The prevalence of **gourmet** restaurants has not kept up with the number of high-end hotels in the region. Most are within the hotels listed on page 49 (in particular Uman Lodge and Hotel El Barranco in Futaleufú, and Espacio y Tiempo in La Junta). South of Coyhaique, upper-end restaurants are few and far between. Nevertheless, the following restaurants (from north to south) are genuinely of a high quality, but even in the most expensive of these restaurants, a couple would be hard-pressed to spend more than US$100 on a single meal excluding wine.

✕ Fogon Cotelé de Jeremy & Pa' Mar Adentro Puerto Montt. Superb quality meat & seafood; page 72.

✕ Isla Verde & Patagonia Green Puerto Aysén. These are both approaching *haute cuisine*; page 162.

✕ Restaurant Ruibarbo Coyhaique. An excellent restaurant that would be equally at home in London or New York; page 177.

PUBLIC HOLIDAYS

1 January	New Year
late March/early April	Easter
1 May	Labour Day
21 May	Navy Day
29 June	Sts Peter and Paul Day
16 July	Virgen del Carmen
15 August	Assumption of the Virgin Mary
18 September	National Day
19 September	Army Day
12 October	Colombus Day
1 November	All Saints' Day
8 December	Immaculate Conception
25 December	Christmas Day

Besides the usual holidays around Christmas and New Year, the main public holidays a visitor to the Carretera Austral is likely to witness are the annual celebrations of individual towns, often based around a rodeo theme, generally in January or February – the exact dates vary from year to year.

SHOPPING

Even the smallest villages have a simple store for basic provisions. If at first they appear closed, knock on the door. However, **supermarkets** (in the normal sense of the word) are found only in the main towns (Chaitén, Hornopirén, Aysén, Coyhaique and Cochrane) and, as a general rule, only the basic necessities are available anywhere outside of Coyhaique. One major benefit of the Carretera Austral

Courtesy of Randy Clouse, international beer expert, resident of (bars in) Bariloche, Argentina

There are at least ten widely available microbrews in the region, and that doesn't include the many handcrafted beers only available on site or within the village of production. On a well-planned two-week holiday you can try a new beer each day. Adding beer-tasting to your itinerary on the Carretera Austral may come with some risks, but you will come away enriched knowing that you have experienced beer that is only available in remote southern Chile. How many others can say that? As more entrepreneurs start adding their creative and sometimes exquisite products to the market, I'm sure the range and quality of craft beers will continue to increase in the region.

Most craft beers use only four ingredients: water, malted barley, hops, and yeast. Generally they are heartier than industrial beers and are not filtered. Don't be surprised if you see a little sediment at the bottom of your bottle; it's just yeast and it's safe to consume. Allow the beer to settle for a minute, pour it slowly in one go so as not to agitate it unnecessarily, and stop pouring before the settled yeast emerges. Newcomers should find they are pouring like a pro within no time.

In the summer of 2015, Puerto Aysén held the Second Annual Beer Expo featuring a number of regional breweries. The festive event is gaining popularity and is a fantastic way for a beer enthusiast to get to know several harder-to-find varieties from small brewers who are on the forefront of the regional craft beer movement.

COYHAIQUE D'Olbek (*Baquedano 1899;* \ *(67) 2232947; www.dolbek.cl*) is the most widely available along the Carretera Austral. Aficionados can tour their facilities, but call ahead to make sure they're open. I went too late one evening and was chased away by some intimidating dogs. The owners guard their elixir at any cost.

Tropera (*www.tropera.cl*) makes a variety of excellent ales available in only two places: their rustic brewpub (*Camino Teniente Vidad, km1.5*) just across the river from town; and the Mamma Gaucha pizzeria (*Paseo Horn 47*) off the main plaza. The brewpub also offers great burgers and other Chilean gastronomic favourites, but the main draw is the highly recommended beer. Depending on the season they usually have five to nine different styles, from light to dark, sweet to bitter, and strong to stronger. The Indian Pale Ale is their most popular. The walk to the brewpub is steep and crosses a swaying bridge over the Río Simpson; don't be surprised if the walk back seems even steeper and the bridge sways more!

Campo D'Hielo (*www.campodhielo.cl*) produces three beers made from the same recipe but incorporating water from different sources: glacier, river and spring water. These have a tendency to be murky. You'll be amazed at the impact the water makes, both in flavour and in appearance, depending both on the pH balance and the minerals, nitrates, and salts it contains. Several restaurants in the area, mostly in Coyhaique, carry these beers on their menus.

Pioneros (⨍ *Cerveza Pioneros*) is also popular, and the varieties include Negra (dark), Roja (red), and Rubia (blond). Many small shops also sell this beer which is recognisable from its label that show black and white photos of pioneers in the region. Although not up there with the best, it does the job.

Caiquén (🅵 *Cerveza Artesanal Caiquén*) is another notable brew. Apparently the brewer started in Villa Cerro Castillo (since that is shown as the origin on the label) but locals informed me that he now produces the beer in Coyhaique. A fine dark or blond ale that goes well either with a sandwich or on its own.

NORTHERN CARRETERA AUSTRAL Leaving the cosmopolitan comforts of Coyhaique doesn't mean giving up on the microbrews. Elsewhere on the Carretera Austral most towns offer a locally brewed beer.

Joost (*Av Pangal 167, Puerto Aysén,* ✆ *(9) 90995682;* e *cervezajoost@ yahoo.cl*), produces three styles: Blond Lager, Red Ale, and Dark Ale.

Using water with low mineral content from the springs around Puerto Chacabuco, **Bravo** is a lager beer also produced in Puerto Aysén. Their three most popular styles are the coffee-and-chocolate-flavoured Lager Negra (dark), caramel Lager Ambar (red), and the bitter and strong Lager Rubia (blond).

Kawiñ (*Carretera Austral 339B, La Junta;* ✆ *(9) 76418823;* e *donald.manque@ gmail.com; cervezakawin.cl*) is from La Junta and uses only Chilean barley without additives or preservatives. They say it's made with respect for the environment. Kawiñ roughly means 'festive social gathering' (ie: party) in the Mapuche language. The two varieties, Golden Ale and Porter, use water originating in the Reserva Nacional Lago Rosselot. Brewery tours (🕐 *10.00– 13.00 & 15.00–20.00*) can be arranged Monday to Saturday in summer.

Hopperdeitzal (*www.puyuhuapi.com*) is brewed just north of Puyuhuapi but has also expanded regionally. Produced with water from Valle Caesar, the three styles are Goldene Jahre Ale, Roter Teppich Ale and Schwarz Back Ale. The stubby bottles add an old-world charm to this delightful beer.

Puerto Cisnes is home to **Finisterra** (page 149). Their 100% organic beer comes in seven varieties: Rubia (blond), Dorada (golden), Negra (dark), Rubia con Calafate (with calafate fruit juice), Rubia con Cauchao, Rubia con Miel (honey) y Rubia con Ají (spicy). The Queulat Mountains are the source of the water. This brewery has been around for a while and has a good reputation. Guided tours of the brewery are a highlight to any visit to Puerto Cisnes.

Futaleufú offers at least three local beers. My personal favourite is **FutaAlhue**, made by Arturo Vivanco Navarete who started brewing back in 2010 at the time of the Chilean bicentennial celebration, and still makes his beer in 20-litre batches giving the beer a special small batch richness. FutaAlhue means 'Place of Big Souls', and is sold in half-litre bottles in three varieties: Golden, IPA (Blood of the Guide), and Oatmeal Stout (Bosque Nativo, 'Native Forest').

Zakingen is brewed for the Antigua Casa restaurant near the plaza, and uses water from thermal springs near Chaitén (Termas de Río Amarillo; page 107) that give their Blond, Red, and Dark beers a unique flavour.

Ruta Siete (only available in Hornopirén) is frankly, mediocre.

SOUTHERN CARRETERA AUSTRAL Further south near Puerto Ingeniero Ibáñez you can find **Dallman**, which is only available on site at the Fundo El Maitenal. It's a German-style beer that supposedly is the perfect thirst-quencher after rock climbing in the area. Gerald Dallman and his wife have been known to share their home brew alongside a true Patagonian *asado*.

The **Cervecería Río Tranquilo** (*Carretera Austral s/n, Puerto Río Tranquilo;* \ *(9) 98955577;* f *Cerveza Arisca*) produces **Arisca** beer, which is also sold in their pub in Coyhaique (page 177). Arisca in English means 'wild', but this refined beer is most drinkable. In the small factory next door they brew three styles: Baya, a light wheat; Alazana, a slightly bitter malty red; and Picasa, a smoky dark with a coffee aroma. Even with 100-litre fermentation tanks, they still have difficulties in meeting demand during the high season, so not all styles are always available.

On the southern shores of the Lago General Carrera, the beer **Olilkel** comes from Chile Chico and can be found in the southern region of the Carretera Austral.

In Cochrane you may be able to find **Baker Beer** (*Cabañas Sol y Luna;* page 239), which made a name for itself in the city according to locals but has temporarily stopped production. Let's hope they continue since it has left a gaping hole in the craft beer industry of Cochrane. Shops and restaurants do carry other regional beers, so beer fans will not be forced into abstinence.

Towards the southern extreme of the Carretera Austral there is a new arrival from Caleta Tortel, aptly called **Tortel**, which is still in its infancy but is on the right track to become a solid player in the south. For now it's only available in the Sabores Locales restaurant (page 250).

is that it is hard to spend money on anything other than food, accommodation and the occasional tour or kayak rental. **Laundries** are less common along the Carretera – those present in villages are listed in the text.

In terms of **food**, outside Coyhaique there are few shops selling more than basic ingredients. Campers can find the traditional array of tomato paste, tinned products, pasta and occasionally dried soya, but beyond the standard camping fare, options are limited. Stock up on more esoteric ingredients in Puerto Montt or Coyhaique. Local edible products are available; in particular marmalades, bottled shellfish, *nalca* stalks and bread are offered in most towns.

The typical **market** stalls found across most of South America selling brightly coloured handbags and purses (apparently from the region but invariably from Peru) are almost non-existent along the Carretera. Coyhaique has a small trinket market on the central square, and Villa Amengual has an impressive co-operative selling locally made handicrafts at reasonable prices. Elsewhere, the Puyuhuapi Carpet Factory sells some amazing (if not overpriced) carpets (page 141). Indeed, one almost wishes there were more shops.

ACTIVITIES ALONG THE CARRETERA AUSTRAL

Chile has consistently been voted one of the leading adventure destinations on earth. The range of activities offered along the Carretera Austral does not necessarily involve jumping from an airplane or ice-climbing, but there is something for everyone: adrenaline junkies will be delighted with the climbing and rafting options while more sedentary visitors may be content with a short trek and a spot of fishing. With the obvious exception of beach activities (water temperatures range from solid ice to merely freezing cold), a degree of adventure and exercise can be incorporated into any itinerary.

TREKKING This is possible almost everywhere. Most parks have extensive networks of marked trails. Some people trek the entire Carretera Austral itself. In the northern section, **Cochamó** has extensive marked trails, including over to Argentina, ranging from day treks to treks taking in excess of one week (pages 84–7). The Cochamó trails connect with those of Puelo and further south, as well as those in Argentina reaching Bariloche. **Parque Pumalín** has a number of trails, including to rare alerce trees (pages 107–8). Treks range from half an hour to a full day, and are some of the more accessible treks for young children or for those with reduced mobility. The **Sendero de Chile** between Palena and Lago Verde (page 121) passes the otherwise inaccessible Lago Palena, and also connects to other trails to the east of the Carretera, making multiple-day treks feasible. **Parque Patagonia** (a park still in development although open to visitors) has relatively few marked trails, but of incredible beauty, in particular the three-day trek to **Reserva Nacional Jeinemeni**. A comparable multi-day trek extends from **Cochrane to Villa O'Higgins** in the extreme south. For the more adventurous it is possible to trek up onto the two ice fields, but generally this requires a guide, and specific experience.

CYCLING This is one the most common means of transport along the Carretera Austral, and the route is considered one of the definitive bike rides on the continent. Mountain bikes can be rented in most towns, but in particular consider Futaleufú, Puyuhuapi, La Junta, around Coyhaique, and Cochrane. As with trekking, the possibilities are almost without limit.

CLIMBING **Cochamó** is widely considered to be one of the best climbing spots on the continent, colloquially referred to as 'the Yosemite of South America' (pages 84–7). There are sufficient routes for dedicated climbers to spend an entire season around Cochamó and never climb the same route twice. Watersports may be the principal activity in **Futaleufú** (pages 118–19); it is also possible to climb. Around Coyhaique there are also decent climbing routes. **Cerro Castillo** (pages 198–200) offers some challenging routes to experienced climbers, but access is limited. Needless to say the ice shelves and glaciers offer ice-climbing options for experienced climbers.

BIRDWATCHING The entire Carretera Austral is an ornithologist's paradise, so this is an almost unavoidable activity. Park maps generally list the most common species. The area around **Coyhaique** is probably the most famous place to see Andean condors (pages 182–3). Thanks to its extensive grasslands and countless lagoons, **Parque Patagonia** has abundant birdlife, including flamingos, owls, condors, ibis and flightless birds such as small native ostriches. The restoration of natural grasslands and native species in Parque Patagonia has resulted in abundant wildlife and ideal nesting grounds for the condor – it is possible to see dozens of Andean condors simultaneously. For sea birds, **Raúl Marín Balmaceda** is worth a visit (page 129). **Villa O'Higgins** offers excellent guided birdwatching treks. Penguins are most easily seen around **Chaitén**. In fact they can be seen along most of the coastline close to the Carretera Austral, but access can be a challenge. They have even been seen in Puyuhuapi.

RAFTING/KAYAKING The thundering rivers around **Palena** and **Futaleufú** are widely considered to offer some of the best white water on earth (pages 118–19), with numerous adrenaline-filled trips possible. Most villages on lakes will have someone, somewhere, willing to rent a kayak, and many hotels will have some for guests. Renting a kayak in **Puyuhuapi** enables a visit to some hot springs (page 142)

The abundant, transparent waters where trout abound, combined with the low number of fishermen, make southern Chile a sport-fishing paradise. From shallow mountain streams to huge rivers, from freshwater lakes to the salty Pacific coast, the variety and range of locations offer a number of options for all experience levels. Most of the common species found in inland waters today were introduced from both North America and Europe over a century ago, dominating the few native species that still exist. Trout species include rainbows, brown and fontalis. Chinook and sakura are the most common salmon species. Salmon farming in the area has increased significantly within the last few decades, especially off the coast, and most of the salmon now found in the area is a by-product of the aquaculture programmes.

Sernapesca (*www.pescarecreativa.sernapesca.cl*) is the government agency that regulates fishing and sells licences both online and in their offices throughout Chile. Some fishing supply stores in Puerto Montt and Coyhaique also sell licences. The main sport-fishing season runs from October to April, with some variation for different types of species and location. A week's licence for foreigners is around $12,000, and a full-season licence is $35,000. Catch and release is mandatory in some bodies of water and always strongly recommended. The licence includes a small booklet with more details.

It is advised to bring equipment with you as it is hard to rent outside of Coyhaique. It will be inspected and disinfected upon entry by border control authorities for a fee and, due to the recent detection of the Didymo algae, the government has started a prevention programme to stop its spread. This invasive algae originated in North America and grows into large slimy clumps in slow-moving rivers and spreads easily, affecting the visibility and oxygen levels of the water.

To help prevent the spread of Didymo, the Chilean government recommends a thorough cleaning of shoes, waders, gear, lines, and anything else that touches the water. Soak it all in a bucket with detergent for one–two minutes, and then dry it all thoroughly. Fortunately many of the larger rivers have not been infected, but it's up to all of us to keep it that way since once Didymo arrives it is nearly impossible to eradicate.

---

accessible only by boat at low tide, and also to see a hidden glacier only visible from the far side of the canal. The other rafting destination is **Puerto Bertrand** and along the Río Baker (page 226). **Puerto Cisnes** has some interesting lake and sea-kayaking options. Obviously almost every village around the massive **Lago General Carrera** is suitable for a range of water activities, and most rent kayaks. Instead of taking a guided tour to the marble caves around **Puerto Río Tranquilo**, consider renting a kayak and spending half a day visiting the caves (page 207). There are countless lakes across the entire region, including around Coyhaique – the options are endless.

HORSERIDING This is deeply embedded in the culture of the entire region. Most villages will have a rodeo, and the gaucho culture is very much alive from north to south. The **Sendero de Chile** route between Palena and Lago Verde is commonly done on horseback (page 121), as is the week-long route between Cochrane and Villa O'Higgins. Horseriding is also common around Cochrane, where many inhabitants will tether their horses on the central plaza while they do a spot of

Serious anglers should plan on bringing all their own gear with them. A portable 7 to 8ft, five- or six-weight rod works well in most situations, and reels and lines that can withstand those 20lb+ trophy fish. A couple of different lines would come in handy: one for floating and one for sinking. Wet flies, dry flies, nymphs, and streamers all may work depending on the conditions. Outside Coyhaique finding gear is difficult so bring everything and spares. Only barbless hooks are permitted for catch and release.

Principal destinations are the rivers Baker, Futaleufú, Simpson, Palena, Rosselot, Cochrane and Cisnes, and also Lago General Carrera, Bahía Exploradores, and Lago Cochrane. The full list of options would require another book unto itself, since the reality is that almost everywhere on the Carretera Austral is close to some body of water with fish. Some of these waters are so transparent and full of fish that even an amateur can have lots of fun without going too far off the beaten path.

Fishing from the coast is fine, but to hook the big catches you'll need a guide or boat. Guides and tour operators can be found locally in nearly all villages, but there are a few that stand out for the international fisherman. Prices and services vary. For example Carlos Benes in Cochrane (*www. hotelultimoparaiso.cl*) charges US$200 per day for two people (including lunch). In Puerto Bertrand you can hire a boat and guide by the hour for $18,000 (two people), and Expediciones Coyhaique offers an all-inclusive per-night rate of US$375 perperson at their lodge near Coyhaique.

A number of great fishing lodges have sprung up in the area as well, including the Robinson Crusoe lodge in Villa O'Higgins, the Green Baker Lodge in Puerto Bertrand, Patagonia Bay Lodge in Bahia Murta, the Coyhaique River Lodge near Coyhaique, and Espacio y Tiempo Hotel in La Junta (see respective chapters for contact details). Most include four- or five-star service, excursions, and full board.

Even if you are not an avid fisherman, you will be tempted to try your luck in these legendary waters. You will probably see more fish than people! If you don't catch anything, this outstanding location alone, with breathtaking views, will bring satisfaction and enough material to tell tales about the one that got away.

shopping. Cerro Castillo also has a number of tails and horses for rent for those preferring to ride rather than hike.

SCUBA/FREE DIVING Although not as common as other activities, Cochrane has an official scuba centre. It is also possible to snorkel on the Río Cochrane, one of the most pleasantly surprising activities along the entire Carretera (pages 238 and 241). The crystal-clear waters of Lago Cochrane are ideal for diving, and it is even possible to take formal PADI courses there. However, outside Cochrane there is no equipment rental and diving is done entirely with your own equipment at your own risk. Snorkelling and free diving are thus more practical, and it is possible to explore the marble caves in both **Puerto Sanchez** (page 202) and **Puerto Río Tranquilo** (page 207) with a decent wetsuit, mask and snorkel. Needless to say water temperatures are somewhat chilly; a 7mm wetsuit is probably the minimum required. Good opportunities can also be found along the coastal road to Hornopirén; along Fiordo Comau; at many places in Chiloé; at Puerto Cisnes; on the islands around Raúl Marín Balmaceda, and in the endless lakes that stretch along the entire route. There are also options to go out to sea with the traditional fishermen living along the coast to the west of Hornopirén (page 89).

OTHER ACTIVITIES Sports such as canyoning, canopy and dirt-bike rentals are emerging each season. Given the popularity of kite-surfing on the Argentine side of the mountains, inevitably this will begin in Chile also. In winter it is possible to **ski** around Coyhaique (page 182), but this is unlikely to become a major attraction for a number of years. There's even a **language school** if you want to improve your Spanish – see page 181 for details.

COMMUNICATIONS

INTERNET Along the majority of the Carretera Austral there is no internet. However, almost every village with a municipal office or library offers free computers and internet access, and some larger towns such as La Junta, Coyhaique and Cochrane offer free Wi-Fi in the central plazas, and if a village is connected to the internet then even basic hostels will offer this for free.

TELEPHONE Mobile phone coverage is patchy, to say the least, and none of three main mobile phone companies (Movistar, Entel and Claro) have universal coverage. In general, Entel seems to have the best coverage at the time of writing, but the ideal solution would be to buy SIMs of all three networks and switch them according to the region (or simply do not rely on a phone!). SIMs are cheap and can be purchased in larger towns (Chile Chico, Puerto Montt, Coyhaique or Aysén) and topped up in most places.

Telephone codes in Chile can be infuriatingly complicated. Along the Carretera Austral there are two main fixed line codes: (65) and (67), most of which cannot

---

DON'T MENTION THE WAR

In October 2014 the team of *Top Gear*, the BBC's popular television series about cars, sparked controversy by driving through Patagonia with a Porsche 928 with the number plate H982 FKL. Argentines assumed this was a discreet reference to the 1982 Falklands War. Whether the choice of number plate was deliberate or coincidental is a matter of some controversy, although the *Top Gear* team and the BBC claim this was a pure chance. All three presenters drove V8 vehicles, and lead presenter Jeremy Clarkson, driver of the offending vehicle, claimed the choice of car was because a Porsche 928 had enabled him to rapidly visit his dying father some years previously. From Bariloche, where the number plate was first spotted, the team drove south and crossed over to the Carretera Austral at Futaleufú (they stayed in the excellent Hotel El Barranco, pages 115–16), and left at Coyhaique. Describing a northern section of the road Clarkson suggests it appeared like the 'set of *Jurassic Park*, petrified forests, mysterious lakes… this is all very odd… if I go round the next corner and there's a brontosaurus I will not be surprised.'

Upon arriving in Ushuaia (Argentina), where sentiments run high regarding the ownership of the Falkland Islands (Islas Malvinas), angry mobs gathered. The *Top Gear* team decided to flee. Pelted with stones, they eventually sought refuge in Chile.

be dialled on Skype Out. Fixed lines are followed by seven digits, but calling *from* a fixed line is relatively challenging, as there are no public telephones. Cellphones must use the local dialling code; calling a cellphone requires a (9) followed by eight digits regardless of the operator or the origin of the call (dial +569 and then the eight-digit code from abroad). Owing to the patchy coverage of all operators, and the mobility of the people, most people (and in particular most companies) have multiple cellphones, in order to be able to receive calls regardless of their precise location. If the first number does not work as the phone is 'out of coverage area', try the second (or third). Until universal coverage is achieved this is as inconvenient for the recipient as the dialler, but bear in mind that large parts of the Carretera Austral simply have no cellphone coverage. Leaving a message is generally a waste of time; it's best to just try again later.

In this guide, telephone numbers are listed in the following order: fixed line first (generally a (65) or (67) prefix, (2) in the case on Santiago phones), followed by the most likely cellphone numbers.

CULTURAL ETIQUETTE

Southern Chile is generally fairly laidback. Although English is not widely spoken, Chileans will generally be delighted to have a chat with foreigners able to converse in even basic Spanish. However, the informality of the Argentine *vos* is not used in Chile, and particularly when speaking to older people of those in authority the *usted* form is more appropriate. Likewise, the Argentine custom of referring to strangers as *che* is not always welcome in Chile. See page 268 for more detail on specific Chilean linguistic idiosyncrasies.

Some topics have to be broached with caution, in part related to 20th-century Chilean history. Southern Chile was generally less adversely impacted by the **Pinochet** military junta (page 17), and indeed some regions positively benefited from Pinochet. Given the constant squabbling with Argentina over the borders separating the two countries, particularly in the south many Chileans believe with some justification that it was Pinochet who protected this region from falling into Argentine hands. However, expressing pro-Pinochet sentiment is often misinterpreted and thus many people, particularly the older generation, are hesitant to discuss this topic. There were also atrocities committed under the military junta in this region, perhaps not to the extent of central and northern Chile, and broaching the topic risks opening old wounds.

The **Falklands War** of 1982 can also raise some lively conversations, but ensure there are no Argentines present. Chile, and in particular Pinochet, supported the UK in 1982, while Chile now officially supports further dialogue and tentatively backs the Argentine claim to the islands. Most locals firmly believe the Falklands are British, but this could equally be discreet national rivalry against their neighbour. Trips to the Carretera Austral inevitably involve border crossings to Argentina, and the topic has a remarkable tendency to crop up, particularly with British citizens. It is best not to enter into a debate on this topic. For anyone under the age of 35 it is usually safer to mention that you were not born at the time and have hardly heard of the dispute. 'What islands?'

Another sensitive topic is **World War II**. A number of German settlers from both sides of the political spectrum arrived both before and after the war, as well as by Sudeten Germans (Czechoslovakian German-speakers) and refugees fleeing the war. Tread cautiously when making sweeping generalisations on this topic.

Chile is a **Catholic** country, but the southern region is relatively areligious. This is not as much a delicate topic of conversation as a non-topic of conversation. There are few historic churches in the region; for those interested in exploring fantastic churches that have played – and continue to play – a central role in society, Chiloé may be a more interesting destination.

The issue of installing **hydro-electric dams** in the region stirred huge controversy and plans were eventually scrapped (see box, pages 172–4). '*Patagonia ¡sin represas!*' ('Patagonia without dams!') stickers adorn most cars and shop windows. Unless you have an extremely valid reason to disagree, it is generally safer to go with the mass consensus and broadly frown upon the idea of flooding much of Patagonia in order to provide electricity predominantly for use in Santiago. It is hard to imagine riot police in the region, but emotions ran sufficiently high in Coyhaique as to prompt full civil unrest, and the topic remains a sensitive one to this day.

Related to the anti-hydro-electric dam sentiment, the US philanthropist Doug Tompkins has historically sparked some controversial and critical sentiment, but nowadays he is largely viewed as a benevolent contributor to the region (and planet in general). Some farmers, however, are positively 'anti-Tompkins'. See box, pages 104–5 for more information.

There is one topic that sparks serious animosity to this day and is of direct relevance to some travellers along the Carretera Austral – the issue of **Israel**. Strong anti-Israeli sentiment exists, and is increasingly vocal and visible; some hostels even place Palestinian flags in their windows as a discreet means to warn that not all foreigners are welcome. It is not generally anti-Semitism, but anti-Israeli. The local people believe that the Israelis travelling in the region are looking out for new land (given the current situation in Israel), and that they particularly like regions with water. This sentiment is more directed towards groups of young Israeli travellers, particularly those having recently completed their military service. Most hostel owners can recount a story of bad behaviour by an Israeli, mostly unsubstantiated, but sufficient to create a strong feeling across the tourism sector. The national parks have the park rules specifically printed in Hebrew (and in no other foreign language). This sentiment was not helped by a fire reportedly started by an Israeli backpacker in Torres del Paine in 2011–12 that burned 176km^2 of Chile's most famous national park. A recent and somewhat disturbing trend is for hitchhikers to declare their nationalities either verbally or on small signs (Chileans often carry a flag) specifically to alert drivers that they are not Israeli, aware that many fear stopping for hitchhikers for this reason. The most obvious solution to this problem is that all nationalities, including Israelis, should consider themselves ambassadors for their countries and do their utmost to contribute to the region and create a favourable impression of their country.

Part Two

THE NORTHERN CARRETERA AUSTRAL

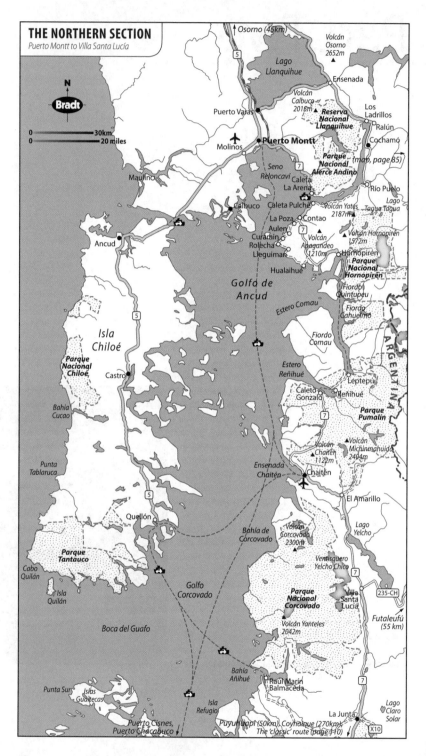

THE NORTHERN SECTION
Puerto Montt to Villa Santa Lucía

Bradt

0   30km
0   20 miles

N

Osorno (45km)

Volcán Osorno 2652m

Lago Llanquihue

Ensenada

Puerto Varas

Volcán Calbuco 2016m

Reserva Nacional Llanquihue

Los Ladrillos

Ralún

Molinos

Puerto Montt

Cochamó

Parque Nacional Alerce Andino

(map, page 85)

Maullino

Seno Reloncaví

Caleta La Arena

Río Puelo

Calbuco

Caleta Pulche

Lago Tagua Tagua

Volcán Yates 2187m

La Poza

Contao

Ancud

Aulen

Curamín

Rollecha

Lleguiman

Volcán Apagandeo 1210m

Volcán Hornopirén 1572m

Hornopirén

Parque Nacional Hornopirén

Hualaihué

Golfo de Ancud

Fiordo Quintupeu

Estero Comau

Fiordo Cahuelmo

Isla Chiloé

Fiordo Comau

Parque Nacional Chiloé

Estero Reñihué

Castro

Bahía Cucao

Caleto Gonzalo

Reñihué

Lepteпú

Parque Pumalín

ARGENTINA

Volcán Chaitén 1122m

Volcán Michinmahuida 2404m

Punta Tablaruca

Ensenada Chaitén

Chaitén

El Amarillo

Lago Yelcho

Quellón

Parque Tantauco

Bahía de Corcovado

Volcán Corcovado 2300m

Ventisquero Yelcho Chico

235-CH

Cabo Quilán

Isla Quilán

Golfo Corcovado

Parque Nacional Corcovado

Villa Santa Lucía

Futaleufú (55 km)

Boca del Guafo

Volcán Yanteles 2042m

Bahía Añihué

Raúl Marín Balmaceda

Punta Sur

Islas Guaitecas

Isla Refugio

Lago Claro Solar

La Junta

X10

Puerto Cisnes, Puerto Chacabuco

Puyuhuapi (50km), Coyhaique (270km), The 'classic' route (page 110)

3

Puerto Montt

Telephone code: 65

Perched on the Reloncaví Sound, Puerto Montt is a bustling frontier city driven by commerce and salmon farming. The city is home to nearly 250,000 inhabitants – approximately double the entire population of the 1,240km region traversed by the Carretera Austral. For those heading south this is essentially the last bit of modernity for a few weeks – make the most of it. The shopping in Puerto Montt is excellent, there are fine restaurants, a thriving nightlife, and the city is an ideal means to prepare oneself for the isolation of the south. The city is the main northern access point to the Carretera Austral, and is surrounded by world-class sights such as the island of Chiloé, the Chilean and Argentine lake districts, and the popular tourist town of Puerto Varas to the north.

And yet, perhaps prompted by some scathing reviews in other guidebooks and online, the majority of visitors leave Puerto Montt as soon as possible in search of wonders further north or to join the Carretera proper. Even within Chile, Puerto Montt does not have a great reputation. It certainly does appear to have more than its fair share of drunks, beggars, derelict or burnt-out buildings, monstrous concrete high-rises, overflowing rubbish bins emitting putrid odours, a bizarre one-way traffic system which does not seem to resolve the endemic traffic problem, E-grade casinos, graffiti, trinket shops selling low-quality Chinese imports, some pretty sleazy neighbourhoods and a McDonald's, but Puerto Montt is an authentic Chilean city, for better or for worse. Scratch the surface and you will find an intriguing, upbeat place which, while not packed with top sightseeing opportunities, does offer those heading south their last opportunity to eat quality sushi, get a high-speed internet connection, go to the cinema, buy some last-minute gear that is impossible to find further south, visit a decent car/bike/motorbike mechanic and enjoy some nightlife – all this as well as stunning views across the Reloncaví Sound and towards the Osorno and Calbuco volcanoes.

HISTORY

Puerto Montt was founded in 1853 when Germans settled here, and was named after the Chilean President at the time, Manuel Montt, who ruled from 1851 to 1861 and was the first civilian president of Chile. Montt himself was of humble origins but he created a presidential dynasty: both his son and nephew went on to become presidents of Chile. Jorge Montt (nephew) was Vice Admiral of the Chilean navy and had served in the War of the Pacific, in which Chile famously denied Bolivia access to the Pacific Ocean, lamented to this day. He was president from 1891 to 1896, during which time he reinstated the gold monetary standard and avoided a skirmish with the Argentines over border disputes by seeking arbitration from the British. He peacefully handed over power to Federico Errázuriz Echaurren in September 1896, and commanded the Chilean navy from 1897 until his retirement from the military in 1913. He was Mayor of Valparaiso from 1915 to 1918, and died in 1922. Ventisquero Montt near Caleta Tortel is named after him.

Manuel Montt's son, Pedro, ruled from 1906 to 1910, but has a chequered reputation and nothing of note named after him. He ordered the Santa Maria School Massacre, in which striking nitrate workers in Iquique were killed by the army on the orders of the president, resulting in approximately 2,200 deaths, including the wives and children of the workers. In fact, a more recent massacre also darkened the history of Puerto Montt; in 1969 heavy-handed police killed eight illegal squatters in the city, and the public outcry that ensued contributed to the downfall of the then president Eduardo Frei to be replaced by Salvador Allende in 1970. Other key moments in the history of the city include the devastating 1960 Valdivia earthquake, the most violent recorded, reaching 9.5 on the Richter scale and killing up to 6,000 people. The city's cathedral was one of the only buildings to survive thanks to its novel construction (page 78).

Although Pedro may have been the last of the Montt dynasty to rule the country, the name resounds in Chilean history to this day. Julio Montt (1861–82) was also a hero in the War of the Pacific. Teresa Wilms Montt (1893–1921) was a writer, poet and anarchist-feminist. Montts have also achieved celebrity status. Cristina Montt (1895–1969) was a movie star, and Marta Montt Balmaceda (1934–) is considered Chile's first supermodel. Andrés Wood Montt (1965–) is an accomplished film director; and Rodrigo Montt Swett (1974–), great-great-grandson of the original Manuel Montt whom the city was named after, is a lawyer and politician, but based in Santiago rather than in the city that bears his name.

GETTING THERE AND AROUND

BY PRIVATE VEHICLE Puerto Montt is 20km south of Puerto Varas (a more manicured tourist base) – see page 28 on the broader access points to the Carretera Austral. This is a public transport hub, but bear in mind that south of Puerto Montt, either in the direction of Hornopirén or via Cochamó and Río Puelo, road quality deteriorates substantially. The Carretera officially starts at the southern exit of Puerto Montt, but there is a valid argument to suppose the entry point via Cochamó is also a key starting point, and avoids one ferry crossing (see page 79 for details).

The southern departure from Puerto Montt along the Carretera Austral is the coastal road heading southeast. It is signposted from downtown, and hard to miss;

PUERTO MONTT
For listings, see pages 69–74

⊙ Where to stay

1	Brisas del Mar	C3
2	Casa Perla	C1
3	Gran Hotel Vicente Costanera	F3
4	Hospedaje Corina	C1
5	Hospedaje Vista del Mar	C2
6	Hostal Benavente	D2
7	Hostal Peumayen	B2
8	Hotel Don Luis	F3
9	Hotel Gran Pacífico	E2
10	Hotel Manquehue	G2
11	Hotel Suizo	B2
12	Hotel Tren del Sur	G1

✪ Where to eat and drink

	Brisas del Mar	(see 1)
13	Club Aleman	F3
14	Cirus Bar	C2
15	El Apa	A3
16	Fogon de Pepe	E2
	Hotel Manquehue	(see 10)
17	Japon del Lago	D1
	Los Navegantes	(see 9)
18	Pa' Mar Adentro	A3
19	Rhenania	F3
20	Saltzberg	E2
21	Sanito	G3
22	Tablón del Ancla	F3

Off map

	Fogon Cotelé de Jeremy	G4

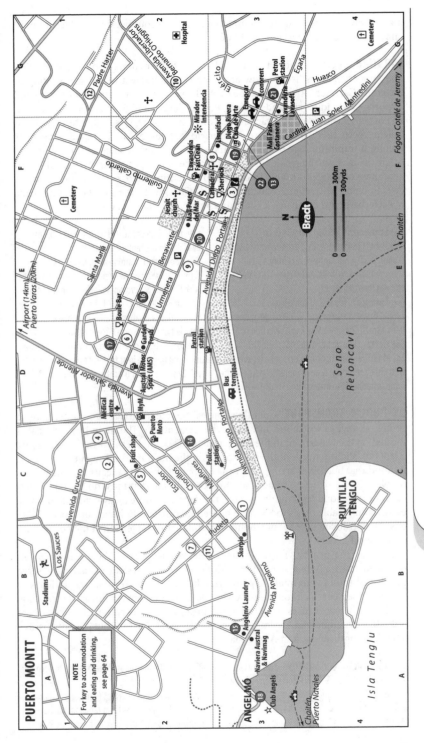

PUERTO MONTT

NOTE
For key to accommodation
and eating and drinking,
see page 64

Padre Harter

Avenida Libertador
Bernardo O'Higgins

Hospital

Ejército

Mirador
Intendencia

Empifacil

Diego Rivera

Casa de Arte

Econrent

Petrol
station

Enerpur

Euroagar

Huasco

Egaña

Lavandería
Lavasoft

Cardinal Juan Soler Manfredini

Fógon Cotelé de Jeremy

Mall Paseo
Costanera

Lavandería
FastClean

Cathedral

Sherlock

Guillermo Gallardo

Cemetery

Jesuit
church

Mall Paseo
del Mar

Benavente

Santa María

Umeneta

Boulé Bar

Garden
Feast

Austral Móvil
Sport (AMS)

Avenida Salvador Allende

Avenida Crucero

Los Sauces

Stadiums

Cemetery

Avenida Diego Portales

Seno
Reloncaví

Chaitén

Airport (14km)/
Puerto Varas (20km)

Medical
centre

Fruit shop

Ecuador

Chorrillos

Mallhones

Rengifo

Hudeto

Skorpio

Petrol
station

Bus
terminal

Puerto
Moto

MyM

Police
station

PUNTILLA
TENGLU

ANGELMÓ

Angelmó Laundry

Avenida Angelmó

Naviera Austral
& Navimag

Club Angels

Chaitén
Puerto Natales

Isla Tenglu

N

Bradt

0   300m
0   300yds

Cardinal Juan Soler Manfredini

65

it's the only road heading in this direction. Heading southwest from Puerto Montt on route 5 leads to the island of Chiloé.

CAR HIRE Puerto Montt has offices of most of the major car-rental companies. The four companies listed below are of particular interest to anyone wanting to travel the Carretera Austral because they all have offices in Puerto Montt (city and airport), Coyhaique (city and airport), Puerto Natales and Punta Arenas which will be convenient for one-way car rentals when the new ferry service starts between Caleta Tortel or Puerto Yungay and Puerto Natales. Most car-rental companies require a minimum age of 22–24 years, a valid driver's licence in the country of origin or a valid international driver's licence, valid passport and a credit card guarantee of US$500–1,000. To cross into Argentina there is a delay of up to ten days to obtain the required documentation. Check with the specific requirements of each car-rental company. It is often easier and cheaper to book online.

Econorent [65 G3] Antonio Varas 144; \(65) 2481264; e reservas@econorent.cl; www.econorent.cl. A full range of cars from a small Chevrolet Spark to 4x4s, daily & weekly rentals (no office in Puerto Natales).

Europcar [65 G3] Antonio Varas 162; \(65) 2368216; www.europcar.cl. A full range of cars from a small Chevrolet Spark to a selection of 4x4s.

Hertz Calle de Servicio 1031; \(65) 2313445; www.hertz.cl. All Hertz vehicles comply with Chile's technical & environmental norms & the company adheres to international quality control standards. One of the widest range of vehicles available in the rental car market.

Seelmann Camino al Tepuala km3; \(65) 2268001; www.seelmann.cl. A company with English- & German-speaking staff that offer unlimited mileage & vehicle drop-off at your hotel. Prices vary dramatically depending on the vehicle type & season. Offices only in Santiago & Puerto Montt, so one-way rentals more expensive, meaning they are best for local travel. Range of vehicles from small hatchbacks to minivans & 4x4s.

BY PUBLIC TRANSPORT Countless **buses** service Santiago and intermediate routes, as well as to Chiloé and Bariloche (Argentina). The main bus terminal is located on the waterfront in the city centre [65 D3] (*Av Diego Portales 1001;* \ *(65) 2283000*), slightly north of the main plaza on the main road through the city. Bear in mind that bus times are highly prone to change; the only means to mitigate this problem is to buy tickets in advance (and considering that most do not take credit cards or telephone reservations), check the departure time a day before, and arrive early. Comfortable buses to Santiago take approximately 12 hours and cost US$50; buses to Bariloche take about 6 hours, depending on congestion at the border, and cost around US$30.

Between the nearby villages (such as Puerto Varas), small blue **minivans** can be hailed from any bus stop. Puerto Montt also has a system of **taxis** that serve established routes with multiple passengers, but there is no obvious way to find out which taxi serves which route – ask at your hotel. The system is somewhat confusing.

The list below focuses on southbound buses only. Two companies offer direct buses to Coyhaique (via Argentina), for approximately $40,000, but it is not possible to embark or disembark in Argentina.

Buses M&M \(9) 54149796. Puerto Montt to Hornopirén: 13.30 & 17.30 Mon–Sat, returning to Puerto Montt at 07.00 & noon.

Buses Río Puelo \(65) 2841200. Puerto Montt to Lago Tagua Tagua, Río Puelo & Cochamó: 07.45 & 16.00 Mon–Sat; Puerto Montt to Cochamó & Río Puelo: 07.45 & 15.00 Sun only. In low season only the 07.45 bus operates (daily). Note that this bus does not cross Lago Tagua Tagua, but synchronises with the ferry & the onward bus at the other side of the lake, reaching Llanada Grande.

Expreso Austral (65) 2369681. Puerto Montt to Hualaihué: 14.55 & 15.55 Mon–Sat, 16.45 on Sun, returning to Puerto Montt at 05.00 & 06.00 Mon–Sat, 12.30 on Sun.

Kemelbus (65) 2253530; www.kemelbus.cl. Puerto Montt to Chaitén: 06.00 & 08.00 daily (in low season 1 bus at 07.00); return at noon; Puerto Montt to Hornopirén: 08.00, 13.00, 14.30 & 16.45 Mon–Fri; return at 05.00, 05.30, 07.30 & 13.00; Puerto Montt to Hualaihué (times vary).

Queilenbus (65) 2253468. Puerto Montt to Coyhaique: 10.35 Mon, Wed & Fri.

TransAustral (65) 2270984. Puerto Montt to Coyhaique: 11.00 Tue (Feb only); Puerto Montt to Futaleufú: 06.30 Tue–Sat.

Transhar (65) 2254187. Puerto Montt to Cochamó & Río Puelo: 07.45, 12.15, 15.30 & 16.00 Mon–Fri, 07.45 & 15.30 Sat & Sun; return 05.30, 06.00, 13.30 & 16.30 Mon–Fri, 06.00, 13.30 & 15.30 Sat & Sun in high season. Substantially reduced service in low season, but always at least 1 bus per day in each direction.

BY FERRY Both Navimag and Naviera Austral are based at Angelmó 1735, heading slightly out of the city towards the Angelmó district, close to the hostel area. Check-in is also here, even if travelling on one of the larger boats which leave from slightly further out of the city – the transfers are free and arranged by the companies.

Cruce Andino Del Salvador 72, Puerto Varas; Mitre 219, Bariloche; www.cruceandino. com. An overpriced daily ferry-bus combination connecting Bariloche (Argentina) with Puerto Varas (Chile, 20km north of Puerto Montt). The route is by bus from Puerto Varas to Petrohué, then by boat across Lago Todos Los Santos to Puella, then a 2nd bus to Puerto Frias (Chilean border control), followed by a 2nd boat across Lago Frías to the Argentine customs. A 3rd bus goes to Puerto Blest, & then a final boat to Puerto Pañuelo, near the Llao Llao hotel, with a final bus to Bariloche. The section from Puerto Pañuelo to Puerto Blest, along an arm of the large Lago Nahuelhuapi, includes an infuriating commentary in multiple languages. 2014–15 rates (excl food) were US$280pp (one-

way); the return is 50% less. The route is beautiful on a sunny day, but for those travelling the Carretera Austral it is comparatively mediocre in terms of attractiveness, & extremely expensive. Take the bus instead – it is quicker (*6hrs*), cheaper (*$30*), does not include an annoying commentary & the route is fairly spectacular, with views over the Volcán Puyehue which erupted in 2011. Book online (take credit card & PayPal) or through a local agent in Puerto Varas or Bariloche.

Naviera Austral [65 A3] (65) 2270430/1/2; ⊕ 09.00–13.00 & 15.00–19.00 Mon–Fri, 10.00–13.00 Sat. Ferries to Ayacara & Chaitén. For other routes not departing or arriving to Puerto Montt, see relevant section (& warning) on pages 45–6.

ESCAPING THE CITY – BOAT TAXIS FROM PUERTO MONTT

Taxi-mar is a new concept in Puerto Montt; these small covered boats hold up to ten people and operate similarly to a taxi – fixed fares for fixed routes, or rent by the hour. Three standard routes are: Puerto Montt to Isla Mailen (across the sound from Puerto Montt) for $40,000; $70,000 to the slightly more distant island of Guar; and $140,000 direct to Caleta La Arena. The last route is ideal for those starting the Carretera Austral but not wishing to do the first section by land (such as cyclists), skipping one of the less interesting parts of the Carretera and promptly taking the first of the southbound ferries. The longest standard tour offered is to the Calbuco archipelago ($160,000). The costs are per boat regardless of the number of passengers.

For details, (9) 96984394, (9) 67891070; e reservas@taximar.cl, or visit www. taximar.cl.

Navimag [65 A3] ☎(65) 2432360;
🕘 09.00–13.00 & 14.30–18.30 Mon–Sat. Ferries
to Puerto Chacabuco or Puerto Natales.
Skorpio [65 B3] Angelmó 1660; ☎(65)
2275643, (65) 2275646; e puertomontt@
skorpios.cl; www.skorpios.cl; also have offices in
Santiago (☎(2) 24771900; e skoinfo@skorpios.cl)
& Puerto Natales (☎(61) 2412714; e natales@
skorpios.cl). These are passenger cruises rather
than ferries, no cars onboard, return itineraries
only. They offer 3 main routes: from Puerto
Montt to Fiordo Comau, visiting Hornopirén,
Fiordo Quintupeu, the Llancahue hot springs
& returning via Calbuco (*winter only; overnight
trip; US$300–400pp depending on cabin choice*);
to Ventiquero San Rafael from Puerto Montt,
stopping in Aguirre (*summer only; 6 days, 5 nights;
approx US$2,200pp*); they also have a ferry service
in the deep south visiting the glaciers around
Puerto Natales, beyond the southernmost extreme
of the Carretera Austral (*4 days, 3 nights; approx
US$1,900pp*).

BY AIR Puerto Montt is served by both Sky Airlines and LAN. Despite the airport
being formally called El Tepual International Airport, no international flights
fly to or from Puerto Montt – destinations include Punta Arenas, Balmaceda
(Coyhaique), Santiago, Castro (Chiloé), and occasional flights *en route* to/from
Santiago via Valdivia. The main airport is 14km northwest of Puerto Montt.

The predominant origin or destination of light aircraft travelling between Puerto
Montt and the Carretera Austral is Chaitén, arriving and departing from the La
Paloma Aerodrome 5km northeast of Puerto Montt.

PUERTO MONTT AIRPORT IN THE MEDIA

At 18.00 on 15 August 1972, an Argentine flight from Comodoro Rivadavia to
Buenos Aires made a routine stop in Trelew, on the Atlantic coast. Unbeknown
to the pilot a commander from a leftist Argentine guerrilla movement was
on the flight, and armed. At 18.30 six guerrillas escaped from Rawson Prison
and made it to Trelew airport in a Ford Falcon and boarded the plane, shortly
after it landed at 19.20. In the ultimate double-bluff, in order to maintain calm
the captain told passengers that this was a simulation of terrorist activity on
account of being located so close to Rawson Prison, where a number of famous
terrorists were incarcerated. Another 19 guerrillas from various organisations
had escaped and were on their way to the airport, but their getaway vehicles
had not arrived meaning they had to travel in three taxis. Meanwhile, fearful
of the Argentine army and police arriving, the hijackers ordered the captain
to take off promptly, to Tepual airport in Puerto Montt, where it refuelled
and continued to Santiago. After some hours of negotiation in Santiago the
hostages were released and the guerrillas were granted safe passage to Cuba
by the Allende government, much to the annoyance of the Argentines. The
plane returned to Buenos Aires that same day, and no hostages were hurt.
The remaining 19 escapees were trapped in Trelew Airport and surrendered
on the condition that they would be returned to jail. However, in the early
hours of 22 August, 16 of the 19 guerrillas were executed in what is now
known as 'The Trelew Massacre'; the official account of the events at the time
suggested that there was a second attempted escape which triggered the
killings, but the three survivors (and public opinion) severely challenge this
version of events, claiming they were led out of their cells, forced to lay face
down and then executed. In 2012, three former army officials were sentenced
to life imprisonment for crimes against humanity, although in reality this has
amounted to mere house arrest.

Airport transfers Taxis to the airport generally charge about $10,000–15,000; if going to the light aircraft airport be sure to specify this to the taxi driver. Alternatively, ETM buses (from the main bus terminal) go to/from the main airport synchronised with the flight arrivals and departures, costing approximately $2,000 per person.

TOUR OPERATORS

It is hardly necessary to use a tour operator for most of the sights and activities in the region; buying a bus ticket and paying an entry fee usually suffices. Tour operators simplify logistics, rather than being formally required in order to do a particular tour. However, if time is tight, or Spanish skills poor, they may be a convenient option. There are various semi-formal operators in the bus terminal, but one operator based in Puerto Montt is worth mentioning. For tours north of Puerto Montt (ie: in the Lake District region of Chile beyond the limits of the Carretera Austral), Puerto Varas is the tourism hub, and has a greater range of operators serving this region.

Laketour Expediciones local 22, P Melipulli; ☏ (9) 81552479; e laketour.expediciones@ gmail.com. A decent, small operator offering all the standard tours, but with some flexibility to design more esoteric combinations, run by Jaime Quezada, who knows the region like the back of his hand & also the political background & history of the places they visit. His tours might be marginally more expensive than the usual off-the-rack tours, but worth the additional attention.

⌂ WHERE TO STAY

Accommodation in Puerto Montt is more varied than anywhere else along the Carretera Austral, including Coyhaique. Generally, it is more reasonably priced, and never fills up entirely as some villages further south are prone to do in peak season. The only missing element is camping opportunities, which are almost unheard of (exception: Casa Perla, page 71). The hotels close to Angelmó and the ferry port tend to be cheaper, although this is a slightly rougher neighbourhood (albeit oozing with character). Safety is reasonable in Puerto Montt but late at night it may be wiser to take a taxi to or from hotels in this neighbourhood. However, to experience genuine Puerto Montt housing, this is the place to be, and the houses tend to be raised above the main city with lovely views over the sound and to the volcanoes. This area is also walking distance to Rengifo, a hive of bars and restaurants. The Hospedaje Vista del Mar (pages 70–1) is a fine example, and very popular. The downtown hotels tend to be less pleasant, although perhaps more conveniently located, and the upper-range options in this district are overpriced. The Hotel Manquehue (page 70), while not as central, is an excellent premium accommodation, and in terms of value for money, one of the best 'treats' in the region. Competition between hotels/hostels is fierce in Puerto Montt, and prices are surprisingly good value compared with further south.

⌂ **Gran Hotel Vicente Costanera**
[65 F3] (70 rooms) Av Diego Portales 450; ☏ (65) 2282995; e reservas@vicentecostanera.cl; www. granhotelvicentecostanera.cl. A beautiful building on the main plaza with rooms facing out to sea. However, the interior is dated & the hotel is characterless. Laundry, Wi-Fi, gym & parking available; credit cards accepted. Most rooms are dbls; US$165 for a junior suite with sea view. Overpriced. **$$$$**
⌂ **Hotel Don Luis** [65 F3] (60 rooms) Quillota 146; ☏ (65) 2200300; e reservas@hdl.cl;

www.hoteldonluis.cl. A homogenous executive hotel with a price to match but lacking the charm or views of others in this category. Conveniently downtown. All rooms with private bathrooms, safety deposit box & cable TV. Laundry, Wi-Fi, parking, gym, sauna, bar & restaurant. Good if there on business, otherwise better options abound. $$$$

🏠 **Hotel Gran Pacífico** [65 E2] (43 rooms) Urmenta 719; 📞 (65) 2482100; e reserva@ hotelgranpacifico.cl; www.hotelgranpacifico.cl. 'Executive' hotel with fantastic views & somewhat less formal than others in this category. Has a restaurant on the top floor boasting 'the best view of Chile Austral', & within Puerto Montt this is probably an accurate description. It's worth visiting this even if you're not staying here. Gym, Wi-Fi, laundry, sauna, jacuzzi & massages. Although this is certainly not a budget hotel, it is worth splashing out & getting a room with a view. Children under 12 are free if they do not require an additional bed; cribs are also free, & they have a babysitter service – ideal for families. Very good upper-end option, only exceeded by the Hotel Manquehue. Can book online & take credit cards. $$$$

🏠 **Hotel Manquehue** [65 G2] (142 rooms) Av Seminario 252; 📞 (65) 2331000; www. hotelmanquehue.cl. Superb hotel, the best in Puerto Montt, complete with a small indoor heated swimming pool & gym. The rooms are spacious, many with good vistas across the sound & city due to its elevated position. Room service, safety deposit box, fully equipped bathrooms (shower only), minibar, & a rapid (overpriced) laundry service. The restaurant & bar area downstairs is positively hip, where the trendy & wealthy hang out at w/ends, but closes at midnight & is far enough from bedrooms to allow a decent night's sleep. The restaurant is excellent (page 72) & includes vegetarian options. The b/fast (inc) consists of copious quantities of almost every conceivable item bar eggs. Funky artwork & wooden sculptures adorn the bar, although the range of artisanal beers could be better. It is a short walk from the centre, up a fairly steep hill – location is about the only mildly negative thing to say about it. Surprisingly good value, particularly if booked online. The suite is generally not offered as this is reserved for visiting dignitaries – the president has stayed here. $$$$

🏠 **Hostal Benavente** [65 D2] (18 rooms) Manuel Rodríguez 214; 📞 (65) 2756630,

(9) 78516607; e hostalbenavente@gmail. com; www.hostalbenavente.cl. Reasonable accommodation near the restaurant district, not far from the centre, & also walking distance to the ferries & Angelmó district. Rooms are with & without private bathrooms (some with a nice view); parking, Wi-Fi & cable TV. Basic b/fast included, also has a restaurant. A little overpriced, but not a bad option. Credit cards accepted. $$$

🏠 **Hotel Tren del Sur** [65 G1] (17 rooms) Santa Teresa 643; 📞 (65) 2343939; e info@trendelsur.cl; www.trendelsur.cl. This hotel, recently upgraded from a 'boutique hostel', has a reputation that possibly exceeds its merit. The train theme is nice enough & the building is certainly quirky, but the rooms are pokey with windows that look out to the corridors rather than the outside world, & do not warrant the price tag. It is located a short walk up the hill from the downtown plaza, smack bang on a main road with electricity cables spoiling any chance of a decent view. All rooms have private bathrooms; Wi-Fi, computers, laundry, limited parking available, & also hire bikes & cars (own & subcontracted). The hotel has established celebrity status & is certainly unique, but better-value options are available. Visiting the restaurant alone (🕐 19.30–23.00; $$$$) is a wise alternative to staying here. Credit cards accepted. $$$

🏠 **Brisas del Mar** [65 C3] (5 cabins) Angelmó 2186; 📞 (65) 2263379. Run by the owners of the restaurant of the same name (page 72). Cabins are not so common in Puerto Montt for some reason, but these sleep 5 or 6 people, fully equipped, & with a fantastic quincho. Nice garden for kids to play, & well located near the ferries & Angelmó, but set back from the main road. Parking $45,000/ cabin. $$–$$$

🏠 **Hospedaje Vista del Mar** [65 C2] (6 rooms) Francisco Vivar 1337; 📞 (65) 2255625, (9) 98194202; e hospedajevistaalmar@yahoo.es; www.hospedajevistaalmar.cl. Located on a quiet street about a 10min walk (uphill) from the bus terminal, this is the finest budget accommodation in Puerto Montt, & consistently well reviewed by all who visit. Open all year & lovingly managed by the owner, Eliana Oyarzún. The 2 sgls are small & cheap, possibly a little cramped if you have a lot of luggage; the 2 twins are much more spacious. Upstairs is the only en-suite room (dbl), with splendid views out to the Reloncaví. The final dbl is also very comfortable, but without a view.

The shared bathrooms are ample even when the hostel is full (it often is), & spotlessly clean, with good hot water, & the downstairs shower has a great view of the Volcán Calbuco. High-speed internet, a computer & printer available for guests, cable TV in each room, a small communal balcony to enjoy the sunsets with a glass of wine, & a comfortable sitting area. Laundry available, & can use the kitchen. Eliana is from Chiloé originally & knows the region very well, including arranging ferries, tours in the region, good restaurants, etc. The b/fast is excellent – much of which is homemade, with fine bread, marmalades, muffins, unlimited decent coffee, fresh fruit, yoghurt, cereals, etc. Although cheaper options exist in this area, it is worth spending a little extra to stay here. Highly recommended, but do make a reservation as it's extremely popular. **$$–$$$**

Casa Perla [65 C1] (4 rooms) Trigal 312; (65) 2262104. Lovely, rustic, traditional hostel in a delightful alerce building of over 100 years old. Wi-Fi, laundry, parking for bikes & motorbikes off-road, cars on the road. B/fast included. Small camping area, free use of kitchen. All rooms have shared bathrooms, 2 dbls, 1 trpl & 1 quintuple. The entire house is wooden, & feels slightly like a museum, the dbl room has a nice view towards the ocean. Reservations by email or phone, no need to make a deposit but call to confirm. **$$**

Hospedaje Corina [65 C1] (6 rooms & camping) Los Guindos 329; (65) 2273948, (9) 82403037; e hospedajecorina@gmail.com; www.hospedajecorina.cl. Reasonable option fairly close to the main hostel region & not far from Angelmó & the bus/ferry terminals, in front of the lovely chapel San Alberto de Sicilia. Rooms are pleasant enough at this price range; 5 dbls (both private & shared bathrooms available) & 1 trpl. Nice patio with views & grass section for sunny days. Camping with b/fast included (*$6,000pp*).

Also offers Spanish classes (*$8,000/hr or multi-day packages inc accommodation*). English, Spanish & German spoken. **$$**

Hostal Peumayen [65 B2] (9 rooms) Buenos Aires cnr with Pudeto 1558; (65) 2711728, (9) 86461999; e hostalpeumayen@gmail.com; www.hostal-peumayen.webnode.cl. Decent hostel with sgls, dbls & trpls; 2 of the dbls have private bathrooms, the rest are shared. Simple rooms; those overlooking the sea are preferable. Laundry, Wi-Fi, kitchen, parking & cable TV. Good continental b/fast included. Has a small terrace for sunny days. Reasonable budget accommodation if the Hostal Suizo, just around the corner, is unavailable. **$$**

Hotel Suizo [65 B2] (9 rooms) Independencia 231; 22716382, (9) 93085533; e rossyoelckers@yahoo.es; ⊕ Dec–Mar. Located in an amazing house that should be declared a national monument in Puerto Montt, this is a charming, slightly eccentric place to stay. The owners are Swiss & Chilean, & the house has been lovingly built over many years reflecting these 2 architectural styles. The rooms themselves are fine, simple wooden chalet-style. The main house is combination gallery/art studio/museum, with a tower offering views over the city. Some rooms are fairly self-contained mini cabins, without a kitchen. Has a quincho, parking, Wi-Fi; the only missing item is b/fast, although guests can use the kitchen to prepare their own nibbles, & tea & coffee is freely available. The owner, Rossy Oelckers, is a well-known artist, & her pictures can be seen in the house & occasionally in local restaurants; she also offers painting & Spanish classes. She comes from the family of the Oelckers of Hornopirén who also have a hostel, cabins & a supermarket (pages 94–5). English, German, French & Italian spoken. Good choice. **$$**

✗ WHERE TO EAT AND DRINK

Puerto Montt has an impressive range of restaurants, and it is worth grabbing a last exotic meal before heading south, where such offerings are largely absent outside of Coyhaique. There is a wide range of cuisines available, from the usual steaks, burgers, fast food and quality pizzas, to sushi, vegetarian restaurants, a huge range of seafood and German cuisine. Particularly in the downtown section, and along Rengifo, it is possible to grab a decent dinner and then hop to a bar next door. Angelmó has a huge range of small restaurants, most of which serve relatively similar good-quality fare, focused on seafood.

✖ **Brisas del Mar** [65 C3] Angelmó 2186; ✆(65) 2263379; www.brisasdelmarrest.cl; ⏰ 13.00–midnight daily. Popular & well-established restaurant approaching the Angelmó district, serving reasonable seafood & meats; the speciality of the house is *concato* – grilled salmon with melted cheese & tomato, also spicy prawns. Decent, but cheaper & possibly more charming options available in Angelmó, & with a nicer view. Also have cabañas (page 70). **$$$$**

⌂ **Hotel Manquehue** [65 G2] Av Seminario 252; ✆(65) 2331000; www.hotelmanquehue.cl; ⏰ until 23.00 daily. An excellent restaurant as would be expected in the Manquehue, popular with residents & locals alike. The menu includes seafood, ceviche, salads, carpaccio, pizzas, sandwiches, vegetarian options &, unusual for Chile, a range of desserts including strudel & a jasmine tea & ginger crème brûlée. Sushi night 19.00–22.00 Thu; lunch buffet 13.00–15.30 Fri; parrilla night 20.00–22.30 Fri. **$$$$**

✖ **Pa' Mar Adentro** [65 A3] Pacheco Altamirano 2525, Angelmó; ✆(65) 2264060; e contacto@pamaradentro.cl; www.pamaradentro.cl; ⏰ noon–midnight daily. One of the top restaurants in Puerto Montt & well worth the lovely stroll to the Angelmó district. Extensive wine list & wide range of fish, shellfish, meats, pastas & desserts. Interesting décor with lamps made of local algae. Bustling atmosphere, reservations required most of the time, especially at w/ends & in high season. Do a mean Pisco sour, & on Sun there is a decent buffet menu for $18,000pp. **$$$$**

✖ **Club Aleman** [65 F3] Antonio Varas 264; ✆(65) 2297000; www.clubalemanpuertomontt.cl; ⏰ 11.00–02.00 Mon–Sat, noon–20.00 Sun. The private club downstairs is not open to visitors, but the bar is lovely, & the restaurant offers a range of German foods. There is a series of black-&-white photos explaining the history of the early German settlers, although not enough to qualify it as a museum. The building was founded in 1860, making this the oldest German Club in southern Chile (others exist in Osorno, Frutillar & Puerto Varas). **$$$**

✖ **Fogon Cotelé de Jeremy** [65 G4] Juan Soler Manfredini 1661, Pelluco; ✆(65) 2278000, (9) 86245285; e jeremy@cotele.cl; www.cotele.cl; ⏰ 13.00–16.00 & 20.00–midnight Mon–Fri, closed Sun & public holidays. This is simply a superb

restaurant. Beware, it is further from Puerto Montt than maps suggest; ideally drive, take a taxi or jump on the frequent buses from Puerto Montt towards Pelluco. It is run by Jeremy, perhaps not surprisingly, who sailed to Puerto Montt from South Africa some years ago & never left. He likes to keep things simple. There are 3 meats – sirloin, rib-eye & fillet. He brings you the raw meat, cuts the exact piece you want, & the price depends on the weight. It is cooked over an open fire by an experienced *parrillero* in the main part of the restaurant with a well-designed chimney to prevent the entire place filling with smoke. There are 2 salads available, & an excellent wine list catering to every budget & taste. 2 things make the restaurant unique. Firstly, the meat is exquisite, probably the best available in Puerto Montt; given the limited menu Jeremy goes to lengths to buy the very best fresh meat possible, which will not be frozen at any stage, & is basted in a special *chimichuri* sauce (unless requested otherwise). Secondly, the setting & atmosphere are utterly geared towards relaxing, unwinding, chatting for hours on end, & feeling as though you are in your own home. It's a small restaurant & booking is sensible, particularly considering the distance from town. Technically the restaurant is on the Carretera Austral – a fine eating option for day 1 on the way south. **$$$**

✖ **Fogon de Pepe** [65 E2] Rengifo 845; ✆(65) 2271527; ⏰ 12.30–15.30 & 19.30–00.30, evening only Sat, closed Sun. Good steaks in a lovely building that has been in the family for 3 generations. Quality of the meat depends on benchmark – this is neither Argentina nor the Fogon Cotelé de Jeremy, but is good nonetheless. Large portions, great service, & the owner wanders around keeping an eye on everything. Centrally located on trendy Rengifo. Good vibe & wide range of local beers. Not great for vegetarians. Fills up quickly so get there early. **$$$**

✖ **Japon del Lago** [65 D1] Rengifo 952; ✆(65) 2231318; www.japondellago.cl; ⏰ 13.00–16.00 & 19.00–23.00 Mon–Wed, until midnight on Thu–Sat, closed Sun. Decent Japanese restaurant, & the last chance to have some sushi before hitting the Carretera Austral. Perhaps not competing with the finest gourmet sushi found in Santiago or Buenos Aires, but the fish can hardly be any fresher, & a nice vibe. The *trucha de salmon* sashimi is fantastic, as are the nikkei. All standard fare – rolls, cones, soups, vegetarian options,

Angelmó opening hours are somewhat random. *Most* restaurants are open *most* days if there are enough people to justify opening, and the owners feel like working that day, but it is not generally possible to make a reservation; Pa' Mar Adentro (page 72) is the exception, with formal opening hours. Saturdays and Sunday afternoons are generally busy and most places are open for lunch, but dinners can be harder to find on Sunday evenings. There are so many restaurants in this district that visitors will not go hungry, but on Sunday evenings outside high season it may be unwise to go to Angelmó.

tempura, as well as fixed menus from 18 to 58 pieces. Lively atmosphere, but fills up quickly so make a reservation. One local beer (Colonos, from Llanquihue). $$$

Los Navegantes [65 E2] Urmenta 719; (65) 2482100; www.hotelgranpacifico.cl/ english/restaurant.php; ⏲ 12.30–23.00 Mon– Sat, no lunch on Sun in low season. Take the glass elevator up to the top floor of the Hotel Gran Pacifico (page 70) for a surprisingly nice & reasonably priced lunch or dinner with excellent views. Set menus are $9,800 (lunch or dinner), & offer a choice of 2 or 3 starters & main courses, & a good buffet dessert. A great place to chill out & soak up the view, & they have a decent internet connection to catch up with emails. Usually not necessary to make a reservation. $$$

Cirus Bar [65 C2] Miradores 1175; (65) 2252016; ⏲ 10.30–midnight, until 01.00 on Sat. Great, fun bar-restaurant located close to many of the hostels & not far from Angelmó & the bus/ferry terminals. Popular with the locals of the area, plus the occasional wondering tourist. Serves a decent ale from Puerto Montt (Trilogía: pale, amber & stout) & good food; seafood features prominently, also *cazuela* (casserole) & ribs. Laidback atmosphere, & a local musician periodically arrives & sings a few folkloric tunes with his guitar. The bar has been operating for over 50 years, & the current owner/manager is the son of the founder. Ocean theme, with flags & boats adorning most of the bar. Hard for a couple to spend over $20,000 without drinking a huge amount of beer. $$

El Apa [65 A3] Palafito 20, Angelmó. A popular choice; does a great fish stew, as well as curantos for those with particularly large appetites. Typical plates are about $5,000, but *loco* & some crab dishes are notably more. $$

Saltzberg [65 E2] Cauquenes 128; (65) 2293000; ⏲ 10.00–02.00 Mon–Thu, 11.00– 03.00 Fri & Sat. Cool brew-pub with 3 decent beers, reasonable food & a great place to watch a football game. When there is not a sports event, the bar avoids blaring music or TVs so possible to have a chat without shouting. They used to have live music, but after endless complaints from the neighbours this was eventually stopped. German & Wild-West theme, with wagons on the walls. Nice atmosphere, & when very full they open the top floor. Hot dogs, meats, sandwiches, pizzas, tapas, chicken curry, salads, cocktails, fruit juices, etc. The 3 homemade beers are Altes Ale (a decent, smooth blond beer), Helles Lager (average amber beer) & Doppel Bock (a delicious dark porter with a hint of bitter coffee); they cannot be bought elsewhere. The Altes & Doppel Bock beers won prizes in the Australia International Beer Award in 2009. In short, this serves decent pub-grub in a nice place to hang out; service is not great, in part to persuade you to drink more beers in the meantime. $$

Sanito [65 G3] Copiapó 66; (65) 2259032; www.sanito.cl; ⏲ 09.00–20.00 Mon–Fri, Sat only in summer, closed Sun. Popular restaurant with organic options, good for vegetarians & carnivores alike, favoured lunch sandwich stop. Proper coffee, wide range of juices, smoothies & soups, 7 sandwiches & 7 salads – that's it! Plus a menu of the day. Does not take reservations & does get crowded at lunch, but can always take out. $$

Tablón del Ancla [65 F3] Antonio Varas 350; (65) 2367555, (65) 2367554; www. tablondelancla.cl; ⏲ 11.00–02.00 Mon–Sat, 13.00–21.00 Sun (until 02.00 in Feb). Ideally located on the central plaza close to the main shopping mall, this is a popular place with locals & tourists alike. Constantly full, & doubles as a bar

3

in the evenings, including yards of ale. Not the quietest venue in town, TVs show sporting events, but a fun & lively place. Sandwiches, hamburgers, meat & the house speciality of *pichinga* (a plate of chips covered in an extensive selection of toppings, good for 2 or more people). Good late-night option when other places close. **$$**

✗ Rhenania [65 F3] Antonio Varas 328; www. rhenania.cl; ⊕ 09.00–21.00 Mon–Fri, 10.00–21.00 Sat, noon–20.30 Sun. Set back from the waterfront near the plaza & main shopping mall, this is a nice place for a quick sandwich, slice of (excellent) cake, (reasonable) empanada or a coffee. The original factory was founded in 1959 in Osorno, & there is also a branch in Valdivia. **$**

ENTERTAINMENT AND NIGHTLIFE

Nightlife in Puerto Montt, particularly at weekends, is surprisingly lively; weekdays tend to be low-key. Many restaurants double as bars, in particular Saltzberg, Cirus Bar, Tablón del Ancla, Hotel Manquehue and Club Aleman. Rengifo has a range of bars as well as restaurants.

☆ **Sherlock** [65 F3] Antonio Varas 452; ☎ (65) 2288888; ⊕ lunch & dinner, closes by midnight in the week & 02.00 Fri–Sun, but hours vary. A very versatile café, restaurant & pub. The restaurant prepares delicious homemade Chilean dishes with outdoor seating for sunny days. Extensive selection of wines, beers & cocktails; try the Pisco sour which is highly recommended by the locals. Downstairs they often have live music or karaoke. This is one of the best pubs in the city to have some drinks, a dance or two & meet the locals. Credit cards accepted.

☆ **Boule Bar** [65 D2] Benavente 435 & Rengifo 920; ☎ (65) 2348973; ⊕ 18.00–late most nights. A good option to relax over a few drinks; the music is not too loud so it is easier to talk. Boule's has many rooms with tables & candle lighting & a broad range of music from 'Hit the Road, Jack' to

hip-hop. Old *Rolling Stone* covers and other musical memorabilia are dotted around the walls. A good bar to carry on late in the evening. Credit cards accepted.

☆ **Club Angels** [65 A3] Pacheco Altamirano 2507; ☎ (65) 2253303; www.discoangels.com. This is a disco dance club, adult entertainment & gay bar.

Hoyts Cinema [65 F3] Illapel 10, Mall Pase Costanera (on the coastal road heading south); www.cinehoyts.cl. The only cinema along the entire Carretera Austral. 5 decent screens, AC, popcorn, & while arthouse movies are rare, does show the occasional non-Hollywood & Latin movies. International films are generally shown with subtitles or dubbed during the day. Some films in 3D.

SHOPPING

This is a large Chilean city with every conceivable shop one might expect. The **Mall Paseo del Mar** [65 E2] (*Urmenta;* ⊕ *10.00–21.00 daily*), close to the Gran Pacifico Hotel, contains an array of shops and a UniMarc supermarket. The department store within this mall is Ripley, selling everything from clothes to camping gear, electronics to make-up. There is a food court on the top floor.

However, this mall pales into significance besides the **Mall Pase Costanera** [65 F3] (*on the coastal road heading south;* ⊕ *10.00–21.00 daily*). Visible from miles away thanks to two gigantic white towers containing office space above, this is a truly impressive feat of commercial real estate, a mere 2km from the official starting point of the Carretera Austral. It contains four separate department stores (Falabella, Ripley, Polar and Paris), and the UniMarc supermarket on the ground floor is as big as any in Chile, with a gourmet section where unusual international food may be found (Twinings tea is available; Marmite, alas, is not). A number of well-known brands have shops, and the food hall upstairs contains all the usual suspects (KFC, McDonald's, Pizza Hut, etc). For those in need of specialised camping equipment, AndesGear (*ground floor;* ✆ *(65) 2315077; www.andesgear.cl*) is a good option, stocking all major brands as well as GPS devices, sleeping bags, technical climbing equipment, ropes, rucksacks and helmets.

Both within the main district of Angelmó and on the main road to Puerto Montt are a number of small **handicraft** shops, mostly selling standard Latin American trinkets found in such markets across the continent. However, for those needing an additional sweater with the iconic llama images across the front, this is the place to buy such items, and at lower prices than in mainstream stores. There are also local handicraft products including food, honey, jams, etc.

OTHER PRACTICALITIES

The **tourist information centre** [65 F3] (*San Martin 80;* ✆ *(65) 2256999*) is located just off the main plaza, offering brochures, leaflets and limited knowledge of the Carretera Austral; its main focus is tours in the region. ATMs and pharmacies are dotted throughout the city.

CAR REPAIRS Car mechanics are abundant in Puerto Montt, including mechanics and dealerships specialising in all major brands.

BIKE REPAIRS

Austral Motor Sport (AMS) [65 D2] Urmenta 996; ✆ (65) 2289956, (9) 95120266; e herbert@ australmotosport.cl; www.australmotosport.cl; ⊕ 10.00–19.30 Mon–Fri, 10.00–14.00 Sat. Probably the best motorbike shop & mechanic in Puerto Montt. Authorised dealer for KTM (motorbikes & bicycles), Polaris, Suzuki, Yamaha, Euromot, Giant & Husqvarna. Can fix most problems on most bikes, & has a good stock of parts for these manufacturers, but can obtain parts for most other manufacturers. More complex BMW repairs/parts might not be possible but MotoAventura in Osorno (see below) can work with these. All types of tyres available, including those suitable for the Carretera Austral, as well as all accessories, clothing, helmets, etc. Can also sell spares to take south (filters, etc).
MotoAventura Chile Gregorio Argomedo 739, Osorno; ✆ (64) 2249127/24/23, (9) 98298077; e info@motoaventura.cl, motoaventura@ telsur.cl; www.motoaventura.cl, www. motoaventurachile.cl; ⊕ 09.00–18.30 Mon–Fri, 10.00–13.00 Sat. The best-equipped motorbike shop in the region, by a wide margin, including in Argentine Patagonia. Predominantly focused on BMWs (authorised dealer, have scanner), but also services & has parts for KTM, Aprilla & Honda. Sell motorbikes & occasionally used bikes, plus all accessories imaginable (gloves, helmets, jackets,

trousers, electronics, GPS, panniers & racks, engine guards, tank bags, boots, body armour, rain gear, sidestands, windscreens, chains & sprockets, etc). Tyres include Bridgestone, Continental, Heidenau, Kenda, MaXXis, Metzeler, Michelin & Pirelli. They also offer motorbike courses & guided tours (including to segments of the Carretera Austral as well as the rest of Chile, Peru, Bolivia, Argentina & Brazil) in English, German, French, Italian & Spanish; 4x4s can accompany guided tours. Perhaps most interestingly they have an extensive motorbike-rental service with 80 bikes available (BMW 650GS, 700GS, 800GS, 1200GS & Triumph 800XCX). Certainly for BMW enthusiasts this is the best one-stop shop in Patagonia, & non-BMW bikers would be well-advised to contact this store.
Puerto Moto [65 C2] Mechanic: Chorillos 1241, main shop: Urmenta 974; ✆ (65) 2266684; ⊕ 09.30–19.30 Mon–Fri, 10.00–14.00 Sat. Motorbikes only, & cheaper brands from India & China, but decent range of accessories, & the mechanics are perhaps not as formal as AMS (see opposite) but perfectly decent. Also range of tyres – slightly lower budget items than AMS.
MyM [65 D2] Vicente Rerez Rosales 150b; ✆ (65) 2273810; ⊕ 09.00–19.30 Mon–Fri, 10.00–14.30 Sat. Small garage capable of basic repairs of bikes & motorbikes.

LAUNDRY This is generally cheaper if done privately at a dedicated laundry rather than relying on a hotel, typically costing about $1,300–1,500 per kg. As well as those listed below, laundry is also available in a fruit shop at Augusto Goeke 298 close to Hospedaje del Mar [65 C2] (9) 84433757; ⊕ *08.00–midnight; same-day service possible).*

Angelmó Laundry [65 A3] Angelmó 2134; ⊕ 08.00–20.00 Mon–Sat. Same-day service available, conveniently close to ferry terminals.
Garden Fresh [65 D2] Manuel Rodríguez 160; (9) 81901244

Lavandería Lavasoft [65 G3] Engaña 82; (9) 96410361
Lavandería FastClean [65 F2] San Martin 167, stall 6; (65) 2258643
Limpifacil [65 F3] Quillota 191; ⊕ 09.00–13.00 & 15.00–19.00 Mon–Fri, 09.00–13.00 Sat

WHAT TO SEE AND DO

Puerto Montt may not be top of any tourist's must-visit list, but it's worth taking a day or two to explore – especially if you like shopping or fancy catching a movie at Chile's most southerly cinema. The city's architecture is varied; the Chilote influence is visible, and colourful alerce tiled woodwork is abundant, ranging from derelict buildings with smashed windows to beautifully restored houses offering a glimpse of the how this city must have looked a century ago. Modern buildings are springing up monthly, perched next to buildings that appear on the verge of collapse. There is a pleasant pedestrian and cycling path along the city's shore, with occasional vendors of local handicrafts, playgrounds for children, a skateboard park and some old trains. The sunset is lovely on a sunny day, best viewed from the restaurant at the top of the Hotel Gran Pacifico (which serves a decent meal; page 73).

Although there is no 'tick-list' of tourist sites, there's a certain charm to be found here that too many are quick to dismiss.

ANGELMÓ Anyone disillusioned with the relative modernity of Puerto Montt will find Angelmó a tonic for the soul, reminiscent as it is of the *palafitos* of Chiloé. The characterful market is bustling with countless seafood restaurants and shops, all set in a pedestrian area on the coast with fishing boats chugging in and out of the harbour, and kids sitting on the pier with basic fishing tackle periodically plucking their dinner out of the water. This is also the last handicraft market for those heading south, and a relaxing place to watch Puerto Montt life go by. On a more practical level, it is close to the main boat ports (Navimag and Naviera Austral) and a 10-minute walk from the central plaza. A trip to Puerto Montt is incomplete without visiting Angelmó (at its best when it's not raining), and both the quality and range of food offerings in this small district will keep even the most fastidious foodie well fed for days.

HERITAGE WALKING TOUR This is the closest thing to a city tour in Puerto Montt. The historic centre is small enough to explore on foot. Maps are available at the tourist information centre on the central plaza, providing a brief explanation of the items of interest as well as the principal route. The walking tour is the main source of historic information about the city since the Juan Pablo II Museum closed. The tour starts at the main dock and follows a trail through the downtown section of the city, visiting the central plaza, the monument to the German settlers, the Diego Rivera Casa de Arte, the cathedral and a Jesuit church. The walking tour takes

For those leaving the Carretera at Puerto Montt or for those with more time before they start their journey south, there are some good opportunities for sightseeing close by which are all beyond the remit of this guide, but here's a few pointers to set you in the right direction.

Endless tour agents (ie: those representing tour operators) litter Puerto Montt, but actual operators are few and far between. The standard tours in the area are the **Petrohué waterfalls**, the **Volcán Osorno**, the **Puyehue hot springs**, **Lago Tagua Tagua**, trips to the **penguin colonies** near Puerto Montt, and excursions to Chiloé (see below). Most of these can be done independently, particularly with a private vehicle. Renting a car offers increased flexibility and is not necessarily much more expensive than an organised tour. The only standard tours towards the south (ie: to the Carretera Austral) are tours to Hornopirén and to the Parque Nacional Andean Alerce.

Perhaps the biggest natural attraction, however, is the island of **Chiloé**. This is Chile's second-largest island (8,400km^2, after Chilean Tierra del Fuego), and although it is not technically part of the Carretera Austral, it is possible to travel to/from Chiloé to regions along the route. It is a wonderful and increasingly popular tourist destination, and visitors can easily spend a few weeks exploring. It is rich in wildlife, including whales in the surrounding ocean, and the entire western side of the island is Valdivian temperate rainforest.

While LAN airlines now services Castro, Puerto Montt is inevitably a key jumping-off point for visitors to the island with ferries crossing the short Chacao Strait southwest of Puerto Montt and planes/ferries from Chaitén. An indirect ferry from Puerto Chacabuco (near Puerto Aysén, on the Carretera Austral) connects the smaller towns of Aguirre, Raúl Marín Balmaceda and Puerto Cisnes, eventually crossing the Golfo de Corcovado to Quellón on Chiloé.

The east of Chiloé is relatively developed and is where most inhabitants live, and the interior is dominated by large national reserves and private parks, with varying degrees of accessibility. The island has a strong maritime culture stretching back 7,000 years, and is rich in history – the traditional churches of Chiloé are world famous, many of which have UNESCO World Heritage status. Its capital, Castro, was founded in 1567, and the island joined the Chilean Republic in 1826. Parque Tantauco, at the southern tip of the island, is owned by business magnate and former President of Chile Sebastian Piñera. Plans to build a bridge across the Chacao Strait were discussed in the 1970s, and although the formal project was cancelled in 2006 due to cost concerns, President Piñera resurrected it in 2012 before leaving his post. The strait is 2km wide at its narrowest point, the current ferries cross a 4km section at the eastern side, so this is indeed a major project.

a couple of hours, and while it is possibly not the most fascinating city tour on the continent due to the size and relative youth of Puerto Montt, it conveniently encompasses the main points of historic interest in the city.

Diego Rivera Casa de Arte [65 F3] (*Quillota 116*; ☏ *(65) 2482638*) In the 1960 earthquake a small art house in Angelmó was destroyed, and the current building was donated to Puerto Montt by the Mexican government as a replacement, thus the name. It is located in the heart of the downtown district and houses a 430-seat theatre which hosts a variety of cultural events, such as classical and contemporary dance, theatre and concerts, as well as four rooms for exhibitions from both local and international artists, the vast majority of which are free. A full list of events is available on www.culturapuertomontt.cl. The *casa* is run by the municipal government and also offers music, dance and theatre classes. Usually held in July, the Casa hosts the Temporales Teatrales – a series of theatre productions from around Latin America.

Iglesia Catedral (Church Cathedral) [65 F3] The somewhat confusingly named Iglesia Catedral is of mild architectural interest, built almost entirely of alerce; construction began in 1856 and was completed 40 years later. The design avoided the use of nails, with all joins made by dowels, affording the building some mechanical play. The effectiveness of this design was proven in 1960 when, despite being the oldest building in all of Puerto Montt, the cathedral was unaffected by a major earthquake that destroyed much of the city.

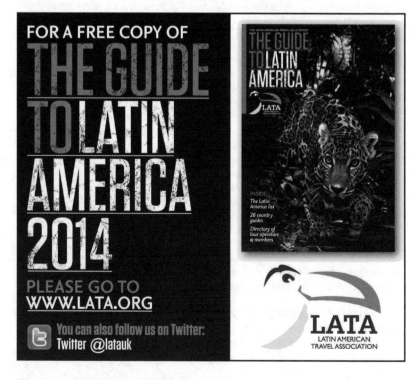

4

Puerto Montt to Villa Santa Lucía

The Carretera Austral officially begins at the southeastern exit of Puerto Montt. The relative modernity of the city rapidly fades only a short distance from the shopping mall at the southern exit and, with the exception of a brief interlude at Coyhaique some 560km south, it is wilderness from here onwards. This northern section is often ignored by visitors to the Carretera Austral, who prefer to join the road further south at Futaleufú. However, doing so misses the spectacular scenery around **Cochamó**, with some of the best treks along the entire Carretera. The scenic coastal road to **Hornopirén** offers a unique insight into the fishing and boat-building traditions of the region, and the ferry from Hornopirén along **Fiordo Comau** besides the northern section of **Parque Pumalín** is a soothing introduction to the wilderness to the south.

From Hornopirén there are a couple of minor detours, but this is basically the end of this section of road. The only way south is via ferry to **Caleta Gonzalo**, on the edge of Parque Pumalín, from where the Carretera Austral continues towards the town of **Chaitén**, destroyed by a volcanic eruption in 2008. South of this, the road passes the first of many lakes bordering the Carretera, before arriving at the crossroads of **Villa Santa Lucía**, the jumping-off point for Futaleufú.

TOWARDS HORNOPIRÉN

There are a number of different route options in this section of the Carretera. The most **direct route** from Puerto Montt involves catching the ferry from Caleta La Arena in the north to Caleta Puelche in the south and then heading along the Carretera to Hornopirén. Along this stretch are the main access points to the Parque Nacional Andean Alerce and the Volcán Calbuco (2,015m), but there is little else of interest. Even with the ferry crossing, this can easily be done in a single day, although cyclists will need to get up early to do so. The only accommodation along this stretch is in Contao.

There is, however, an **alternative and more scenic** means of reaching Caleta Puelche that avoids both the ferry and Puerto Montt. The departure point for this 'back route' is Ensenada, at the eastern tip of Lago Llanquihue. If heading to the Carretera Austral from Bariloche (Argentina), this is a shorter option, and also more interesting than the developed road through southern Puerto Montt suburbia. From Ensenada a decent paved road heads southeast to Ralún, at which point the gravel begins. Ralún is situated at the head of the Reloncaví Sound, but is of little interest, catering mostly to the salmon farmers in the region. The road then continues 15km south to the picturesque town of Cochamó, on to the less picturesque town of Puelo, and along the southern edge of the sound to Caleta Puelche. Prior to the ferry connection at Caleta Puelche this was the only way to reach Hornopirén, thus the residents of the region have a valid point in claiming that this is in fact the original Carretera Austral.

On arriving in Caleta Puelche, one final decision remains before arriving at the town of Hornopirén. The road continues for 10km (paved) until the town of Contao where it forks. The 'official' Carretera Austral heads directly south through the interior of this peninsula, but there is a lengthier **coastal road** heading southwest from Contao, eventually joining the Carretera Austral approximately 23km from Hornopirén. Indeed, this is one of the few segments of the entire Carretera Austral where the alternative route is more interesting than the 'official' route. The coastal road passes through a number of lovely villages, along stretches of open sandy beaches, past some historic churches, and boasts extensive wildlife and lovely views out to the Golfo de Ancud and to some of the islands of Chiloé.

For those with a time constraint, it is possible to travel from Puerto Montt directly to Hornopirén in half a day via the short ferry crossing between Caleta La Arena and Caleta Puelche and by heading directly south through the peninsula on the Carretera (100km driving in total). For those with a little extra spare time, the detour along the coastal route to Hornopirén is worth the effort. However, the more significant detour via Cochamó and Puelo is certainly a consideration if time permits, particularly for those connecting with Argentina.

See map on page 62 for the options.

DIRECT ROUTE FROM PUERTO MONTT TO HORNOPIRÉN (*99km; 2hrs drive, 1hr ferry crossing; paved*) The road is paved to Caleta La Arena (*45km; under 1hr*), where the ferry departs to Caleta Puelche (see page 45). Initially the road heads through southern Puerto Montt suburbia, and then passes through a number of small villages of marginal interest. It is likely that most departing from Puerto Montt will aim to arrive in Hornopirén the same day, which is also possible if travelling by the slightly longer coastal route south of Caleta Puelche. It is 54km to Hornopirén from Caleta Puelche, and takes approximately 1 hour. The road is entirely paved, with no places to stay or eat. Besides the Parque Nacional Alerce Andino there is relatively little of interest until Hornopirén.

Getting there by bus Kemelbus and Buses M&M offer frequent daily services between Puerto Montt and Hornopirén – see pages 66–7 for details.

Sightseeing and excursions along the route Given the prevalence of spectacular parks along the Carretera Austral, both parks listed here may be of less interest to most visitors who intend to travel further south. As of mid 2015 the Volcán Calbuco, a key highlight of both parks, remains inaccessible due to the April 2015 eruption. Further south, Parque Pumalín provides extensive opportunities to view towering alerce trees and visit two volcanoes (Chaitén and Michinmahuida).

Reserva Nacional Llanquihue (*www.conaf.cl/parques/reserva-nacional-llanquihue*) Located to the east of Puerto Varas and Puerto Montt, and south of Ensenada, the Reserva Nacional Llanquihue is arguably the first point of interest along the Carretera. Its principal highlight is the **Volcán Calbuco** (2,015m), a rarely climbed volcano that erupted as recently as April 2015 with spectacular images of electrical storms and billowing ash clouds reaching the international media. As of May 2015 the volcano was not accessible to tourists and it's not known when the situation will change. Assuming it does open during the lifetime of this guide, there are two main access points to the volcano: south of Puerto Montt towards

Correntoso and Lago Chapo; or north of Puerto Montt close to Ensenada, along the 'back route' to Caleta Puelche (see below). A guide is highly recommended for either route. From Correntoso, at the edge of the Parque Nacional Alerce Andino, the road continues 7km north towards the volcano to a car park. From here the Los Alerces del Río Blanco trek (*20km; full day; medium*) heads north for 1½ hours alongside the river to a bridge, before continuing north to a refuge. It then leaves the forest, heading northeast to the summit. There is no park ranger in this reserve, and only one hiking trail (to the volcano).

The northern access to the Volcán Calbuco passes through the private property of Casa Ko B&B (page 82); it's a nice place to stay, so to climb the volcano it is best to overnight here. Permission is required to pass through this private property, and the owner of Casa Ko, Rafael, is able to guide visitors to the volcano. However, given the April 2015 eruption of Calbuco, it is not currently clear if and when this trek will reopen.

Parque Nacional Alerce Andino (65) 2486401; *e parque.alerceandino@ conaf.cl; www.conaf.cl/parques/parque-nacional-alerce-andino; $1,500, but note that there is not always a ranger on duty, so you can pay on exit*) This park borders the Reserva Nacional Llanquihue to the north and is the main point of interest between Puerto Montt and the first ferry crossing. There are a number of lakes and well-marked trails within the park. Fauna include pudú, puma, kodkod (the smallest cat in the Americas), and the equally elusive *monito del monte* (no obvious translation in English, a very small marsupial that could be mistaken for a hamster and lives exclusively in this region of Chile and across the border in Argentina). Birds include the condor, the black woodpecker and huet-huet. Trees include larch, coigüe Magallanes and lenga. A number of short to medium-length trails are clearly marked, generally to lakes within the park.

There are two entry points to the park. The first begins some 7km southeast of Puerto Montt at Coihuín. The road to Correntoso is paved, and the road beyond towards Lago Chapo is a decent, wide, gravel road. Heading south the road deteriorates; it narrows and traverses steeper sections with tighter curves. There is also a narrow, challenging gravel back road from Correntoso to the Carretera Austral passing through Chamiza that runs parallel to the paved road on the north side of the river, although this is of little interest. However, for those wishing to avoid doubling back on themselves, this is an option. From Correntoso, it is also possible to continue further north towards Volcán Calbuco, if permitted given the recent eruption.

The second entry point is from Chaica, on a poor quality, steep gravel trail with tyre ruts, only suitable for a car with good clearance. It's a single-lane track with blind corners, some of the worst quality road encountered on the Carretera.

THE BACK ROUTE FROM PUERTO MONTT TO CALETA PUELCHE VIA COCHAMÓ

(*174km; 3hrs; paved to Ralún, then gravel*) The alternative northern entry point to the Carretera Austral by road is at **Ensenada** (where there is accommodation). Instead of heading south from Puerto Montt, head north to Puerto Varas (*17km; paved*) and then east along the southern coast of Lago Llanquihue (*47km; paved*). For those with sufficient time available, this is the recommended northern entry point to the Carretera Austral by road. In addition to being more scenic than the direct route from Puerto Montt, this back road also passes through **Cochamó**, an adventure hub colloquially referred to as 'the Yosemite of Chile', and the destination point for those trekking from Argentina via Paso Río Manso. Although **Río Puelo** is of less interest, those trekking from Argentina via Paso Río Puelo in the south usually end up here. In fact, these two treks from Argentina to either Río Puelo or Cochamó are connected via a 24km route between Torrentoso (southwest of Paso Río Manso) to the main road towards Llanada Grande. Although logistically a little more complex, these two border crossings provide an interesting alternative means for those without a vehicle to begin the journey along the Carretera Austral. It is even possible to trek all the way to Hornopirén, but get local information before embarking on this route. Maps are available at the border and also at the destination towns of Río Puelo (the town, as opposed to the river and border of the same name), Cochamó and Hornopirén.

If travelling from (or to) Bariloche or east of Lago Llanquihue, this route is no slower than the direct route, particularly in high season, as there is generally less traffic and no need to take the ferry, which often involves a queue.

This route also enables access to the northern trek to the Volcán Calbuco accessed through **Casa Ko**, although following the April 2015 eruption it is not clear when this trek will once again become feasible.

There is a minor detour to **Petrohué** shortly after Ensenada, which is a popular weekend retreat for Puerto Montt locals, and also the start point of the bus/ferry route to **Bariloche** (*www.cruceandino.com*). For those heading south this is not an important detour, but is a potential (and expensive) means to connect the north of the Carretera with Bariloche.

Getting there by bus There are regular buses from Puerto Montt to Cochamó and Río Puelo offered by Transhar and Buses Río Puelo (see pages 66–7 for details); however, the latter go via Lago Tagua Tagua, which involves a ferry crossing, making the journey slightly longer.

Towards Cochamó (*47km from Ensenada; under 1hr; mostly paved*) The 32km road from Ensenada to Ralún is paved; it then continues for 15km to Cochamó on mostly reasonable gravel which is currently being paved. However, the winding section prior to arriving in the town is treacherous, narrow and has blind corners, so take care.

🏠 *Where to stay and eat*

🏠 **Casa Ko B&B** (6 rooms) 37km east of Puerto Varas, 10km west of Ensenada; 📞 (9) 77036477; e casako@casako.com; www.casako.com. A lovely B&B with great views over the lake & towards the Calbuco, Puntiagudo & Osorno volcanoes. The turning from the main road between Puerto Varas & Ensenada is signposted 'El Tepu', & the B&B is 3km up this trail. Frequent buses traverse the main road. Dbl rooms with & without bathroom, full b/fast included. Wi-Fi, laundry & wide range of movies (no TV in rooms, only in nice communal sitting area). This is a remote location, but fortunately dinner is available, including vegetarian options, for guests (**$$$**). The location is ideal: close to the lake as well as the Petrohué waterfalls, convenient for the Cruce Andino bus–boat combination to Bariloche (page 67), & ideal

for accessing the Carretera Austral via Cochamó. The owner, Rafael, can take guests to the summit of Volcán Calbuco, & speaks English, Spanish & French. They also arrange tours (kayak, canyoning, fishing, mountain biking, horseriding, etc). Accepts credit card. **$$$**

🏠 **Complejo Montaña – Ensenada** (5 rooms, 3 cabins, camping) Ensenada junction; 📞 (65) 2212088, (9) 84085859; e turismoensenada@gmail.com; www. turismomontana.com. Around 44km from Puerto Varas, this hostel/campsite is well located at the junction to the Carretera Austral (via Cochamó), the road to Petrohué (where the boat from Bariloche arrives/departs) & the road north towards Entre Lagos, the Volcán Osorno & on to Argentina. Decent rooms with private bathroom,

Wi-Fi, cable TV & beds sleeping 4–6 people; b/fast included. The cabins are cosy, wooden, rustic affairs, with fully equipped kitchen, dbl bed & 4 sgls; more expensive than the rooms & prices depend on occupancy (b/fast not included). The camping, somewhat unusually, boasts private bathrooms on the premium sites, & direct access to the lake. **$$–$$$**

Cochamó and around Founded in 1979, Cochamó (population approximately 4,500) is a delightful town situated on the Reloncaví Sound. It has a pleasant central square and church, and great views when the sun shines. However, shopping options are limited, and there is neither a petrol station nor ATM in the town, so come prepared and fill up at Ensenada or Hornopirén. While there's not a great deal to keep visitors occupied within the town itself, the surrounding region, and in particular the interior mountainous section towards the Argentine border, has been christened 'the Yosemite of Chile' by climbers and hikers alike. The Valle Río Cochamó is accessed 5km south of town on a northeastern detour. It may not compete with the parks of Torres del Paine and Cerro Castillo further south, but the region is certainly worth a visit.

Tourist information and tour operator On the main road next to the library is a small tourist information centre (⊕ *08.30–20.00 Mon–Fri, until 17.30 in low season*), with maps and information relating to tours in the region. As well as the listed tour operator, there are a few guides offering horse/trekking tours and recommended by the information centre.

Guides
Cristian Igor ☏(9) 90772361
Victor Contreras ☏(9) 99112890
Ida Delgado ☏(9) 99372042 (one of the only female guides)
Fabian Sandoval ☏(9) 84072559 (speaks basic English)
Jose Villega ☏(9) 84539755

Tour operator
Experiencia Patagonia Juan Jesús Molina 77; ☏(9) 93349213, (9) 82439937; e maurok@live. se; www.experienciapatagonia.cl. Operating out of the Hostel Maura, Mauricio is a registered guide offering fly-fishing trips, horseriding, kayaking & trekking around Cochamó, including along the trails to Argentina.

Patagonia Nativa Avenida Aerodromo at the northern entrance to Cochamó; ☏(9) 93165635; e cochamo@patagonianativa.cl; www.patagonianativa.cl. Run out of the hostel of the same name, Patagonia Nativa is one of the best-established tour operators in Cochamó, & speak English. All trekking options are available, including those to Argentina. Climbing available in the nearby 'Yosemite of Chile', kayak tours with certified guides on both the rivers & in the sound, & mountain bikes also available for rent. For those wishing to hike over to Argentina (although a guide is not strictly necessary as the routes are well sign-posted), it might be wise to spend an evening in this hostel & find out more information about the trails.

🛏 **Where to stay**
🏠 **Las Dalias Cabins** (2 cabins) Northern entrance to Cochamó; ☏(9) 94423583, (9) 68103638; e janecita.eve@hotmail.com. Pleasant cabins for 4 or 6 people; Wi-Fi, cable TV, direct access to the sound, full kitchen, laundry service & good parking facilities. Frequented by motorcyclists. The owner also works in the municipality tourist information centre, so has a wealth of information about the region, including all the guides & tours available, maps, etc. **$$$**

🏠 **Hostel La Ollita** (8 rooms) Principal; ☏(9) 88072716, (9) 81665225.Decent sgl, dbl & trpl rooms accommodating up to 18 people in total. B/fast included; part of restaurant of the same name. Wi-Fi not available, but laundry is. Decent communal sitting area & kitchen. Reservations required in peak season, deposit normally required but some flexibility with foreigners. Owner has a boat & can arrange trips to the sound. Credit cards accepted. **$$**

🏠 **Hostel Maura** (7 rooms) Juan Jesús Molina 77; 📞(9) 93349213, (9) 82439937; e hostalmaura@outlook.com; www.experienciapatagonia.cl. A charming & well-equipped hostel 100m from the church & even closer to the coast – it's one of the best in the town. Sgl, dbl & trpl rooms available, all with an excellent b/fast included. Rooms are simple, & most with shared bathroom; south-facing rooms enjoy a wonderful view over the sound. For larger groups a quincho is also available. In peak season the owner sparks up the sauna & hot tub in the garden. Laundry service available on site. Decent off-road parking – motorcyclists often stay here. The hostel was founded by the owner, Nory, in 1996 & her son, Mauricio Mora, is the founder of tour operator Experiencia Patagonia (page 83), & offers kayak trips, horseriding, trekking in the valleys, boat trips on the sound & to the hot springs, plus private transport. For those wishing to hike over to Argentina, Mauricio is able to guide such routes. Nory speaks Spanish only, but Mauricio also speaks English & Swedish. **$$**

🏠 **Hostel Patagonia Nativa** (6 rooms) Av Aerodromo at the northern entrance to Cochamó; 📞(9) 93165635; e cochamo@patagonianativa.cl; www.patagonianativa.cl. Decent, simple sgl, dbl & trpl rooms; b/fast included, rates slightly higher for a private bathroom. No Wi-Fi, but laundry & parking available. Great view over the sound; perhaps a 5min walk downhill to the coast. The main attraction to this hostel is that it is run by one of the most experienced guides in the region, Cristian Cea (page 83). **$$**

🏠 *Where to eat and drink*

✕ **La Ollita** Principal; 📞(9) 88072716, (9) 81665225; ⊕ 10.00–02.00 daily. The largest restaurant in town, lovely views from terrace, great b/fast. Specialities are seafood & ceviche, but in particular the *puyi* – a fish that is sometimes confused for an eel, but is in fact a fish so small that its fins are barely visible – delicious & hard to find. All food is either homemade or from the region. Doubles as bar in the evenings, popular with both locals & tourists. **$$$**

✕ **Restaurant Reloncaví** Catedral 16 (uphill from church); 📞(9) 97965764; ⊕ all year, closes at 23.00. Specialises in local seafood dishes, adequate selection of wines & beers. **$$$**

✕ **Restaurant del Pueblo** Next to Hostel Maura. A reasonable new addition to the culinary offerings of Cochamó, cheap fresh fish dishes, decent view if you can get one of the window seats, annoying TV blaring but provides a rare opportunity to watch the news. **$$**

Sightseeing and excursions Cochamó may appear a sleepy town, but there is a huge amount to do in the surrounding region, with excellent trekking, riding and climbing (see www.cochamo.com/climbing for more detailed information). There are also kayaking options, but given the abundance of alternatives further south it is perhaps not something to prioritise here. There are currently around 160 marked climbing routes, although this is growing, with 100 big-wall routes, including a 1,200m route (Tigres del Norte, 5.12d). Pitches range from 5.6 to 5.13. For kayaking, speak to Christian Cea at Patagonia Nativa (page 83), who speaks English, offers tours, and knows all the guides in the region.

The trekking options are extensive, and of particular interest to those travelling the length of the Carretera Austral is the option to hike directly to or from Argentina (described on page 86; see trail map on page 85).

Trekking in Valle Río Cochamó (*Map, opposite*) For those wishing to combine a journey along the Carretera Austral with some trekking, the trek between Cochamó and Argentina is one of the best options in the region, which connects with an array of trails extending as far south as Hornopirén. Leave Cochamó on the main road south, and turn left at the bridge heading east. The gravel trail continues for about 8km, accessible by road but, at the park ranger station, the road ends, and from this point it is accessible by horse or on foot only. The main destination is La Junta, 13km from the park ranger station, where basic accommodation and

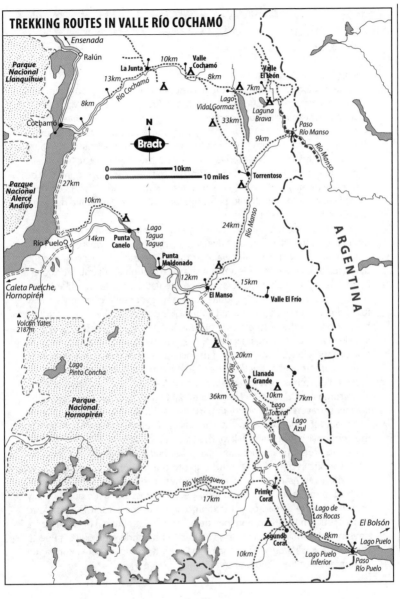

TREKKING ROUTES IN VALLE RÍO COCHAMÓ

Ensenada
Ralún
Parque Nacional Llanquihue
La Junta
10km
Valle Cochamó
13km
Río Cochamó
8km
Valle El León
7km
Lago Vidal Gormaz
33km
Laguna Brava
Paso Río Manso
9km
Cochamó
8km
N
Bradt
0   10km
0   10 miles
Parque Nacional Alerce Andino
27km
10km
Torrentoso
Río Manso
24km
Río Manso
Río Puelo
14km
Punta Canelo
Lago Tagua Tagua
Punta Maldonado
12km
15km
El Manso
Valle El Frío
Caleta Puelche, Hornopirén
Volcán Yates 2187m
20km
Lago Pinto Concha
Río Puelo
Parque Nacional Hornopirén
36km
Llanada Grande
10km
7km
Lago Totoral
Lago Azul
Río Ventisquero
17km
Primer Coral
Lago de Las Rocas
El Bolsón
8km
Lago Puelo
Segundo Coral
10km
Lago Puelo Inferior
Paso Río Puelo

A R G E N T I N A

food are available. From La Junta a number of short hikes are available, but you can also continue onwards to the Argentine border at Paso Río Manso. Campsites are available along the route and a number of detours are possible to Lago Vidal Gormaz, lagunas Brava and Obscura, and to Valle El León. Alternatively one can head south from Paso Río Manso to Torrentoso (9km, camping and food available) and a further 24km to the trails originating in Puelo (page 87), ultimately crossing the border to Argentina further south at Paso Río Puelo and onto El Bolsón (Argentina). Although there is limited formal accommodation in this region, it is highly advisable to carry a tent.

TREK FROM LA JUNTA (IN VALLE COCHAMÓ) TO ARGENTINA

By David Sparkman

(35km; 3–4 days; medium)
From La Junta, an often-muddy and occasionally braided old pioneer trading route goes for three to four days' travel to the Argentine border. Maps of this route are available through Sendero de Chile (*www.senderodechile.cl*; page 121), who are working to develop the route more for tourism and establish homestays with local families along the way. Ask before camping anywhere as most of this route is on private land. The route, while not technically demanding, is clear, but requires fording up to three small rivers and can be extremely muddy in the rainy season. It also requires some patience in trail identification, but this should be mitigated as Sendero de Chile develops the route more for tourism.

From La Junta, the standard trek begins on a well-worn path eastward for 5 hours, fording a couple of rivers, to camp at El Arco, where there is an old *puesto/refugio* in case the weather turns. The camp is just past the Río del Arco ford, where there is a nice waterfall through a beautiful rock arch. From El Arco, the trail meanders through the flat river valley for 45 minutes or so, occasionally becoming quite faint and eventually climbing steadily for another hour to a low pass at Laguna Grande/Espejo. From here the trail heads down to the northern side of Lago Vidal Gormaz, where a couple of families live and camping is available. The main trail then follows the western side of Lago Vidal Gormaz, passing the occasional home, eventually arriving at the southern end of the lake after 3 to 4 hours (camping is available). The trail then descends for another hour or so to Valle Río Manso, where there is more camping. Once at Río Manso, the trail begins to climb, heading to the northeast traversing the northern part of Valle Río Manso. A few hours after first seeing the Río Manso the trail arrives at El León and Paso Río Manso at the border with Argentina. Ask for the Carabineros office in El León if leaving Chile; the Argentine immigration is another half hour away. Ask around for more specific information on how to get to the Argentine immigration and cross the river. As of 2015, there was someone stationed at the site of an old bridge (no longer in use) to ferry people across the river, but this may change as there is road construction going on in the area. It is possible to do this route in less time, and may be possible with minimal gear and food, staying with families along the way. Check with Sendero de Chile in Puerto Varas and/or ask around in Cochamó or La Junta for up-to-date information on homestay options and trail conditions.

The trails from both Cochamó and Río Puelo offer a viable means to connect the Carretera Austral with Argentina through spectacular scenery and don't require a high level of expertise – they are not technical, meaning they are accessible to anyone of reasonable fitness equipped with the necessary camping gear. The trails are well marked, and a guide is optional. In high season it is likely other trekkers will appear periodically along the way. Owing to the array of inter-connected treks it is highly advisable to obtain a map, available to download at http://municochamo.cl/turismo/MapaCochamoFull.jpg. Alternatively, you can purchase one from Stanfords (page 271).

Where to stay and eat Camping and basic accommodation is also available, but check with the park rangers to make a reservation.

Refugio Cochamó La Junta; www.cochamo.com/lodging. This is one of the last formal accommodation options whilst trekking in the region, & a meeting place for climbers & trekkers offering bunk rooms (bring bedding) & a private room for 2 (bedding included), although at the time of writing it was currently closed for refurbishment. Keep an eye on their website for the latest. The website also contains local info, trail maps & a notice board for visitors. **$$–$$$**

Río Puelo

A further 27km south of the bridge to the Valle Cochamó (or 32km south of Cochamó) is the nondescript village of Río Puelo – travellers are advised to push on further south. Its main virtue is being the start/end point for treks across to Argentina that utilise the crossing at Paso Río Puelo as opposed to the slightly more northern Paso Río Manso, which is closer to Cochamó. As with most of the gravel road along the southern edge of the Reloncaví Sound, this road is treacherous, often with deep gravel and blind curves, so take care and avoid driving at night. Expect oncoming vehicles often travelling at high speed and drifting towards the centre of the road. The road narrows to a single track in places, and weaves along steep precipices into the sound; it is poor quality until Caleta Puelche, 36km southwest of Puelo.

Where to stay and eat

Hostel and Cabins El Arrayan (7 rooms; 3 cabins) 1 block towards coast from central plaza; (9) 88819677. Dbl rooms with & without private bathrooms; b/fast included .Cheaper cabins also available for 4 or 6 people. **$**

Sightseeing and excursions

Lago Tagua Tagua The detour to Lago Tagua Tagua is wonderful, if only to enjoy the winding road climbing through the valley up to the edge of the lake. It is the starting point of more trails over to Argentina which connect with the routes from Cochamó. The detour is perhaps 1km north of Puelo to the east, and continues for 14km (gravel) to the ferry port at Punta Canelo (*3 Naviera Puelche ferries daily, 07.30, 09.00 & 13.00, return 08.15, noon & 16.30; $6,500 one-way with car, $1,000 for pedestrians*), where there is food and camping available. The ferry crosses to Puerto Maldonado (cars permitted), where the road continues 32km south to Llanada Grande and 20km further to Primer Coral, at which point only travel by horse or on foot is possible.

Trekking routes   *Map, page 85*

There are three main trekking options from Río Puelo. The first is a new route to Hornopirén (seek information in Río Puelo as this is a long, isolated trek suitable only for experienced hikers), and there's also a possibility to trek from Río Puelo (town) up to Lago Tagua Tagua along the northern shore of Río Puelo (river). However, the most common routes start in Puerto Maldonado on the southern edge of Lago Tagua Tagua and connect with an array of trails, including those that head north towards Cochamó (pages 84–6) and south towards Llanada Grande, Primer and Segundo Coral, and eventually to Paso Río Puelo.

Make sure you pick up a map at the information centre in Río Puelo or Cochamó prior to departing. The treks towards Llanada Grande, Primer and Segundo Coral are relatively well trodden, and not far from the road. However, the more isolated treks towards Valle Ventisqueros, Hornopirén and Cochamó are not as well traversed, thus obtain local information prior to departing.

Río Puelo to Caleta Puelche (*36km; under 1hr; gravel*) From Puelo the road continues 36km to Caleta Puelche along the southern shore of the Reloncaví Estuary. Caleta Puelche is where the ferry from Caleta La Arena arrives. This section of road is gravel, with steep cliffs, occasional rocks in the road, blind corners and the occasional oncoming vehicle in the middle of the road. As with this entire stretch of road along the estuary, take care and drive slowly. The views over the estuary are beautiful on a sunny day, but there is relatively little to do along this largely uninhabited section.

THE COASTAL ROUTE FROM CONTAO TO HORNOPIRÉN (*73km; 3hrs; gravel*) From
Caleta Puelche the road continues 10km (paved) southwest until Contao. From here there are two routes to Hornopirén: the direct route, along the 'official' Carretera Austral (pages 80–1); or the longer coastal route. The latter is recommended for those with time to spare, and is mostly gravel; it adds approximately 30km versus the direct route through the peninsula, but there are various places worth visiting, so budget at least 3 hours to get to Hornopirén from Contao via the coast. A vehicle with high clearance is advisable along this section. If at all possible avoid sleeping in Contao, but in an emergency **Hostel Sofia** (✆ *(9) 95920114;* **$**) offers accommodation (breakfast included) that will seem worryingly familiar to anyone who has ever spent a night in jail. Gloomy but cheap rooms are provided, of interest primarily to cyclists unable to reach Hornopirén or Puerto Montt that day, with breakfast included.

This coastal region is home to a number of boat-builders as well as traditional fishermen using compressed air and garden hosepipes to dive for shellfish, often staying underwater for hours at a time in 11mm wetsuits. The activity is not particularly safe, and accidents are common. Fortunately decompression chambers are available in Puerto Montt and on Chiloé, but alas those that practise this activity are not always aware of the dangers of extended periods at depth. Anyone wishing to dive with the traditional fishermen does so entirely at their own risk; although such fishing methods are generally deemed unsafe, an exemption was made to permit so-called traditional fishing, but this does not extend to tour operators. There are no authorised dive centres or equipment rental stores, so snorkelling or free diving might be safer.

Getting there by bus There are only two services (Kemelbus and Expreso Austral) that traverse the coastal road, but they do not go all the way to Hornopirén – they terminate at Hualaihué, around 30km east. See page 67 for details.

South from Contao (*16km to Curamín; 1hr; gravel*) The first village along the route is **La Poza**, approximately 10km south of Contao. According to local guides there is a lake here, but pond might be a fairer description. However, the San Nicolas de Tolentino chapel is truly a highlight of the region. Dating back to 1860, this is the oldest chapel in the area, and although in a desperate state of disrepair, still functions as a working chapel when the priest from Hornopirén comes once a month to deliver mass. It is entirely built of local wood and adorned with alerce tiles. The church bell is Spanish, and apparently one of only five in the country. To visit the church knock on the doors of neighbours until someone with a key appears – they are usually delighted to receive an inquisitive visitor interested in their village.

A further 4km south is the **San Miguel de Aulen chapel**, built almost a century later (1958) but in a similar style. Of particular interest is the cemetery, visible on the neighbouring island, with colourfully decorated graves. Fishermen can offer a quick shuttle service for those wishing to visit the graveyard, but to some extent viewing it from the mainland is as interesting. The annual festival of San Pedro is held on the island nearby on 29 June.

Curamín Along the 7km stretch between Aulen and Nao is the surprisingly pleasant village of Curamín, where, on a sunny day, the views out to the Golfo de Ancud are impressive. The village consists of the four key things to warrant an overnight stay: a shop, reasonable accommodation, a decent restaurant and access to boats. The shop is run by a fishing family, and has a large sign outside reading 'Mariscos' (shellfish), although it also sells basic food supplies, drinks, local jams and shellfish in jars. The family have a boat (↘ (9) 77266828) and can arrange fishing trips, or visits to the islands. For those with a wetsuit it is conceivably possible to hitch a ride out to sea with the family on a fishing excursion to observe the insanely dangerous hosepipe diving, but be aware that this is entirely at your own risk.

Where to stay and eat The family who own the shop also have a **cabin** available for rent across the road, with spectacular views out to the gulf.

✕ **El Fogón Costero Curamín** 500m further south from the shop along the road; ↘ (9) 76565121. This is a gem, without a doubt the finest place to eat along the entire coast, & apparently the only restaurant in the region to have ever made it into a magazine (the Dec 2014 edition of *Destinos Chile*), which the owner has on proud display. Meat dishes are available, but the focus is the seafood, including a seafood buffet, & it's a good opportunity to taste the much sought-after loco. The restaurant itself is simple, entirely made of wood, with a warm stove & sweeping views over the gulf. This is simply *the* place to eat along the coast, popular with locals & the occasional visitor alike, as well as catering for parties in the region. Excellent & reasonably priced. $$

The Nao Peninsula to Hornopirén *(58km; 2hrs; gravel)* The **Nao Peninsula** is approximately 6km south of Aulen, and at low tide it is possible to walk over to a small island. However, it's all too easy to get stranded on the island, so check tide times locally, and let a local fisherman know your plans prior to departing. The peninsula has a small village, and it is possible to visit boat-builders here.

Rolecha, approximately 26km south of Contao, is the largest community along the coastal route, and roughly halfway to the junction with the main Carretera to Hornopirén. It is home to a chapel, built in 1940, and also boasts an impressive sandy beach, but beach-lovers are advised to head 14km further south to Lleguiman. **Chauchil**, shortly before Lleguiman, has a school, an impressive yellow church, and free camping. The beach at **Lleguiman** is where the locals go to bathe, and the river is good for fishing. **Accommodation** is sometimes available at the house of Emiliano (↘ (9) 82976823; $), with breakfast sometimes included. Bear in mind that this is a region entirely unfamiliar with tourism, so services are comparably chaotic and informal.

Next you'll reach **Hualaihué** port, the final inhabited spot along the coast. There is a chapel dating from 1930, and a small mountain (Cerro La Silla) that can be easily hiked in a couple of hours; it boasts a small lake at the top, as well as lovely views across the peninsula towards the mountainous interior and out to the gulf. Hualaihué is home to potentially the first dedicated tour operator along this stretch of coast, Don Neftali Moños Diaz (↘ (9) 84605448). While the operation may be basic, he is so far the only local person dedicated to tourism, and can guide the trek up Cerro La Silla.

From Hualaihué port, the road continues north for approximately 6km, passing through the Hualaihué Estuary, where ample birdlife can be observed. Just 1km before the road meets the Carretera Austral (23km from Hornopirén) is the **final accommodation option** along the route (Residencia Yoanna; page 94), ideal for those seeking an abundance of religious icons and kitsch décor. The more discerning traveller may prefer to push on to Hornopirén.

HORNOPIRÉN

As with Chaitén and other towns along the Carretera Austral, many visitors use Hornopirén as a mere stopping-off point on their journeys north and south. In fact Hornopirén, on a sunny day, is a delightful town worthy of a day or two for those keen on trekking; it has a certain charm, and the surrounding area has abundant wildlife and trekking options to the lakes and volcanoes. One notable criticism of the town, however, is the lack of restaurants, and in peak season, accommodation can also be a problem, so it is wise to plan ahead.

HISTORY Although there is evidence of pre-Hispanic visitors to what is now the town of Hornopirén and the surrounding region of Hualaihué, the region was visited by the Spanish during their search for the mythical Ciudad de los Césares (see box, pages 92–3). The first settlers arrived around 1890, principally for the abundant alerce wood in the region and to raise animals. Local families often have distinct surnames revealing their origins from the neighbouring island of Chiloé. During the 19th century such was the value of alerce that planks of the sought-after wood were used as a currency. In the late 1950s, the North American logging company BIMA (a subsidiary of the Simpson Timber Company) established a base in what is now Contao and began deforesting the region, forcing the local inhabitants to seek alternative livelihoods, principally fishing. As a result, the population of Hornopirén swelled from 427 in 1960 to 1,126 a decade later. However, the prohibition of alerce extraction in 1976 and the arrival of Salvador Allende persuaded the Americans to leave the zone, and the Hornopirén population fell to a mere 365 by 1992.

In 1965, a tragic landslide on the volcano bearing the name of the town killed 28 people. The remnants of this landslide can be seen on the hike to Lago Cabrera.

The latest phase of immigration to the area has been fuelled by extensive salmon farming. The name Hualaihué means 'place of aquatic birds', so it is perhaps no surprise that the history of this section of the Carretera Austral is intimately related to the natural resources in the region. The town was formally founded in 1979, and the Carretera Austral reached Hornopirén in 1984; it now has around 3,000 inhabitants.

One intriguing element of Hornopirén's recent past concerns its lovely church on the central plaza. The priest is a Dutchman named Father Antonio van Kessel who has lived in the region much of his life, after arriving in Hornopirén 25 years ago. During the Pinochet years Father Antonio was imprisoned twice, accused of communist tendencies for his support of the poor, and was a personal friend of Father Ronchi (see box, page 125), whose influence extends across much of the Carretera Austral. Father Antonio built the church in 1991, and it was inaugurated on 18 December of that year. He managed to obtain 15 authorised reprints depicting the various stages of the Crucifixion, originally painted by Adolfo Pérez Esquivel, the Argentine Nobel Peace Prize winner in 1980. In 1993 these reprints were stolen, and have never been recovered; nevertheless, a stubborn Father Antonio obtained a second set of authorised reprints, copies of which are visible in the church to this day, and are worth perusing.

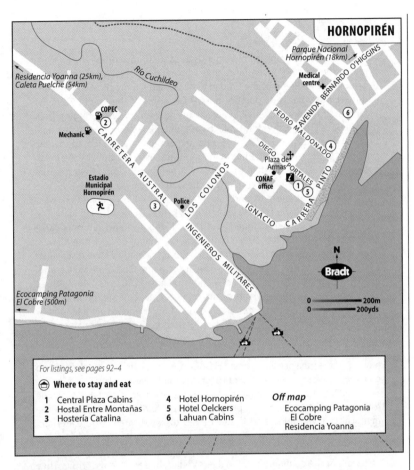

Residencia Yoanna (25km),
Caleta Puelche (54km)

Río Cuchildeo

Parque Nacional
Hornopirén (18km)

Medical
centre

COPEC

Mechanic

Estadio
Municipal
Hornopirén

Police

Plaza de
Armas

CONAF
office

DIEGO PORTALES

PEDRO MALDONADO

AVENIDA BERNARDO O'HIGGINS

IGNACIO CARRERA PINTO

CARRETERA AUSTRAL

LOS COLONOS

INGENIEROS MILITARES

Ecocamping Patagonia
El Cobre (500m)

N

Bradt

0 — 200m
0 — 200yds

For listings, see pages 92–4

🛏 **Where to stay and eat**

1 Central Plaza Cabins
2 Hostal Entre Montañas
3 Hostería Catalina
4 Hotel Hornopirén
5 Hotel Oelckers
6 Lahuan Cabins

Off map
   Ecocamping Patagonia
      El Cobre
   Residencia Yoanna

TOUR OPERATORS

Ecoturismo Hornopirén Expediciones ☎(9) 93570261; e hornopirenexpediciones@gmail.com; www.hornopirenexpediciones.com. They offer a 5-hour round-trip tour to Lago Cabrera; tours to Parque Hornopirén & volcano; to the hot springs in the Comau & Cahuelmó fjords; plus shorter tours around the town.

Patagonia El Cobre Playa el Cobre; ☎(9) 82275152, (9) 78090799; e patagoniaelcobre@ gmail.com; www.patagoniaelcobre.cl. Experienced tour operators with a campsite of the same name (page 94). Tours to all 3 volcanoes in the region (Yates, Hornopirén & Apagado); mountain bikes for rent (including guides); offers 3–10-day kayak trips in the fjords including multi-day guided trips down the fjord to the Cahuelmó hot springs; plus trips to seal colonies, penguins & dolphin-spotting.

Turismo Lahuan Cahuelmó 40; ☎(65) 2217239, (9) 84090231; e info@turismolahuan.com; www. turismolahuan.com. Owned by those with the cabins of the same name (page 92), this company also offers tailor-made tours in the region. These include a tour along the coastal route towards Puerto Montt – often missed by visitors to the region & well worth visiting. For those without a private vehicle this is a good means to visit the Hualaihué region, & the company can also pickup or drop-off at the ferry port (ie: one-way trips). They also offer ascents of Hornopirén & Apagado volcanoes; trips to the lakes & hot springs (they have their own boat); kayaking; visits to the sea lion colonies & boat tours along the canal to Cahuelmó & Quintupeu fjords; & trips to Parque Nacional Hornopirén. Perhaps more expensive than other operators, but that's expected of private, bespoke tours.

The vastness of Patagonia allows legends to abound, and combining its sheer size with the passing of centuries, plus a liberal dose of religious mysticism, the result is the legend of the Ciudad de los Césares, a mythical city of silver and gold. But what is its point of origin? Did some of the Knights Templar escape their coming downfall in Europe in the 14th century, bringing their most famous charge, the Holy Grail, to Patagonia? Is it still buried somewhere beneath the vast and barren Meseta de Somuncura, which spans the provinces of Río Negro and Chubut in Argentina? Or was it built by the Incas, escaping from the Spanish in the north of Argentina, bringing their treasure with them to establish a new colony in the wilds of Patagonia?

In 1515 the Spanish explorer Juan de Solis and his expedition were attacked by local Indians while exploring the area around Buenos Aires. The survivors of his party continued south into Patagonia, and rumours came back that they had discovered a fantastical city inhabited by white men. In 1528, another Spanish explorer, Francisco César, claimed to have discovered a city rich in gold and silver, and he gave it the name Ciudad de los Césares. In 1540 a shipwreck in the Straits of Magellan claimed 200 lives. Twenty-three years later, two of the survivors of the original crew emerged in Chile with stories of a city rich in treasures, silver and gold. Such legends were fanned by two separate flames: firstly, the local indigenous population were more than happy to send colonialist explorers off to the depths of Patagonia in search of mythical cities of gold; secondly, the monarchies of Spain and Britain may have used the idea of a Patagonian El Dorado to motivate their explorers, and give them a reason to establish outposts in remote Patagonia.

In 1783, the explorer Francisco Menendez left from the island of Chiloé together with 16 indigenous people intent on finding the location of the mythical city. He didn't find it, but he did discover three large waterfalls, which themselves generated mythical status. In 1961, a group from the 'Centro Andino' of Bariloche in Argentina retraced his trail and discovered the waterfalls at the confluence of the rivers Vodudahue and Vidal Gormaz. They did not, however, find the Ciudad de los Césares.

The only 'evidence' (and this term is used lightly) of the city seems to be the existence of the 'Argentine Fort', situated 15km from the city of San Antonio in the province of Río Negro on the Atlantic coast. While this fort appears to be a natural phenomenon, it would undoubtedly have been a useful strategic fortress were it inhabited. A rather mysterious group of Argentine investigators called the Delphos Foundation claim to have discovered engravings related to the Knights Templar in the fort, including a stone engraved with their cross. A map produced in 1865 by the explorer

🏠 **WHERE TO STAY AND EAT** *Map, page 91*

For some reason Hornopirén is light on restaurants; the best options are either within the hostels and hotels listed, or are at small, informal stalls dotted around the town or in the market, just west of the plaza. The restaurants in Entre Montañas and Central Plaza are probably the best options, but few come to Hornopirén for the food.

🏠 **Lahuan Cabins** (3 cabins) Calle Cahuelmó 40; ☎ (65) 2217239, (9) 84090231; e info@   turismolahuan.com; www.turismolahuan. com. Top-quality, fully equipped & positively

Juan Antonio Victor Martin de Moussy marks the site of this natural fortress as 'Abandoned Fort', suggesting they had come across something more than just a natural formation. The group carried out a number of expeditions here in the 1990s, but they never found the Holy Grail.

Legend has it that the Knights Templar set up three such fortresses: the 'Argentine Fort' near the Atlantic coast; another fortress at the same latitude on the Pacific coast, near what is now Osorno in Chile; and a third fortress further south in Patagonia, which is as yet undiscovered. Terms vary as to whether these were various 'Cities of the Casares', or whether the various fortresses were set up to protect and serve the one 'City'.

But what were the Knights Templar doing in Patagonia? The Templars were founded in the early 12th century as warrior-monks, primarily to escort pilgrims to the Holy Land. Their role, wealth and importance expanded throughout Europe and the Holy Land.

In the early 1300s Pope Clement V and King Philip IV of France demanded the arrest of all the Knights Templar in order to sequestrate their vast wealth. Some may have escaped from La Rochelle in France with their most important treasures (including the Holy Grail) and subsequently travelled to the American continent.

Rosslyn Chapel in Scotland, long associated with the Knights Templar, has engravings in its stone window arches of maize and aloe vera cactus plants, which did not exist in Europe when it was built in the 15th century. As the chapel was constructed before any Europeans had officially 'discovered' the American continent, this has been presented as evidence, albeit circumstantial, of Knights Templars' travels in the American continent.

A competing theory is that the city was inhabited by Incas fleeing the Spanish after a failed attempt to rescue their leader Pablo Inga in 1535 in the area now known as Santiago del Estero, Argentina. Don Pablo had been working as a guide for the Spanish colonialist Diego de Almagro, but when his posse was forced to flee by the Spanish, they took much of their wealth with them and founded their own city in the remote safety of Patagonia.

Patagonia may well be a vast region, but despite the advent of aviation, GPS, satellite photography and mapping, as well as a large number of expeditions specifically searching for the Ciudad de los Césares, there appears still to be no evidence of its existence. However, if on your travels along the Carretera Austral you wander off the beaten track and happen to stumble upon a fantastical city full of silver and gold, please let us know. *City of the Césares: The Bradt Guide* would be a novel addition to the Bradt list.

comfortable cabins for 6–8 people; bath as well as shower in the largest cabin. Wood-stove heating, decent sitting area, parking & play area for children; laundry service offered. Views over Fiordo Comau or towards the mountains. Walking distance from centre. The owners, Luis & Betty, are locals & know the area extremely well. They also operate a tour company (page 91), with their own boat & van, & can offer a range of excursions. Credit cards accepted. **$$$$**

🏠 **Central Plaza Cabins** (9 cabins) Lago Pinto Concha shortly before coastal road; ☎ (65) 2217247, (9) 81376188; e Luciano.jara@hotmail.com. Excellent, cosy 2-storey cabins sleeping from 4 to 8 people. Wi-Fi, off-road parking & laundry available. Decent restaurant with a pool table which doubles as a bar in the evenings & is a favourite amongst locals, so might be wiser to rent a cabin at the further end of the complex to get a quiet night's sleep. In the summer the owner, Luciano, hosts regular roast meat BBQs. Large garden with a treehouse, plenty of space for kids to play, ideal for groups & families. Very homely feel. Can also arrange tours in the region. Accepts credit cards; strict cancellations policy & requires reservations. $$$

🏠 **Hostería Catalina** (6 dbl & 4 sgl rooms, 2 cabins) Ingenieros Militares, between the police station & the COPEC petrol station; ✆ (65) 2217359, (9) 90860912; e hchornopiren@hosteriacatalina.cl; www.hosteriacatalina.cl. The friendly owner, Vladimir, has lived in Hornopirén for decades & is knowledgeable about the area & history. Rooms are comfortable but simple; central heating & even electric blankets for the cold winters. Good, large restaurant for guests, large sitting area & quincho; full b/fast included. Wi-Fi, off-street parking, but no laundry service. A slight walk to the centre of town, but on the Carretera Austral if arriving from the north. Rooms with private bathrooms available; rates slightly lower in low season or with a shared bathroom. Can also arrange trekking & horseriding in the area. Accepts credit cards. $$$

🏠 **Hotel Hornopirén** (10 rooms) Ignacio Carrera beyond Pedro Maldonado; ✆ (65) 2217256; e h.honopiren@gmail.com. One of the few remaining buildings dating back 70 years, with the charm & rickety wooden floors to match, & a view over the fjord. The hotel is old: walls are thin, ceilings are low, & for those seeking a modern, plush establishment this might not be the best choice, but undoubtedly one of the most charming hotels in the region, almost entirely made of alerce. The sunrises & sunsets are lovely, when the town is not shrouded in cloud. The owner, Oly Bräuning, founded the hotel in 1984, & has a wealth of information about the region. The perpendicular street, Pedro Maldonado, is named after her late husband. This was the hotel that Doug Tompkins stayed in when he first began exploring the region. Sgls, dbls & trpls available with & without shared bathroom; try to get a room facing the fjord. B/fast included; it is extensive & features a range of jams, homemade bread & some tasty pastries. Wi-Fi & laundry available, private parking, wood-stove heating; deposit usually required. Oly can also offer lunches & dinners for guests, arranged in advance. $$$

🏠 **Hostal Entre Montañas** (8 apts, 4 cabins) Ingenieros Militares, 100m south of COPEC petrol station; ✆ (65) 2217352, (9) 94397505, (9) 56422463; e contacto@hostalentremontanas.cl; www.hostalentremontanas.cl. Good, basic rooms, all sleeping 4 people. Gas heating, Wi-Fi, electric blankets, all private bathrooms; b/fast not included, off-street parking. Decent family-run restaurant onsite (🕐 08.00–23.30 daily; $$$) offering good-value fish & meat dishes. Can also arrange local activities. $$

🏠 **Hotel Oelckers** (18 rooms, 2 cabins) Lago Pinto Concha & Los Colonos; ✆ (65) 2217450; e info@hoteloelckers.cl; www.hoteloelckers.cl. Sgl, dbl & trpl rooms available; cabins are more expensive & sleep 2–6 people. A modern & comfortable option; rooms all have private bathrooms, cable TV, Wi-Fi, & central heating. Full homemade b/fast included; has a restaurant for guests only. Off-road parking available, but no laundry service offered. Takes credit cards. $$

🏠 **Residencia Yoanna** (8 rooms) Hualaihué, 1km south of El Varal junction; ✆ (9) 76553182. One of the few options to stay along the coastal road, kitsch to the extreme & laden with religious icons, but a cheap option close to the birdwatching region of Hualaihué. Shared bathrooms, b/fast included. No Wi-Fi & laundry service offered. $–$$

Å **Ecocamping Patagonia El Cobre** (20 sites, some covered) Playa El Cobre; ✆ (9) 82275152, (9) 78090799; e patagoniaelcobre@gmail.com; www.patagoniaelcobre.cl. Turn left off ferry & head 500m towards the end of the beach. This large waterfront café has accommodation for up to 7 people. Camping surrounded by trees, private sites, some with fire pits available as well as a covered communal fire pit. Shared bathrooms with hot showers ($4,000pp, $8,000pp inside the café). At high tide, austral dolphins are visible from the café. Organic vegetables available for purchase, or pick mussels at low tide (free). Everything gets recycled here. Kayaks & mountain bikes available to rent. Various high-quality walkways through the bush along nature trails, with trees labelled. Very helpful owner, Robert Catalan, speaks English & Spanish, & can advise on all trekking enquiries in the region (page 91). Check out his impressive waterwheel used prior to the arrival of electricity in Hornopirén. $

OTHER PRACTICALITIES The **tourist information centre** is on the southern corner of the plaza, which can provide maps of the town and some trekking routes, but has uncertain opening hours. The best-stocked **supermarket** in town was on the western corner of the plaza (Oelckers). However, it suffered a fire in January 2015 and it is uncertain when it will reopen (keep an eye on www.bradtupdates.com/schile for the latest information). There is a petrol station at the northern entrance to the town, but no ATM.

Mechanic As well as the mechanic listed below, there is another option on O'Higgins behind the Hotel Hornopirén. Services include soldering, bodywork, etc, but available for diesel engines only. No motorbike servicing.

Servicio y Mantención Automotriz Antonio Celedon Opposite COPEC petrol station at northern entrance to town; ☎ (65) 2217353, (9) 94397505; e automotrizceledon@gmail.com; ⏰ 08.00–18.00 Mon–Sat. Best bet in town; can do basic repairs on motorbikes & bicycles. Credit cards accepted.

PARQUE NACIONAL HORNOPIRÉN

(*www.conaf.cl/parques/parque-nacional-hornopiren; CONAF park office is on western side of Hornopirén plaza; park entrance & maps free*) Containing 482km² of rugged Andean mountains and virgin Valdivian temperate rainforests, Parque Nacional Hornopirén borders the northern portion of Parque Pumalín with Volcán Yates (2,187m) and Volcán Hornopirén (1,572m) bordering the western boundaries of the park. It is the highlight of the region and includes treks to Lago Pinto Concha (3km from park entrance) and on to the town of Río Puelo, thus connecting with the treks over the Argentine border mentioned on pages 84–6. Hiking Volcán Hornopirén is possible without a guide. Opinions vary as to whether a guide is required for volcanoes Yates and Apagado, but we would recommend using one.

GETTING THERE To reach the park from Hornopirén, head for 11km northeast on Avenida Lib Bernardo O'Higgins; this road is reasonable-quality compact gravel. A fork in the road directs visitors to the park to veer left for a further 7km on poor-quality, pot-holed gravel. At the end of this section there is parking; and from here, the trek described below begins. There is no public transport to the park, but hitching is an option, or you can get a taxi from Hornopirén.

TREKKING ROUTES Fit trekkers should try the **two- or three-day trek** (depending on whether you climb the summit), which features three main highlights: the millennial alerce forest (larch); the picturesque Lago Pinto Concha; and the crater of Volcán Yates, from where panoramic views of the park, Lago Pinto Concha, and Fiordo Hornopirén are visible.

In addition to the trek below, there are routes north to Lago Puelo, but these are poorly signed and a guide is highly recommended. In February each year, a guided tour takes both visitors and locals north of Lago Pinto Concha and down the Río Puelo to arrive at the village of the same name. For more information, see www.hornopiren.net. Note that campfires in the park are illegal.

Day one (*10km one-way; 5–6hrs; medium*) From the car park, the first day passes initially through private farmland on a well-marked trail crossing multiple swing bridges across crystal-clear rivers. An old lumber trail continues up a steep incline before levelling out at a plateau and then continuing a further 4.5km up a gradual slope to the park boundary. This is the official park entrance, and where the alerce trees start. The track then continues to climb 3km gradually under the cover of mature bush (including some alerce trees) to the shore of Lago Pinto Concha. There is a CONAF ranger shelter on the southwest side of the lake with information for tourists in the summer months and a basic camping area on the western side of the lake, with neither cooking facilities nor drinking water available, although you can drink water from the lake.

Day two (*7km round trip; 4–5hrs; medium*) The second day reaches the crater of Volcán Yates and is suitable for any experienced trekker with a high level of fitness. From the campsite, the well-marked trail continues uphill through the larch and lenga forest to the base of the volcano, before weaving its way up the southern edge of the crater passing over volcanic rock and scoria. Spectacular panoramic views from the top make it all worthwhile. It is possible to see into the crater of Yates as well as across the entire park with views of Lago Pinto Concha and Fiordo Hornopirén. It is possible to return to Hornopirén on the third day.

⊕ AS THE CONDOR FLIES

Hornopirén is 65km from Puerto Montt and 780km from the end point of the Carretera Austral at the border crossing to El Chaltén.

TOWARDS CHAITÉN

The ferry ride through Fiordo Comau that separates the majority of the Carretera Austral from the main road network of Chile is a dramatic introduction to what lies in store further south. It arrives at Caleta Gonzalo on the edge of Parque Pumalín (pages 103–8), one of the most important private conservation projects on earth. From here, the Carretera continues south to Chaitén, El Amarillo and Villa Santa Lucía.

FIORDO COMAU Entirely within the boundaries of Parque Pumalín (northern section), this fjord runs directly south of Hornopirén to Leptepú on the Huequi Peninsula. Ferries to Caleta Gonzalo traverse the length of it, at which point a 10km gravel road connects to the other side of the peninsula at Fiordo Largo, where a second ferry traverses the short stretch to Caleta Gonzalo, entry point to Parque Pumalín and on to Chaitén. Along the length of Fiordo Comau are two smaller fjords to the east. The first, **Quintupeu** (meaning 'Place of Five Waterfalls'), is of historic interest. Following the 1915 Battle of the Falkland Islands, the only surviving German vessel, the *Dresden*, is rumoured to have hidden in this fjord, reportedly leaving immense treasures hidden. Quintupeu offers impressive views of the surrounding volcanoes, and vertical cliffs of 600m altitude. Alerce trees of 3,600 years old remain in this fjord, as well as numerous waterfalls.

Approximately 10km further south is a second fjord, **Cahuelmó**, with hot springs. Neither fjord can be accessed by land, nor do the scheduled ferries visit either; private boat is the only means of access. On the western side of the fjord, on the Huequi Peninsula around 10km south of Cahuelmó and 10km north of Leptepú are the **Porcelana Hot Springs and Geysers**, also accessible only by boat.

The only means to reach these destinations, other than for visitors with a private boat, is through a tour operator in Hornopirén (page 91).

CHAITÉN

The town itself is of mild interest beyond witnessing the aftermath of a major volcanic eruption. All basic services are available, but most visitors spend their time in Parque Pumalín or depart Chaitén after a meal, refuelling and perhaps doing some laundry. For those heading north without a ferry ticket, the first port of call might be the Naviera Austral office to secure a place on the boat. Those without vehicles can simply buy a northbound bus ticket which includes the ferry crossing, removing one potentially serious headache. Chaitén is also a useful base from which to access Parque Pumalín – both the northern section (between Chaitén and Caleta Gonzalo) and the southern section (accessed from El Amarillo). In addition to the ferries, passenger boats visiting the sea lions and whales depart from Chaitén.

HISTORY The earliest record of permanent habitation in Chaitén suggests there were three houses in 1933. However, the town began to grow as boats wishing to

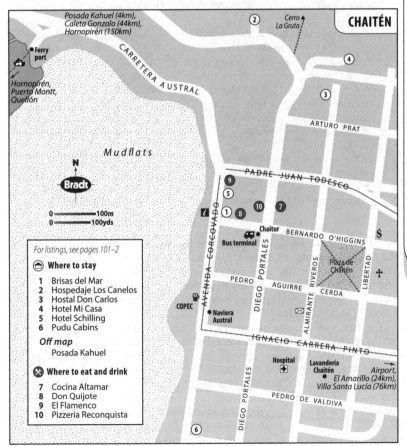

CHAITÉN

Posada Kahuel (4km),
Caleta Gonzalo (44km),
Hornopirén (150km)

Cerro La Gruta

Ferry port

Hornopirén, Puerto Montt, Quellón

CARRETERA AUSTRAL

ARTURO PRAT

Mudflats

N

Bradt

0 ——— 100m
0 ——— 100yds

PADRE JUAN TODESCO

Chaitur
Bus terminal

BERNARDO O'HIGGINS

AVENIDA CORCOVADO

DIEGO PORTALES

PEDRO AGUIRRE CERDA

ALMIRANTE RIVEROS

Plaza de Chaitén

LIBERTAD

COPEC

Naviera Austral

IGNACIO CARRERA PINTO

For listings, see pages 101–2

Where to stay
1 Brisas del Mar
2 Hospedaje Los Canelos
3 Hostal Don Carlos
4 Hotel Mi Casa
5 Hotel Schilling
6 Pudu Cabins

Off map
Posada Kahuel

Where to eat and drink
7 Cocina Altamar
8 Don Quijote
9 El Flamenco
10 Pizzeria Reconquista

Hospital

Lavandería Chaitén

DIEGO PORTALES

Airport,
El Amarillo (24km),
Villa Santa Lucía (76km)

PEDRO DE VALDIVIA

A BRIDGE TOO FAR?

The 'gap' in the Carretera Austral between Hornopirén and Caleta Gonzalo is far more political than it initially appears. Two rival proposals are on the table. Firstly, the **current plan** of the Ministry of Public Works is to extend the Carretera Austral entirely by land from Hornopirén along the east of the Fiordo Comau to Caleta Gonzalo, through territory which is mostly within Parque Pumalín. So far only two sections of this route have been completed: 35km south of Hornopirén to Pichanco, and a 10km stretch across the Huequi Peninsula between Fiordo Largo and Leptepú. Four major problems jeopardise this proposal. First, there are two large fjords along the route (Quintupeu and Cahuelmó). Going around the fjords, or building bridges across them, is expensive. Some estimates suggest it could be up to 50 times more expensive than the proposed alternative. Second, this will involve further environmental damage to the region, including within Parque Pumalín – a Nature Conservancy. Pumalín cannot deny the Chilean government access to its land to build a public highway, but this is somewhat contradictory to the entire purpose of creating such a conservancy. Thirdly, this so-called 'interior route' would be more expensive to maintain and involve greater fuel consumption for those that use it. And, finally, this route would take 20 years to build!

The **proposed alternative** is to operate an efficient ferry from Hualaihué (just west of Hornopirén) to Poyo, on the north of the Huequi Peninsula. There is already a road from Poyo south to Ayacara and on to Buill, from where a second ferry would head initially to Caleta Gonzalo. The road from Chumildén, just west of Caleta Gonzalo, to Chaitén is not yet finished. Once this is completed, the ferry would go from Buill directly to Chumildén, passing the villages of Refugio, Chana and Santa Bárbara. This could be launched almost immediately, and would actually benefit the villages along the route.

One argument against the proposal requiring ferry connections is that southern Chile has a mixed record when it comes to running a reliable service. The ferries between Hornopirén and Caleta Gonzalo aren't exactly known for their efficiency (see box, pages 46–7), but those from the mainland

access Lago Yelcho needed to traverse the Río Yelcho which connects the lake to the Golfo Corcovado at Chaitén. However, Chaitén's history is dominated by the volcanic eruption of May 2008, evidence of which is still visible. As a result of the eruption, Chaitén temporarily lost its status as capital of the province of Palena, when most governmental activities moved to Futaleufú. Some of these activities are reverting back to Chaitén.

The first visible signs of the eruption are the various channels of debris left from the volcanic ash and trees destroyed by the volcano, passing under bridges on the Carretera Austral between Caleta Gonzalo and Chaitén. Within the town most of the debris has been removed, and gradually the downtown section of Chaitén is returning to normality. However, as a result of the accumulation of debris along the shore, Chaitén's coastline actually shifted about 1km out to sea, and in its place is a barren wasteland where the remnants of vehicles and houses can still be seen. The coastal road now seems somewhat out of place, offering views out to what appears to be a to Chiloé function well. Other critics of the ferry proposal suggest that this would imply ongoing subsidies, at a cost to the state. But constructing a road would be vastly more expensive so this also involves a massive implicit subsidy. Or would this be a toll-road, in which case many of the inhabitants probably could not afford the fee to traverse it? Either route will involve a subsidy, one way or the other.

One of the myths surrounding Parque Pumalín is Doug Tompkins's apparent refusal to allow a road through 'his' park in a deliberate attempt to thwart development in the region and to divide Chile geographically. This is simply untrue. The Chilean government can requisition terrain from any private individual, and the possibility of a road through Pumalín was incorporated into a memorandum of understanding (MoU) between Pumalín and the Chilean government a decade ago. It is even considered on the COPEC Road Atlas! Furthermore, Doug Tompkins does not *own* Parque Pumalín; it is a foundation managed by a board of seven directors (five Chileans, plus Doug and his wife Kris). It is true that Pumalín are generally in favour of the ferry alternative, but not because they refuse to allow a road through the park – a road would attract additional visitors. Rather, they believe it is an unnecessarily expensive and environmentally damaging proposal with a viable alternative solution.

But here lies the political motivation. The terrestrial route would traverse precisely the same route that the proposed electricity pylons from the currently halted HidroAysén dam project would utilise (see box, pages 172–4). Building a road along this route would facilitate the subsequent construction of electricity transmission enormously, and this serves the economic interests of the mining sector.

A well-run ferry service across this section would be cheaper, more environmentally friendly, of greater service to the local communities, quicker to implement, and easier to maintain. Alas political and economic interests are likely to obfuscate the issue, and in the meantime connectivity will remain a problem for all those living in this region or wishing to visit it.

gigantic rubbish dump. It is possible to hike to the caldera of the volcano in Parque Pumalín (page 108).

One of the less fortunate impacts of the volcanic eruption was that the Río Blanco changed course as a result of this excess of water and debris, and the new path runs straight through the middle of Chaitén. The town was evacuated, and many suggested it would not be reconstructed given the significant danger to residents. Chaitén's fate seemed sealed when Chile's interior minister, Edmundo Pérez Yoma, announced in January the following year, 'We are not going to invest public funds in a city that ought not to be located here'. However, residents did return, and slowly but surely the town is emerging from the ashes. The town currently has approximately 3,500 residents.

However, the reconstruction of Chaitén is far from complete and most visitors find it a slightly depressing and drab town with little to offer. Surrounded by the marvels of Parque Pumalín to the north and south, and onwards to Futaleufú and La Junta, there is little reason to stay in Chaitén for more than a day or two other than to use it as a base to explore the surroundings.

GETTING THERE
About the route

Caleta Gonzalo to Chaitén (*44km; 1hr; gravel, last 5km paved*) Comprising reasonable-quality gravel passable in any vehicle, but beware of pot-holes, particularly at the ends of bridges. Undulating hills will exercise the legs of cyclists. The road passes a number of bridges where the debris from the volcanic eruption of 2008 is clearly visible. The two main lakes to the west of the road are Río Negro and Río Blanco, both with hiking trails and camping options. The last 5km to Chaitén is paved. The road passes a barrier, usually open, and widens to 50m. Keep to the far eastern side of this stretch – the reason why the road widens is that this is Chaitén's landing strip. Cars, motorbikes and cyclists are not allowed onto the main landing area. However, use of this airstrip is being phased out as a new paved airport has been recently constructed in Santa Bárbara, just off the Carretera Austral. Most of this section passes through Parque Pumalín, with various trails of varying lengths (pages 107–8) and also offers spectacular views of Volcán Chaitén.

By bus Kemelbus have a daily service to Puerto Montt (page 67). A number of companies offer daily buses to Futaleufú and Palena, and Buses Becker offer a twice-weekly bus south to Coyhaique (via La Junta, Puyuhuapi and Puerto Aysén, but can stop elsewhere if required). There's also a thrice-weekly service to Caleta Gonzalo.

Bus routes and times are notoriously flexible. Many depend on connecting ferries or synchronise with other buses. However, bus connections from Chaitén are generally quite reliable, and all buses depart from the central bus station run by the main tour operator, Chaitur (page 101). The advantage of going via Chaitur is that there is no need to deal with the individual bus companies. If only such a service existed in all towns along the Carretera Austral!

By ferry Naviera Austral offer services from Puerto Montt to Chaitén twice a week (*9hrs*), plus a weekly service between Chaitén and Quellón (Chiloé) (*5hrs*). The route between Chaitén and Castro features on the Naviera Austral website and maps, but does not currently operate. There are two daily ferries between Caleta Gonzalo (58km north of Chaitén) and Hornopirén (*7hrs*). See page 45 for times and prices.

By air Chaitén is one of the few places along the Carretera Austral with scheduled flights. Most other regions are by charter flights only, and substantially more expensive. Flights to Puerto Montt, the only scheduled destination, cost approximately $40,000–$50,000 one-way and take 45 minutes. The Santa Bárbara airstrip is 10km north of Chaitén, where light aircraft fly to and from the La Paloma airstrip in Puerto Montt, not the main commercial airport. Purchase tickets at Chaitur (page 101) or directly from the airlines.

For those with a vehicle, including bicycle, flying is not an option. However, foot passengers may find this convenient – it saves substantial time for a reasonable cost, but does mean missing out Hornopirén and surrounds. It also removes the necessity to take the ferry from Caleta Gonzalo – although this is a beautiful ferry ride through the Fiordo Comau, it is often hard to secure a seat. The flight is equally spectacular on a clear day.

✈ **Aerocord** ☏(65) 2262300, (9) 76694515; e aperez@aerocord.cl; www.aerocord.cl. Puerto Montt to Chaitén: 09.30 Mon–Sat, returning at 10.30.

✈ **Cielo Mar Austral** ☏(65) 2264010, (9) 94437740; e cielomaraustral@surnet.cl; www.cielomaraustral.cl. Puerto Montt to Chaitén: 09.30 Mon–Fri, returning at 10.30.

✈ **Pewen Air Services** ✆(65) 2224000, (9) 97341413; e ventas@pewenchile.com; www. pewenchile.com. Puerto Montt to Chaitén: 09.00 & 10.00 Mon–Sat, returning at 10.00 & 11.00.

TOUR OPERATORS

Chaitur O'Higgins 67; ✆(65) 2731429, (9) 74685608; e nchaitur@hotmail.com; www. chaitur.com; Ⓢ nicolaslapenna. This is currently the only show in town. In addition to selling bus tickets & running the bus terminal, Chaitur can arrange flights & excursions in the region. Tours include trips to the Palena & Pumalín parks, the Volcán Chaitén, the Yelcho & Michinmahuida glaciers, hot springs, mountain biking, rafting & boat trips to the sea lion colonies, etc. English-speaking.

Kahuel Tours 4km before Chaitén approaching from north; ✆(9) 81566148; e horacio@kahuel.cl; www.posadakahuel.cl. Operated out of the hostel of the same name (see below), Kahuel offers guided kayak tours & treks in the region, & boat trips. They have a 7m open boat for up to 7 passengers to visit the sea lion colonies, watch dolphins, & potentially see whales.

WHERE TO STAY   *Map, page 97*

🏠 **Brisas del Mar** (9 cabins) Av Corcovado 278; ✆(65) 2731284, (9) 95158808; e cababrisas@ hotmail.com. Clean, slightly dated cabins on the coastal road. Central heating, Wi-Fi, cable TV, off-road parking, laundry, fairly complete kitchen (no microwave) with seating area, plenty of natural light thanks to large windows. Sgl beds double as sofas. Larger cabins for up to 7 people are better value. No deposit necessary, but call a day or 2 before arriving to confirm. A short walk to the plaza, by the sea, close to the Naviera Austral office. **$$$$**

🏠 **Hotel Schilling** (10 rooms) Av Corcovado 230; ✆(65) 2731295; e hotelschilling@hotmail. com. Located at the northern entrance to Chaitén, this is the only formal hotel in town, with a corresponding price tag. B/fast included; parking, cable TV & Wi-Fi, all rooms with private bathroom. No credit cards & do not offer laundry service. Dbl/ twin, trpl or quadruple. Comfortable, but poor value for money. **$$$$**

🏠 **Hospedaje Los Canelos** (4 rooms, 3 cabins, 1 apt) Av Norte, 200m past junction; ✆(65) 2731417, (9) 81882423; e migonzat54@ gmail.com. Decent accommodation slightly out of town, lovely rooms, some with ocean views. All with private bathrooms, hot water, heating (wood-stove & gas), Wi-Fi & cable TV. Laundry not possible, but available in town. A 10min walk to the central plaza, so perhaps easier for those with private vehicle. Ample off-road parking. Extensive b/fast included for those staying in the rooms in the main house. Guests cannot use the kitchen. **$$$**

🏠 **Hostal Don Carlos** (22 rooms) Almirante Riveros 53; ✆(65) 2731287; e doncarlos.palena@ gmail.com. A decent choice for downtown Chaitén at reasonable prices. Kitsch is about the only negative comment possible. All the standard features: Wi-Fi, hot water, large off-road parking, cable TV, basic b/fast included. Most room types are possible, sgl, dbl, twin, with & without private bathroom. Walls are thin so quality of sleep depends on the noise from neighbouring rooms. Ideally avoid the stuffy interior rooms without windows. Rooms are clean, wooden fixtures, decent bathrooms, & a comfortable sitting area downstairs. There is neither restaurant nor laundry, but both are within walking distance of the hostel. Endless china trinkets adorn the common area; be careful with kids, it is extremely easy to smash a porcelain duck in this place. For bikers or cyclists not requiring a cabin this is a good option. **$$$**

🏠 **Hotel Mi Casa** (17 rooms) Av Norte 206; ✆(9) 76084895, (9) 78988045; e malynam@ hotmail.com. Founded in 1980, this was once a fine hotel, but has suffered from years of neglect in part due to the volcanic eruption in 2008. Located slightly out of town up a hill, it is one of the few options with a fine view over Chaitén & out to sea. All rooms include a simple bathroom & basic b/fast. A sauna, hot tub & gym are available for an additional fee. Wi-Fi available, no laundry services but available in town. The owner, Maria Angelica, can put visitors in contact with known tour operators if required. The restaurant closed after the eruption & has not reopened. **$$$**

🏠 **Posada Kahuel** (6 rooms, 1 cabin) km4 north of Chaitén towards Santa Bárbara; ✆(9) 81566148; e horacio@kahuel.cl; www. posadakahuel.cl. Perhaps not ideal for those without a vehicle, but a great option for those wishing to stay slightly outside Chaitén. Comfortable, recently built rooms for up to 4 people, all with central heating, cable TV, lovely wooden floors & views out to the forest, tastefully decorated, & walking distance to the coast within the same property. The cabin sleeps 8. Basic b/fast included, also has a restaurant (mainly but not exclusively for guests) offering pizzas & a range of local foods rotating every 3 days. Wi-Fi available, & unusually for Chaitén, laundry service also offered. The icing on the cake, however, is the on-site micro-brewery, producing a modest supply of blond & red ales, EsPumalín and Trapananda. Also offer tours (page 101). Takes credit cards. **$$$**

🏠 **Pudu Cabins** (8 cabins) Av Corcovado 668; 📞(9) 82279602, (65) 2731336; e puduchaiten@ hotmail.com. Established in 1997, this is a decent budget option & a favourite amongst motorcyclists. The smallest cabin sleeps 3, & is fairly basic, paper-thin walls & dated. The larger cabins, for 4 to 7 people, are notably superior & positively comfortable. Wi-Fi, wood-stove heating, hot water & laundry service offered. For larger groups a quincho is available. B/fast is not included; it can be arranged for a $3,000pp surplus, but is nothing special. Decent off-road parking. The owners, Anita & Juan, were some of the first people to return to Chaitén after the eruption, & can provide extensive information on the region. Book ahead as fills in the summer season, deposit not required but call to confirm, popular with motorbikers. **$$$**

🍴 WHERE TO EAT AND DRINK *Map, page 97*

🍴 **Don Quijote** O'Higgins, opposite bus terminal. Very laid back restaurant that becomes an informal bar in the evenings. The owner, Javier, was one of the first back to Chaitén after the eruption, & his knowledge of the region is phenomenal. The menu is limited but very good quality. The congrio with homemade chips is worth trying. Also a hostel, but not recommended. **$$$**

🍴 **Cocina Altamar** Portales 258; 📞(9) 81708983; ⊕ 08.00–23.00 daily in high season, 08.30–17.00 Mon–Sat rest of year. The best-value meals in Chaitén, if not along the entire Carretera Austral. The portions are gigantic, & reasonably priced. The speciality of the house, the Chilote curanto, could feed a small family. The first bowl contains fresh mussels & clams in abundance. Then arrives the 2nd plate, cooked in the same pot, with a sausage, chunk of pork, a decent chicken portion, a homegrown potato & some less identifiable potato-/wheat-based

items. The paella is equally filling, more like a seafood soup, & delicious. Standard dishes such as merluza are also available, & in very generous portions. The restaurant was originally started as a co-operative following the eruption in 2008 & has become a favourite amongst locals. Wine & beer available also. The most expensive dish on the menu is $6,000. **$$**

🍴 **El Flamenco** Av Corcovado 218; 📞(65) 2731301; ⊕ 10.00–midnight daily. Massive sandwiches, reasonably priced, local beers available. Slightly drab atmosphere, blaring TV but good place to catch a football game or the news. On the coast at entrance to Chaitén from the north; take credit cards & have Wi-Fi. **$$**

🍴 **Pizzeria Reconquista** Portales 269; ⊕ 10.00–23.00 Mon–Sat. Decent pizzas to eat in or take-away for about $7,000. Also offer b/fasts, cheap beer, sandwiches & lemon pie. **$$**

OTHER PRACTICALITIES There is a **tourist information centre** by the COPEC petrol station on the main road into town from the north, but the office is minuscule; Chaitur is probably more helpful (page 101).

Mechanic

Baaltech Automotriz Camino aeródromo at southern exit of Chaitén; 📞(9) 98323886; e baaltech@gmail.com; ⊕ 09.00–13.00 & 15.00–19.00 Mon–Fri. The best, if not only, mechanic in Chaitén. They can certainly look at most problems

for most vehicles & motorbikes, including basic electric work. The main problem is obtaining spare parts, but given the proximity to Puerto Montt this can potentially be resolved. Other options exist for tyres only.

Laundry

Lavandería Chaitén Pasaje Los Carreras 540; ✆(65) 2731185; ⊕ 09.00–21.00 Mon–Sat. Hard to find, although there is a small signpost. Enter from either Ignacio Carrera Pinto or Pedro de Valdivia streets; the laundry is located in the middle of the block east of the main street Almirante Riveros, but ask if you can't find it – everyone knows where the only laundry in town is. They have dryers, so if you leave clothes in the morning they will be washed & dried by the evening. Min price $5,000.

WHAT TO SEE AND DO This section of the Carretera Austral is dominated by Parque Pumalín. Chaitén itself is not a cultural centre, and often used as a mere laundry stop on the way north or south, or as a base for exploring Pumalín. However, there are **sea lion colonies** accessible by boat from Chaitén and **hot springs** in the area. As a government-designated Nature Conservancy, **fishing** is not permitted in Pumalín, but is permitted south of the park, particularly around Lago Yelcho. Just south of Puerto Cárdenas is a short trek to **Ventisquero Yelcho**, taking about 3 to 4 hours to reach the ice wall, a little less if only trekking the marked trail. No need for a guide, but one can be arranged at Yelcho en la Patagonia (page 109) if desired. In addition to hiking and fishing the main additional activity is exploring the **marine life** in the region, including the potential prize of spotting blue whales. Kahuel and Chaitur can arrange such trips (page 101).

PARQUE PUMALÍN

(*Park office Klenner 299, Puerto Varas;* ✆ *(65) 2250079;* **e** *info@parquepumalin.cl; www.parquepumalin.cl;* ⊕ *all year*) If ever there was a reason to visit the northern section of the Carretera Austral, it is Parque Pumalín. US conservationist Doug Tompkins acquired the Reñihué farm in 1991 and over the following years the US foundation The Conservation Land Trust added substantial land to create the park. In 2005 the park was declared a nature sanctuary, which affords it the highest level of environmental protection in Chile. As a result, it is entirely prohibited to fish, even with a permit. The park is managed by the Chilean Fundación Pumalín, and covers an area of approximately 300,000ha.

Many visitors to the Carretera miss this section in favour of entering or leaving via Futaleufú. This may save the minor inconvenience of having to take two or three ferries to eventually connect with Puerto Montt, but visiting the northern section of the Carretera is worth the effort. If using the Futaleufú border, do consider the 76km (mostly paved) detour to Chaitén and on to Parque Pumalín.

There are two main sections to the park. **Pumalín Norte** is actually the more difficult to access, as visitors need to hire a boat from Hornopirén. Information on this section of the park is available at the Puerto Varas information centre. **Pumalín Sur** is more accessible. This part of the park is broadly divided into **two sub-regions**: the various trails and campsites located between Caleta Gonzalo and Chaitén; and those accessed from the extreme south of the park at El Amarillo.

The first park ranger station is located just north of the (old) landing strip approximately 10km north of Chaitén. South of Chaitén the Carretera is paved, and touches the park once more, at the southern extremity of Pumalín. This southern entrance is called '**El Amarillo**', and located in the village of the same name. The village of El Amarillo has undergone a major urban beautification scheme, sponsored by Conservacíon Patagónica (CP).

Where the Carretera Austral buckles south towards Lago Yelcho at the exit of El Amarillo, continue straight ahead into the park. The second park ranger and tourist information kiosk is on the right-hand side, and able to provide maps and

Perhaps no contemporary couple have so divided opinions in Chile as Douglas and Kristine Tompkins. Pioneering conservationists, or evil destroyers of Chilean culture. Supporters claim they have demonstrated a practical means to save the delicate ecosystem of the planet from imminent collapse. Detractors suggest they are part of a plot to seize control of Chile's water supply, breed pumas to kill the sheep of local farmers, and intend to obstruct the development of southern Chile by preventing passage through their land stretching from the ocean to the Argentine border. Some have even claimed they were attempting to establish a Jewish state, despite both Doug and Kris being born and raised Anglicans!

Such criticisms do not stand up to even the mildest scrutiny. Most of the land acquired has been donated to the state, and they allow free access to most of it which they still own privately. The only breeding programme they operate is to raise Great Pyrenees dogs to protect the sheep of local farmers from predators. The difficulty (and corresponding expense) of constructing a road through Pumalín is largely due to two fjords, and the only requirement is that such a road have minimal impact upon the environment – hardly an unreasonable request in a state-designated Nature Conservancy.

Doug Tompkins is an avid skier, climber, kayaker, pilot and explorer. He set up The North Face in 1964 initially as a retail store selling camping and climbing equipment, and sold it in 1969 for a modest profit. He made most of his money with the Esprit clothing company. By the late '70s Esprit had annual sales surpassing US$100m. Disillusioned with the environmental impact of the fashion industry he sold his shares in 1990 and become a professional conservationist. He invented the first tents that did not require a central pole.

He established the Foundation for Deep Ecology in 1990 (*www.deepecology. org*), which goes far beyond standard 'green' issues. Through advocacy, grants, publications and education the foundation seeks to fundamentally alter the mindset of 21st-century mankind. Nature is not a resource to be harnessed by man, but rather man is an integral and interconnected part of a complex ecology. Alas, man is destroying the entire ecosphere. Rather than recycling plastic bags and cycling to work once a week, the foundation believes a fundamental re-alignment of core values is required to prevent ecological disaster. Nature possesses inherent rights comparable to those of mankind. This more profound belief of the planet as a harmonious system stems from the work of Norwegian philosopher Arne Naess, and suggests that economic growth is not a panacea for global problems, but a cause of these same problems. The dash to globalise, mass urbanisation and overpopulation are problems that need to be addressed directly. Blind faith that technology will eventually resolve all problems is naïve.

Putting such beliefs into action, Doug began acquiring land in what is now Parque Pumalín (*www.parquepumalin.cl*) in 1991, with the purchase of Reñihué farm. In 1992 he founded the Conservation Land Trust (*CLT; www.theconservationlandtrust.org*), the main way by which land for parks is acquired. CLT purchased land around Reñihué farm, often from absentee landowners. Under the Lagos Government the park was converted to a Nature Conservancy in August 2005 and was donated to Fundación Pumalín the same year, managed by a board of five Chileans, along with Doug and Kris.

The land between Hornopirén and Chaitén is almost entirely owned by Fundación Pumalín. One exception is the 340km² owned by the San Ignacio del Huinay Foundation towards the southern end of the Fiordo Comau. In 1994

CLT and US philanthropist Peter Buckley acquired 840km² of forest destined for logging, adjacent to land owned by various governmental agencies including the Chilean Armed Forces. On the basis that the combined territory be converted to a national park, CLT offered the property to the Chilean state. In 2005 President Lagos accepted the offer, forming the 2,940km² Parque Nacional Corcovado.

Lands established by Doug Tompkins are not entirely devoted to pure 'hands-off' conservation. Sustainable organic farms raise sheep and cattle, and produce honey, cheese, berries and vegetables. He was also an active supporter of Patagonia Chilena Sin Represas (see box, pages 172–4).

Kris Tompkins has kept a lower profile than her husband, but has had an equally profound impact in southern Patagonia. She was former CEO of the Patagonia clothes brand, married Doug in 1993, and set up Conservación Patagónica (*CP; www.conservacionpatagonica.org*) 'to create national parks in Patagonia that save and restore wildlands and wildlife, inspire care for the natural world, and generate healthy economic opportunities for local communities'. Her first project was to create Parque Nacional Monte Leon in southern Patagonia, the first coastal national park in Argentina. She then embarked on a more ambitious project between Cochrane and Lago General Carrera, to restore the over-grazed Estancia Valle Chacabuco to its former glory and merge it with two existing national reserves to form Parque Patagonia. The combined park will be approximately 650,000 acres and one of the most important in the Americas. It will be donated to the Chilean national park system, and form a transnational park with the adjacent 130,000-acre Parque Nacional Patagonia in Argentina.

To the greatest extent possible Kris seeks to revert land to its original state, with minimal intervention once the damage has been corrected. Grasses grow wild, pumas eat guanacos, animals roam freely, and nature gradually restores the equilibrium inherent in this complex ecological system. She believes that this needs to be seen to be believed: entry to the park is free and campsites are reasonably priced. CP arranges school trips for local children to learn about conservation and has awarded 50 scholarships for children to continue their education beyond the secondary school offered in Cochrane.

Philanthropic conservation is a relatively new phenomenon in Chile, and was initially greeted with suspicion, particularly when large areas were purchased by non-Chileans. Removing livestock, the main source of income, sparked animosity. However, as local communities see the transformation of these regions, and as tourism plays a growing role in the local economy, fears of covert plots of foreigners trying to control the water supply of Chile are fading.

The trajectory of Estancia Chacabuco, as well as many other large-scale sheep farms in Patagonia, was very clear – bankruptcy. Having resurrected this land, a world-class park complete with trails and facilities will soon be donated to the state for the benefit of future generations. The fragile ecosystem will be restored after a century of exploitation. And this has been accomplished by two successful 'ecobarons' determined to correct the unbalanced development of the 20th century, and in the process create state-owned parks.

A tangential goal of the Tompkins is to demonstrate a model for sustainable conservation. In 2005 President Piñera founded Parque Tantauco in southern Chiloé along similar lines to Pumalín, as well as many other Chileans who have founded their own private conservation parks over the last 20 years. Perhaps 'ecopioneer' is a better description?

local information (☏ *(65) 2203107*). The road continues straight to the El Amarillo hot springs, or left into the park and to the trails and four campsites (Puente Carlos Cuevas, Vuelta del Río, Grande and Ventisquero El Amarillo). The Ventisquero campground, at the foot of Volcán Michinmahuida, is considered one of the most dramatic and spectacular settings for a campground in Chilean Patagonia.

Hot springs are dotted along the length of the Carretera Austral, with perhaps the most famous being the Puyuhuapi Lodge and Spa (page 138). If not staying at the Termas Río Amarillo Lodge (page 107) the **El Amarillo hot springs** (⊕ *ask in El Amarillo for opening times; $4,000pp/day*), about 5km northeast of the park's southern entrance, are worth visiting. There are various pools filled with thermal water originating from Volcán Michinmahuida, said to possess healing properties, and undoubtedly containing sulphur. The springs are located amongst lush vegetation, well beyond the reach of cellphone coverage, and with ample picnic areas.

The village of **El Amarillo** underwent a 'beautification' project supported by Pumalín shortly after the eruption in 2008. Almost all the local residents participated in upgrading both the public use areas, and private residences in the village, and constructing new facilities such as a supermarket. Pumalín's landscape architects and builders painted houses, planted trees and flowers, and transformed the village in a very visible manner.

🏠 **WHERE TO STAY AND EAT** From Caleta Gonzalo to Chaitén there are currently six **campsites**, which are free. From north to south, they are as follows: Caleta Gonzalo, convenient for connecting with the ferry to/from Hornopirén; Laguna Tronador and Cascadas Escondidas, 12km and 14km south of Caleta Gonzalo; Lago Negro and Lago Blanco are 20km and 25km south of Caleta Gonzalo; and El Volcán, close to the trail to Volcán Chaitén and the closest campground to Chaitén (approximately 30km from both Chaitén and Caleta Gonzalo). The Vodudahue campsite near Leptepú is located north of Caleta Gonzalo in the Valle Vodudahue.

All campsites have dedicated sites for campers as well as communal sites. Bathrooms (with cold showers) are available as are basic washing facilities for clothes. Rules are simple: no camp fires, camp only in designated areas (and leave no trace), you must use only authorised bathroom facilities, and must not destroy the habitat. Parks may post additional rules specific to the region.

In the El Amarillo region of the park there are three main campgrounds: the Carlos Cuevas campground, with views of Mount Tabique, a camping shelter and bathrooms; the Vuelta del Río campground with similar facilities, around half a kilometre further; and the Ventisquero campground, around an hour further, with stunning views of the valley and glaciers of Volcán Michinmahuida– considered by some to be one of the most breathtaking campsites along the entire Carretera Austral.

In addition to the campsites within the park, between Caleta Gonzalo and the Chaitén airstrip there is only one place to stay, in Caleta Gonzalo itself, which is also the only place to eat in this region.

🏠 **Caleta Gonzalo Cabins** (9 cabins) ☏ (65) 2250079, (9) 74967173; e reservas@ parquepumalin.cl; www.parquepumalin.cl; ⊕ all year. 7 excellent cabins accommodating between 2 & 5 people (without kitchen but b/fast included); 2 smaller cabins for 2–4 people have a kitchen. All with well-equipped bathrooms. Electricity is generated from a mini turbine located a few hundred metres along the nearby Cascadas trail, & provides heating for the cabins. The beds are comfortable, the views are breathtaking, & the cabins are entirely made of wood, with open timber ceilings & extensive windows. This is a remote region, & Wi-Fi, cellphone coverage

& laundry facilities are not available. The neighbouring **restaurant** (⏰ *09.00–14.00 & 16.00–20.00 Mon–Sat;* **$$$$**) is the only option between Caleta Gonzalo & Chaitén airport. Food is mostly locally produced, & decent organic wine is available. A fine & full b/fast is included with most accommodation. The cabins currently do not accept credit cards, although this is planned for 2015/16 season. However, most bookings are made through the Puerto Varas office where credit cards can be used (📞*(65) 2250079*). The cabins fill up promptly, & it is highly advisable to book in advance, particularly in high season. This is a convenient location to make ferry connections, situated under 100m from the pier. The cabins & restaurant are owned & operated by Parque Pumalín, & can provide information on local trails & campsites. Although accommodation may be more expensive than Chaitén, these are top-quality cabins in an utterly unique setting, surrounded by park on 3 sides, a fjord on the 4th, stars above on a clear night, & guaranteeing a good night's sleep. **$$$$**

🏠 **Grizzly Cabins** (3 cabins) El Amarillo, 700m west of the park entrance; 📞(65) 2241908; e elguetangel@gmail.com; ⏰ Nov–Mar. Named after a large dog of the same name, these are a good option for those wishing to sleep close to the southern entrance of the park in El Amarillo without camping. Well equipped with 2 twin rooms in each, tastefully decorated, high ceilings, wood-stove heating, a decent deck for watching the sunset, proper wine glasses & a reasonable kitchen. Bathrooms are complete, Wi-Fi available, off-road parking. Angelica, the friendly owner, is originally from Chiloé, & can provide information about the region & park. US$110 per night regardless of occupancy. **$$$$**

🏠 **Termas Río Amarillo Lodge** (2 rooms) 30km south of Chaitén, 4.6km from El Amarillo; 📞(9) 93120447; e contact@termasrioamarillolodge.cl; www. termasrioamarillolodge.cl; ⏰ all year. One of the finest B&Bs along the entire Carretera Austral. Not cheap, in the middle of nowhere, but worth every peso. Accessed through the main El Amarillo hot springs. 1 smaller dbl room has a glass roof to observe the stars. The huge, beautifully decorated deluxe room has 2 large dbl beds & a sgl, all of which are extremely comfortable, plus a roaring wood stove for heating, & a private bathroom. It overlooks a bend in the Río Amarillo & the only sound in the evening is the lapping of water. An excellent b/fast is included, & visitors can use the kitchen, which is a serious consideration given the lack of nearby restaurants or shops – buy food for dinner in the shop in the village of El Amarillo or in Chaitén before arriving at the lodge. The lodge is owned by a charming couple, Catalina & Gregorio, who also brew their own beer, Zakingen, using water from the hot spring. The lodge is powered by a homemade hydro-electric generator & solar panels. The truly unique perk of this lodge is the private stone-lined thermal hot spring within the building, with a view towards the forest & stars which saves the $4,000 entrance fee to visit the public hot springs next door! Reservations are required, particularly in Jan & Feb, with a 100% deposit. It is possible to pay with PayPal (facilitating the use of credit cards). There is no laundry service or internet access, & the owners only check email in town every 3 days, so do not expect a prompt reply. They also offer fishing & trekking tours in the region. **$$$$**

WALKING TRAILS There are seven trails in the park between Caleta Gonzalo and Chaitén. Seek more up-to-date information, as new trails may open and existing trails may close, or be undergoing temporary maintenance. Although maps are available from the tourist information kiosk, the trails are very well marked and it is easy to do them independently. The main ones along this section (from north to south) include:

Caleta Gonzalo–Cascadas trail 6km round-trip; 2–3hrs; easy. A loop following a river to the waterfalls. Well-maintained path with frequent boardwalks spanning wet sections.

Tronador trail 5km; 4hrs round-trip; difficult. An initial ascent along a gorge, views over snow-

capped Volcán Michinmahuida, arriving at the amphitheatre Lago Tronador where the campsite is located.

Alerce trail Under 1hr loop; easy. A short trail through a section of forest housing a number of impressive alerce trees approaching 3,000 years of age. The alerce has been cut to near-extinction over the previous 2 centuries for their valuable wood. The path is well maintained & contains occasional explanatory boards.

Cascadas Escondidas trail 4km round-trip; 2hrs; medium. A fantastic trip alongside a river, to a series of increasingly impressive waterfalls. Wooden boardwalks are well maintained, but take care when climbing the wooden ladders which may be slippery. A small detour on the way down goes via approximately half-a-dozen alerce trees of impressive size.

Volcán Michinmahuida trail 24km round-trip; 10hrs; difficult. Probably the most physically demanding of all the trails in this section of the park.

Volcán Chaitén trail 4km round-trip; 3hrs; medium. This trail heads to the edge of the Chaitén crater, where steam emerges from the ground on the far side. One of the most accessible volcano hikes on the entire Carretera Austral, and well worth the effort. Having lain dormant for nearly 10,000 years, in May 2008 this volcano erupted, causing massive devastation to the nearby town carrying the same name.

Darwin's Frog trail 2.5km round-trip; easy. An informative loop explaining how forests grow following logging or fire. Pick up the interpretive guide in the tourist information centre at the entrance to the park. Darwin's frog is endangered & rather small, but can be seen along this trail although perhaps only by those with a trained eye.

Ventisquero El Amarillo trail 20km round-trip; 6hrs; easy. An excellent trail to the base of a glacier protruding from the south side of Volcán Michinmahuida.

EL AMARILLO TO VILLA SANTA LUCÍA

The road south of El Amarillo passes two points of interest before reaching Villa Santa Lucía: the impressive **Yelcho en la Patagonia** on the beautiful Lago Yelcho, which is excellent for fishing, and the **Ventisquero Yelcho Chico**, the most northerly accessible glacier along the Carretera. However, compared with the other glaciers, hikes and lakes in the region, this stretch could be passed through without stopping.

Villa Santa Lucía itself, located as it is 76km south of Chaitén and 68km north of La Junta, exists as a crossroad, and for little other reason. The scenic 30km road up to Puerto Ramírez and on to Futaleufú (an additional 48km) and Palena (an additional 43km) begins here, as well as the first two vehicular border crossings to Argentina. The village was named after Pinochet's wife during the construction of the Carretera Austral. There is no petrol, and little reason to stay in the village other than to pop into a shop to grab some supplies. As a key junction along the Carretera Austral, Villa Santa Lucía's principal function is as a bus stop (located at the junction of the Carretera Austral and the eastward road towards Futaleufú and Palena) where hitchhikers also await a ride. No public transport exclusively serves this stretch, but southbound buses from Chaitén and northbound buses from La Junta will stop at Puerto Cárdenas and Villa Santa Lucía if required.

GETTING THERE
About the route
Chaitén to Villa Santa Lucía (*76km; 1hr; partly paved, partly poor gravel*) A decent 24km paved road from El Amarillo to Chaitén. The further 19km on to Puerto Cárdenas at the northern end of Lago Yelcho is fairly nondescript until the lake, passing through agricultural regions with mountains to the east. The gravel section begins at Puerto Cárdenas and is being prepared for paving, so is likely to improve, but in the meantime is terrible: loose gravel; exposed rocks; when raining the water runs along the length of the road for extended sections; corrugations and pot-holes. It is 33km to Villa Santa Lucía, the first 10km of which skirt the lake and pass Yelcho en la Patagonia after 8km, and a further 6km to the glacier.

WHERE TO STAY AND EAT

Illampu hospedaje and cabins
(6 cabins, 2 dbls) Villa Santa Lucía; ✆(65) 2731502, (9) 81441927; e illampu@hotmail.cl. Despite relatively few reasons to stay in the village, Illampu is a welcome haven for those left stranded here overnight without a tent. Lovely building, & the owner worked in the military service constructing the Carretera Austral so has some amazing stories. Located at the northwestern corner of the plaza. **$$**

Yelcho en la Patagonia (8 rooms, 6 cabins, camping) Northern end of Lago Yelcho, 27km south of El Amarillo & 25km north of Villa Santa Lucía; ✆(65) 2576005/8; e reservas@yelcho.cl; www.yelcho.cl. This is a top-quality, full-service hotel with a price to match. The rooms boast all the usual features of such an establishment, with central heating, full b/fast included, safety deposit box, laundry service, full private bathroom, etc. Every room & cabin has a lake view. Fishing is firmly the focus, & the hotel arranges half- & full-day fishing trips, although is not allowed to enter the Parque Pumalín for such activities. The lake is unusual for containing all species of trout & landlocked salmon. Fishing lessons for beginners are also available, as are trips to the local glacier & guided horse rides within the grounds. The restaurant sources most ingredients locally, many vegetables are grown on site, & the ice cream, bread, desserts & pastas are all homemade. Local beers also available. Spectacular views over the lake from the upper floor sitting area, with a small library & a shop laden with fishing accessories. An excellent option for those keen on fishing, possibly not the best value for those without such a passion. *Camping* **$$**, *main lodge* **$$$$$**, *restaurant* **$$$$**

SIGHTSEEING AND EXCURSIONS A short **hike** to **Ventisquero Yelcho Chico**, just south of Puerto Cárdenas, is a pleasant detour (*8km round-trip; 3hrs; easy*) and an introduction to the abundant glaciers further south. Guides are available at Yelcho en la Patagonia, but aren't essential. The route starts at the Puente Ventisquero (bridge) 6km south of Yelcho Lodge, and parking is available. There are also **fishing** opportunities on and around Lago Yelcho. South of the glacier there is relatively little of interest until the junction of Villa Santa Lucía (17km), where the road to Futaleufú and Palena begins. To the west of the road lies the **Parque Nacional Corcovado** (*www.conaf.cl/parques/parque-nacional-corcovado*), also originally acquired by Doug Tompkins/Conservation Land Trust, but unlike Parque Pumalín to the north and Parque Valle Chacabuco (soon to be renamed as Parque Patagonia; see pages 229–35) much further south, Corcovado is largely inaccessible. The Ventisquero Yelcho Chico offers about the only glimpse of the park possible. The park contains two volcanoes, Corcovado (2,300m) and Nevado (or Yanteles, 2,042m) and extends south to the border between Los Lagos and Aysén regions. Access is perhaps easiest from Raúl Marín Balmaceda (page 129), where fishermen will take die-hard tourists to Bahía Tic Toc, but even here there is no public infrastructure for entering the park on land.

⊕ AS THE CONDOR FLIES

Villa Santa Lucía is 220km from Puerto Montt and 620km from the final end point of the Carretera Austral at the border crossing to El Chaltén. A southbound condor would be almost exactly one-third of the way.

Puerto Montt to Villa Santa Lucía   EL AMARILLO TO VILLA SANTA LUCÍA

4

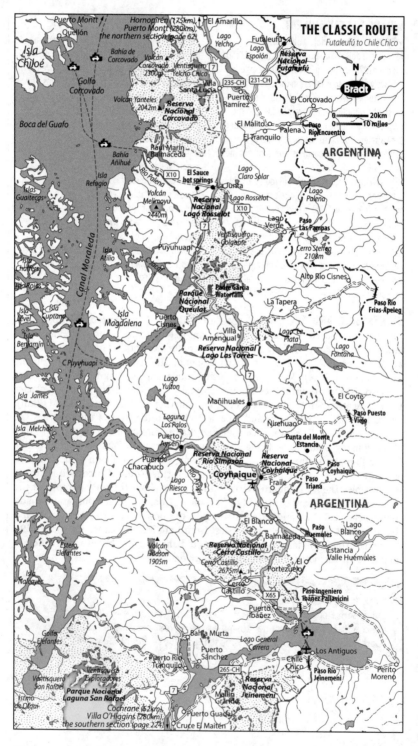

THE CLASSIC ROUTE

Futaleufú to Chile Chico

N

Bradt

0 — 20km
0 — 10 miles

Isla Chiloé

Puerto Montt

Quellón

Hornopirén (75km)
Puerto Montt (280km),
the northern section (page 62)

El Amarillo

Lago Yelcho

Futaleufú

Lago Espolón

Reserva Nacional Futaleufú

El Corcovado

Bahía de Corcovado

Volcán Corcovado 2300m

Ventisquero Yelcho Chico

235-CH

231-CH

Golfo Corcovado

Volcán Yanteles 2042m

Santa Lucía

Villa

Puerto Ramírez

Paso Río Encuentro

Reserva Nacional Corcovado

El Malito

Palena

Boca del Guafo

El Tranquilo

ARGENTINA

Raúl Marín Balmaceda

Bahía Anihué

Río Palena

X10

El Sauce hot springs

La Junta

Lago Claro Solar

Lago Palena

Isla Refugio

Islas Guaitecas

Volcán Melimoyu 2440m

Reserva Nacional Lago Rosselot

Lago Rosselot

X10

Lago Verde

Paso Las Pampas

7

Cerro Steffen 2108m

Isla Atilio

Puyuhuapi

Ventisquero Colgante

Isla Chaffers

Jurac

Alto Río Cisnes

Isla Rojas

Isla Level

Isla Cuptana

Isla Magdalena

Parque Nacional Queulat

Padre García Waterfalls

La Tapera

Paso Río Frías-Apeleg

Isla Benjamín

Canal Moraleda

Puerto Cisnes

Villa Amengual

Lago La Plata

C Puyuhuapi

Reserva Nacional Lago Las Torres

Lago Fontana

Isla James

7

Lago Yulton

Isla Melchor

Laguna Los Palos

Mañihuales

El Coyte

Ñirehuao

Paso Puesto Viejo

Puerto Aysén

Punta del Monte Estancia

Puerto Chacabuco

Reserva Nacional Río Simpson

Reserva Nacional Coyhaique

Paso Coyhaique

Lago Riesco

Río Aysén

Coyhaique

Fraile

Paso Triana

ARGENTINA

El Blanco

7

Estero Elefantes

Volcán Hudson 1905m

Reserva Nacional Cerro Castillo

Balmaceda

Paso Huemules

Lago Blanco

Isla Nalcayec

Cerro Castillo 2675m

El Portezuelo

Estancia Valle Huémules

Cerro Castillo

7

X65

Paso Ingeniero Ibáñez Pallavicini

Puerto Ibáñez

Golfo Elefantes

Bahía Murta

Puerto Sánchez

Lago General Carrera

Los Antiguos

Ventisquero Exploradores

Ventisquero San Rafael

Puerto Río Tranquilo

Chile Chico

Perito Moreno

Istmo de Ofqui

Parque Nacional Laguna San Rafael

265-CH

Reserva Nacional Jeinemeni

Paso Río Jeinemeni

7

Mallín Grande

Cochrane (52km),
Villa O'Higgins (280km),
the southern section (page 224)

Puerto Guadal

Cruce El Maitén

Part Three

THE CLASSIC ROUTE

5

Futaleufú to La Junta

Located some 80km east of the Carretera Austral by the Argentine border, **Futaleufú** is a key access point to the road, and the start of the 'classic' route. Many visitors to the region enter or leave via Futaleufú to/from Argentina, skipping the northern section of the Carretera altogether. This beautiful, mountainous region is home to some of the best rafting and kayaking on the planet, with huge forests, lakes and rivers. **Palena**, a 91km drive south, is also a pleasant town with a lesser used border crossing to Argentina.

While this region is of particular interest to those keen on white-water rafting, there are a number of good treks of varying lengths, including a section of Chile's longest – the **Sendero de Chile**. On top of this, there are lush national parks, excellent horseriding opportunities, exciting mountain-biking routes, fly-fishing possibilities, and fine accommodation and food.

The road west of Futaleufú and Palena is spectacular, weaving along thundering rivers, past isolated lakes, beneath steep cliffs, traversing the southern edge of Lago Yelcho (the first of the 'great lakes' of the region), before finally arriving at Villa Santa Lucía on the Carretera Austral. Heading south, you come to nondescript **La Junta**, the crossroads to two of the most spectacular detours from the Carretera Austral. To the east, **Lago Verde** is the central point for the horseriding route between Palena and La Tapera, and a fantastic (albeit somewhat rough) drive through one of the more isolated sections of the region. To the west lies **Raúl Marín Balmaceda**, one of the most recommended detours in the guide, with abundant marine wildlife, spectacular views of Volcán Melimoyu, and access to the Parque Nacional Corcovado and hot springs.

Many choose this entry/exit point for its proximity to Bariloche (Argentina), but it can be easily reached by car or direct bus from Puerto Montt, trekking across the border from Cochamó, or driving from Cochamó via Lago Llanquihue. So, for those with limited interest in rafting or horseriding, traversing the northern section of the Carretera Austral is recommended.

IF YOU'RE COMING FROM VILLA SANTA LUCÍA...

For those not joining the Carretera at Futaleufú, but instead making this town a detour from Villa Santa Lucía, leave Villa Santa Lucía on the Ruta 235 heading 30km east towards Puerto Ramírez where the road splits and becomes the 231 (towards Futaleufú) and the 235 (towards Palena). Further details of this route are given on, page 114.

FUTALEUFÚ

Upon arrival it becomes pretty apparent what the main draw to 'Futa' is. There are as many kayaks as cars in the town, and every other business is somehow related to kayaking or rafting. The town is surrounded by mountains and retains a frontier feel to it, reminiscent of towns in Alaska. The inhabitants are generally pretty laidback and, when not in the water, the central plaza is a good place to relax and have a fruit juice. Fly-fishing and trekking are also possible, but the Río Futaleufú is considered one of the top rivers worldwide for rafting, and most visitors come here to dip their toes in the water.

HISTORY Futaleufú was not connected to the Carretera Austral until 1980. Until then, the primary contact with the outside world was with Argentina, and to this day the town has a strong Argentine ambience. It temporarily became the provincial capital following the Chaitén volcanic eruption, but administration is slowly moving back to Chaitén.

As with many towns in this region of Chile, the history of Futaleufú is poorly documented and interspersed with legend. The first settler was Don Ceferino Moraga, originally from Chiloé. He and his family arrived in 1912 via Argentina. What is now called Futaleufú, meaning 'Great River' or 'Great Waters' in the native language, was an inhospitable dense forest at this time. Slowly the family cleared enough land to raise cattle, sheep and oxen. Moraga jealously guarded his territory, and resisted the arrival of other settlers who wished to exploit the fertile land. According to legend, all the men in the Moraga family were thus slain between 1919 and 1920 by Chilean pioneers who wished to populate the region and, given the lack of any authorities in the region, the crime went

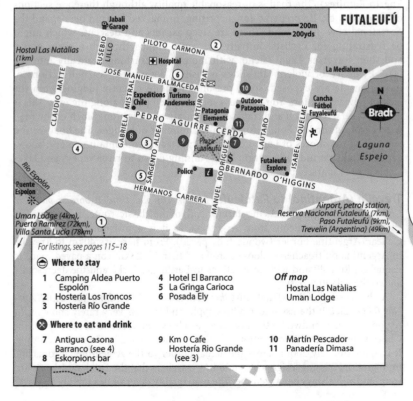

FUTALEUFÚ

For listings, see pages 115–18

Where to stay

1 Camping Aldea Puerto Espolón
2 Hostería Los Troncos
3 Hostería Río Grande
4 Hotel El Barranco
5 La Gringa Carioca
6 Posada Ely

Off map
Hostal Las Natàlias
Uman Lodge

Where to eat and drink

7 Antigua Casona Barranco (see 4)
8 Eskorpions bar
9 Km 0 Cafe Hostería Rio Grande (see 3)
10 Martín Pescador
11 Panadería Dimasa

5

unpunished. However, this cavalier approach to law and order came to a halt in 1929 when Police Chief José Felmer Patof and a group of surveyors arrived and subsequently founded the village on 1 April that year. A single house from this period remains on Lago Espolón, and to this day serves as a warehouse. Settlers continued to arrive to the region, and slowly inhabited the regions of El Espolón, Las Escalas, Río Azul and Loncanao. Since the arrival of this single pioneering family the population of Futaleufú has swelled to an impressive 2,300 according to the 2012 census.

✪ AS THE CONDOR FLIES

Futaleufú is 210km from Puerto Montt and 645km from the border south of Villa O'Higgins to El Chaltén. Palena is 600km from this border, and 255km from Puerto Montt. From either town it is approximately a 950km drive to Villa O'Higgins including one ferry crossing.

GETTING THERE
About the route
Villa Santa Lucía to Futaleufú (*78km; 2hrs; reasonable quality, sections of exposed rock*) For those making a detour from Villa Santa Lucía on the Carretera Austral, the road ascends 30km to Puerto Ramírez. Futaleufú is a further 48km (*1hr*) from Puerto Ramírez along Ruta 231 (northeasterly from the junction at Puerto Ramírez). The road is of reasonable quality, although there are sections of exposed rock. Be prepared for surprising, unmarked hairpin bends, and the occasional cow in the road. There are steep ascents and descents which might be frustrating for cyclists. Initially the route climbs through a steep gorge, and then traverses Lago Yelcho, with mountains crashing vertically into the lake. Evidence of violent landslides is visible: deforested, scarred sections of mountainside are exposed, some presumably quite recently judging from the lack of new vegetation. You will pass snow-capped peaks along the way. This is a well-traversed section and traffic is comparatively common. Much of the road winds around the Río Futaleufú, crossing a number of bridges. The final section runs along the shores of Lago Lonconao: spectacular mountain scenery; snow-capped peaks periodically; virgin bush running down to river valleys and lakes – this area is sparsely populated.

Trevelin (Argentina) to Futaleufú (*49km; 1hr plus time at border; paved in Chile, gravel in Argentina*) As the start (or end) of the 'classic' route, many travellers enter (or leave) Futaleufú from Argentina, as it is approximately 9km to the Chilean/Argentine border (wonderfully paved). From here, it's 40km to Trevelin in Argentina on treacherous loose gravel and then it's 23km (on a paved road) to Esquel on Ruta 40 and with connections to Bariloche, Tecka and the deep south, and to the Atlantic coast.

At the crossing of Paso Futaleufú (*9km from town;* ⊕ *Dec–Mar 08.00–21.00, Apr–Nov 08.00–20.00*) the usual formalities apply, and there is very rarely snow in the region so even in midwinter this border is passable without chains or snowtyres. The Chilean customs and immigration are efficient and housed in a modern building. It is approximately 200m across the actual border to the Argentine customs and immigration, passing a signpost reminding travellers that the Falkland Islands are, were, and will always be, Argentine. The road quality deteriorates rapidly to gravel.

By bus There are regular buses to **Puerto Montt** (offered by Feryval, Transportes Pavez and Transaustral) going via Osorno, but passengers should note that they cannot get on or off in Argentina. Buses Cárdenas and Buses Cumbres Nevadas offer frequent services to **Chaitén**, and Buses Becker have a twice-weekly service to **Coyhaique** in high season. Frontera del Sur has a few buses a week to **Palena**. If you want to get to **Argentina**, Transportes Futaleufú offer a daily minivan to the border, which synchronises with an Argentine bus that continues to Esquel.

Times and prices vary widely – best to confirm upon arrival, and in peak season book a seat in advance. The Feryval office is on the corner of Gabriela Mistral and Pedro Cerda. The **post office** (*cnr of Jose Manuel Balmaceda & Arturo Prat, 1 block north of central plaza*) also sells bus tickets and ferry tickets for Naviera Austral (and secondhand clothes). If direct buses to more distant locations are not available, or the routes are not served in low season, it is always possible to get to Chaitén (north) or La Junta (south) where onward connections are possible.

TOUR OPERATORS

Bio-Bio Expeditions m (2) 1964258, (USA) +1 800 2467238; www.bbxrafting.com/futaleufu-rafting-multi-sport. US-based adventure tour operator, geared mainly towards package trips for dedicated kayakers. Not geared towards walk-ins.

Expeditions Chile Gabriela Mistral 296; (65) 2562639, (USA) +1 208 6295032; www.exchile. com. Founded by Chris Spelius, US Olympic kayaker, who sometimes guides the trips. Started entirely with kayak & rafting tours, now also offers mountain biking, trekking, horseriding & canyoning.

Futaleufú Explore O'Higgins & Riquelme, on exit road to Argentina; (9) 74334455; e info@ futaleufuexplore.com; www.futaleufuexplore. com. Another decent operator with Chilean & international guides. Focus is on the rivers, but also offer trekking, fishing & horseriding trips. Have own lodging on the Río Futaleufú.

H2O Patagonia (USA) +1 828 3334615; www. h2opatagonia.com. More focused on all-inclusive 1-week adventure package tours rather than walk-ins. Have own accommodation, transport, boats, etc, & while focus remains on white water, also offer other activities. Prices start at US$3,600pp.

Outdoor Patagonia Manuel Rodriguez 127; (9) 85702407; e raftingoutdoor@gmail.com. Well-respected operator in town with local guides, offers half-, full- & 2-day rafting/kayaking tours with access to their own lodge along the river for the longer tours. Ranges from class III to V, suitable for all abilities. Also offer kayaking courses & fly-fishing trips.

Patagonia Elements North side of plaza; (9) 74990296, (9) 92619441; e info@ patagoniaelements.com; www.patagoniaelements. com. A well-respected operator with Chilean staff, many of whom live in the region & have many years of experience with the company. Offers fly-fishing, horseriding, trekking, guided mountain-bike trips & bicycle hire.

Turismo Andesweiss Balmaceda 358; (9) 83825133; e asilva@andesweiss.cl; www. andesweiss.cl. Outdoor operator offering a wide range of treks in the region including in Reserva Nacional Futaleufú, fly-fishing trips, canopy descents, horseriding, rappelling & mountain biking. For those less interested in rafting or kayaking, this is a good alternative.

WHERE TO STAY *Map, page 113*

Hotel El Barranco (10 rooms) Av Bernado O'Higgins 172; (65) 2721314, (9) 76977574; e hotel@elbarrancochile.cl; www.elbarrancochile.cl; Aug–Apr. A gem of a hotel with a hidden swimming pool for sunny afternoons. The hotel itself is entirely made of wood, all rooms with private bathrooms & fantastic, large beds. Wi-Fi available, including on the deckchairs by the pool. There is no television in the hotel – this is a place to unwind. Security box, central heating & fridge in all rooms. Complete buffet b/fast included, consisting of yoghurt, cereals, cheeses, meats, jams, juice, etc; also has a restaurant (pages 117–18). For cold evenings a Finnish sauna & massages are available after a hard day kayaking. The finishing touch: a car-wash prior to departure. A few blocks' walk from the centre, views fluctuate between mountains & forest. Parking for 5 cars, & additional space for motorbikes. Free use of bicycles. Wheelchair accessible. English & Spanish spoken. The owner is very knowledgeable about all local activities, & is able to arrange guided fly-fishing trips, rafting, kayaking, trekking, canyoning, mountain biking & horseriding in the region. An upper-end option, but well worth splashing out. This is where the *Top Gear* team stayed when visiting Futaleufú (page 58). Kids under 12 are free. **$$$$$**

🏠 **Uman Lodge** (16 suites) Fundo la Confluencia; ◌ (65) 2721700 e info@umanlodge.cl; www.umanlodge.cl. The premium accommodation in the region. Set in an impressive 500ha estate, the lodge has incredible views over the town & towards the mountains, as well as over the confluence of the Futaleufú & Espolón rivers. Huge dbl beds look out over the valley, some with views of the river, each with a balcony, a small sitting area with comfortable furniture, large TVs for those who tire of the view. Facilities include Wi-Fi, laundry, sauna, jacuzzi, indoor & outdoor heated pools, a massive deck with panoramic views over the valley, massages & treatments, a gym, a top-quality restaurant (also available to non-guests with a reservation; **$$$$**), & glorious rooms. Beautiful, spacious & modern building, albeit something of an eyesore from the valley; also home to a working farm. Despite the size of the building it possesses a sense of intimacy due to the limited number of rooms & large open spaces. Quite possibly the finest hotel in the entire region, but certainly winner of the most *expensive* hotel in the region, with prices starting at approximately US$420/night. However, the restaurant is no more expensive than many in downtown Futaleufú, boasts the inspiring view enjoyed in the rest of the building, & the wonders of a renowned chef Lucas Trigos Foussadier, so if the budget doesn't stretch to a night in this lodge, lunch or dinner is not a bad option. **$$$$$**

🏠 **Hostería Río Grande** (13 rooms & 1 apt) Bernado O'Higgins 397; ☎ (65) 2721320, (9) 97560818; e renzo@pachile.com; www.pachile.com. Reasonable, mid-range accommodation. All rooms come with private bathrooms & off-street parking is available. Complete b/fast included; decent restaurant (page 118). The staff speak French, Italian, Spanish & English. US$80 for a sgl, US$110 for a dbl, US$130 for a trpl, US$150 for the 6-person apt. Centrally located 1 block from the plaza. Wi-Fi. Decent but overpriced. Credit cards accepted. **$$$$**

🏠 **La Gringa Carioca** (4 rooms) Sargento Aldea 498; ☎ (65) 2721260, (9) 96599341; e lagringacarioca@gmail.com; www.hostallagringacarioca.cl. Charming upmarket boutique hostel on the outskirts of town with a view over the Río Espolón. The cottage is wonderfully decorated to a quality rarely found in the region, & each room is distinct, with private bathroom. B/fast is a positive feast, & all services are included (laundry, Wi-Fi, credit card payment, etc). English, Spanish & Portuguese spoken by the outgoing owner, Adriana, who is from Brazil & bought the hostel in 2005. In fact, it was one of the first in Futaleufú, dating back to 1990. The style of the house is hard to pinpoint – Laura Ashley *à la Latina*! Adriana doesn't get directly involved in tours, but can point guests in the right direction, & can also arrange food for larger groups. Certainly at the upper end of the hostels along the entire Carretera Austral, with a price to match – dbls/trpls US$120/160. **$$$$**

🏠 **Hostal Las Natàlias** (6 rooms) 1km along northwest exit of Futaleufú; ☎ (9) 96311330, (9) 89033571; e hostallasnatalias@gmail.com; www.hostallasnatalias.cl. Wonderful, rural setting with mountain & river views, & yet walking distance to town. Ideal for trekkers wishing to visit Cero Teta, Lago Espolón, Las Rosas & Noreste lakes & the Garganta del Diablo. The owner, Nathanial, is a very experienced kayak guide & instructor. He can arrange fly-fishing trips, treks, any variety of watersports, & rents bicycles. 2 dorms with 3 bunk beds, 2 private rooms with dbl beds, all with shared bathroom. Also 1 dbl room with bunk beds for a family. English & Spanish spoken. Cash or PayPal only. B/fast is not included, but visitors have full use of a well-equipped kitchen. Off-road parking & Wi-Fi. **$$**

🏠 **Posada Ely** (6 rooms & 1 apt) Balmaceda 409; ☎ (65) 2721205; e posada.ely.futaleufu@gmail.com. Decent budget accommodation 2 blocks from the centre run by Betty, who prepares an excellent b/fast (included) which even contains fruit juice, real milk & homemade jams. All rooms with private bathroom, heating & hot water; apt has a stove & fridge. No English spoken, but familiar with hand signals for most requirements; can arrange laundry. **$$**

🏠 **Hostería Los Troncos** (4 rooms: 2 with 3 beds & 2 dbls) Piloto Carmona 541; ☎ (65) 2721269, (9) 94591281; e lostroncosfuta@gmail.com. Basic, clean budget option, shared bathroom but with plans to incorporate en-suite bathrooms. Basic continental b/fast included. Large off-road parking, Wi-Fi, & guests can use kitchen; no laundry. Only 2 blocks from the plaza. Owner is a keen fisherman & can advise or guide visits to local rivers. **$**

⚐ **Camping Aldea Puerto Espolón** Southern entrance to Futaleufú; ☎ (65) 2721509, (9) 53240305; e puertoespolon@gmail.com; http://aldeapuertoespolon.blogspot.co.uk. Pleasant campsite a short walk from the centre, dome tents for rent (*$15,000/couple*), camping $6,000pp with hot water, bathrooms, quincho, electricity, facilities for handwashing clothes & access to the Río Espolón (return catch). Arturo Vivanco, the owner, is also the creator of the Futalhué beer. **$**

✖ **WHERE TO EAT AND DRINK** *Map, page 113*

✖ **Barranco** Av Bernado O'Higgins 172; ☺ Aug–Apr. Probably the best restaurant in town, but not necessarily for budget travellers. Includes local delicacies, such as wild boar, hare & the usual salmon dishes. It's a pity not to try hare while visiting Futa as it's rarely on the menu elsewhere, & Barranco has a decent sample. Excellent service but not the cheapest place in town. $$$$

✗ **Martín Pescador** Balmaceda 603; \(65) 2721279; e restaurantemartinpescador@yahoo.cl; www.martinpescador.cl. Founded in 2003, this is a fine restaurant that doubles as a bar later in the evenings. All food is organic &, where possible, produced within 200km of the restaurant – beef, wild boar, hare – & all seafood is caught by local fishermen. Decent selection of wines (including organic), beer on tap, & local cheeses. This has the look of a formal establishment built in the style of a fishing lodge, with tablecloths, nice wine glasses & very good service – not typical along the Carretera. But it also has a laidback atmosphere, with sofas & wacky art, a bar, a fireplace, housed in a large space of wooden construction & wide windows to watch Futa life go by. You can also sit out on the deck on a warm evening. The US/Chilean owners are very knowledgeable about the region, activities, rafting options, etc. Mitch is a fishing guide & Tatiana is the chef. Not large portions, so if you're ravenous, it might not be the best value meal in town. Best to reserve a table in high season. Take credit cards. $$$$

✗ **Hostería Río Grande** Bernado O'Higgins 397. Reasonable food in the hotel of the same name, with dishes including great locally caught salmon, good pork, but mediocre wines. Also serves as one of the town's main bars. $$$

✗ **Km 0 Cafe** Arturo Prat 262-B, west side of the Plaza; \(65) 2721510; ⊕ 09.30–21.00 daily. A conveniently located café/fast-food restaurant selling hotdogs, burgers, milanesas, sandwiches, fruit juices, salads, beef steak or salmon with chips. Rustic décor with old wooden floors painted green, rough sawn timber half walls & a sack-like cloth ceiling likely covering a multitude of amateur carpentry & electrical sins. A bit dark if you choose a table away from the main window, but don't worry, the food is good. $

✗ **Panadería Dimasa** Pedro Aguirre Cerda 458, half block from the plaza; \(65) 2721337; ⊕ 07.00–22.00 daily. This bakery makes pizzas, sandwiches & hamburgers to eat-in or take-away, plus a good selection of fresh hot bread. The mouth-watering meat empanadas are not to be missed, with decent chunks of hand-cut meat & whole olives especially prepared by the owner. $

✗ **Antigua Casona** Main plaza. A reportedly decent restaurant but invariably closed. Serves the local Futahué beer.

♀ **Eskorpions bar** Gabriela Mistral 265; ⊕ until late. Nightlife in Futaleufú is mostly limited to the hotels, but this bar offers a slightly wilder alternative. Beware of women sitting at your table without any formal invitation & asking for drinks at suspiciously elevated prices and dressed in attire more suited for a beach. But often the only place in town for a beer.

OTHER PRACTICALITIES The **tourist information centre** is on the south side of the plaza (*O'Higgins 565*), but better information is available in the hostels/hotels. The rafting outfits are clustered around the central blocks of the town, and it is worth shopping around for a suitable deal, depending on the duration and difficulty level. Equipment hire is generally included in a guided package, but some will rent gear for use on the more peaceful rivers and lakes. There is no laundry in Futaleufú, but most hostels/hotels will wash clothes for a fee. The **petrol station** is located approximately 1km east of town on the main road (Ruta 231) towards the Argentine border.

Mechanic

Jabali Garage Cnr of Piloto Carmona & Eusebio Lillo; \(9) 74975920. Owned by English-speaking Leonardo, who is a very competent mechanic with a range of equipment. The only thing he does not do is tyres, but there are 3 tyre specialists in town. He works with most cars & motorbikes as well as bicycles, although the latter are not his speciality. Spare parts are the main bottleneck (some sourced in Esquel, Argentina if necessary), but he will attempt to fix most things. He also has a tow truck for emergencies in the area. As a side business Leonardo also hunts the hares that appear on the plates in some restaurants.

SIGHTSEEING, ACTIVITIES AND EXCURSIONS The main attraction in the region is world-class **rafting** and **kayaking**. Professionals from across the world visit this town specifically to raft the river, so if you have never rafted before but were always curious, this is possibly the finest place in Latin America to do so. Up to Class V rapids offer even the most experienced kayakers a serious challenge, and the **Río Futaleufú** is notably safe as the main white-water sections are invariably followed by more tranquil waters which makes rescue operations easier. Although tours can be booked in town at the agencies listed on page 115, most use one of four operators located outside the town and situated along the river. For those listings in the US, for example, this has to be arranged in advance via phone or online. The **Río Espolón** has Class III rapids suitable for less experienced rafters, and offered by most of the operators listed. Usually held in late February, the annual **FutaFest** event (*www.futafest.cl*) brings competitors from across the world for a three-day extravaganza of extreme rafting and kayaking competitions.

At the northeast corner of town lies the all-important rodeo, **La Medialuna**. Horse-related activities are taken very seriously both here and in Palena, a consequence of the gaucho legacy. Next to the rodeo is a small lake, **Espejo**, and a short trail around the north shore of the lake leads up to a viewing platform – Torre de Agua, with sweeping views over the town and valley.

A number of **horse**, **hiking** and **mountain-biking** trails surround Futaleufú for those less interested in rafting, generally following the main rivers. To the northwest of town are a number of lakes and trails, as well as fishing options. Day treks include Lago Azul, Lago los Cedros and Piedra del Águila – Las Cascadas del Lago Espolón. Multi-day treks are possible around Espolón. There are also rock-climbing routes in the region – ask at Las Natàlias (page 117).

The 12,000ha **Reserva Nacional Futaleufú** (*www.conaf.cl/parques/reserva-nacional-futaleufu*) lies to the south of the town and has a number of trails and refuges as well as abundant flora and fauna.

PALENA – A DETOUR

The rodeo is taken extremely seriously in Palena. The town, correctly named Alto Palena, maintains a strongly Argentine feel, and the gaucho culture more typically found on the east of the Andes is dominant here, at least in part due to the historic confusion over the precise border. The rodeo stadium seems disproportionately large for such a small, sleepy town, and the Rodeo de Palena, held over the last weekend of January, is a spectacle to be seen by anyone remotely interested in horses. Palena attracts fewer tourists than neighbouring Futaleufú, and its border is less frequently traversed. Agriculture and animal husbandry is the main economic activity of the region, although tourism is growing. It is the southernmost town in the X Region (Los Lagos) and has a population of 1,700.

Palena was originally inhabited by Tehuelche Indians and was named by Nicolás Mascardi, a Jesuit explorer. It was founded in 1929, the same year as Futaleufú. From a tourism perspective there is relatively little to do in Palena compared with neighbouring Futaleufú. The main attraction is the hike/horse ride south to connect with the Sendero de Chile (page 121).

There is a **petrol station** in Palena.

GETTING THERE
About the route
Puerto Ramírez to Palena (*43km; 1hr; gravel*) Palena is situated 5km (paved) west of the Paso Río Encuentro (Argentine border), and 43km southeast of Puerto Ramírez. From Puerto Ramírez it is either 30km west to the Carretera

ONE OF MANY BORDER DISPUTES

The Paso Río Encuentro at Palena has an unusual history, as possibly one of the most hotly contested borders in the area. The Chileans and Argentines have squabbled over the precise border for centuries. In 1893 both countries agreed to determine the line of the border according to an apparently simple geographic principle: Argentina would 'hold in perpetuity all territory to the east of the line of the highest peaks which divide the waters while Chile was to hold in perpetuity all territory to the west of that line'. As sensible as this might sound, the ridge connecting the highest peaks does not always coincide with the water divide line, thus opening up the potential for continued bickering. The King of the United Kingdom was to arbitrate in the case of disputes, and in 1902 formally declared the lie of the border. However, the demarcation posts were placed too far apart, in particular around Palena. Residents of both countries began entering this nebulous no-man's-land for agriculture and grazing, and eventually agreed to resubmit the case to the Queen rather than risk an all-out war over such an obscure plot of land. And so in 1966 the border was redefined, with 21 intermediate posts designed to avoid any subsequent dispute. 'The boundary shall cross the Palena to the mouth of the River Encuentro.'

Another border dispute was eventually settled in 1994, awarding the Laguna del Desierto to Argentina. Travelling from Villa O'Higgins to El Chaltén in Argentina requires a boat trip across this lake – now the newest official region of Argentine territory. To this day a border section within the southern Patagonian ice field of some 80km remains undefined. In 2006 Argentine president Néstor Kirchner invited Chile's president Michelle Bachelet to define the border, but the Chileans declined. However, perhaps the greatest source of border tension lies not on the South American continent at all, but rather in Antarctica. The claims of Argentina, Chile and the UK overlap almost entirely, and such claims are of the utmost strategic importance, as the region encompasses the entire Antarctic Peninsula, the main access point to the frozen continent.

Austral, or 48km northwest to Futaleufú. The road quality from Puerto Ramírez to Palena fluctuates violently, from pleasant gravel to rough, loose gravel, often with corrugation. At times the road is two lanes wide, at others a single track. There are also some major ascents and descents, which must make this one of the most challenging sections for cyclists, with descents as difficult as ascents given the corrugations and blind corners. The road is also home to a number of cows and dogs, so additional care is required.

By bus Cumbres Nevadas offer weekday buses to Chaitén, and there are three services a week to Futaleufú with Frontera del Sur.

WHERE TO STAY AND EAT Food options are limited in Palena, and accommodation is modest and scarce. Consider **El Huaso** (*Pedro Montt 908;* ☏ *(65) 2741244;* **$$**) or **Altas Cumbres** (*Pedro Montt 828;* ☏ *(9) 95846729;* **$$**) for *comida casera* (typical Chilean fare).

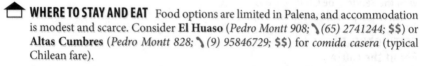

Hospedaje Horzas (6 rooms) ☏ (65) 2741380; e horzas_palena@hotmail.com; ⏱ Jan–May. New option in town for reasonable prices. Also has a restaurant. **$**

Hospedaje Palena Mio (3 rooms) 🔌 (9) 98737294; e hectorcasanova.r@hotmail.com. A reasonable budget option in a town with few alternatives. Comfortable rooms, decent b/fast, heating & hot water, off-road parking, Wi-Fi & laundry service. Shared bathroom. **$**

Los Ñires Cabins (3 cabins) Perez Rosales 368; 🔌 (65) 2741206. Can sleep 4, 6 or 7 people for approximately $10,000pp. Wi-Fi, kitchen, reasonably equipped. Laundry service available. **$**

SIGHTSEEING AND EXCURSIONS While Palena can't be described as a 'must-see' of the Carretera Austral there are endless **horse-related activities** for those with equine interests. **Kayaking** is also an option on the Río Palena although enthusiasts are better advised to get their fix in Futaleufú. Palena is the access point to the **Sendero de Chile** (see below) meaning excellent **horseriding and trekking trails** traversing mountains and lakes to Lago Verde and then on to La Tapera. Keep in mind, though, that for those travelling by private vehicle, this would involve some substantial backtracking later. Further to the east, along the Argentine border but also extending down to Lago Palena, is the **Valle California**. By walking west along the north shore of the lake this trail connects with the Sendero trail, allowing a circuitous route. From Palena it is hard to make a mistake, but consider that there are two roads south – Valle California some 4km to the east of the town towards the border, and El Tigre directly south of Palena.

Another group of hiking trails lie to the south on the road towards Puerto Ramírez, back towards the Carretera Austral, forming a separate natural loop. Some 20km west of Palena on the main (only) road is the village of El Malito. From here it is possible to walk (or drive) a further 10km to El Diablo, a pleasant meander

---

SENDERO DE CHILE   (*www.senderodechile.cl*)

This is an ambitious plan to create the longest trek in the world: 8,500km of trails connecting the entirety of Chile, from the Atacama Desert to the remote regions of Tierra del Fuego/Magallanes. Within this area, the full trail spans from Lago Palena to Lago Verde (*55km; 1 week one-way*), with trails connecting to it in La Tapera (page 153) and Palena (page 122); there's also a section of the sendero in Cerro Castillo (page 197). As it is not yet a tourist attraction in its own right, organised tours along the route are not readily available so treks must be arranged ad hoc in La Tapera, Lago Verde or Palena. Camping is possible along most of the route, and there are occasional refuges; it is wise to go on horseback and with a guide. Maps are available locally, or from e ana.caravantes@senderodechile.cl in either paper or electronic format. There are no permits or fees, but do advise the tourist information centre (on the plaza) or CONAF who is going, and to request permission to stay at the refuge at the end of day one.

The original name for this part of the Sendero de Chile is '**La Huella de los Troperos**' (literally 'footprint of the cattle ranchers'), and the journey falls into four sections. The first (*5km*) departs from Lago Palena, and is the most challenging section, ideally done with horses, or with light rucksacks. It ends at the Sánchez Pobre refuge, where there are places to camp. The second leg (*15km*) is an easy walk to the shore of Lago Quinto where it is possible to camp. The third leg (*15km*) is slightly more strenuous due to steep inclines, with mud and branches, slowing travel by horse, ending at the Río Quinto refuge. The final stretch is an easy hike (*20km*) to Lago Verde along the Río Quinto. The entire trail is clearly marked with 35 guideposts.

5

through virgin forest to the northwest. The trail then heads southwest (hiking or horse only) 14km towards El Tranquilo on the Río Palena, passing two lakes (Golondrina, with camping available, and Negra). From El Tranquilo it is 20km northeast to El Malito along the southern shore of the river (there's a bridge over the river approximately 1km before the village), or the trail continues to Palena via El Tigre and a second Laguna Negra. This latter trail does actually connect to the main trail south from El Tigre.

If you want to connect with the Sendero de Chile (see box, page 121), you can trek 'The Patagonian Andes Lake Palena Heritage Trail' (*33km; 2–3 days one-way; horse & guide advisable*) from Palena to the lake. It could be argued that this is the precursor to the Carretera Austral, as it was the route used by ranchers to bring cattle to market, and such trails stretch much of the length of the Carretera Austral, generally hugging more closely the Andes than the current Carretera. Be sure to advise CONAF or the tourist information centre of your intention to traverse this route (no fee). Head out of Palena on the road to El Tigre and El Azul. After 5km you'll come to an information sign, at which point the road forks south running parallel to the Río El Tigre. This is the formal starting point of the trail (marked by 35 guideposts), which involves various river crossings, passes snow-capped mountains, waterfalls, former homesteads revealing the agricultural past of this now remote region, and passes various forests with magnificent cypress trees and other interesting flora. It is not advised to cross the Río El Azul on foot (check with locals in advance of attempting this), and thus this section is usually done on horseback.

PUERTO RAMÍREZ

Heading back towards the Carretera Austral, this village is located 6km west of the junction to Villa Santa Lucía, and is usually skipped by most. Those *en route* from Futaleufú or Palena may find this a useful stop, and westbound cyclists who can't make it all the way to Villa Santa Lucía 30km away may sleep here. There are actually a number of mostly unmarked trails in the region, opportunities to go fishing, a waterfall, and one accommodation option.

For route details connecting Puerto Ramírez to Villa Santa Lucía, see page 114.

 WHERE TO STAY AND EAT

Cabañas Cumbres Nevadas (1 cabin)
Main intersection of Puerto Ramírez; ✆(65) 2241926; e cumbres.nevadas@hotmail.com; www.cumbresnevadas.cl. 1 decent equipped cabin for up to 5 people, Wi-Fi & quincho available, $45,000/day regardless of number of guests. Very close to Lago Yelcho (page 108), offer full-day

fly-fishing trips in region with food for $180,000/2 people. Owned by the family of 1 of the original settlers in the region & same company that runs the Cumbre Nevada bus service between Palena/ Futaleufú & Chaitén. Useful for cyclists who don't make it to Palena or Futaleufú. **$$$**

LA JUNTA AND AROUND

Having joined the Carretera Austral at Villa Santa Lucía from Futaleufú/Palena, or arriving from Chaitén/El Amarillo/Lago Yelcho in the north, the road continues 68km southwards on gravel to La Junta. Although set within an impressive valley, the transport hub of La Junta is little more than a large **petrol station** (situated at the northern end of town) and stopping-off point *en route* to other places. La Junta is at the confluence of two rivers as well as two roads and, as such, much is made of the 'joining' concept (the Spanish verb *juntar* means to meet or join together), but do not forget that *junta* is also a name for the military dictatorship, although the town was named prior to Pinochet's arrival. Throughout the 19th century La Junta was a strategic hub for those in the region wishing to bring animals for sale in Puerto Montt, using the ports of Raúl Marín Balmaceda or Puyuhuapi. As with Villa Santa Lucía to the north, La Junta has relatively little to offer visitors, most of whom will prefer to push on to Puyuhuapi (47km south) or along one of the detours (pages 127–31). It does, however, boast an impressive and rare monument to Pinochet revealing the favourable sentiment to the former dictator.

HISTORY It is not only the roads that unite in La Junta, but the Figueroa/Rosselot and Palena rivers. The town was not founded until 1963, and opened its first school in 1970, of which Father Ronchi (see box, page 125) was its first teacher. However, the logistical benefits of being situated at an important junction, the development of the Carretera Austral (connecting La Junta in 1986), and fertile agricultural and grazing land around the confluence of two rivers eventually created the main hub in the region.

The original name of La Junta was Medio Palena (Middle Palena), as it lies a little over halfway from Alto Palena (High Palena, the full name for the town now referred to simply as Palena) and Raúl Marín Balmaceda, which was originally called Bajo Palena (Low Palena). It is no coincidence that the Río Palena runs through all three towns.

⊕ **AS THE CONDOR FLIES**

La Junta is 280km south of Puerto Montt, and 555km from the border south of Villa O'Higgins to El Chaltén.

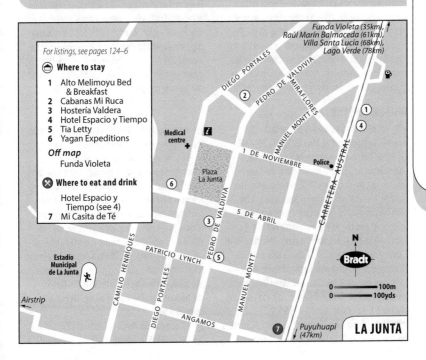

For listings, see pages 124–6

🛏 **Where to stay**
1   Alto Melimoyu Bed
    & Breakfast
2   Cabanas Mi Ruca
3   Hostería Valdera
4   Hotel Espacio y Tiempo
5   Tia Letty
6   Yagan Expeditions

Off map
    Funda Violeta

🍴 **Where to eat and drink**
    Hotel Espacio y
    Tiempo (see 4)
7   Mi Casita de Té

Funda Violeta (35km),
Raúl Marín Balmaceda (61km),
Villa Santa Lucía (68km),
Lago Verde (78km)

DIEGO PORTALES
PEDRO DE VALDIVIA
MIRAFLORES
MANUEL MONTT
1 DE NOVIEMBRE
CARRETERA AUSTRAL
Medical centre
Police
Plaza La Junta
5 DE ABRIL
PEDRO DE VALDIVIA
PATRICIO LYNCH
CAMILIO HENRIQUES
DIEGO PORTALES
MANUEL MONTT
ANGAMOS
Estadio Municipal de La Junta
Airstrip

N

Bradt

0 _____ 100m
0 _____ 100yds

Puyuhuapi (47km)

LA JUNTA

GETTING THERE
About the route
Villa Santa Lucía to La Junta (*68km; 1hr; gravel*) The road from Villa Santa Lucía to La Junta is pleasant, with fast, excellent gravel and some paved sections – this stretch will soon be completely paved. There are lovely views of snow-capped mountains on both sides of the road and occasional views of the river, but there are no lakes along this section. Halfway along this stretch, just passed La Vanguardia, is the border between Region X (Los Lagos) and Region XI (Aysén). The only decent accommodation and restaurant is also close to La Vanguardia – Funda Violeta (page 126). The entire region to the west of this stretch of road is Parque Nacional Corcovado, without access points.

By bus La Junta is a transport hub, with buses to/from **Coyhaique** and **Chaitén** passing through here (see pages 100 and 170–1 for more information), and Buses Entre Verde (◥(9) 95103196) have three services a week to **Cisnes** via Puyuhuapi. **Lago Verde** is extremely hard to reach by public transport; however, Bronco Bus (◥(9) 66105214) stop here a couple of times a week on their way from Coyhaique, and hitchhiking is viable. **Raúl Marín Balmaceda** is slightly easier to reach by public transport, and Heriberto Klein (◥ (9) 66075746) and Transportes Willy (◥(9) 66084854) offer frequent buses.

TOUR OPERATOR
Yagan Expeditions 5 de abril 350; ◥(67) 2314352, (9) 84599708; e info@yaganexpeditions.com; www.yaganexpeditions.com; ⓢ yagan.expeditions. The only operator in town, run by knowledgeable Bruno who has lived in La Junta since the late 1990s. Offer a range of tours as well as accommodation (page 126). Rafting on the Río Figueroa for the more adventurous, or kayaking on Lago Rosselot or the Río Palena for those seeking a more relaxed afternoon. Also offer horseback rides from Lago Claro Solar towards the Sendero de Chile (full day), & trips to the El Sauce hot springs, plus 5- or 6-day packages to/from Balmaceda airport with transport, hiking, mountain biking, horseriding in the region, trips to Puyuhuapi & the Ventisquero Queulat. Can also organise tailor-made expeditions across the Futaleufú–Palena–Lago Verde–Puyuhuapi region, & arrange the full 4-day kayak trip from Palena to Raúl Marín, run once a year for around 200 kayakers & rafters in Feb. They have their own transport, work with Turismo Valle del Palena & can arrange tours in Raúl Marín accordingly.

 ## WHERE TO STAY *Map, page 123*
🏠 **Alto Melimoyu Bed & Breakfast** (8 rooms) Carretera Austral, km375; ◥(67) 2314320, (9) 91586421; e info@altomelimoyu.cl; www.altomelimoyu.cl. Decent rooms along the Carretera Austral, just south of the COPEC petrol station. The building is constructed entirely from wood, & the beds are top quality. Dbl or twin rooms are a little overpriced, but the B&B does boast a hot-tub & a sauna. All rooms have cable TV, central heating, Wi-Fi. Laundry service offered, & a cabin is also available. The bonus is that they also arrange bicycle tours, treks, rent kayaks, & tours to Raúl Marín Balmaceda for those without private transport. Off-road parking available. Credit cards accepted. **$$$$**

🏠 **Hotel Espacio y Tiempo** (9 rooms) Carretera Austral 399; ◥(67) 2314141, (9) 92229220; e info@espacioytiempo.cl; www.espacioytiempo.cl. Probably the finest accommodation in town, with a very good restaurant (page 126) & gorgeous manicured garden. All rooms with central heating, cable TV, a safe, private bathrooms, wooden finish & a view over the gardens. Wi-Fi, laundry service & full b/fast. Patios for outdoor eating, & large cosy communal seating areas with a roaring log fire. While the hotel does not offer tours they have all information & contacts. This is a positively pleasant hotel with a corresponding price tag, but worth the splurge if feeling like a treat. If this breaks the budget, consider dinner alone. Takes credit cards. **$$$$**

🏠 **Cabanas Mi Ruca** (4 cabins) Libertad 220; ◥(9) 82090455; e lisveth_hellriegel@hotmail.

com. A good-value option with 4 new & tidy mid-range cabins with well-maintained grounds. Cabins are fully equipped, sleep 4 & have a dbl room & a 2nd room with bunk bed, with cable TV & Wi-Fi. Secure parking on a quiet street. There is a kitchen/dining room with a cosy wood-fired heater. Laundry provided. Credit cards accepted. $$$

⌂ **Tia Letty** (7 rooms) Antonio Varas 596; ✆ (9) 87635191; e tialety2009@hotmail.com; ⊕ all year. A charming family-run hostel. All rooms have 1 shared bathroom, & the ceiling in 2 of the upstairs rooms is a mere 1m from the floor – fine for kids, less so for adults wishing to sit up in bed. Towels provided, off-road parking, visitors cannot use the kitchen.

THE LEGEND OF FATHER RONCHI

Father Ronchi, the self-proclaimed 'rascal priest', came from a small village in Italy in 1960 to remote Chilean Patagonia with the sole goal of transforming the region. Three decades of total devotion forever changed the destiny of more than 50 towns in the regions of Aysén and Chiloé with his influence extending the entire length of the Carretera Austral. He founded three new villages, created an extensive network of radio and television stations, built dozens of chapels, schools, lodges, boats and workshops, and developed a number of projects that nowadays might well be described as 'social enterprises'. He had many loyal followers and friends within Aysén, but he also had critics. Many of his peers did not agree with his focus on the poorest and most isolated communities of the region, while others did not approve of his methods. For his life's work parliament granted him Chilean nationality. Today he is adored in all corners of southern Patagonia.

Ronchi was sent to Chile in 1960, to work in a shelter in the city of Rancagua with the Mother of the Divine Providence Mission. The following year he moved to the Shelter San Luis of Puerto Cisnes in the Region XI of Chile – his official arrival in Patagonia. In addition to his pastoral services he proactively worked closely with several local authorities and businesses to encourage them to help the local inhabitants progress in their spiritual, personal, social and economic development. In 1967 he moved back to Rancagua to become the local parish priest but lasted only five years until he was sent back to his beloved Puerto Cisnes. He worked in the Parish of Nuestra Señora del Trabajo (Our Lady of Work) and for more than 20 years he worked predominantly in the most remote towns in the region. Many such villages had neither roads nor communications and were surrounded by dense forests, mountains and fjords. Thus one of Ronchi's first accomplishments was to install FM radio antennas and television transmitters. Such was the impact of connecting such villages to the outside world that to this day the FM transmitter remains a Historic Monument and is marked on maps. Ronchi established various social projects with food supplies he managed to get from the Catholic Church in Europe. He built chapels and lodges, workshops for handicrafts, boats, small docks and infrastructure necessary to develop the local community. He did all this inspired by the belief that God wanted the people to lead dignified lives and for them to be happy.

Father Ronchi died on 17 December 1997 in Santiago, aged 67. He was buried in the cemetery of Puerto Aysén. Today he has a foundation named after him, the Fundacion Obra Padre Antonio Ronchi (Foundation for the Works of Father Antonio Ronchi) that seeks to keep his legacy alive and continue the works that he started.

For more information on Father Ronchi, see www.bradtguides.com/schile.

However, there is a superb b/fast consisting of a variety of homemade jams & bread, local cheeses & scrambled eggs. Better value in low season. **$$$**

🏠 **Yagan Expeditions** (1 cabin, 2 apts) 5 de abril 350; 📞(67) 2314352, (9) 84599708; e info@ yaganexpeditions.com; www.yaganexpeditions. com; 🅂 yagan.expeditions. Good, simple accommodation owned by the tour operator of the same name. 1 fully equipped cabin for up to 4 people, b/fast not included but has kitchen. 1 apt for a couple, 1 with a dbl bed & a sgl bed, b/fast included. All accommodation includes Wi-Fi, off-road parking, towels & laundry service. A good option, particularly if doing tours with Yagan – the only operator in La Junta (page 124). **$$–$$$**

🏠 **Funda Violeta** (8 rooms) Valle Frio, Ruta 7, km300 (23km south of Villa Santa Lucía just north of La Vanguardia); e violetavmonjes@gmail. com. On entering this rambling farmhouse, one might be excused for mistaking the restaurant/ hostel for the set of a western movie. The bull skulls with horns at the entrance indicate that this is no normal residence. The interior is tastefully decorated with a gaucho cowboy horse theme, complete with rustic rough sawn timber finish & log roof structure. The friendly & talkative hostess, Violeta, will ensure a pleasant stay, & speaks basic English. This doubles as a roadside café (**$$**) with a large deck & beautiful mountain views, offering basic meals. The simple accommodation has 4 dbls & 4 sgls all with shared bathroom. A decent b/fast is included comprising farm-cooked eggs, homemade jam & fresh baked bread, fruit juice & coffee. Along this stretch of the Carretera there are few accommodation or food options, & this is a pleasantly quirky surprise. There is access to the river below the road for good trout fishing. **$$**

🏠 **Hostería Valdera** (13 rooms, 1 cabin) Antonio Varas, 1 block south of plaza; 📞(67) 2314105; e luslagos@hotmail.es. Sprawling hostel with various rooms of various sizes, with or without private bathroom. Decent parking area, laundry, cable TV. Restaurant & bar (**$$**). **$$**

✘ WHERE TO EAT AND DRINK *Map, page 123*

✘ **Hotel Espacio y Tiempo** Carretera Austral 399; 📞(67) 2314141, (9) 92229220; e info@ espacioytiempo.cl; www.espacioytiempo.cl. A fine choice – excellent food, decent-sized dishes & good service. Range of local beers & wines, good salads & puddings, plus daily specials. Cosy atmosphere with views out to garden. Top choice in town. **$$$$**

✘ **Mi Casita de Té** Carretera Austral, cnr of Varas & Lynch; 📞(67) 2314206, (9) 78020488; e elypaz. cortes@gmail.com; ⊕ all day, serving b/fast, lunch, & dinner. Popular with locals & travellers, this cosy restaurant comes highly recommended for the reasonable prices & local food, & is more than a tea house. Personal service from the owner herself, who cooks up fresh home-cooked Chilean specialities like stew or chicken. Nice salads & good espresso as well. The best-value option in La Junta for a sit-down meal. Dish of the day usually around $7,000, or order off the limited menu starting at $5,000. **$$**

SIGHTSEEING AND EXCURSIONS La Junta is the key access point to the 12,725ha **Reserva Nacional Lago Rosselot** (*www.conaf.cl/parques/reserva-nacional-lago-rosselot*). The Río Figueroa flows into Lago Rosselot, within the park, and the Río Rosselot flows from the lake towards the Pacific, joining the Río Palena west of La Junta. Besides the beautiful lake itself, surrounded by mountains, the national reserve provides ample fishing opportunities and has trails accessed from the La Junta entry point. It is possible to see the rivers and Volcán Melimoyu in the distance.

Some 18km north of La Junta is a small turning to the east towards **Lago Claro Solar**, with wildlife, fishing and trekking options. These trails eventually connect to the trails heading north up through the **Valle El Quinto**, ultimately forming part of the Sendero de Chile trail heading up to Palena (page 122). Despite some maps suggesting otherwise, it is possible to drive around Lago Claro Solar and reach the road from Lago Verde to La Junta, some 15km east of the junction. This section is best done in a 4x4 or at least in a high-clearance vehicle – road quality is poor, there are exposed rocks and high ridges along the centre of the gravel road. It's also rarely transited.

La **Ruta de Palena** is a four-day organised descent of the Río Palena in early February, from La Junta to Raúl Marín Balmaceda by kayak or canoe. The first two days are spent on the river, camping approximately halfway to Raúl Marín. On the third day various events are arranged in Raúl Marín including treks, and then return to La Junta on the fourth day. The event changes each year; for more information contact **e** rutadelpalena@gmail.com.

The **La Junta Rodeo** takes place on the second weekend of February.

RAÚL MARÍN BALMACEDA – A DETOUR

If a visitor to the Carretera Austral has time for only one of the various detours off the main road, this is possibly the most interesting. Founded in 1889, Raúl Marín is actually the oldest inhabited place in the entire province of Aysén, in part for being an obvious access point for the early settlers from Chiloé. It is situated at the confluence of ocean, river and fjord, barely populated (under 500 inhabitants), and boasts spectacular wildlife and vistas. Accessible from La Junta (61km) via a short ferry ride, or by boat from Chiloé twice a week, and sandwiched between Volcán Melimoyu to the south and Parque Nacional Corcovado to the north, it is hard to find somewhere quite as remote as this even elsewhere along the Carretera Austral. With the possible exception of thriving nightlife, there is something in this small village for everyone, from birdwatching to sailing; sitting on sandy beaches to eating fine seafood; and from hot springs to kayak trips.

Raúl Marín is currently expanding its port. At the time of writing, the most useful ferry sails to/from Quellón on Chiloé (page 45). It is also on the slow ferry route visiting the coastal villages between Chiloé, Melinka and along the coast to Puerto Chacabuco (page 45).

GETTING THERE
About the route
La Junta to Raúl Marín Balmaceda (*70km; 2hrs inc boat crossing; gravel*)
This road was completed in 2009, some 120 years after its founding, and is truly spectacular, one of the highlights of the region. Depending on traffic, the short boat ride (⊕ *08.30–13.00 & 14.00–19.00; free*) across the Río Palena takes only 5 minutes, but the boat can take only six vehicles. This is where the jungle canopy to the north meets the forest canopy to the south. The initial section of the road is flat, easy gravel until the El Sauce hot springs (page 129). Thereafter the road becomes more treacherous and narrow, with occasional steep sections and tight curves. The river widens as the road approaches Raúl Marín, and is periodically visible in its turquoise splendour. Beware of oncoming vehicles, particularly trucks that often travel in the middle of the road at high speed. There are extended sections of loose gravel. The forest encroaches on the road at times, creating a tunnel effect. The few signposts that exist, invariably warning of dangerous curves ahead, are barely visible as the forest covers them. Huge nalca plants (the oversized rhubarb leaves) can be seen along the way. Towards Raúl Marín the road passes a swamp area. The final section after the boat crossing is increasingly sandy, so particularly difficult for cyclists and motorcyclists.

By bus See page 124 for details.

By ferry Raúl Marín Balmaceda is connected to Quellón on Chiloé by a twice-weekly service (page 45). To book tickets in Raúl Marín speak to Jonathan at

Hostería Valle del Palena (see below), or ideally book tickets as much in advance as possible at any Naviera Austral office.

TOUR OPERATORS

Kawelyek Expeditions 1 block above Av Rosselot; \(9) 75429056; e Kawelyekexpediciones@gmail. com; www.kawelyek.cl. Besides the various services offered out of the Hostería Valle del Palena (page 128), this is about the only tour operator in town. The name means 'refuge of dolphins & whales'. They offer tours to the Las Hermanas islands, where it is possible to observe all manner of seabirds, the southern & Chilean dolphin, orcas & blue whales (if you're extremely lucky), the southern right whale (known locally as *franca austral*), & sea lions. The other tours explore the Estero Pitipalena, the Fiordo Pilan & further up the Río Palena (by kayak).

Turismo Valle del Palena Las Hermanas; \(9) 66089537/8. In addition to a decent hostel, a small shop, a marmalade business & a fine restaurant (see below), Jonathan Hechenleitner is also a tour operator. Increasingly he is subcontracting this side to his business to trusted third parties rather than doing the tours himself, but he is a wealth of knowledge & contacts & can arrange or advise on almost any conceivable tour in Raúl Marín.

WHERE TO STAY

Fundo Los Leones (4 cabins) 1km before Raúl Marín Balmaceda; \(9) 78982956, (9) 65973986; e fundolosleones@gmail.com; www. fundolosleones.cl. A truly unique destination, in an old organic farm previously owned by Doug Tompkins, but the new owners still retain a strong conservation objective. It is located shortly before the entrance to Raúl Marín from La Junta (at km72), & the landing strip is at the northern end of the property. Visitors tend to arrive either by road from the main Carretera, or by chartering a flight from Puerto Montt (the owner, Mery, can arrange the flight). Prices vary depending on the number of visitors, from approximately US$150 for a sgl to US$250 for a trpl (less in low season). The cabins vary in size & décor, all with private bathroom, comfortable beds, full b/fast included, & a deck overlooking the Fiordo Pitipalena & mountains. Internet is available only in the main house, but this is a place to unwind, boxed-in by nature. The property has direct access to an extensive beach, where sea lions & dolphins can be seen as well as abundant bird species. Guests can wander freely around the working sheep farm, visit the beehives, or use the kayaks to explore the area. Mery can also arrange fishing expeditions in the area, including to some remote spots, as well as trips to the nearby attractions of Raúl Marín, such as the sea lion colonies or the hot springs, as well as to the Tic Toc marine reserve (accessible only by boat). Lunch or dinner can be arranged for approximately $20,000pp consisting of principally organic food sourced locally (vegetables, steak, fish & lamb). An excellent, if not the only, upper-end choice for hundreds of kilometres. $$$$$

Hostería Valle del Palena (6 rooms, 4 cabins) Las Hermanas; \(9) 66089537/8; e isladelpalena@gmail.com. Surprisingly good accommodation for such a remote village. All rooms with private bathroom, cosy wooden effect, decent heating & hot water, friendly owners who seem to know everything & everyone in the village. Laundry available, Wi-Fi. Besides the decent rooms, owner Jonathan Hechenleitner is something of a guru on the region. He can arrange any tour, speaks English, has a fair-sized shop across from the hotel & to top it all, runs a superb restaurant (see below). Accept credit cards. $$

Residencial y Cabañas El Viajero (7 rooms, 5 cabins) Av Costanera; \(9) 66084858, (9) 84206181; e turismoelviajero@hotmail. com. Reasonable rooms, b/fast included, shared bathroom, & cabins under construction. No Wi-Fi or laundry, but do offer boat trips in the area. $$

WHERE TO EAT AND DRINK

Isla del Palena Las Hermanas; \(9) 66089537/8. Best place in town, beneath the Hostería Valle del Palena; lively atmosphere, doubles as bar in the evening. Excellent seafood, reasonable selection of wines but no local ales. Serves an excellent puye dish. $$$

Restaurant El Faro Las Hermanas; \(9) 76002860. Simple food, no alcohol available – only had tap water when we visited. Local dishes, plenty of seafood, appears to be the main sitting room of someone's house. Pleasant enough. $$

OTHER PRACTICALITIES There is no petrol station, garage, laundry or ATM in Raúl Marín, so fill up in La Junta and take clean clothes. The **tourist information office** is on the central plaza (🕽 *(9) 79636241;* **e** *informacionturistica.raulmarin@ gmail.com).*

SIGHTSEEING AND EXCURSIONS
El Sauce hot springs (🕽 *(9) 94522711, (9) 87375645;* **e** *alejvc@hotmail.com; ⊕ from Dec–Feb/Mar 09.30–20.30; $5,000/4,000 adult/child, camping is $8,000pp with access to the hot springs inc)* Hot springs of varying qualities litter the Carretera Austral, but El Sauce, some 17km from La Junta on the road to Raúl Marín, is one of the finest and cheapest. Run by Claudio Berger, the springs are lovingly maintained in lush vegetation, and there is one large communal pool and two smaller private pools. The water emerges from the spring at 84°C and is mixed with cold water from the river to reach 40°C. Those who choose to camp here can use the pools outside normal opening hours – useful as the site is popular at weekends. Claudio can arrange private transport, or visitors can combine with the bus to/from Raúl Marín, but this requires walking 3km to/from the main road. There's no food available at the campsite so be sure to bring supplies. You can make campfires in authorised spots. Claudio also offers local fishing excursions; call ahead to ensure the water level is high enough.

Other hot springs are found at the estuary of the Río Rodriguez, upstream of the Fiordo Pitipalena, accessible only by boat from Raúl Marín.

Wildlife watching The village is technically an island, with the sea to the west (the Golfo Corcovado and Bahía Añihue), the estuary of the Río Palena to the southwest, and the Fiordo Pitipalena to the east. As a result of this confluence of water, and a lack of major human interference, marine life flourishes. Whales, otters, penguins, sea lions, pelicans and dolphins are frequently observed. The Las Hermanas islands, 30 minutes by boat from Raúl Marín, have permanent sea lion and penguin colonies – every hotel and restaurant in the village can arrange a boat trip here. Trips further out to sea to spot whales, or to visit Tic Toc (access to Parque Nacional Corcovado) have to be arranged especially and prices depend mostly on distance and the interest of the fisherman himself in visiting that area. The Golfo Corcovado is one of the best places in the entire southern hemisphere to observe blue whales, but the national park is not readily accessible (page 109).

Trekking For a leisurely stroll, the **Sendero Chucao** trail head is at the northern end of the village, a short trail that takes approximately 20 minutes through a small but dense forest of ferns, coigües and old man's beard, up to the sand dunes facing the open sea. From here walk down the sand dunes and head around the sandy peninsula back to town. The slightly longer but equally easy **Sendero Los Arrayanes** *(3hrs)* begins at the entrance to the town just past the landing strip.

LAGO VERDE – A DETOUR

A frontier town without a frontier. Alas, the Argentine side of the border has not been completed, and while in theory it is possible (and permitted) to cross the border, the absence of a critical bridge makes this a treacherous crossing. Generally the water level of the Río Pico is low enough to cross safely only a few days per year so, in all likelihood, this is a 160km spectacular round-trip drive beginning and ending in La Junta. Those intrigued by isolated communities perched in the middle of nowhere will find it interesting, but make sure the fuel tank is full and the spare tyre is inflated before departing.

The region was originally inhabited by Tehuelche Indians, and the first known permanent inhabitants were the family of Don Antonio Solís Martínez, of Chile. Owing to the proximity to Argentina, and the lack of a road connection (the road connecting Lago Verde to the Carretera Austral was completed in 1992), many of the subsequent immigrants were from Argentina. Indeed, the village was entirely dependent on Argentina until the landing strip was constructed in 1945. Although founded in 1936, this village didn't have its own municipality until 1979.

Given the lack of through traffic, to describe Lago Verde with its population of just 1,000 souls as 'sleepy' risks understatement. There is minimal tourist infrastructure, very poor cellphone coverage and almost no services. Consequently, it is easier to arrive in the village and go straight to the tourist information centre rather than attempt to arrange trips in advance. Many residents have no telephone.

The main highlights, beyond the journey itself, are centred on **trekking and horseriding**: a stroll down to the spectacular lake takes just 30 minutes from the centre of the village and there's a short trek to see local **cave paintings** (*4hrs; 12km*). Horseriding opportunities range from a few hours to over a week. **Boat trips** and **fishing** around the lake are also options.

GETTING THERE
About the route
La Junta to Lago Verde (*78km; 2hrs; gravel*) As with the Raúl Marín Balmaceda detour, this is one of the most beautiful roads of the region. It is initially flat, passing the northern edge of Lago Rosselot. Shortly after, the road enters a valley which increasingly narrows to a gorge, winding alongside the Río Figueroa. The road is single track and barely visited, but take care of oncoming vehicles and do not stop on curves however tempting the photo opportunity might be. There are steep inclines, hairpin bends and loose gravel, with sheer drops down to the river. Approaching Lago Verde the road emerges from the gorge onto a plain, with a final section of straight road that ends in the village of Lago Verde. Before this connecting road was constructed in 1992, the route took up to a fortnight to traverse. Note the border is not passable for most vehicles most of the year.

By bus It's possible, albeit difficult, to reach Lago Verde by bus – see page 124 for details.

EDUARDO SIMON

A person of great influence in the village was Eduardo Simon, a Frenchman who arrived in Lago Verde in 1950 and bought substantial lands which formed the Estancia Cacique Blanco. He developed the region quickly, installing drinking water and electricity, and perhaps most heroically, he bought an airplane from the USA which finally connected Lago Verde to Coyhaique. The plane was used for the *estancia*, but also to transport pregnant women and people with medical emergencies to Coyhaique. He also used the plane to take children to (boarding) schools in the nearby towns, avoiding the need to make a substantial trek. He originally served in the French army as a parachutist in occupied France, and in 2011 was awarded Chilean nationality for his services to the country.

TOUR GUIDES Claudio Soto (↘ *(9) 91566856;* e *claudiosotosolis@hotmail.com*) is probably the most easily contacted guide in the region. He offers the southern Sendero de Chile tour (see box, page 153) as well as fishing and trekking trips, but also knows all the other guides in the village. He can advise on the northern route to Palena, but does not offer it as a standard tour. There are five listed **horseback** guides, two guides offering **lake tours**, and two guides offering **trekking** and **fishing** trips – call in at the new tourist information office on the plaza to make arrangements.

WHERE TO STAY AND EAT There are only two places to stay in Lago Verde, both also housing the only restaurants in the village.

Residencial Nina (12 rooms) Trapananda 214; ↘ (9) 89005120, (9) 56549745; e ninapatagonica@hotmail.com, gm435977@ gmail.com; ⊕ all year. Dbls & sgls with & without private bathrooms, central heating, hot water, can use washing machine, parking, (sketchy) Wi-Fi, food available (**$$**). Located in village so more convenient for those without transport. **$$**

Residencial El Mirador (7 rooms, 1 cabin, camping) Camino a la Frontera; ↘ (9) 84769191, (9) 73831473; e hernanbal@yahoo.es; ⊕ all year.

Located 1km past the Chilean border post up the hill. If you are stopped by the border police clarify your intention to go to the hostel rather than into Argentina. 2 dbls & 5 sgls, shared bathroom, no Wi-Fi or English, but do offer laundry & full b/fast included. The small restaurant has simple meals available (**$$**). The cabin does not currently have heating, is suitable for up to 3 people & costs $40,000. Camping costs $5,000pp, & has 4 covered sites as well as various exposed sites. Bathrooms with cold showers available. Great views. **$–$$**

OTHER PRACTICALITIES There is no **petrol** in Lago Verde, so be sure to refuel in La Junta, nor is there an ATM. **Bus tickets** to La Junta can be purchased at the Santa Teresita store on Los Baguales 247 between Caique Blanco and Los Maitenes. Other shops include: Minimarket Nina, next to Residencial Nina, which also has a public telephone (*Trapanada 221*); Minimarket and bakery San Daniel (*Pioneros 294, camping also possible*); and Supermarket Paulina Alejandra (*cnr of Los Baguales & Los Radales*).

All information and maps are available at the new **tourist information centre** which was opening at the time of research on the western side of the central plaza. There is currently no website or telephone.

6

La Junta to Puyuhuapi and Cisnes

The Comuna de Cisnes stretches from Raúl Marín Balmaceda and La Junta in the north to Puerto Cisnes and Villa Amengual in the south. It is home to some 6,000 people, and covers 17,450km². Within this region lie two of the most historically fascinating towns along the entire Carretera Austral – **Puyuhuapi** and **Puerto Cisnes**. This is a stunning section of the Carretera, passing through the sub-tropical rainforest of the **Parque Nacional Queulat**; skirting glaciers, enchanted forests, beautiful lakes and jaw-dropping scenery. There are ample treks in the region, kayak and rafting opportunities, fly-fishing, and remote islands to explore by boat. However, the most intriguing aspect of this section is the history – Mussolini, Hitler and Pinochet; World War II refugees; vanishing submarines and Sudeten German settlers make up the rich history of the region, with a healthy dose of magic, astrology and mythology added for good measure.

This chapter begins where the previous chapter finished: at La Junta. It includes the larger towns of Puyuhuapi and Puerto Cisnes, as well the smaller village of **Villa Amengual**, notable only for lying on the Carretera Austral close to an important but little-known detour to the Argentine border at Río Frías.

For those in a rush Puyuhuapi may be little more than a petrol and lunch stop. Puerto Cisnes is a detour from the Carretera Austral, although it is also an increasingly important entry/exit point with ferries to the remote islands as well as direct connections to Quellón on Chiloé. The Parque Nacional Queulat is fast becoming one of the must-see places to visit along the entire Carretera and well worth the short hike to the glacier.

PUYUHUAPI

On a sunny day there are few places more beautiful than Puyuhuapi along the entire Carretera Austral. Although it might not compete with the likes of Futaleufú for adventure activities, or with Cerro Castillo for trekking options, it boasts great food, lovely accommodation, a pioneering history, and a superb place to unwind overlooking the canal of the same name. The nearby Parque Nacional Queulat is one of the finest parks in this region of Chile, competing with Parque Pumalín in the north and Parque Patagonia in the south, and is home to one of the more accessible glaciers. Many visitors pass through Puyuhuapi without stopping. For those that pause, discover a little of the history, and perhaps rent a kayak to visit the hot springs in the bay from where another glacier becomes visible, this is truly a highlight of the entire Carretera.

PUYUHUAPI

EcoCamping Playas Arrayanes (5km),
Angostura campground (12km),
Lago Puma (12km), El Pangue Lodge (18km),
La Junta (47km)

Río Pascua

CALLE 6
CALLE 3
PASADA POR PUYUHUAPI
CALLE 7
OTTO UEBEL

CIRCUNVALACIÓN AYSÉN
HAMBURGO
PEDRO LLAUTUREO
DIEGO PORTALES
BERNARDO O'HIGGINS
GABRIELA MISTRAL
VICTORIA
CALLE 10

Experiencia Austral

Hospital
Catholic church
Football ground

AVENIDA OTTO UEBEL
Tyre repairs
Bus station
Police
Plaza Puyuhuapi

Alfombras de Puyuhuapi

AVENIDA COSTANERA
N

COPEC

Bradt

Fiordo Puyuhuapi

0 ——— 100m
0 ——— 100yds

Puyuhuapi Lodge and Spa (15km),
Parque Nacional Queulat (23km),
Padra Garcia waterfalls (42km),
Bosque Encantado (50km),
Puerto Cisnes (91km)

For listings, see pages 138–40

Where to stay

1 Camping La Sirena
2 Casa Ludwig
3 Hospedaje Aonikenk
4 Hospedaje Isabel
5 Hostal Evelyn
6 Hostería Alemana
7 Residencia Doña Nury

Off map
Angostura campground
EcoCamping Playas Arrayanes
El Pangue Lodge
Puyuhuapi Lodge and Spa

Where to eat and drink

8 Café/restaurant Los Maníos del Queulat
9 Restaurant El Muelle
10 Restaurant Getzemaní

There is perhaps no better place along the entire Carretera Austral to appreciate the pioneering spirit of the region than Puyuhuapi. Fortunately the history of the village is well documented in an excellent book published in 2011 by Luisa Ludwig (page 137), daughter of one of the original settlers who still lives in Puyuhuapi and runs arguably the finest hotel in the village (page 139) – Casa Ludwig. A close competitor is the also magnificent and historic Hostería Alemana (page 139), run by the Flack family, also direct descendants of the original settlers.

HISTORY Puyuhuapi all started with a book.

A group of young Sudeten Germans had enthusiastically read Hans Steffen's book about the region of Aysén. Steffen was an avid explorer, and the glacier north of Caleta Tortel is named after him. So enthused were these impressionable adventurers with this book that they visited Hans in Switzerland in 1932. As tensions were rising in the inter-war years, Walter Hopperdietzel and a group of friends were considering emigration, including to Australia or Canada. They lived in the small town of Rossbach in Czechoslovakia, close to the border with Germany. The combination of Steffen's book and the offer of free land to settlers persuaded these hardy pioneers to select southern Chile. It even had the same damp climate as Czechoslovakia!

Sudeten Germans were Czechoslovakians by nationality, but ethnically German. Indeed, prior to World War I they had been Austrian. In the annexation of the Sudetenland during World War II the nationality of most Sudeten Germans was changed to German. In the case of the settlers of Puyuhuapi, this placed them in a bind: renounce their German citizenship and become Chileans, or lose any right to free land. In a bold act of bridge-burning, they opted for the former.

A wealthy businessman called Robert Uebel financed the emigration in an effort to create a form of colony, or outpost, as war loomed. The idea was to establish a base and then bring over new settlers, but the war dampened the feasibility of others joining them. Robert was a sympathiser of Konrad Henlein, founder of the German Sudeten Party, which supported the annexation of Sudeten Germany, albeit subsequently aligning members with Nazi Germany following the annexation in 1938.

Carlos Ludwig and Otto Uebel arrived in Chile in 1933 and 1934, and began scouting out suitable locations. They first looked around the region of Llanada Grande (between Cochamó and Río Puelo), but eventually settled on a plot at the northern end of a canal (now called Canal Puyuhuapi) some 45km north of Puerto Cisnes. Puerto Cisnes was uninhabited at this point. So isolated was this spot that those leaving Puyuhuapi would speak of 'returning to Chile'. Steffen and fellow explorer Augusto Grosse had previously, albeit independently, explored this channel, and had discovered one abandoned (and extremely basic) house, and piles of seashells typical of prior visits from Chono canoeists (likely centuries old).

Thus in 1935 Puyuhuapi was founded. Walter Hopperdietzel arrived in June, and Ernesto Ludwig in August. Along with Carlos and Otto, these were the four founders of Puyuhuapi. Although Augusto Grosse was part of the initial group, he left shortly afterwards and is consequently not considered one of the true founders. In fact, in 1941 Grosse was placed in charge of the construction of the Ofqui Canal (page 208), and purchased all the timber required for the project from Puyuhuapi.

The Canal Puyuhuapi was named prior to the village, after the Poye islands at the mouth of the Fiordo Queulat where it joins the main canal. *Huapi* means 'island' in Mapuche.

Utterly unprepared, these sprightly settlers had to learn everything the hard way, building a village from scratch, from clearing land to cutting trees to build the first basic accommodations. Pipes used to transport water were hollowed-out tree trunks. They knew very little about farming in Patagonia, a modest amount about agriculture, and almost nothing about fishing. They learned how to raise pigs, but grew fond of them, and slaughtering them was always a problem. (It seems their fondness of sausages outweighed this minor obstacle.)

Initially they depended entirely on passing boats travelling between Puerto Montt and Puerto Aysén for equipment and supplies. They would row out to Patience Island (not visible from the Carretera Austral, directly north of Puerto Cisnes at the mouth of the Canal Puyuhuapi where boats would traverse the Jacaf Canal) and hail a boat, sometimes having to wait for days in pouring rain.

Their first two houses flooded, having built them a little too close to the shore. The third burned down during a warm summer due to a fault in the chimney.

The Chilean government had initially offered 5,000ha to each settler, but following the outbreak of war, Chile severed ties with Germany and ceased granting land to any foreigners, by which point the settlers had inadvertently become German following the annexation of the Sudetenland. By becoming Chilean they could claim only 600ha. However, by assuming a public sector duty, albeit unpaid, this was extended to 1,000ha, and thus they all assumed nominal public-sector duties in order to obtain more land.

Initially they relied on food from Puerto Montt, before starting to grow basic crops in 1936. The first experiment with cattle was not entirely successful, as their food was sufficiently coarse to grind down their teeth, and half starved to death in the winter of 1937. The next herd of cattle was even less successful – they suffocated in an inadequate container on their way to Puerto Montt for sale. The health authorities were unimpressed by this cavalier attitude to farming. However, by 1940 the settlers worked out, with some advice from farmers in the region, how to raise cattle, and produced a dairy which subsequently supplied cheese and butter to the village and Puerto Montt.

Summer labourers from Chiloé were initially hired, but it was not until 1938 that Chilote families moved and stayed in the village. In 1942 the first hydro-electric plant was constructed. This provided electricity first to the dairy, and subsequently to the houses. Around this time they upgraded the sawmill with more suitable equipment obtained in Osorno, and timber soon became an important source of income for the village.

All finances were managed in Germany, until the outbreak of war, and subsequently from Puerto Montt where Carlos spent most of the time. Employees' salaries were invariably spent on buying provisions from the small store run on a cost-covering basis. Money was used only occasionally. In practice the settlers had created something akin to a co-operative, but over the years this was gradually replaced with more usual commercial relationships. Otto was the de facto leader of the commune; he came from a rich family that owned carpet factories – a skill that would come in handy in subsequent years.

In 1943 a key event took place, engraved on the minds of residents to this day: the somewhat ironically named 'taking of Puyuhuapi'. A boat arrived in the village with English soldiers searching for spies. The settlers were Nazi sympathisers, and Otto and Carlos were on a blacklist. But their Nazi sentiment was divorced from the realities of Germany, and was more concerned with supporting the reunification of ethnic Germans in the Sudetenland with Germany. However, the settlers were suspected of supporting German submarines, and when it became painfully obvious there were neither submarines nor German soldiers in the village, they were questioned about the radio communications. When the soldiers asked some of the locals what the Germans did in their free time and discovered they would climb mountains, they believed this was where the radio must be hidden, so demanded to be taken up the mountain, but were unfit to do so. Embarrassed and apologetic, the naval officer in charge of the inquisition compensated the settlers with a dinner aboard the frigate – an act which cost him his job.

In 1943 Walter built some basic looms based on sketches he had copied in Germany. Initially they produced tweed and plaid, but in 1948 the factory began producing carpets, initially to provide employment to the women, with wool purchased in Lago Verde. The carpets were of high quality and readily sold in Puerto Montt and subsequently in Santiago. Over the following decades wool production became less profitable and the wool factory eventually closed. Imported carpets were cheaper than those produced in Puyuhuapi, and nowadays carpets are made only to order. Given the infrastructure and logistics of the mid 20th century it is impressive that such a quality cottage industry was so successful in Puyuhuapi.

After all Germans were expelled from Czechoslovakia in 1947, Helmut Hopperdietzel and Ernesto's family moved to Puyuhuapi. In 1949 the settlers built the first decent boat belonging to the village, the *Paloma*. In 1951, Helmut set up the first public radio. In 1954 the first major calamity struck the village: typhus likely brought from Chiloé. The disease was transmitted by lice bites and spread rapidly due to unsafe funeral practices; the Germans were unaffected as they did not attend these funerals. Walter secured antibiotics from Aysén and the disease was stopped immediately, albeit having claimed 15 lives in two months.

The following years saw a stream of disasters. In 1958 an electrical short-circuit caused a fire in the carpet factory, which was largely destroyed. The factory was rebuilt thanks to a loan. An earthquake struck the village in 1960 (no casualties). And in 1964, the village was infested with rats – an event firmly fixed in the memories of the inhabitants. So abundant were the rats that wild cats, usually hard to spot, were clearly visible in trees ready to pounce. For some inexplicable reason one day the rats all ran into the water and drowned, in a rare case of 'mass-rat-suicide'.

Construction of the village continued unabated. Between 1955 and 1956 the first formal education of children in the village began, and the first school was established in 1958. In 1966 the first Catholic church was constructed, in traditional Chilote style. Up until the early 1970s Puyuhuapi was not a 'village' in the traditional sense. The region was privately owned and those living there were first and foremost employees rather than residents. This changed in 1971, when the Chilean state formally recognised Puyuhuapi. Two years later, in the coup, Pinochet's troops arrived, suspicious of this unusual German-run collective, and one person was reportedly killed for having left-leaning tendencies (although not one of the original settlers). By the mid 1970s Father Ronchi (see box, page 125) began playing an increasing role in the village, initially building a small chapel at the cemetery, and subsequently installing an additional radio antenna and television. However, TV stations had begun to encrypt their signals, and the only channel freely available in the village was from Mexico. According to Walter Hopperdietzel this led to the children picking up Mexican slang!

The year 1982 was pivotal for the residents of Puyuhuapi – many signs of which are visible to this day. Firstly, Pinochet inaugurated the Carretera Austral, passing through the centre of the village. In fact the Carretera Austral was inevitably to pass through Puyuhuapi, as the village had already built significant sections of the road north and south in order to facilitate the movement of cattle. However, due to the difficulty and cost of crossing the Fiordo Queulat the Carretera veered westward, over the Queulat Pass, rather than continuing south along the coast, much to the annoyance of Eugenia Pirzio Biroli, Mayor of Puerto Cisnes. The first regular bus service connected Puyuhuapi to Coyhaique (Becker Buses, still operating to this day). Ursula, the wife of Helmut, opened Hosteria Alemana which is still one of the finest accommodation options in the village. She has since handed day-to-day control over to her daughter, Hildegard. And finally, Walter installed the first petrol station (now replaced by a COPEC station, next to the carpet factory).

Telephones arrived in 1988; state-operated electricity the following year; cellphones in 2007 and internet in 2008. The Parque Nacional Queulat was formed in 1983, but the first trails were not opened until 1994, which resulted in a notable increase in tourism to Puyuhuapi. In 2011, Casa Ludwig was the first private residence in Aysén to be declared a Historic Monument, and remains open to guests to this day. In this same year Luisa Ludwig, owner of Casa Ludwig (page 139), published her historical account of the village, *Curanto y Kuchen* (pages 137 and 270). The landing strip was paved in 2012. Perhaps the last major historical event was the launch of Hopperdietzel beer in 2013.

Ernesto Ludwig died in 1969, aged 57. Otto Uebel died in 1975, aged 69. Helmut Hopperdietzel died in 1979, aged 58, and Carlos Ludwig died in 1996, aged 90. The last of the original settlers, Walter Hopperdietzel, died in 1996, aged 85. While many of the descendants of the 'original four' have left Puyuhuapi, some have remained. Ursula and Hildegard still run the Hosteria Alemana, and Luisa Ludwig (daughter of Ernesto) lives in and runs Casa Ludwig with her husband James Falkowski. All the Hopperdietzel descendants still live in the village, and besides their various other accomplishments, their beer is one of the finest artisanal beers along the entire Carretera Austral.

CURANTO Y KUCHEN – PATAGONIAN PIONEERS

The history of Puyuhuapi is perhaps no more remarkable than that of many villages along the Carretera Austral, but two key factors make the village unique from a historical perspective. Firstly, many of the buildings and people, or rather, their descendants, remain integral parts of the village. Secondly, the history is written down. Puyuhuapi *knows* where it comes from. Many villages, even larger towns along the Carretera Austral, display a cavalier attitude to history. And, as migration from other parts of Chile continues, this is likely to deteriorate further. Coyhaique is only now, in 2015, constructing a proper museum. Eugenia Biroli's house lies abandoned in Puerto Cisnes. The museum of Father Antonio Ronchi in Villa O'Higgins is a modest affair, to put it mildly. Oral history passed down through the generations is fine for as long as the custom is maintained, but in the 21st century, with increased migration, urbanisation, mobility of residents, and expanding university attendance inevitably drawing the youth to other parts of Chile, can Chile rely on oral records to record its own origins?

Luisa Ludwig's wonderful book *Curanto y Kuchen* contains an insightful and charming personal account of the lives of the early settlers and the sheer magnitude of forming a village in so remote a location. The book is packed with colourful anecdotes from various perspectives. The name is not easily translated to English – *curanto* is a traditional dish originating in Chiloé, prepared in a hole in the ground, while *kuchen* is the name of German pastries and cakes common across southern Chile where German settlers played such a role in the development of the region. Thus the title of the book reflects these two vital cultural influences upon southern Chile.

The Carretera Austral is so unique, and not simply for its endless glaciers and pristine rainforests. It emerged in relative isolation from the outside world, and its history is both fascinating and under threat. The early residents are ageing – the time to write the history of the Carretera Austral is now. Let Luisa's work be an example to other villages. The book is available to buy from Casa Ludwig (or via e curantoykuchen@gmail.com), and will be available in English in 2016. For more information on the book, see www.bradtguides.com/schile.

GETTING THERE
About the route
La Junta to Puyuhuapi (*47km; 1hr due to roadworks; partly paved but poor condition*) Although a short stretch of road, at the time of writing, it was possibly in the worst condition of any section along the entire Carretera Austral. It is currently being prepared for paving, requiring heavy bulldozers to flatten the road and widen it from a single-track lane. This involves removing the dense vegetation on either side of the road (this section passes entirely through the Rosselot and Queulat parks) as well as using dynamite to remove huge rocks. The first section, from La Junta to El Pangue Lodge at the northern end of Lago Risopatrón, is fine, paved, and reaches approximately halfway to Puyuhuapi (26km). Thereafter take extreme caution: there are bare exposed rocks, extended sections of wet mud, substantial pot-holes, adverse cambers as well as heavy trucks and bulldozers. The final section to Puyuhuapi is reasonable gravel.

By bus The village does not have its own public transport service, although all buses from Coyhaique to La Junta (and further) pass through, as do all southbound buses heading towards Coyhaique.

TOUR OPERATOR

Experiencia Austral Av Otto Uebel 36; \(9) 87448755, (9) 77661524; e contacto@ experienciaustral.com; www.experienciaustral. com. The only operator in town. Rents kayaks (*$6,000/hr for a dbl; $4,000 for a sgl*), & also offers kayak tours. Bicycle rental (*$2,000/hr or $12,000/ day*). Treks in the region include to Ventisquero

Queulat, Laguna de los Pumas & the Bosque Encantado trail. They also offer multi-day trips including airport pickup (to/from Balmaceda airport). The owner, Adonis Acuña, has a boat available for longer trips along the fjord, or to Isla Magdalena (prices vary according to length of trip).

 WHERE TO STAY *Map, page 133*

Puyuhuapi Lodge & Spa (30 rooms) Bahía Dorita, 15km south of Puyuhuapi; m (2) 22256489; e info@puyuhuapilodge. com; www.puyuhuapilodge.com. Something of a legend in the region, this is one of the better-established upper-end accommodations along the Carretera Austral, with good reason. If budget constraints limit stays in such locations to a single splurge, this would be a serious contender. The location is unique: accessed by boat from a dedicated pier approximately 15km south of Puyuhuapi or 8km north of the entrance to the Parque Nacional Queulat (arranged when the accommodation is booked). The buildings are simply superb, with an impressive spa housed in a magnificent high-ceilinged wooden complex with stunning views over the Puyuhuapi Canal – ideal for a relaxing massage! There are 3 thermal pools of varying temperatures, ranging from moderate to positively hot, 1 of which is close enough to the canal to enjoy a quick dip in the cold water after an invigorating soak at 35°C. Dense vegetation encroaches on all sides. The hotel underwent a major restoration in 2014, & the rooms by the canal are of excellent quality, each with fully equipped private bathrooms (the hot water comes from the hot springs; leave tap running a while as the pipes are long). The decks are raised above the beach at low tide, & at high tide the water laps underfoot. Kayaks available, as are guides, & there are 2 nature trails to observe the abundant vegetation of the region. Construction in this isolated spot actually begun in 1982 but it was not until Eberhard Kossman bought the land in 1988 from a creditor bank that it was finally converted into a hotel in 1989. Considering the logistical hurdles of operating with 50 staff in so isolated a

spot, the price tag is actually quite reasonable for a truly fantastic location – these are the best hot springs in this region of Chile. The spa & indoor swimming pool is fantastic. The rooms are spacious & comfortable, & the view on a sunny evening over the canal towards snow-capped mountains is simply world-class. Even the communal areas are a pleasure to sit in & enjoy a cold beer, with impressive wooden beams & wood/stone finish. The bar stocks the local Hopperdietzel beer, as well as a decent wine list & quality cocktails. All services provided except Wi-Fi, & there is no cellphone coverage. In all senses this is a getaway, a place to disconnect from everything, even from the Carretera Austral. While the b/fast is excellent (probably the only place on the Carretera Austral serving boiled eggs in proper egg cups), the dinner on our visit was average – the only possible criticism of an otherwise delightful location. The lodge can arrange tours in the region, although there are sufficient activities on site to keep one busy for a couple of days, including with children. Packages including lunch &/or dinner & access to the spa increase the cost, but there is nowhere else to eat. Discounts for longer stays & for children. **$$$$$**

El Pangue Lodge (8 rooms & cabins) Carretera Austral, 18km north of Puyuhuapi, 30km south of la Junta; \(67) 2526906; e info@ elpangue.com; www.elpangue.com. At the upper end of the accommodation spectrum in the region, this lodge is a pleasant surprise. All basic services provided (Wi-Fi, laundry, English/German spoken), but also a number of additional ones: heated swimming pool, sauna, hot tubs, a bar & pool table, a large quincho & a small library. The lodge was founded in 1987, & is perched on the northern end of Lago Risopatrón amongst immaculate gardens. They offer 4 to 7-person cabins (excl b/fast, but full kitchen provided) with spacious sitting areas & en-suite bathrooms, plus 8 rooms in the main lodge (b/fast included). All are centrally heated. They also offer guided kayak tours, fly-fishing (including classes), boat trips & horseriding, & it is possible to swim in the lake. In the main lodge is a restaurant (**$$$$**) that serves b/fast, quick lunches (or lunch boxes for those doing an excursion) & full dinners, including venison & hare as well as the usual Chilean seafood & meat dishes. If not staying, be sure to book ahead. The lodge & cabins are located in a 16ha park with trekking trails, entirely surrounded by native forest. Many of the rooms & cabins overlook the fjord & surrounding mountains. This is a wonderful place to unwind from the Carretera Austral. **$$$$**

Casa Ludwig (10 rooms) Av Otto Uebel 202; ☏ (67) 2325220; e info@casaludwig.cl; www.casaludwig.cl; ⏰ Oct–Mar. Probably the finest accommodation in the village, located at the southern exit. The building was the first private residence in Aysén Province to be declared a Historic Monument, & is immaculately maintained to this day. Owned & run by Luisa Ludwig, daughter of Ernesto Ludwig (one of the initial founders of Puyuhuapi) & author of the definitive text on the history of the village (page 137), & her husband James Falkowski. You can quiz Luisa on the history of this region – reason enough to consider a stay at this B&B. The cheaper, upper rooms have shared bathrooms, but otherwise all rooms have private bathrooms & are very comfortable, some with views over the canal. B/fast (included) is fantastic & filling, with unlimited coffee available all morning. English, German & Spanish spoken, & James has a workshop downstairs where minor repairs can be carried out. Kitchen use & Wi-Fi. Rooms can accommodate 1 to 5 people. The sitting room is replete with an extensive library, ample seating, a large table (for b/fast or catching up with emails), a great view of the village, canal & the western mountains, & is a very relaxing place to read a book on a rainy day. Very popular so reservations required. **$$$**

Hospedaje Aonikenk (6 rooms, 6 cabins) Hamburgo 16; ☏ (67) 2325208; e aonikenkturismo@yahoo.com; ⏰ all year. Decent rooms with private bathrooms, clean, electric heating, rustic beds, spacious with big windows & hot water. Ask for upstairs rooms if possible, some have a balcony. Fills up in Jan & Feb. Pleasant upstairs sitting area with television in main building. The cabins do not include b/fast, but all rooms (with private bathrooms) do. No laundry service on site, but it can be arranged. Reservations without a deposit are possible if reconfirmed a few days prior to arrival. Parking available. No English spoken. The charming owner, Veronica Gallardo, can also arrange tours in the region. Takes credit cards. **$$$**

Hostería Alemana (9 rooms) Otto Uebel 450, ☏ (67) 2325118, (9) 62058309; e aflackk@gmail.com; www.hosteriaalemana.cl. This hostería is still run by the family of some of the earliest German settlers to Puyuhuapi. Beautifully designed, tastefully decorated, large rooms with large beds & private bathrooms. Heating is via gas or wood stoves. An outstanding b/fast true to German cuisine. This is a serious contender for the top accommodation in Puyuhuapi. It is popular with motorcycle groups, & reservations are required. English & German spoken. Accepts credit cards. **$$$**

Residencia Doña Nury (17 rooms) O'Higgins 40; ☏ (67) 2325109, (9) 90813232; e marciavidalgomez@gmail.com; ⏰ all year. A wide range of room sizes to cope with almost any combination of guests, all with a basic b/fast included. There is heating & hot water, & visitors can use the kitchen. Particularly good for families, & they have 4 rooms on the ground floor suitable for people with limited mobility. Off-road parking. Another perk is that they have an on-site tyre repair service. The owner's pet peeve is visitors with wet rucksacks that dirty the rooms! Reservations without deposit are possible. **$$–$$$**

Camping La Sirena (camping, 4 rooms) Costanera 148; ☏ (67) 2325100, (9) 78806251; e lasirenapuyuhuapi@gmail.com. 40 tent sites with a roof overhead (for the incessant Puyuhuapi rain; $4,000pp) with hot water, a communal wood-fired stove doubling as a means to dry clothes. There are 3 dbls & 1 sgl, all with a shared bathroom for $7,000pp. B/fast not included, but can use kitchen. Right by the fjord; 2 of the bedrooms have great views. New mini bakery onsite offering fresh empanadas, bread & pastries. Wi-Fi available. **$**

Hospedaje Isabel (5 twin rooms) Otto Uebel 166; ☏ (9) 76623535; e isa_sala75@

hotmail.com. Very basic. Use of kitchen costs $1,500. Shared bathrooms. Wi-Fi available. **$**

🏠 **Hostal Evelyn** (9 rooms) Otto Uebel s/n, opposite Hospedaje Isabel; 📞(67) 2325114; e Leonor.escandon@hotmail.com. Very basic sgl, dbl & trpl rooms all with sgl beds. Can use kitchen. A favourite amongst budget travellers. Wi-Fi available, & the hostel also has a small shop. Shared bathrooms. **$**

🏕 **Angostura campground** A lovely, small campground on Lago Risopatrón set in dense forest only 12km north of Puyuhuapi, with access to the lake. Basic bathroom facilities available. **$**

🏕 **EcoCamping Playas Arrayanes** 5km north of Puyuhuapi; 📞(9) 85493679; e campingarrayanes@gmail.com; www. campingarrayanes.com. A superbly located camping option, along a sandy beach on Lago Risopatrón in 4ha of land, run by 2 local vets. 3 sites with a basic roof, 7 without. Quincho & communal cooking area available. Fishing possible (return catch). Hot showers, bathrooms & facilities for handwashing clothes. Also rent kayaks, canoes, & a water-cycle. The campsite has 3 trekking paths, including access to some volcanic caves. The beach is sufficiently shallow that the water warms in summer. No electricity. Firewood available. **$**

✖ WHERE TO EAT AND DRINK *Map, page 133*

✖ **Restaurant El Muelle** Av Otto Uebel, towards southern exit of Puyuhuapi; 📞(9) 76543598; e elmuellepuyuhuapi@gmail.com; www.elmuellepuyuhuapi.cl; ⊕ Sep–May noon–16.00 & 19.00–23.00 daily. Despite Puyuhuapi being located at the end of a glorious fjord, this is the only restaurant with a view of the canal. Wide range of dishes, local beers (including Hopperdietzel from Puyuhuapi, Joost & Finisterra), & a deck for those rare occasions when the sun shines. Specialities of the house are merluza, certified organic steak & a number of German dishes, including a potato purée dish blending German & Chilean influences from an original recipe of Snra Ursula, the wife of one of the first pioneers (page 136). Vegetarian dishes available. Spectacular views along the fjord, decent service, cosy atmosphere, & the owners – Agustin & Pamela – are from the region & were formerly fishermen. They also rent kayaks, & do guided trips to the Goñoti hot springs (page 142). Finest place in town. Take credit cards. **$$$–$$$$**

✖ **Café/restaurant Los Maníos del Queulat** Circunvalación s/n; 📞(9) 76649866; www. losmaniosdelqueulat.cl; ⊕ noon–16.30 & 19.00–23.00 daily. A decent range of homemade cakes & pies, as well as a full restaurant serving hamburgers, pizzas, salmon, steaks & salads. A little overpriced, & seating only for a dozen people, but high-quality food. Wi-Fi unavailable as the owner (wisely) thinks visitors should speak to one another while eating. Take credit cards. **$$$**

✖ **Restaurant Getzemaní** Costanera 172; 📞(9) 76000083, (9) 82708393; ⊕ Nov–Mar, informal hours but stays open until midnight. The only late-night option in Puyuhuapi is little more than a small heated hut next to a very basic campground. Cleanliness could be improved, but if not put off by first impressions it is actually an exceptionally nice restaurant for bargain prices. The merluza is simply excellent, & portions are huge; it would be feasible to share 1 dish. The restaurant has crooked, rickety walls, hosting an otter skin, what appears to be the stuffed torso of a cat with a wooden moose head attached, & a large dried trout peering ominously at visitors. The floor, tables, walls & ceiling are not very clean, but the plates & cutlery are. The owner, Sareallas Salidaz, is lovely, & a well-accomplished cook. She grows many of the ingredients in her garden behind the restaurant, the chips are hand-cut, the bread is freshly baked, & her rhubarb jam is delicious. She used to work in the Puyuhuapi Carpet Factory, of historic importance in the region (page 141). All meals cost $5,000. She also has a campsite, costing just $3,000pp, the cheapest in town, but also the most basic. **$**

OTHER PRACTICALITIES Along the main street, within a block of the plaza, lie a number of shops, a bakery, the bus stops, police, fire station, the sole tour operator, and the rather useful **tourist information office**. **Tyre repairs** are possible at Residencia Doña Nury (page 139) and at a *gomería* puncture-repair shop at the northern entrance to the village before reaching the plaza, but there is no mechanic.

The COPEC **petrol station** is on Aysén Street just off the northern side of the bridge at the north of the village. There is neither a laundry nor an ATM.

SIGHTSEEING AND EXCURSIONS Quintessentially quaint, Puyuhuapi is the 'historical heartland' of the Carretera Austral. For those interested in the early settlements and history of the construction of the route, this is a fascinating village to explore. The walking tour covers the main places of interest, but ultimately it is by conversing with the residents that one can truly understand the history. In terms of attractions in the region, the Ventisquero Queulat dominates most itineraries, closely followed by the hot springs for those with a more flexible budget.

Puyuhuapi village tour (*2hrs*) For those interested in history, this is a pleasant way to explore the village on a sunny day. Pick up a map at the tourism office on the plaza. The tour starts at the southern entrance to the village and ends at a lovely viewing platform overlooking the canal, mountains and village, traversing much of the lower section of the Río Pascua. Points of interest along the route include: various original German houses and the German graveyard with a monument naming the original founders of Puyuhuapi; the old path to Lago Risopatrón; the original school built in 1958 and the Catholic church built in 1966 (the first priest was the legendary Father Antonio Ronchi; see box, page 125); the old boat yard; some wetlands with various birds; the old hydro-electric water wheel; the distinctive architecture of Puyuhuapi homes; and finally the carpet factory, before the trail ends at the viewing platform.

Alfombras de Puyuhuapi (Puyuhuapi Carpet Factory) (*Aysén;* ✆ (9) 93599515; e *alfombras@puyuhuapi.com; www.puyuhuapi.com;* ⊕ 09.00–11.30 & 14.00–18.30 Mon–Fri, 10.30–noon w/end & public holidays; optional tour $2,000pp (40mins)*) Founded in 1945, this is one of the key historic buildings of the village and region (page 135). Alas, these days production has dwindled to a trickle and the factory now functions largely as a museum offering a glimpse into working life in the village. You can still see the original looms and materials. The factory does still sell a limited number of carpets which can be purchased.

Ventisquero Colgante/Parque Nacional Queulat (*www.conaf.cl/parques/ parque-nacional-queulat;* $4,000/$1,500 foreign adult/child, $2,000/500 Chilean adult/child; 10 camping sites within the national park: $6,000pp plus the cost of entrance to the park; bathrooms including hot water & showers on site*) This is the main park along the central route of the Carretera Austral. Although access points to the park are limited to Lago Témpanos and the famous hanging glacier, it is well worth a visit. The glacier protrudes from a high valley, with occasional chunks crashing down onto the rocks beneath and eventually melting into the lake. The park is 1,541km² and contains extensive evergreen forests, snow-capped mountains and prolific flora and

> **NOTE**
>
> The Termas Ventisquero hot springs, located along the Carretera Austral 6km south of Puyuhuapi, are not recommended. Run down and overpriced – we advise heading either to the cheaper and better El Sauce springs at La Junta (page 129), or splashing out and heading to the Puyuhuapi Lodge and Spa (page 138).

fauna, and allows easy access to Ventisquero Colgante which emerges from a high valley and melts into Lago Témpanos. A short trail from the car park to the lake is easily done in under half an hour, and a small boat offers tours where the trail ends at the shore offering the chance to get up close to the glacier. However, for a truly spectacular view, the longer trail up the northern side of the valley is worth the 3-hour round-trip. The trail crosses an impressive hanging bridge over a violent section of river that is simply hypnotising.

Goñoti hot springs (*Free entry*) These hot springs are situated on the west side of the canal and are accessible by kayak or boat from Puyuhuapi. From this side of the canal one can see Ventisquero Chico, not visible from either the Carretera Austral or Puyuhuapi itself. Check with locals regarding the best times to visit the hot springs, as they are submerged at high tide.

Padre Garcia waterfalls (*Approximately 8km before the entrance to the Bosque Encantado if travelling from the north*) A mere 200m from the Carretera are some interesting waterfalls named after a Jesuit priest who was searching for the mystical lost City of the Césares (see box, pages 92–3), and instead stumbled across these waterfalls. Beautiful, verdant green, and worth the half-hour round trip on a clearly marked, short trail. No formal parking, so leave the car by road, but not on the bend where the path begins.

Bosque Encantado (*4km from Cisnes Junction travelling from the north; 4km round trip; 2hrs; medium, difficult if heading to the base of the glacier*) A pleasant opportunity to stretch the legs after a long drive, this is another wonderful trek up a fairly steep but reasonably marked trail. Dense vegetation and various muddy sections, so it's advisable to wear decent boots. One river crossing towards the upper section is required in order to reach the base of the glacier and the lake, but many visitors complete only the forested section of the trail and return at the river crossing. Probably not wise to attempt the crossing with children. The trail passes through very dense forest before emerging at a river and lake with a glacier visible above – on a cloudy day the glacier may not be visible.

Lago Puma (*12km north of Puyuhuapi across the road from the Angostura campground; 10km round-trip; 4hrs; easy but steep ascent*) This is a lovely, well-marked hike to a little-visited lake through dense virgin rainforest ending on an open grassland with views of the surrounding mountains.

PUERTO CISNES – A DETOUR

When it's not bucketing down with rain, this is a delightful town. It is perched at the foot of towering mountains at the widest point of the Puyuhuapi Channel, and is the main access point to the remote communities of Puerto Gaviota, Puerto Gala and Melimoyu. Puerto Cisnes is accessed via a (mostly paved) 32km detour from the Carretera Austral (the 'Cisnes Junction'), weaving along the Río Cisnes through a dramatic evergreen valley with lofty cliffs and the occasional waterfall.

The usual array of activities are available: kayaking, fly-fishing, trekking, relaxing on beaches (in-between showers), mountain biking, visiting hot springs, admiring the stunning scenery and wildlife spotting. It is also a functioning fishing town and port, with both local boats to nearby communities and longer-distance ferries connecting this central region of the Carretera directly with Chiloé. There are

PUERTO CISNES

Virgen de
las Rosas

Sendero
Cerro Gilberto

Puyuhuapi (91km)

JUAN JOSÉ LATORRE

Ferry port,
Bahía Allanao

Patagoni-K
Expediciones

SÉPTIMO DE LINEA

RAFAEL SOTOMAYOR

DIEZ DE JULIO

Naviera
Austral ⑥

21 DE MAYO

AVENIDA ARTURO PRAT

Buses
Pandera

④

JOSÉ MARÍA CARO

Hospital

Finisterra
micro-brewery

Police ✝ ℹ Central
Plaza

GABRIELA MISTRAL

PEDRO AGUIRRE CERDA

⑩ ①

ARTURO
ALESSANDRI

CHORRILLOS ✝

Fiordo
Puyuhuapi

② ⑦
⑧ COPEC

CARLOS CONDELL

Buses
Sao Paulo

AVENIDA ARTURO PRAT

③

PILOTO PARDO

SANTIAGO AMENGUAL

DOCTOR STEFFENS

Sendero
La Lagunas

AGUADA

DE S DOLORES

⑨

Football
ground

N

Buses
Terraustral

Lago Escondida

0 ——— 100m
0 ——— 100yds

Bradt

For listings, see pages 147–8

🛏 **Where to stay**

1 Cabañas y Quincho Gilberto
2 Guairao Cabins
3 Hospedaje La Panchita
4 Hostal Amanda
5 Hostal y Cabañas Bellavista
6 Hostal y Cabanas Michay
7 Hostería El Gaucho
8 Lafquén Antú Hostería

✖ **Where to eat and drink**

 Guairao Restaurant (see 2)
 Lafquén Antú Hostería (see 8)
9 La Panchita
10 Panadería Cotty

reasonable accommodation and eating options and some pleasant treks in the surrounding area, but Cisnes is worth visiting for one reason above all others: the history. Cisnes's sleepy appearance belies a turbulent political past.

HISTORY The history of Puerto Cisnes, and the life of its enigmatic mayor, Eugenia Pirzio Biroli, are inseparable.

Eugenia Pirzio Biroli was born on 15 May 1906 in Turin, Italy. She was a keen sportswoman, tennis player, sprinter and discus thrower, winning various European championships. She established the first ever women's rowing club in Rome.

Her father was a commanding officer in the Italian army, and spent from 1921 to 1927 in Ecuador, likely sowing the seeds of curiosity for Latin America in the mind of the young Eugenia. In 1941 Biroli was promoted to General, and served as Governor of Montenegro from 1941 to 1943, crushing an uprising in 1941. In 1942 he ordered the execution of 50 hostages for every Italian soldier killed, but only ten for a wounded soldier. He told his troops: 'I have heard that you are good family fathers. That is good at home, but not here. Here, you can't steal, murder and rape enough.' He was declared a war criminal in the United Nations War Crimes Commission, but was never tried and lived out his old age in Rome.

This somewhat heavy-handed administrative style may partially explain the authoritarian leadership approach of Eugenia.

Biroli's time in Ecuador likely convinced Eugenia to learn Spanish, and it was while attending Spanish classes at the Spanish Academy that she met her future husband Genaro Godoy Arriaza, of Chile. They married in 1932. In addition to Spanish and Italian, Eugenia studied Greek and Latin, and spoke good English.

Eugenia and Genaro moved to Chile after World War II. Genaro was an opera singer and a philologist, but it is not entirely clear what Eugenia did until she began working with some local charities in Santiago, and quickly developed a passion for working with abandoned children. In 1952 the Chilean government donated some land in a remote spot in the region of Aysén to a charity called Obra Don Guanella, which then built a dedicated school and safe environment for abandoned children from Santiago. Eugenia visited the spot in 1957, and never quite left. According to her account of her arrival there were only four houses in the village.

Puerto Cisnes had been founded, as a nascent village, in February 1955. Thus Eugenia lived in Cisnes almost from inception, and was a key player in the formation of the town. The first mayor was David Solis, a retired policeman, and Eugenia was one of the four councillors. Through her friendship with then-president Jorge Alessandri, Eugenia was able to secure some surprising public-sector works in Puerto Cisnes despite its minuscule size. Alessandri, for example, ordered the construction of the municipality, an agricultural school, a landing strip and installed electricity. Eugenia also built the first church, and subsequently the library. In fact she spent her entire inheritance developing the town. She was renowned for being stubborn, frequently travelling to Santiago and sitting for hours, knitting, outside the offices of national ministries until government officials agreed to hear her requests. She would lobby government and companies on behalf of Puerto Cisnes, and secured the town's first ambulance from Fiat. Her refusal to take no for an answer is evidenced in the disproportionate development of Puerto Cisnes compared with other towns in the region. Even today it is possible to observe a greater role of the state in the day-to-day activities of Puerto Cisnes compared with other communities such as Puyuhuapi, which was always somewhat sceptical of public-sector intervention and far preferred to 'go it alone'.

While Eugenia secured astonishing developments for the town, she spent her life living very modestly and never accumulated personal wealth. Genaro never moved to Puerto Cisnes, and apparently visited only rarely. It took at least four days to reach Santiago. Despite this slightly unorthodox marriage Eugenia and Genaro had two children, one of whom died. Estanislao became a geologist and professor at the University of Chile, and still visits Cisnes sporadically. Her husband, Genaro, died in 1979, although Eugenia continued listening to cassettes of his operas for the rest of her life.

In 1960 Father Antonio Ronchi came to Chile, and the following year to Puerto Cisnes. Ronchi soon became the self-named 'rascal priest' (see box, page 125). Ronchi contributed immensely to the economic and spiritual welfare of Cisnes and the surrounding region, as far afield as Villa O'Higgins in the south and north to La Junta, while Eugenia had only one interest above all others – the development of Puerto Cisnes. Ronchi's style was more collaborative, and he appears to have made fewer enemies. The two never got on.

Puerto Cisnes was upgraded to a formal commune in May 1965 under the Frei presidency, with authority over La Junta and Puyuhuapi (which is resented to this day). In 1971 a new mayor was elected and Eugenia continued working as councillor, until the coup d'état on 11 September 1973. Eugenia was appointed mayor by Pinochet in November that year, and held this position for 17 years, narrowly losing an election in 1989 shortly before Pinochet was replaced by Patricio Aylwin. Her friendship with Pinochet is subject to much speculation, and critics refer to her as 'Pinochet's Witch' on account of her uncanny astrological readings. Pinochet fiercely believed in astrology, and visited Eugenia in Puerto Cisnes to consult with her on numerous occasions. Relations between the two soured when Eugenia failed

She is still a divisive character in Puerto Cisnes. Her authoritarian style was perhaps necessary to achieve the development she desired, but it isolated parts of the community. Her close association with the Pinochet regime may have served her and the town during that era, but nowadays pro-Pinochet sentiment is not openly stated. Similarly, some older residents in town are hesitant to speak too openly about Eugenia. Younger residents seem oblivious to the history of Puerto Cisnes, particularly as many are recent arrivals to the town. Some supporters of Eugenia speak of her with almost religious fanaticism, believing her contribution to the town, and astrological prowess, was little short of divine. While her accomplishments were impressive, in neighbouring villages she is less popular, accused of putting Puerto Cisnes before broader regional development.

Her contribution to Puerto Cisnes is undeniable, still visible in the form of infrastructure projects she managed to secure for the town during the Pinochet years, yet there is no museum about her life or work, and scant information online or in the library she built. Her house, opposite the hospital, lies abandoned and overgrown with vegetation. The Guairao Restaurant in Cisnes is the closest thing to a museum that exists (page 148) and there is a bust of Eugenia in front of the town hall (donated by the military). Compare this to the memory of Father Ronchi: photos of him adorn walls the length of the Carretera Austral and the boat from Puerto Yungay to Río Bravo is named after him. It is not clear why this is. Ronchi's actions had a broader impact in the region, for sure. But the view of Pinochet in 21st-century Chilean culture is complex, and perhaps Eugenia's friendship with Pinochet places her too firmly in a chapter of Chilean history that many wish to forget.

The only book written about Eugenia is the Italian/Spanish *La Italiana de Patagonia*, written by her niece Idanna Pucci, containing marvellous photographs of Eugenia from infancy to late in life, as well as testimonies from various people impacted by her works. Idanna Pucci also made a documentary, *Eugenia of Patagonia* in 1992, containing extensive video footage and interviews with Eugenia, which won the Audience Award at the Turin Film Festival in 2005. Although not currently available in Puerto Cisnes, these can be purchased directly from Idanna Pucci (e *idannapucci@gmail.com*). They offer a fascinating glimpse into the life of one of the most charismatic and influential mayors of (southern) Chile.

to predict an unsuccessful attack by the Frente Patriotico on Pinochet's convoy as it made its way to his weekend retreat in 1986.

Perhaps one of Eugenia's greatest regrets was that the Carretera Austral did not pass through Puerto Cisnes, but did pass through the rival village of Puyuhuapi. Indeed, the Carretera Austral could conceivably have traversed a more coastal route through Puerto Cisnes, or even a more easterly trajectory through La Tapera. Eugenia had to make do with a 35km connecting road to the Carretera Austral, which was completed in 1982, but resulted in Puerto Cisnes being a detour.

Eugenia died in Coyhaique on 22 February 2003 aged 96. She had moved to a home for the elderly run by the charity Obra Don Guanella, the same charity that had first persuaded Eugenia to head south nearly half a century previously.

She is buried in the Cisnes Cemetery (which she also built), and she wrote her own epitaph: 'Here rests her body, but her spirit remains vigilant in the skies over Cisnes.'

GETTING THERE
About the route
Puyuhuapi to Cisnes (*91km; 3–4hrs due to roadworks; road under improvement*) This section competes with the stretch just north of Puyuhuapi as some of the worst road quality found along the entire Carretera Austral. At the time of writing, this stretch was closed from 13.00 to 17.00 in order to allow heavy machinery to clear and widen the road, and for the use of explosives. This complicates matters for those wishing to visit two important destinations along this otherwise beautiful section of road: the Parque Nacional Queulat (the 'hanging' glacier, or Ventisquero Colgante), and the Sendero Bosque Encantado (Enchanted Forest Trail); see pages 141 and 142.

The hours when the road is closed sometimes, but not always, extend to seven days per week. All travel along this section is impossible between these times. However, with decent planning it is possible to avoid this inconvenience: the Sendero Bosque Encantado can be done in a couple of hours, and – while the Parque Nacional Queulat takes at least half a day to explore thoroughly – there is camping on site (of particular interest to cyclists). It is also possible to reach the park either from the north or south before 13.00, explore the park while the Carretera is closed, and push on either south or north at 17.00 with plenty of time to reach the next village before nightfall. At the time of writing, information about road closures was best obtained locally. Signposts explaining the formal opening hours of the road were subject to change. The only secure means to guarantee being able to traverse this section is to travel early in the morning or late afternoon.

Roadworks continue outside these hours but generally involve closing only one lane and stopping traffic with manual traffic signals. Waits can often reach half an hour even when the road is technically open. It is a treacherous stretch of road with sharp, steep hairpin bends, often with exposed rock and mud. The road ascends to the Queulat Pass, and then descends with a similar series of dangerous hairpin bends.

From Puyuhuapi the road is initially fine to the Termas del Ventisquero (6km), but deteriorates from this point on. Some 15km later is the entrance to the Parque Nacional Queulat, and the Bosque Encantado entrance is 4km before the Cisnes Junction.

From the junction the condition improves, and is paved almost all the way to Puerto Cisnes – only the last 15km is gravel. The road runs alongside the Río Cisnes with dramatic views to the other side of the river. By the time the gravel begins the road is close to sea level and flat, so there are no ascents or descents on gravel.

By bus There are frequent buses south to **Coyhaique** (with Buses Pantera, Buses São Paulo and Buses Terraustral), as well as a few services a week north to **La Junta** (via Puyuhuapi) with Buses Entre Verde.

By ferry As well as the weekly service to Quellón (*Wed; 11hrs*), there is also a slow ferry that serves the route Chacabuco–Puerto Aguirre–Puerto Gaviota–Puerto Cisnes–Isla Toto–Melimoyu–Santo Domingo–Raúl Marín Balmaceda–Melinka–Quellón. See page 45 for more information on these.

TOUR OPERATORS

Patagoni-K Expediciones Av Arturo Prat 1037; \(67) 2346584. The only tour operator in town offers bike hire, kayak rental & tours, & treks in the region including up Gilbert. Bilingual staff; takes credit cards.

Tours Bellavista Septimo de Linea with Rafael Sotomayor; \(67) 2346408; e contacto@ tourbellavista.cl; www.tourbellavista.cl; ⊕ all year. Operating out of the hostel of the same name (see below), offers a range of standard & tailor-made tours in & around Cisnes, such as kayaking, fishing & boat trips in the bay, including to Isla Magdalena & to the sea lion colonies. Takes credit cards.

WHERE TO STAY *Map, page 143*

There are no formal campsites in Puerto Cisnes, but **camping** is permitted, and free, on the bay to the south of town. It is also tolerated on the main beach in Cisnes in an emergency.

Cabañas y Quincho Gilberto (3 cabins) Gabriela Mistral 504; \(67) 2346440; e roloriffo@ hotmail.com; ⊕ all year. Reasonable cabins at a reasonable price, a little dated, but centrally located. Cabins with 2 & 3 bedrooms; Wi-Fi, hot water, gas heating, single-glazed windows, TV, full kitchen without microwave & off-road parking. B/fast not included. Excellent quincho for larger groups. Good bread shop/mini supermarket next door. Owners have lived in Cisnes for 60 years, & Gueseita founded the first school in Cisnes. **$$$**

Guairao Cabins (9 cabins) Costanera 352; \(67) 2346473; e elguairao@yahoo.com; www. guairao.cl. All cabins sleep 5 people, have hot water, stoves for heating, Wi-Fi, off-road parking & a living area. The newer, more expensive cabins are spacious, have a full kitchen & a dining area, 2 bathrooms, a shared quincho & are worth the extra money. The smaller cabins are a little darker, more cramped, & do not have a kitchen, but are still reasonable value. Reservation required, as they also serve corporate clients & fill up rapidly. One of the better, more upmarket options in town. The owners, Luis Carrasco & his wife Norma Mansilla, were personal friends of the charismatic mayor of the town, Eugenia Biroli (see box, page 145), & have a wealth of information & photographs of her life. Good value for money for one of the higher- standard cabins in town. They also run the Guairao Restaurant (page 148), a similarly upmarket option. **$$$**

Hostería El Gaucho (8 rooms) Augusto Holemburg halfway up block; \(67) 2346514; e miri.latorre@gmail.com. The first hostel in Puerto Cisnes, rich in history. The owners arrived in 1946 & converted the house to a hostel in 1963. Set slightly above 'downtown' Cisnes, it has sweeping views across the bay. 6 twin rooms, 1 dbl, 1 sgl, all with private bathroom & cable TV. B/fast included; although is not the best-value hostel in Cisnes, it is worth considering for its historical significance – you can ask the owners questions about the history of the region. Wi-Fi & off-road parking are offered, & the owner (Eliana Rosales, daughter of the original family) will prepare lunches or dinners for guests if required. **$$$**

Hospedaje La Panchita (9 rooms) Arturo Prat 805; \(67) 2346130, (9) 88380562; e gloria. cadagan@gmail.com; ⊕ all year. Pleasant budget option a short walk from the centre, but with lovely views on the few days of sunshine in Cisnes. Sgl, dbl, trpl & quadruple rooms, some overlooking the bay towards the mountains. All bathrooms are shared, & rooms towards the back are a little gloomy. Wi-Fi, laundry service & some off-road parking. Very good b/fast with a decent serving of scrambled eggs. The menu of the day is very good value (page 148), & they have a quincho available. Take credit cards. **$$**

Hostal Amanda José María Caro 7; \(9) 84213189; e amandahostalybazar@hotmail. com. Simple hostel with sgls & dbls, Wi-Fi, cable TV & basic b/fast included. Also sells bus tickets for Pantera buses. **$$**

Hostal y Cabañas Bellavista (12 rooms, 2 cabins) Septimo de Linea with Rafael Sotomayor; \(67) 2346408; e contacto@tourbellavista.cl; www.tourbellavista.cl; ⊕ all year. Recommended budget accommodation in Cisnes. Rooms are tastefully decorated, comfortable & spacious, often with views over the bay. Decent restaurant (**$$**), shared bathrooms, Wi-Fi & cable TV. Also has 2 cabins sleeping 5 people. The owner has run the hostel since 1992, & since 2005 has also run a tour company (see above). Deposits are required, can be taken by credit card. **$$**

Hostal y Cabanas Michay (6 rooms, 2 cabins) Gabriela Mistral 234; ✆(67) 2346462, (9) 87240475; e hostalmichay@gmail.com; ☺ all year. A traditional home in a good location converted to a hostel in 1990. All rooms (2 or 3 persons) have private bathrooms &, although a little dated, this is an insight into the traditional housing of Cisnes. The owner, Valeria Adasme, arrived in Cisnes in the late 1960s & offers a wealth of information on the region & its history. Deposits are not necessary but do confirm the booking by phone the day before. Basic b/fast included. **$$**

Lafquén Antú Hostería (7 rooms) Arturo Prat 213, cnr with Carlos Condell; ✆(67) 2346382, (9) 76078885; e marisolgabriela@hotmail.com; www.lafquenantu.cl; ☺ all year. A new hostel with dbl, twin & sgl rooms with full b/fast included. Shared bathrooms with hot water. Large communal areas with a computer & video games, & restaurant/bar downstairs (see below). Good meeting place for travellers. Reservations do not require a deposit but do confirm the day before. No English spoken. Lovely location overlooking the Puyuhuapi Canal towards Isla Magdalena. **$$**

✗ WHERE TO EAT AND DRINK *Map, page 143*

✗ Guairao Restaurant Costanera 352; ✆(67) 2346473; e elguairao@yahoo.com; www.guairao.cl. This is probably the best place to eat in a town with surprisingly few options. Seafood is the speciality, including eel, salmon, puye (small eel-like fish – wonderful), & the usual fare of fish & shellfish. Family-run business with decent service, the same business that runs the cabins. The only restaurant in Cisnes recommended in the magazine *Gourmet de la Patagonia*, which the owner can produce on demand. Good presentation of food, & when the restaurant fills up it has a good atmosphere, overlooking the Puyuhuapi Canal. Only possible gripe is that with so many craft beers from the region, & a focus on local ingredients, the only beers available are international brands. **$$$$**

✗ Lafquén Antú Hostería Arturo Prat 213; ✆(9) 76078885, (9) 88655925; e lafquenantucomidas@gmail.com; www.lafquenantu.cl; ☺ 24/7. Part of the hostel of the same name (see above), this is a decent restaurant, which is also good for a quick beer or cup of tea

admiring Isla Magdalena in the distance – it's a delightful place on a sunny evening. Service can be a little slow & perhaps it's not best value for money, but scores highly for location & ambience. Wooden interior, local beers (Caiquen, Campo D'Hielo, Finisterra & Hopperdietzel), friendly owners & occasional live music. Specialities include a wide range of seafood, but in particular the *puyes pil pil*. **$$$**

✗ La Panchita Arturo Prat 805; ✆(67) 2346130, (9) 88380562; e gloria.cadagan@gmail.com. A simple, family-run restaurant serving decent portions & with good service as long as the restaurant doesn't fill up. Seafood is the main speciality, meat dishes also available. Cosy atmosphere, & upstairs in the hotel (page 147). Good budget option in Puerto Cisnes – be sure to grab a window seat for lovely views. **$$**

✗ Panadería Cotty Pedro Aguirre Cerda just above Arturo Prat. Excellent homemade empanadas, savoury & sweet pastries, & a small shop. **$**

OTHER PRACTICALITIES The **tourist information centre** is on the central plaza, as is the municipality building, the library (with free use of computers with internet) and the bust of Eugenia Biroli. The COPEC **petrol station** is on the corner of Piloto Pardo and Carlos Condell. There is neither an ATM nor a laundry in Puerto Cisnes.

SIGHTSEEING AND EXCURSIONS On a sunny day, there are plenty of options for visitors to Puerto Cisnes. Perched as the town is on the edge of the Puyuhuapi Canal and close to the Río Cisnes, there are mountains and lakes within walking distance of the centre. Isla Magdalena is visible across the bay, and the town's rich history is simply fascinating. However, incessant rain can dampen enthusiasm.

A good starting point, and a useful way to get to grips with some of the history of the region, is a trip to the **central plaza**, home to the tourist information centre

above left **Ventisquero Colgante – Queulat's 'hanging glacier' –
protrudes from the Northern Ice Field, where occasional
chunks of ice crash onto the rocks below**
(DMP) pages 141–2

above right & inset **Puyuhuapi is one of the best-preserved historic villages in
all of Aysén – its traditional houses and carpet museum
offer an insight into the working life of the pioneers**
(RO) pages 133–6 and 141

below **The southern road along Lago General Carrera, Chile's
second-largest lake, offers magnificent vistas of the
distant ice fields** (HS) pages 211–23

above The almost alpine Lago Verde is a spectacular detour from the Carretera Austral

(EZ) pages 129–31

left The thundering rivers around Futaleufú are home to some of the greatest white-water rafting in the world

(SS) pages 118–19

below The descent towards Cerro Castillo, with a series of hair-raising switchbacks, is one of the most dramatic sections of the whole route

(EZ) page 193

above left A rare monument to Pinochet in La Junta, who was responsible for connecting some of Chile's remotest regions with the Carretera Austral (HS) pages 13–16

above right The Carretera Austral often weaves precariously along cliff edges – pictured here, the impressive Piedra del Gato viaduct on the way to Villa Amengual (EZ) page 150

below The marble caves at Puerto Río Tranquilo are the best in the region, and are particularly stunning on a sunny day (EZ) page 207

bottom Crossing rivers was one of the major challenges in the construction of the Carretera Austral – pictured here, the beautiful Puente General Carrera in Chile Chico (EZ) page 218

above **Lago Bertrand is one of the most photogenic spots along the whole route** (HS) page 226

left **A *huaso* (Chilean gaucho) by the El Salto waterfall** (WH) page 242

below **Approaching the Argentine steppe in Parque Patagonia, where mud-flats and open plains replace the lush vegetation and fjords** (HS) pages 229–34

above   The small chapel close to Villa O'Higgins was built by Father Ronchi, the self-proclaimed 'rascal priest' (HS) page 259

right   The only inscribed grave on the mysterious Isla de los Muertos (HS) pages 246–7

below   Crossing the Río Aviles in Parque Patagonia on the Aviles trail, which connects Valle Chacabuco with Reserva Nacional Jeinemeni (WH) page 233

above The globally threatened huemul (*Hippocamelus bisulcus*) is the Carretera Austral's most iconic mammal, pictured here beside the ice floes of Ventisquero Montt (HS) page 6

left The guanaco (*Lama guanicoe*) is one of South America's four remaining camelids (HS) pages 104–6

below The rocky shores of Raúl Marín Balmaceda are bursting with marine mammals and birds; such as pelicans and South American sea lions (*Otaria flavescens*) (HS) page 7

right   Llamas on the back route from Puerto Ibáñez (WH)

below left   Andean condors (*Vultur gryphus*) are prolific in the region, particularly around Coyhaique where the Punta del Monte Estancia presents a rare opportunity to get up-close with these massive creatures (AJ/S) pages 182–3

below right   Austral parakeets (*Enicognathus ferrugineus*) are common forest-dwellers (RL/S) page 8

bottom   Known locally as *nalca*, the large and somewhat Jurassic giant rhubarb plants (*Gunnera tinctoria*) adorn the asphalt of the Carretera Austral (WH) page 9

PURA
AVENTURA
To travel is to live

Curious about the
Carretera Austral?

We can help.

Thoughtfully tailored holidays in the great outdoors
of Spain and Latin America

01273 676 712
pura-aventura.com

with a map of an **interpretive trail** around the town. The trail covers all the main sights, including the coast and viewpoints, with occasional opportunities to stop for a coffee or local ale – it takes at least 2 hours, but you could easily spend a day pottering along. The library on the plaza is a surprisingly beautiful building, resembling a small wooded Greek temple, and well equipped with information on the region. It is next to the municipal building of Cisnes, with a statue of Eugenia on the plaza in front.

It is a pity to traverse the Carretera Austral without trying the local ales along the route, and of the micro-breweries open to the public, the **Finisterra micro-brewery** (*José María Caro 297;* \ *(67) 2346407, (9) 66599146;* e *cervezafinisterra@gmail.com; www.cervezafinisterra.cl*) is the one to visit. It began a decade ago, and is one of the largest in the region, producing approximately 3,200 litres per month. Tours are free, and operated by the master brewer Camilo, son of the founder. He explains the process and ingredients used, the differences between the various beers they produce, and is usually preparing a batch during the tour, so don't be surprised if Camillo has to pause to alter temperatures or add ingredients. The main beers are blond, golden and award-winning porter. The blonde beer is also mixed with seasonal fruits, honey and chilies to produce four other beers. The spicy beer is unusual, an acquired taste that some people love, others detest, with chilies imported from Mexico. The beer is fairly widely available along the Carretera, and the tour around this family-run business is delightful – a very good use of an hour or so, particularly if it's raining in Cisnes. They also offer a 'menu of the day' lunch in high season.

The cove to the south of Puerto Cisnes boasts a beach fit for **swimming**, Balnearios; it's not particularly impressive, but it has the advantage of a lifeguard in high season. If you're looking to swim the open sea there are finer places than this mediocre offering, albeit without the benefits of a lifeguard. Beyond the beach, it is possible to continue on by foot, car or bicycle up the Río Cisnes and return to the town via the **Sendero Las Lagunas**, a 1-hour hike along the main road towards the eastern end of Santiago Amengual Street, taking in two small lakes with plenty of opportunity for wildlife spotting.

To see the town and bay from up high, follow the **Sendero Virgen de las Rosas** (*1km round-trip; 1hr; easy*) – a short trek up to a lookout, nicely lit at night, beginning at the end of Rafael Sotomayor Street.

The **Sendero Cerro Gilberto** (*2 days; difficult*) is a substantial hike to the summit of the mountain that looms over Puerto Cisnes. It is a hard climb over two days and if you're attempting the summit, you're advised to take a guide (ask at the tourist information centre or either of the tour operators listed on page 147). The view from the summit is spectacular, extending across the canal to the islands, and mountains to the east. **Fishing** on the Río Cisnes (which originates 160km upstream at the Argentine border) is possible; guides aren't necessary providing you have a fishing licence, but tour operators and the tourist information centre can arrange guides. Tours Bellavista can arrange a boat if you intend to fish the less accessible parts of the river by the estuary, including combining such trips with visits to the sea lion colonies or Isla Magdalena.

Kayaking is another option, either on a guided tour or independently. It's 4 hours upstream to **Lago Escondida**. Other options include kayaking to the sea lion colonies or visiting the waterfalls north of Cisnes along the canal.

To the north, heading along the Puyuhuapi Canal, lies the **Allanao beach**, with short hikes to the estuary of the Río Anita and also to a small lake (Laguna Cipress). This can be visited by boat or kayak. It is then possible to cross the canal over to the hot springs at **Parque Nacional Isla Magdalena** (*www.conaf.cl/parques/parque-nacional-isla-magdalena-2*), accessible by boat only, due to distance, currents and tides.

During the last weekend in January thousands of people descend upon the town for the three-day **Fried Fish Festival**. People come to enjoy music, local customs and delicious fried merluza, a staple fish in the southern fjords. Each year before the festival, the community selects a local family in need of a new house, which is constructed with municipal funds, and then placed on a trailer and manually towed through town to its designated site. This is also the period when Puerto Cisnes elects the town Queen. A wonderful celebration of tradition and community spirit.

VILLA AMENGUAL AND A DETOUR TO PASO RÍO FRÍAS-APELEG

Very few people stop at Villa Amengual. It is one of the least interesting villages along the Carretera Austral, and without even a petrol station there is little reason to pause here. It was founded in 1983 following the construction of the Carretera Austral. Its main claim to fame is that it is the nearest village to the turning towards Villa La Tapera and on to the rarely transited Argentine border at Paso Río Frías-Apeleg. However, before dismissing this village entirely, there are two **good accommodation** options nearby with excellent food, a lovely lake, an impressive church built by the original Chilote immigrants, and a small market selling local handicrafts. The road to the border is magnificent, but rough, and best done in a car with decent clearance if not a 4x4. Villa Amengual lies on a sparsely populated stretch of the Carretera Austral, some 60km north of Mañihuales and 90km south of Puyuhuapi, and is thus a useful break for weary cyclists.

Most people will visit Villa Amengual either on their way west to/from Puerto Cisnes, eastbound up the Río Cisnes towards Villa La Tapera and the border, on their way south towards Coyhaique, or north through the Parque Nacional Queulat towards Puyuhuapi.

GETTING THERE
About the route
Cisnes Junction to Villa Amengual (*34km; 30mins; paved*) A beautiful stretch of paved road sandwiched between towering cliffs and the Río Cisnes. There is an impressive viaduct at Piedra del Gato running alongside the mountain. The old road is still visible, precariously hugging the side of the cliff. The road zigzags up to magnificent views over the Valle Río Cisnes and continues to Villa Amengual.

Villa Amengual to Paso Río Frías-Apeleg (*106km one-way; 2½hrs; 2km paved to junction, 104km of tough gravel*) This offshoot is spectacular, weaving along the Río Cisnes with almost no traffic – the border receives only 400 crossings per year. Dramatic canyons, verdant lush grass (suitable for camping), cows, goats, sheep and hares at every turn plus plenty of birdlife. Miniscule **Villa La Tapera** is approximately halfway from Villa Amengual to the border (page 152), one of the more isolated, and dilapidated places on the entire Carretera Austral. There is little reason to stop here unless you need somewhere to stay travelling to/from Puerto Cisnes/the border, or if you're planning on doing some fishing in the region. It is 4 hours to Coyhaique.

In general, this border crossing is only convenient for those travelling directly to Puerto Cisnes from Argentina; most will use the more northerly border at Palena (page 120), or the more southerly Paso Puesto Viejo (page 155), which is better quality and a more direct route to Coyhaique.

Most of the road is rough and accessible only with a 4x4 or a high-clearance 2x4 travelling with caution, although in good weather and with sufficient patience it could qualify as a 'regular gravel road' in many places. However, given the length of the journey from Villa Amengual to the nearest town in Argentina, this is a long journey and best done in a vehicle with higher clearance. Expect slow travel, hairpin bends, steep ascents and descents and a narrow road.

Paso Río Frías-Apeleg is open from November to March between 08.00 and 21.00. The Chilean border post (❨ *(67) 2567096*) is manned all year, but may close in June and July if the road becomes impassable. The Argentine border post (❨ *+54 2945 496074*) is located 4km east of the actual border. Outside these months it is essential to call ahead to find out if the border is open (ie: April to October; it is invariably closed entirely in June and July due to snow). Outside the summer months the border, if open at all, closes at 20.00. A 4x4 is highly advisable, and chains are obligatory in winter. If closed, paperwork must be completed in Aldea Apeleg, approximately 25km southeast of the actual border. It is obligatory to stop at this border post when the other is closed, and the Chilean authorities will call the Argentine authorities to advise them of a border crossing, and vice versa.

Given the uncertainty of using this border outside the summer months it is wiser to use the Palena/Futaleufú crossings to the north (pages 120 and 114), or the Puesto Viejo crossing further south (page 155).

The nearest **petrol station** to the border is at Puerto Cisnes or Mañihuales. Consider that the Argentine side of the border is relatively isolated and the nearest petrol stations are still a distance into the country. Officially it is not permitted to take fuel in a container across the border, so top up the tank from any such container before crossing.

Reports are mixed as to the road quality on the Argentine side of the border but, as of early 2015, this crossing was possible without a 4x4 in summer, although a high-clearance vehicle is generally highly advisable not only on the Argentine side, but also for reaching the Carretera Austral. Aldea Apeleg is relatively convenient for connecting with Gobernador Costa and Tecka in Argentina, but there is very little traffic in this region and no public transport.

By bus There are no scheduled buses beginning or ending in Villa Amengual, but buses heading north and south inevitably pass through and stop, as does the twice-weekly Buses Aranda (❨ *(9) 97642062*) service from Coyhaique to Alto Río Cisnes via Villa La Tapera.

🏠 **WHERE TO STAY AND EAT** For those wishing to stay in the region, the two best options are slightly out of the village, and both offering fine food.

🏠 **Hostería Casona del Bosque** (8 rooms, 1 cabin) 500m south of Villa Amengual on the east side of Carretera Austral; ❨ (9) 53537484; e tatianaturismo@gmail.com. A delightful discovery, this hostel is run by Tatiana & her husband Victor Hugo, both highly accomplished chefs. The rooms are simple but pleasant; dbl & twin rooms with either shared bathroom or ensuite, 1 trpl, & the cabin sleeps up to 5 people. Gas heating, Wi-Fi, off-road parking, superb b/fast (included with rooms, not with cabin) & a comfortable sitting area to relax by the fire. They also have an excellent restaurant serving homemade local food, local beers, & some surprisingly good cocktails ($$$). English spoken, as Tatiana was the English teacher in Villa Amengual for nearly a decade. A lovely, family-run business offering top-notch food. $$$

6

🏠 Fundo Lago Las Torres (5 rooms, 7 cabins, 1 house) 5km south of Villa Amengual on west side of Carretera Austral; ✆(64) 2232514, (9) 98222685; e jlgalvez@lagolastorres.cl; www. lagolastorres.cl; ⊕ all year. Another gem location offering a wide range of accommodation options within 2,800ha of land, which includes a lake. The main building feels like stepping back in time a century, to gain a glimpse of true Patagonian life before the advent of smartphones. Energy is generated from a small hydro-electric plant on site (with lights occasionally dimming according to the water level) & heating is via wood-stoves. Good hot water once the stoves are fired up. Laundry available, but no Wi-Fi & internet coverage is only via 3G Movistar. Most visitors are self-catering, but food can be prepared if arranged in advance, including a mouthwatering cordero asado (roast lamb). The property has been in the family for 80 years, & the estate operating for the last 30. This is one of the most authentic, rustic Patagonian accommodations along the entire Carretera Austral, & surprisingly good value for money. They also offer fly-fishing on the lake & in the nearby rivers, including Río Cisnes, & can arrange classes for beginners if required. Ample trekking & horseriding opportunities within the estancia. The property has a boat, & can reach remote & unknown spots, including a hidden lake that involves hauling the boat 500m over land. Can arrange airport transfers, & the owners are true locals, so can arrange any tour imaginable. Nature-lovers might be a little put off by the puma skins, but these were presumably killed many decades ago! The Ventisquero El Elefante is visible from the property, which also doubles as a working farm. All too easy to drive past this highly recommended establishment. **$$**

🏠 El Indio (5 rooms, camping) Carmen Arias 10; ✆(67) 2215434, (9) 85078137. Basic accommodation with shared bathrooms, 4 dbls & 1 sgl, extra for full b/fast, laundry & Wi-Fi available. $5,000/tent including Wi-Fi & hot shower. Dinner or lunch available (**$**), can do an asado for groups if booked in advance. **$**

🏠 Hospedaje Sebastian (4 dbl rooms) Pablo Águila St (1 block from plaza), Villa La Tapera; ✆satellite phone only in Villa La Tapera: (02) 1960528/9, Coyhaique: (67) 2242334; ⊕ all year. There are no phones here so, to make a reservation, call Guillermo Matamala on the numbers above; he can relay messages to the owner, Vilma Becerra. While it's rarely full, it is worth reserving in Jan & Feb because this is currently the only option in the village, & there is nothing else until well over the Argentine border, or in Cisnes/Puyuhuapi/ Villa Amengual. Simple rooms with 2 shared bathrooms, hot water & heating. Restaurant also serves lunch or dinner (**$**). No internet in hostel, but the village does have internet after 17.00. No English spoken. Laundry service available. Good value, b/fast included. Vilma's husband is a guide & can arrange local fishing trips or horseriding. **$**

SIGHTSEEING AND EXCURSIONS There are limited options in Villa Amengual – a church built by Father Ronchi (see box, page 125), and a small handicraft store selling local woollen products from the region at reasonable prices (cash only). Historically this was a huge wool producing region, with women working for private farms or for the state. However, with the over-grazing of the estancias and the global competition of cheaper wool from overseas, wool production has declined dramatically and is now a niche activity employing very few people, and destined principally for handicraft markets rather than mass production. Without even a petrol station, few people stop in the village.

Villa La Tapera
Some 50km east of Villa Amengual, there is a valid reason why Villa La Tapera appears so rarely in guidebooks. With a population of approximately 400 people, it must be one of the remotest inhabited spots in the entire region accessible by road. It was founded in 1970, and has grown slowly ever since. The border crossing to Argentina is rarely used (see page 151) and there are very basic services including a police station, two mini-supermarkets, a medical centre, a school and one hostel (see above), and it will shortly have its first pub.

CONNECTING WITH THE SENDERO DE CHILE

It is possible to connect with the Sendero de Chile (see box, page 121) from La Tapera by heading north to Lago Verde (*59km; 3 days, 2 nights; horse & guide advisable*). This section follows the same trail taken by the traditional gauchos centuries earlier and is utterly disconnected from the outside world, passing lakes, crossing rivers, and entering thick, barely visited forest. A good local guide is **Claudio Soto** (page 131). The trail is not technically difficult, and passes two high-altitude points with impressive views of mountains and glaciers: the Portezeulo Los Contrabandistas and Golondrinas.

Estancia Alto Río Cisnes Just before the Argentine border, as the terrain flattens out to Patagonian steppe, a vast shearing shed with the name 'Río Cisnes' written in huge letters across a bright red roof looms ominously. Besides this building is a landing strip. This is a 130,000 hectare functioning sheep farm called Alto Río Cisnes, dating back to 1904. There were three major concessions granted to mega-estancias in the early 20th century: The Industrial Society of Aysén (SIA, land predominantly around Coyhaique); the series of companies that managed the land between Valle Chacabuco and the Baker Delta (see page 164); and Alto Río Cisnes.

The ranch at Alto Río Cisnes was formed in 1904 as the Anglo-Chilean Pastoral Company, consisting of land granted to Joaquín Rodríguez Bravo and Antonio Allende. By 1924 the ranch converted to a new legal structure, renamed the 'Río Cisnes Ranch Cattle Company'. Many of the residents of La Tapera work on the ranch. Some of the buildings were declared National Historic Monuments in 2009, and it is possible to tour the facilities by prior arrangement – call or visit their office in Coyhaique (*Baquedano 776;* ☎ *(67) 2233055 or (2) 1964513 for satellite phone, expensive to call*). This remains a working farm to this day, with 40,000 sheep and some cattle. It is possible to tour the farm.

✪ AS THE CONDOR FLIES

Villa Amengual is 368km south of Puerto Montt, and 470km north of the border crossing at Villa O'Higgins to El Chaltén in Argentina.

6

SEND US YOUR SNAPS!

We'd love to follow your adventures using our *Chile: the Carretera Austral* guide – why not send us your photos and stories via Twitter (@BradtGuides) and Instagram (@bradtguides) using the hashtag #schile. Alternatively, you can upload your photos directly to the gallery on the Carretera Austral destination page via our website (*www.bradtguides.com*).

7

Puerto Aysén and Chacabuco

As the Queulat sub-tropical rainforest fades away, the road continues south beyond the rather obscure detour to La Tapera towards Puerto Aysén and eventually Coyhaique. The Carretera initially continues south from Villa Amengual to a small town often overlooked by visitors – **Mañihuales**, where a landslide in 1966 altered the entire province of Aysén.

Besides a few minor roads to the east, the main points of interest between Mañihuales and Coyhaique are the ports of **Aysén** and **Chacabuco**. Strictly speaking a trip along the Carretera Austral bypasses both these towns and heads directly south to Coyhaique on a gravel road (page 170), so this could be considered a detour. Puerto Aysén's former glory faded thanks to massive deforestation beginning in the 1940s, causing excess sedimentation in the region to clog the port for all but small vessels. The port subsequently moved 14km southwest, and Coyhaique soon took over as the principal city of the region, both economically and culturally. Today, the landscape is characterised by newly planted pine forests and agricultural land, interspersed with lush meadows of brightly coloured lupins and the occasional farm, and the town itself retains a certain charm.

Chacabuco port remains important for local commerce and as an entry/exit point for some visitors, and is also an access point to the **Ventisquero San Rafael** further south. There are some lovely parks in the region, including the **Reserva Nacional Río Simpson**, some decent accommodation and food, and a surprising number of activities.

MAÑIHUALES AND AROUND

Founded in 1962, **Mañihuales** seems to attract only those in search of petrol, with relatively little of interest in the vicinity. It is the closest town for access to the unattractive Toqui mine (although this is not open for visitors and can hardly be described as a highlight) and is consequently home to a number of miners. Mining operations began in 1983, and in 2011 Belgian mining conglomerate Nyrstar acquired the mine and expanded production. The mine produces zinc, lead, silver and gold, and employs 417 people. The region surrounding Mañihuales was routinely destroyed by slash and burn timber practices for much of the early 19th century, evidence of which can be seen to this day. Large sections along the Carretera Austral appear nothing more than tree graveyards, and the mountainsides are scarred with the impact of relentless logging and the subsequent erosion this produces. There is actually a **national reserve** by the town, but it is rarely visited and the tourist information centre closed some years ago. For those genuinely interested in the history of the region it may be worth spending a day in the town, but it is unlikely to qualify as a highlight of a trip along the Carretera Austral. Besides the petrol station there are limited services – there's no ATM or laundry, few shops and little to recommend. The main event of historic importance was the landslide of 1966 which destroyed a large part of the town and had major repercussions across the region, yet is largely forgotten in the annals of history (page 158).

Some 12km **south of Mañihuales**, the Carretera Austral splits (confusingly) into two roads both marked 'Carretera Austral': the gravel route southeast to Coyhaique (page 170) and the paved road southwest towards Aysén and Chacabuco (page 159). Note that the roads around the Toqui mine tend to be in poor condition, periodically destroyed by heavy trucks. Branching off from the direct route to Coyhaique, there is a pleasant detour to **Ñirehuao** and on to the Argentine border along reasonable gravel and undulating hills. This is the only inhabited village in the region, with a hostel (page 156), shop, police station and an emergency medical post. Perhaps for those crossing the border late at night, wishing to get to the border early in the morning, or cyclists, it might be worth a stop. Small ostriches frequent the region, and the road passes various lakes. It also involves a number of minor river crossings, so a high-clearance car might be a wiser choice.

The short road connecting the borders of **Paso Puesto Viejo and Paso Coyhaique** is beautiful. It traverses the border with Argentina, and rarely is the contrast between the two countries so visible: barren wasteland steppe to the east; increasingly green, undulating and populated (mostly by animals) sections to the west. However, this stretch is on very rough gravel, and only suitable for a 4x4.

However, unless actually intending to pass into Argentina, or visit one of the parks in this region, there is little to see and do. For most people, it may be wiser to spend your time further south, or continue north with a full tank of petrol (for those heading south there is no need to refill necessarily, as there is ample petrol in Aysén and Coyhaique).

GETTING THERE
About the route
Villa Amengual to Mañihuales (*57km; under 1hr; paved*) Pleasant paved road with relatively few detours or activities *en route*. The road passes Lago Las Torres and the **Fundo Lago Las Torres** (page 152) to the west, with nice places to picnic. The region is a large valley with flat pastured farmland on either side, flanked by mountains. The scars of deforestation are still visible.

Towards Ñirehuao and Paso Puesto Viejo (*28km from Villa Ortega to Ñirehuao & a further 25km to border; 1hr; gravel*) The few roads to the east of the Carretera in this region are gravel and a high-clearance vehicle capable of minor river crossings is required. The roads to the north head towards the Toqui mine and some minuscule villages along the Argentine border, but it is not possible to cross into Argentina here. The most southern roads in this region are the two main border crossings closest to Coyhaique (Paso Triana and Paso Coyhaique), and in-between lies the largest village in the region – Ñirehuao, 28km east of Villa Ortega. It is a further 25km to the Argentine border. Very limited services are available in this entire region, and cellphone coverage has not reached most of this section.

By bus Mañihuales benefits from its relative proximity to Coyhaique and Aysén and abundant buses pass through the town both south and northbound. Some traverse the longer but paved route via Puerto Aysén, others the direct gravel route to Coyhaique – the time difference is marginal. Mañihuales does not have its own dedicated bus company. There is no formal bus company serving Ñirehuao or on to the border.

WHERE TO STAY, EAT AND DRINK On the plaza above the children's playground in Mañihuales there's an unnamed **bar**, which is the only place in town to get a beer once the restaurants close. Frequented predominantly by employees from the local Toqui mine, it is an interesting opportunity to pay over the odds for mediocre beer and hang out with drunk and occasionally aggressive miners.

La Ruka Cabins (2 cabins) Eusebio Ibar 865, Mañihuales \(67) 2431376, (9) 78003768; e egcaro@hotmail.es. Pleasant cabins on the right-hand side as entering Mañihuales from the south. 2 cabins completed, 2 in construction, all for 4 people (1 dbl bed, 2 sgls). Well-equipped kitchens including microwave, sitting/dining area, Wi-Fi & cable TV, wood-stove heating, hot water. Cash only, but working to resolve this. **$$$**

La Posada del Viajero Bernado O'Higgins 420, Ñirehuao; \(9) 99367701, (9) 66046321; e c-j-hernandez@hotmail.com. The closest accommodation to the Argentine border, & has a small restaurant ($). Contact via email, as there is no phone coverage in Ñirehuao. It is located up the hill from the police station, & is one of the first houses on the left when arriving in the town from the Carretera Austral. **$**

Residencial Mañihuales (5 rooms) Eusebio Ibar 280, Mañihuales; \(67) 2431403; e Pablo.caromansilla@gmail.com; ⊕ all year. The best hostel in town just south of the bridge. Rooms are spacious & light. The room above the kitchen is the warmest, & looks out over the river. The friendly owner, Maria Chiguay Alvarez, has run the hostel for 15 years, & her husband built the bridge. She can provide extensive current information about Mañihuales, having moved here shortly after the flood. Shared gender-specific bathrooms. Basic heating, rickety floorboards, $2,500 for b/fast. No English spoken. The owner will cook meals for guests if arranged in advance. Off-road parking. **$**

La Cocina de Yussef Eusebio Ibar 240, Mañihuales; \(67) 2431469, (9) 76103078; ⊕ noon–23.00. Situated next to Residencial Mañihuales, this place has an impressive collection of hats & a slightly less impressive menu. Cheap, with decent portions. A good chance to catch up on Chilean news with TV blaring permanently. **$–$$**

Cafeteria Luis Nick 250m north of bridge, Mañihuales; \(9) 85285259; ⊕ 07.30–20.00 daily. Located on the Carretera Austral at the northern exit of Mañihuales, this is an ideal place for a quick sandwich, slice of cake or empanada. **$**

PUERTO AYSÉN/PUERTO CHACABUCO

The two towns are often considered a single location connected by a 14km paved road. In reality Chacabuco is a port and little else – unless taking a boat, there is very little reason to visit Chacabuco. The road to Mañihuales, to the northeast, is pleasant but relatively nondescript, although the road to Coyhaique carves straight through the Reserva Nacional Río Simpson. The regions to the immediate north and south of Aysén are worth a visit.

HISTORY What is now Puerto Aysén had been populated since the mid 19th century, principally by Chilotes, German settlers and Argentines, attracted by farming opportunities and cypress extraction. In the early 20th century the Chilean government began awarding concessions, and most importantly to the SIA (page 164). Puerto Aysén was founded in 1913, principally as the location for shipping products out of the region for the SIA. It was the principal population centre of the region and in 1927 was declared the capital, and upgraded to a 'city' in 1928. It soon became the main transport hub between Puerto Montt and Punta Arenas, driven principally around timber and agricultural products. The Ibáñez Bridge over the Río Aysén was inaugurated in 1968, and is the longest suspension bridge in Chile. It was declared a National Monument in 2002, and was the scene of riots of 2012.

Sedimentation began to clog the port of Aysén in the 1960s, and eventually Puerto Chacabuco replaced Puerto Aysén as the principal port in the region. The

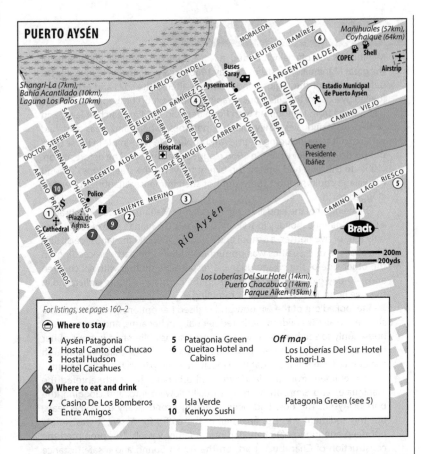

PUERTO AYSÉN

Mañihuales (57km), Coyhaique (64km)

Shangri-La (7km), Bahía Acantilado (10km), Laguna Los Palos (10km)

Buses Saray

Aysenmatic

COPEC Shell

Airstrip

Estadio Municipal de Puerto Aysén

CAMINO VIEJO

Hospital

Puente Presidente Ibáñez

CAMINO A LAGO RIESCO

Police

Plaza de Armas

Cathedral

Río Aysén

Bradt

N

0 ———— 200m
0 ———— 200yds

Los Loberías Del Sur Hotel (14km), Puerto Chacabuco (14km), Parque Aiken (15km) ▾

For listings, see pages 160–2

🛏 **Where to stay**

1 Aysén Patagonia
2 Hostal Canto del Chucao
3 Hostal Hudson
4 Hotel Caicahues
5 Patagonia Green
6 Queitao Hotel and Cabins

Off map
Los Loberías Del Sur Hotel
Shangri-La

❌ **Where to eat and drink**

7 Casino De Los Bomberos
8 Entre Amigos
9 Isla Verde
10 Kenkyo Sushi

Patagonia Green (see 5)

population of Coyhaique had surpassed that of Puerto Aysén by the late 1950s, and in 1975 Puerto Aysén lost its status as capital of the Aysén region to Coyhaique.

Between January and April 2007 a series of earthquakes struck the Fiordo Aysén. The largest of these struck on 21 April (magnitude 6.2) and caused landslides on the surrounding mountains which in turn created waves of up to 6m. Eleven people died, and a number of salmon farms were damaged. The earthquake was felt as far away as Santiago. Aysén's mayor at the time, Óscar Catalán, had complained bitterly that the region had not received sufficient help from the government, and when President Bachelet visited the region she was met with protests and inhabitants waving black flags. Catalán was briefly arrested, according to police for a minor traffic offence. The event raised awareness of the danger of tsunamis in the region, and in particular in narrow fjords where they can occur almost spontaneously from landslides and travel quickly. This event prompted the government to install tsunami warning signs and evacuation routes, which are visible along most coastal regions (especially in Caleta Tortel).

In 2012, Puerto Aysén was the epicentre of a series of protests led by the Movimiento Social por Aysén. The movement was prompted by an ever-increasing cost of living, reduced fishing quotas for local inhabitants, and was also related to the Patagonia Chilena Sin Represas movement (see box, pages 172–4). On 7 February a group of fishermen seized the Ibáñez Bridge. A week later they took over

Mañihuales was officially founded in November 1962, and yet knowledge of the great Mañihuales landslide of May 1966 is scarce. In the 1940s substantial deforestation of the region fundamentally altered the soils and ecosystem, fuelled by a desire to build houses rapidly and to export timber. Juana Carrillo had arrived from Llanquihue with her parents in 1953 in search of land, and settled in Mañihuales. They planted potatoes, wheat and peas and had various fruit trees including cherries and apples. Life was simple in those days, but particularly heavy rains in 1966 clogged the bare soil. The deforestation, visible to this day, had limited the extent to which the steep slopes around the village could support the weight of such immense quantities of water-clogged earth.

On the night of the landslide, the residents of Mañihuales were celebrating a Chilean national holiday in style at the rodeo. On Juana's side of town were only four or five houses, a school and a winery. At 03.00 the landslide struck. The absence of casualties was presumably due to the party proceeding on the other side of the village. Juana, a responsible mother with six children and a 40-day-old baby, had retired from the party some hours earlier, and in the wee hours heard an ominous rumbling.

She looked out of the window and realised her options were limited. She shouted to all the children, gathered her baby in her arms, and fled from the house, only to see her entire worldly possessions obliterated in front of her eyes. Other family members took care of Juana and her children, although she pointedly mentioned that they received no help from the government.

The sediment from this landslide (and others to the south) entered the Mañihuales and Simpson rivers, eventually flowing into, and clogging, the port of Aysén. The port had been suffering economically for some years, but this sediment was the final nail in the coffin for Aysén: it was simply not deep enough to offer safe harbour to larger vessels. This prompted the construction of Chacabuco port, on the Aysén Sound and a safe distance from the estuaries of these rivers. Chacabuco gradually took over as the principal port of the province. Today the town of Aysén bears few signs of its former glory as the main trading hub of the province.

When asked if she ever considered leaving Mañihuales after this event, Juana categorically declared that the idea did not even occur to her, nor after the 1971 eruption of Volcán Hudson that showered the village with ash. What will the ongoing development of the Carretera Austral mean for the village of Mañihuales? Juana believes increased traffic will be good for the village, as they will be able to sell things to people passing through, but some aspects of modernity concern her. 'Before families used to have many children, but no television. Now we have television, but very few children.'

the airport in Melinka. On 14 February 300 people blocked access to Puerto Aysén and Chacabuco, for the first time directly confronting the police. The following day saw protests escalate, with access to Balmaceda airport and the landing strip at Puerto Aysén blocked and various barricades were established in Coyhaique. On 16 February, Coyhaique suffered electricity cuts, a few shops were looted and large parts of the city were blockaded. The following day the road to Mañihuales was blocked, as was the Cruce El Maitén, restricting access to Chile Chico or further south. Gradually media attention shifted towards Coyhaique, where the main police brutalities occurred. Meanwhile the movement reached as far as Villa O'Higgins, at the extreme south of the Carretera Austral, where protesters took over the landing strip.

On 22 February, armed police and Special Forces attempted to retake the Ibáñez Bridge, with full body armour, helmets and shields, riot shotguns and tear gas. Nine people were wounded and five arrested, but the citizens of Puerto Aysén were able to drive back the police by the early hours. The police attempted again to secure the bridge, attacking three groups of journalists from Radio Santa Maria, Chilevisión and Canal 13. Two people lost their eyesight in the fighting that ensued. The director of the National Institute of Human Rights declared: 'there was a disproportionate use of riot shotguns, used as a deterrent, but it seems according to all the data and testimonies gathered – that guns were aimed not pointing upwards (the correct procedure), but directly at the people.'

Civil unrest has largely ceased, but remains a latent danger in the region – most of the demands of the protestors have not been met. The HidroAysén project remains on hold, but not cancelled, thanks to the Bachelet government. Meanwhile a lesser-known hydro project to be run by Energía Austral (a joint venture between Swiss Glencore and Australian Origin Energy) is located a mere 45km from Puerto Aysén, damming the Río Cuervo. This 640 MW plant was approved by the state in 2013. Environmental activists submitted a plea to the Supreme Court, but on 21 August the court granted the environmental permits for construction to begin.

GETTING THERE
About the route
Mañihuales to Aysén (*57km; under 1hr; paved*) Excellent paved road for the first 12km, where the road forks. The western fork continues to Puerto Aysén, the eastern fork to Coyhaique. Somewhat confusingly both are referred to as the Carretera Austral. In fact, the direct, gravel route to Coyhaique is the original Ruta 7, and the road to Aysén is Highway 240.

Beyond the junction the paved road is reasonable quality all the way to Aysén, weaving alongside the Río Mañihuales through lush fields of purple, pink and white lupins. Some 10km past the junction heading south, the road crosses the river at Puente Mañihuales – a spectacular bridge worth a photo stop. Note the deforestation still visible along this section of road – the dead tree trunks are vestiges from the timber industry stretching back to the 1940s. Smallholder farmland with horses, cattle and sheep dominate this region: from here until Lago General Carrera agriculture and livestock farming is a major industry. This is a pleasant road with plenty of sweeping views over the valley, and endless hairpin bends – great fun on a fast motorbike but be careful when the road is wet.

Aysén to Chacabuco (*14km; 15mins; paved*) This section passes Parque Aiken (pages 163–4), but is otherwise nondescript.

By bus Frequent buses travel between Aysén/Chacabuco and Coyhaique (such as the hourly service with Buses Suray). Some northbound buses from Coyhaique do not go via Puerto Aysén, but head directly north along the gravel section of the Carretera towards Mañihuales, so it is often necessary to travel to Coyhaique first for connections.

By ferry A twice-weekly service operates between Chacabuco and Quellón (Chiloé), but this is quite slow (*28hrs*) – it is quicker to take the direct ferry that

7

stops only in Melinka. Ferries also run twice weekly between Puerto Montt and Chacabuco, but this is a long journey (*24hrs*). See page 45 for details.

TOUR OPERATORS

Atex Patagonia   km3.4, Camino Lago Riesco, Puerto Aysén; ✆(9) 89454078, (9) 83383247; e atexpatagonia@gmail.com; www. atexpatagonia.webnode.cl. Note this is not the access road to Lago Riesco from Chacabuco but along the south side of Río Aysén. Bilingual guides (English, Portuguese, German & French) offering a range of trips & logistics in the region, as well as kayak courses. Kayaking, floating, trekking & fishing along Río Blanco & Río Simpson. Also offer tours to further locations, including to the Campo de Hielo Norte (Northern Ice Field). Guided tours within the Reserva Nacional Río Simpson. Can also arrange multi-day treks to the spectacular mountain range beyond Lago Los Palos into Campo El Tabo. Do not offer accommodation, but have a hydro-massage spa within an arrayan forest at their Río Aysén base.

El Pionero   Camino Lago Riesco, Puerto Aysén; ✆(9) 90885898; e elpioneroaysen@hotmail.cl; www.elpioneroaysen.cl. A simple tour operator

offering trips in an 8-person boat along the Aysén Sound to a series of islands & some hot springs in the Cinco Hermanas National Monument.

Fishing Naked   km7, towards Lago los Palos, north of Puerto Aysén; ✆(9) 94194974, (9) 90790660; e fishingnaked53@gmail.com. (Fully clothed) sport & fly-fishing trips on Lago los Palos & along the Río Palos (salmon, trout, chinook, etc), $20,000pp for 2hrs, max 4 people. Also rent kayaks – ½ day is $10,000/15,000 sgl/dbl, $20,000 for the whole day regardless of size. Bicycle hire by hr/½ day/full day for $2,500/9,000/18,000 respectively. Can also arrange trips to other regions, & transport to/from Aysén for an additional cost.

Patagonia Green   Lago Riesco 350, Puerto Aysén; ✆(67) 2336796; e infogreen@ patagoniachile.cl; www.patagoniagreen.cl. The hotel & restaurant of the same name run a variety of tours, but the main one is to the Ventisquero San Rafael. Most visitors stay for 2 or 3 days to combine with this day trip. Bike rental also available.

WHERE TO STAY

Aysén   *Map, page 157*

Below we have listed those places we would recommend, but there are other options in town if the following are booked up.

Aysén Patagonia   (9 sgls, 5 dbls) Sargento Aldea 560; ✆(67) 2330928, (9) 97896938; e recepcion@hotel-aysenpatagonia.cl; www. hotel-aysenpatagonia.cl; ⊕ all year. The most upmarket hotel in town, all standard facilities provided, including off-road parking, laundry, central heating & good-quality service. Late check-outs are possible. The hotel has a decent restaurant (⊕ 08.00–23.00, 15.00–23.00 on w/ends; $$$) & a reasonably priced menu of the day. It is located 1 block from the plaza, & despite catering principally to business clientele the hotel retains a Patagonian feeling. A convenient, well-located & well-maintained upper-end option boasting all the facilities a weary traveller from the Carretera might require. Reservations do not require a deposit, & foreigners do not pay VAT reducing the price by approximately 20%. Credit cards accepted. $$$$

Patagonia Green   (6 rooms, 4 cabins) Lago Riesco 350; ✆(67) 2336796; e infogreen@

patagoniachile.cl; www.patagoniagreen.cl; ⊕ all year. Probably the best accommodation option in Puerto Aysén. It is located across the Río Aysén approximately 15mins' walk from the city centre, & is more suited for those with private transport, although the hotel has a private van & taxis are easily arranged. However, this is an exceptional place to stay. The cabins are centrally heated & offer Wi-Fi, a full kitchen & comfortable seating area. They range in size & can accommodate from 2 to 5 people, but don't include b/fast. There are 3 dbl & 3 twin rooms, each with balconies & b/fast included. Staff are friendly & knowledgeable, & speak Italian, English, Spanish & German. The entire facility has been built gradually over a 15-year period to a very high standard. The 'green' refers both to the lush vegetation that surrounds the entire hotel & cabins, & also to a focus on environmental sustainability. The hotel recycles where possible, uses low-energy lighting, has central heating without burning wood, & is certified by the Responsible Tourism Institute. Particularly child-friendly, with a large lawn & playground (without direct access to the river). Also offers tours (see above). Credit cards accepted. $$$$

Hostal Canto del Chucao (6 rooms, 3 cabins, 3 large tunnel tents) Teniente Merino 724; (67) 2330187, (9) 96820822; e cantochucao@gmail.com; www.cantodelchucao.cl. Close to the central plaza, currently expanding to the next door property adding an additional 7 rooms, basic b/fast included. Tunnel tents are a novelty, 3 beds, a bathroom & reasonable ceilings, reminiscent of a Mongolian *ger*. Run by a pleasant, chatty family. Can arrange laundry. Wi-Fi, off-road parking, but no English or central heating (but this is planned). Stoves in the cabins & the tunnel tents. Reservations by phone or email, no need to leave a deposit. Not good value as it is a little run down – there is more comfortable accommodation available at this price. **$$$**

Queitao Hotel and Cabins (2 rooms, 5 cabins) General Marchant 640; (67) 2336635, (9) 62368335; e reservas@queitaopatagonia.cl; www.queitaopatagonia.cl. Ocean theme runs through the main building, with a bar that looks like a boat & old scuba kit on display. Basic restaurant/cafeteria (**$$**), only 2 rooms of average quality but overpriced albeit with b/fast included, & located just above the restaurant. Cabins are better value, accommodating up to 7 people, good sitting area & well equipped. Caters to companies mainly. Speak English, Wi-Fi, parking, laundry. Redeeming feature is the spa (hot-tub, dry sauna & various treatments). Not best value in town. Accepts credit cards. **$$$**

Shangri-La (4 dbls, 3 4-person cabins, 3 7-person cabins) km7, Camino al Lago los Palos; (9) 77381406, (9) 63040655; e complejoshangri.la@gmail.com; www.shangrilapatagonia.com; ⊕ all year. A relatively new option on the road to the Lago Los Palos. Set in a large pasture with access to the river, this is certainly a peaceful option away from the relative chaos of Aysén. The rooms are simple, & the cabins are probably a wiser choice. They are well equipped with a full kitchen, decent beds & a sofa-bed for 2 people.

The larger cabins have a dbl bed in 1 room, & bunk beds in the 2nd room with a sgl bed on the floor, & a dbl sofa-bed in the sitting area. Hot water a wood-stove for heating. They work closely with the Eco Lodge next door & can arrange fishing, boat trips, kayaking & horseriding. Has cellphone coverage despite being 7km from Aysén. Does not offer food, as most guests are self-catering, but a neighbour runs the 'Buena Vida' food service nearby. Can pay by credit card if booked through Queitao (see opposite). **$$$**

Hostal Hudson (10 dbls) Teniente Merino 1080; (9) 99645253; e hostalhudson@hotmail.com; www.hostalhudson.cl; ⊕ all year. A basic, good-value hostel by the river, 3 blocks from central square. Wi-Fi available, can arrange tours & also offer laundry. Large homely communal area complete with projector & screen. Shared bathrooms. **$$**

Chacabuco

Los Loberías Del Sur Hotel (60 rooms) José Miguel Carrera 50, Puerto Chacabuco; (67) 2351112; e info@loberiasdelsur.cl; www.loberiasdelsur.cl. The only official 5-star hotel in the province of Aysén, & the largest hotel in the entire region. This is a fully fledged luxury hotel with all the trimmings – heated pool, sauna, games room with a decent pool table, gym, events room, laundry, Wi-Fi, decent restaurant (**$$$$**), bar, small business centre, & b/fast inclded. The only thing they don't offer is massages. Lovely views out to the Aysén Sound, & the port itself is visible from the hotel. The company also owns the nearby Parque Aiken for hikes & water activities, & a catamaran that services the Ventisquero San Rafael – one of the highlights of the entire region. Packages combining such tours are available. The rack price is punchy, but most guests combine with a package trip to the glacier. A very comfortable & convenient option for those wishing to visit the glacier (page 163). English spoken. Credit cards accepted. **$$$$$**

✕ WHERE TO EAT AND DRINK *Map, page 157*

The following entries are in Puerto Aysén – for eating options in Chacabuco, Los Loberías Hotel (see above) has a restaurant.

✕ Entre Amigos Sargento Aldea 1077; (67) 2333433; ⊕ 18.00–02.00 Mon–Sat. The place to go for a good parrilla in town – piles of various meats & a generous helping of potatoes for up to 6 people. The menu also has all the Chilean classics

& standard dishes you could hope for: sandwiches, various options a lo pobre, a whole slew of pizzas. Locals say the place is of higher quality than other dining options in Aysén, though the price remains reasonable. **$$$**

161

✘ **Patagonia Green** Lago Riesco 350; ☎(67) 2336796; e infogreen@patagoniachile.cl; www. patagoniagreen.cl; ⏰ 12.45–14.30 & 19.45–22.00 Mon–Sat. Excellent restaurant, gourmet but informal – can wear shorts & flip-flops & not feel awkward. Wide range of seafood dishes, but the speciality is the conger eel. Short walk over the bridge from downtown Aysén, but worth the effort. Also offer accommodation & tours (page 160). **$$$$**

✘ **Isla Verde** Teniente Merino 170; ☎(67) 2334583; ⏰ noon–16.30 & 20.00–23.00 daily. The most formal place in Aysén, doubling as a mini museum, with some interesting black-&-white photos of the town before the flood of 1966, & a selection of clocks & old telephones. The food is decent, & the prices are surprisingly reasonable for the décor. The speciality is seafood, & the eel soup is exquisite. On Sun it is one of the only restaurants open. The only downside is the annoying background music. **$$$**

✘ **Kenkyo Sushi** Sargento Aldea 633-B; ☎(67) 2524039, (9) 71372306; ⓕ Kenkyosushi; ⏰ noon–midnight Mon–Sat, 14.00–22.30 Sun. A gem of a restaurant run by an entrepreneurial woman, Valeska, with big ambitions to create Aysén's finest Asian restaurant. Ingredients are locally sourced when available, from fresh salmon from the fjord to local boutique regional beers. Standard sushi options available, but with some interesting local adaptations. The Aysén roll, for example, contains avocado, asparagus, meat & cheese, a combination

rarely found in Japan. There is also a range of exotic Pisco sours made from local fruits & berries, such as the calafate Pisco sour, well known in town, & other variations include blueberry, rhubarb, rose mosqueta, ginger & cardamom. The food itself is surprisingly good & reasonably priced. This is a rare opportunity to deviate from standard Chilean fare. The local community was slow to adopt sushi into their diets & the restaurant catered mainly to tourists, but within a year Valeska had convinced them of the merits of raw fish, & the restaurant now has a thriving take-away business, & has recently expanded to this more central location. Also serve proper coffee, cakes & sandwiches. Takes credit cards. **$$$**

✘ **Casino De Los Bomberos** Teniente Merino 600; ☎(9) 97392096; ⏰ 08.30–22.00 Mon–Sat, 09.00–17.00 Sun. A local favourite with excellent-value tasty food & large portions. The service is good, with friendly staff, & the food arrives quickly. The blackboard menu of the day includes an entrée, main, dessert, fruit juice & tea or coffee, though you need to arrive early. The main is usually salmon, merluza, turkey or beef with the choice of a salad, mashed potatoes or chips. An adequate selection of beer & wine is available. The atmosphere leaves a bit to be desired; all the walls are painted with lime green paint & there is no further attempt to furbish the restaurant. It is also a café between main mealtimes with a selection of cakes. No reservations. **$$**

OTHER PRACTICALITIES There is **petrol** available in Aysén (COPEC and Shell) and Chacabuco (COPEC). For **shops**, options are limited in Chacabuco, but you'll find a couple along Aysén's main street (Sargento Aldea), and the **tourist information centre** is on Jose Miguel Carrera on the eastern side of plaza just past Banco Estado.

Laundry
Aysenmatic Sargento Aldea 1415, Puerto Aysén; ☎(67) 2330433, (9) 83674219; ⏰ 09.30–14.30
& 16.00–20.00 Mon–Fri. Laundry & dry-cleaning service. Priced per kg.

WHAT TO SEE AND DO For those not intending to head further south or with less time (and a bigger budget), Puerto Aysén offers the opportunity to visit one of the Carretera's undisputed highlights, the spectacular **Ventisquero San Rafael**, as well as opportunities to visit various nearby lakes and parks. Puerto Aysén is also used as a base from which to visit the **Reserva Nacional Río Simpson**.

Bahía Acantilado A modest beach. The fact that it is so popular in summer with the residents of Puerto Aysén may be more a symptom of the lack of any other beaches in the vicinity rather than the inherent beauty of this beach. It is, as the name suggests, next to a cliff.

Laguna Los Palos A lovely detour on a sunny day, through verdant forestation of arrayan trees and up to a sparkling lake surrounded by snow-capped mountains. The views across Laguna los Palos are breathtaking, and if ever you had any concern about the impact of salmon farming, observe the impact simply upon the view over the lake of the bizarre and solitary salmon farm which was permitted in this otherwise pristine environment. In fact the salmon farm, owned by Aqua Chile, was abandoned approximately five years ago and the company never bothered to clean up the mess it had left, spoiling the view for generations to come.

Head north out of Puerto Aysén on Eusebio Ibar Street, until leaving the main inhabited area, and turn left along Pangal towards a small, scenic bridge with some small fishing boats (Puerto Palos). After the bridge turn right (ie: north) towards Lago los Palos, or continue straight towards Bahía Acantilado. Reaching the beach is possible in any vehicle, but head north towards Lago los Palos only with a car capable of traversing moderate gravel. Beyond the end of the lake, a 4x4 is required. The road weaves through spectacular mountains, snow-capped peaks visible, some farmland, and then a few cabins. Various outfitters along the road offer a range of activities, from treks to horseriding, kayaking, boat trips, fishing excursions and cycling trips. It is possible to continue beyond the lake to Campo El Tabo, but this is private property and has to be arranged through a tour operator. **Atex Patagonia** (page 160) offer multi-day treks in this region.

SIGHTSEEING AND EXCURSIONS
Ventisquero San Rafael (*www.loberiasdelsur.cl/en/tarifas*; *prices from US$240 to US$380pp, under-5s pay half, discounts for over-55s, packages combining accommodation plus glacier trip available*) Despite being located some 200km north of the Ventisquero San Rafael, Puerto Aysén is one of only two main access points (the other being from Bahía Exploradores, accessed from Puerto Río Tranquilo – page 209) for those wishing to visit the glacier. And, although tours from Puerto Aysén travel a substantially greater distance, the experience is five-star, compared with the more arduous trip available in the south. All tour operators and hostels offering this tour are ultimately selling the same service, provided by the same company that owns Los Loberías del Sur Hotel and Parque Aiken. The round trip takes a full day, travelling by fast, comfortable catamaran. The frequency of boats depends on the time of year: there are between 11 and 15 trips per month from October to April, and weekends only the rest of the year (except July), and the price includes all food and drink, plus the zodiac trip to the glacier through the icebergs. The glacier is spectacular and undoubtedly a highlight of the entire Carretera Austral (see page 209 for a full description).

Parque Aiken to Lago Riesco (✆ (67) 2351112) The park is owned by Loberías del Sur and accessed via a short gravel road approximately 4km before arriving at Chacabuco. The 250ha park has four trails, and contains a simple visitor centre able to provide information and maps. The **River Trail** (*2km one-way*) follows the El Salto Creek from the visitors' centre to a waterfall, and the **Waterfall Trail** (*1km round trip*) connects the road to the waterfall. The longest trail is the **Arrayanes Trail** (*2.5km one-way*), which can be extended to the quincho by the lake by walking a further 600m (technically the **Lake Trail**). Bilingual guides are available. Vegetation includes cafayate, michay and Chilcos shrubs, plus the common maqui shrub which is able to grow in burnt and eroded soils, producing a small fruit that is used as a colorant for wines and other drinks. The park has various ferns, lichens and mosses, including the *Lophosoria quadripinnata*, which is apparently unique

7

to the region around the waterfall at the end of the River Trail. Trees include the arrayan, notros, tepa and myrtaceous, as well as a 300-year-old Chilean myrtle (*Luma apiculate*). Animal species include pudús and pumas (apparently), huet huet, kingfishers, foxes, woodpeckers, and Chucaos. The large bandurria (*Theristicus caudatus*) is common across the park as well as the region, clearly visible prodding the ground or marsh searching for small insects, spiders and frogs. The park also includes a small botanic garden located approximately halfway along the road through the park, with 32 native trees and bushes. Alas the view over the lake has also been spoilt somewhat by an ugly salmon farm. From November to April it is possible to fish in the lake (with a licence; brown trout are common).

Other lakes south of Puerto Aysén It is possible to drive along the south side of the Río Aysén and then along the Río Blanco to **Lago Portales**, or continue along the Río Riesco towards **Lago Riesco** (the southeastern side of the lake, as opposed to access from Parque Aiken which reaches the northern extreme of the lake). The road continues to the smaller **Laguna Alta** and **Laguna Baja**.

RESERVA NACIONAL RÍO SIMPSON

(*www.conaf.cl/parques/reserva-nacional-rio-simpson; entrance $1,000*) Situated on the main road between Puerto Aysén and Coyhaique, the Reserva Nacional Río Simpson is a small (41,620ha) reserve that covers the mountains and valleys to the west and northwest of Coyhaique. It was established to restore the delicate ecosystem following environmental damage caused by deforestation in the early 20th century. The Río Simpson is the main watercourse in this region. There is a small native forest and wildlife information centre at the park headquarters, where a description of the El Pescador trail is available in English or Spanish. There is a **CONAF campsite** (*$6,000pp; booking not essential*) on the river 2km towards Coyhaique from the park headquarters. There are ten camping sites that consist of a covered hut suitable for wet weather, with a concrete floor, table and bench seat and a built-in barbecue area. There is also a large quincho for 30 people. The park can also be accessed from Coyhaique via the Área de Protección del Huemul Río Claro (a protected area within the national reserve where huemules reside) along a 16km trail passable only in a 4x4.

One of the first explorers in this region was Captain Enrique Simpson whose name was bestowed upon the river. At the beginning of the 20th century the first settlers opened up this route to provide access from the port of Aysén to Coyhaique. In 1904 the livestock company SIA (Sociedad Industrial de Aysén) hired people to build this notorious road. It is said that the forest lumberjacks had to cut 100,000 4m-long coigüe poles, cut in half to cover 20km of swamp land to complete this route. In 1920 and 1948 extensive fires ripped through this valley due to cut and burn agriculture practices in this period in order to clear bush land for farming purposes. The subsequent land erosion in the Valle Río Simpson, from the 1966 floods (page 158), was catastrophic and is partly responsible for the closure of the port at Puerto Aysén due to river sedimentation blocking the river from larger boats. As a result of this manmade disaster, the Chile Tax Authority acquired private land in the valley to form the Reserva Nacional Río Simpson to protect this fragile ecosystem.

Today the Río Simpson is renowned for its great **fly-fishing** and is considered to be one of the top four fly-fishing rivers on the planet. There is also a new, well-maintained **trail** that follows the northern river bank and is suitable for children.

ABOUT THE ROUTE
Puerto Aysén to Reserva Nacional Río Simpson (*31km; 30mins; paved*)
Follow the main road (Ruta 240) between Puerto Aysén and Coyhaique, driving through the main 'T' intersection at km17 where the Carretera Austral heads north towards Villa Mañihuales. Follow the Río Simpson into the river valley for a further 14km. The entrance for the reserve and the trail is directly across from the shrine of San Sebastian. After leaving the reserve, the **road to Coyhaique** continues through temperate rainforest with stunning views of the river to rolling grassland within a few kilometres. Coyhaique is 32km south of the reserve entrance.

By public transport Buses Suray run hourly between Puerto Aysén and Coyhaique – ask the driver to drop you at the park's entrance (but be vigilant in case he forgets). To continue from the park to Coyhaique, simply flag a passing bus down.

THE EL PESCADOR TRAIL (*The Fishermen's Trail; 2.5km; 1½hrs one-way; easy*) is part of the original trail used by the early explorers and settlers and winds through beautiful native forest with stunning river views. The trailhead is 32km north of Coyhaique towards Aysén or 31km east of Aysén. The changing landscape from Coyhaique evolves from rolling grassland to temperate rainforest within a few kilometres. The entrance for the reserve and to the trail is directly across from the shrine of San Sebastian. The hike starts in a pine forest which is part of a reforestation initiative but soon enters the native forests of the temperate rainforest ecosystem. It follows the Río Simpson for the entire trek, from sections of relative calm to roaring white-water rapids. Keep eyes peeled for a variety of wildlife and plant species. The native vegetation is mainly the mixed forest of common coigüe and lenga with some ñire in the humid sectors. There is also a mix of exotic shrub species introduced to try and control the erosion after the deforestation. The chilco (*Fusia magallanica*) is abundant and has adapted very well to this environment – many of those who live in sub-tropical climates will easily recognise this distinctive bright red-and-purple flower as the common fuchsia that grows prolifically in many gardens.

After the moss-covered stone house is a section with challenging rapids that are popular with local kayakers. Thereafter the trail leaves the forest and emerges into a section predominantly covered with the giant leaves of the nalco plant – a rhubarb plant on steroids – and an impressive display of the colourful red flowers from the Chilco bush.

⊕ AS THE CONDOR FLIES

Puerto Aysén is 435km from Puerto Montt and 395km from the border crossing south of Villa O'Higgins at the extreme southern end of the Carretera Austral. Southbound condors are a little over halfway to their final destination.

8

Coyhaique

Telephone code: 67

Coyhaique is the only city of notable size along the Carretera Austral. Previously visitors would rarely stop here for anything more than a change of clothes, a bite to eat, to pick up provisions, repair vehicles or to catch a bus north or south. However, this situation is starting to change. The shopping possibilities have grown substantially, to include camping gear, clothing of all qualities, bicycle accessories, well-stocked pharmacies and most of the essentials one might expect, albeit at elevated prices. There is even a book shop! The city boasts an ever-increasing array of restaurants, including sushi and Peruvian cuisine (there is not yet an Indian restaurant). There are garages, roadside cafés, ATMs, tour operators, hotels of every conceivable price range, and a very fine micro-brewery. It is the logistical hub for the entire region – book ferry tickets and flights here. Nightlife is reasonable in high season, but there is no cinema. The weather is pleasant in the summer, occasionally reaching the high 20s (centigrade), but a raincoat is required all year. Ironically for so remote a city in such a pristine environment, pollution is a problem in winter, mainly due to wood-burning stoves. The city is safe, laidback, surrounded by forests, mountains and rivers, and increasingly bohemian.

However, the architecture is fairly drab and beyond the few blocks comprising downtown Coyhaique there is relatively little to do. Public transport is chaotic, confusing and frustrating to arrange. It is likely that within a few days the call of the Carretera Austral will lure visitors away from the city and back into the stunning region of which Coyhaique is the capital.

HISTORY

Prior to the arrival of the settlers, mainly of Spanish descent, this region was occupied by the various nomadic tribes of the Tehuelche (also called Aonikenk), Kawésqar (Alacalufes) and Chonos. Most had been driven away, killed or died of disease by the mid 19th century. The first documented record of what is now the city of Coyhaique was by Rear Admiral Enrique Simpson Baeza, who visited the area in December 1872 while studying the lakes and rivers of the region. Permanent inhabitants began arriving in the late 19th century, followed shortly thereafter by large cattle herders.

Settlement was facilitated by the state awarding large tracts of land to private individuals, as in other parts of the province. In 1903 Luis Aguirre, originally from Punta Arenas, was awarded a 22-year concession over the valleys of Coyhaique, Mañihuales and Ñirehuao. These were subsequently ceded to the wealthy industrialist Mauricio Braun, who formed the Sociedad Industrial de Aysén (SIA – Aysén Industrial Society; page 164). Braun was the industrialist behind the failed development around Caleta Tortel which resulted in the mysterious deaths of approximately 80 people in the winter of 1906 (see box, pages 246–7). SIA established its main facilities at the confluence of the Coyhaique and Simpson rivers, and began mass deforestation in order to create space for cattle grazing. This involved cutting and burning large tracts of native forest (some estimates suggest as much as three million hectares), the damage of which is still visible to this day.

SIA failed to comply with the terms of the concession, namely in building roads, the government began to intervene more forcefully in the 1920s, and in 1927 created the Territory of Aysén, with its capital in Puerto Aysén. The following year Luis Gonzalez Marchant established the village of Baquedano, which was formally incorporated on 12 October 1929.

Naming the village in honour of the Chilean military commander Manuel Baquedano González turned out to be unwise, as post invariably was sent to the better-known town of Baquedano in northern Chile. Thus, in January 1934 the state decided to change the name of the town to to Coyhaique. The origin of the name is the subject of some dispute. In Mapudungun, the language of the Mapuche people of the region, *koi* meant 'water', or 'lagoon'. However, in the language of the Tehuelches, *coi* meant *coihue* (the tree). Given that the region has abundant trees and water both explanations seem reasonable. *Áiken* in Mapudungun means 'camp', while *aike* in Tehuelche means 'place' – comparable meanings. Thus the name Coyhaique broadly means 'place of water or trees'.

The population grew as more settlers were attracted to the region for its rich logging opportunities. The town also became the hub for livestock trading. By 1940 there were over 4,000 inhabitants in the town, but it was still eclipsed by Puerto Aysén, with nearly 6,000, and the dominant port of the region. The slightly confusing pentagonal plaza in downtown Coyhaique was built in 1945, but it was not until July 1947 that Coyhaique became a formal municipality, and built the town hall the following year. By 1959 the town's population had overtaken that of Puerto Aysén and Coyhaique was upgraded to a department. In part this was likely due to Coyhaique's location serving as a trade hub for the region, being closer to the Argentine border, and also for the relative demise of the port at Puerto Aysén in the 1960s.

A livestock crisis in the 1970s left the region heavily dependent on public investments, and following the overthrow of Salvador Allende in 1973, Pinochet decided to move the regional capital from Puerto Aysén to Coyhaique. The following year work resumed on building road connections in the region in what subsequently became the Carretera Austral.

According to the 2012 census Coyhaique has just under 60,000 inhabitants.

GETTING THERE

ABOUT THE ROUTE

Puerto Aysén to Coyhaique (*63km; 1hr; paved*) The road is initially flat and opens out into a wide valley, leaving the snow-capped mountains of Puerto Aysén in the distance. Road quality is good and there is reasonable traffic along this route, connecting two of the most populated towns of the entire Carretera Austral. However, take care of unexpected pot-holes and subsidence when approaching Coyhaique. The road follows the Río Simpson and passes through the centre of the Reserva Nacional Río Simpson, with the valley gradually narrowing to offer some fantastic views down to the river, and passing through the only tunnel along the entire Carretera Austral (Túnel Farelló). Various waterfalls can be seen along the route, and plenty of farmland and fields bursting with purple and white lupins, with

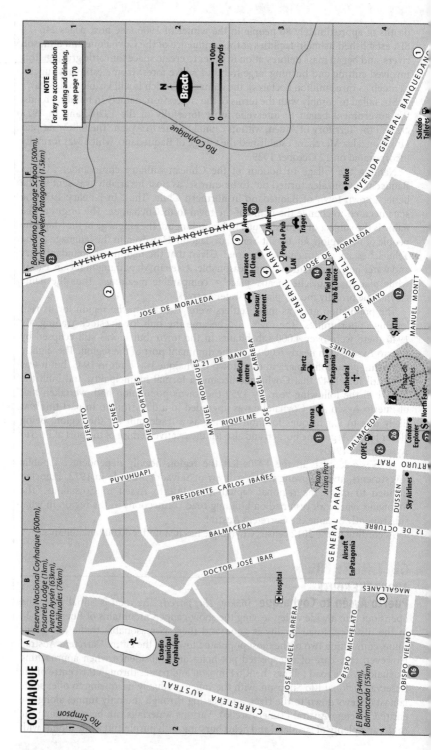

COYHAIQUE

168

NOTE
For key to accommodation and eating and drinking, see page 170.

Río Coyhaique

Baquedano Language School (500m),
Turismo Ayelen Patagonia (1.5km)

Reserva Nacional Coyhaique (500m),
Pasarela Lodge (1km),
Puerto Aysén (63km),
Mañihuales (76km)

Estadio
Municipal
Coyhaique

Río Simpson

CARRETERA AUSTRAL

El Blanco (34km),
Balmaceda (55km)

AVENIDA GENERAL BANQUEDANO

Police

Aerocord
Akelarre
Pepe Le Pub
Trager
LAN

Lavaseco
All Clean

Piel Roja
Pub & Dance

Recasur/
Econorent

JOSÉ DE MORALEDA

JOSÉ DE MORALEDA

21 DE MAYO

Medical
centre

Hertz

Pura
Patagonia

Cathedral

Varona

EJERCITO

CISNES

PUYUHUAPI

PRESIDENTE CARLOS IBÁÑES

BALMACEDA

DOCTOR JOSÉ IBAR

DIEGO PORTALES

MANUEL RODRIGUES

JOSÉ MIGUEL CARRERA

RIQUELME

Hospital

Plaza
Arturo Prat

Airsoft
EnPatagonia

Sky Airlines

Condor
Explorer

North Face

COPEC

BALMACEDA

ARTURO PRAT

DUSSEN

12 DE OCTUBRE

GENERAL PARA

MAGALLANES

OBISPO MICHELATO

OBISPO VIELMO

JOSÉ MIGUEL CARRERA

Plaza de
Armas

ATM

ATM

MANUEL MONTT

BULNES

PARRA

GENERAL

CONDELL

Salcedo
Talleres

0   100m
0   100yds

N

Bradt

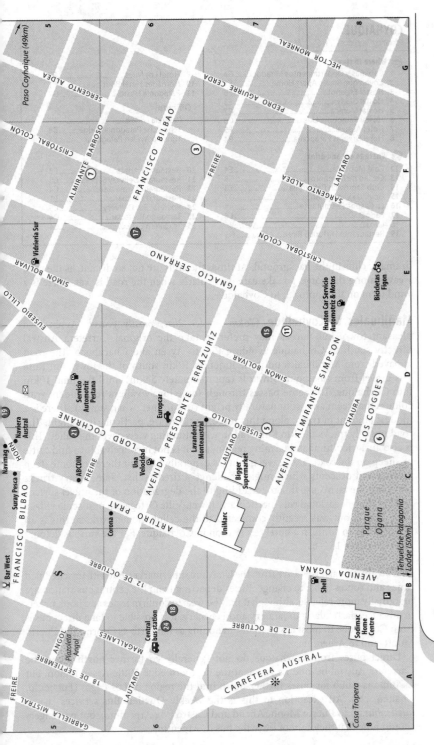

Paso Coyhaique (49km)

SERGENTO ALDEA

ALMIRANTE BARROSO

CRISTÓBAL COLÓN

FRANCISCO BILBAO

HÉCTOR MONREAL

PEDRO AGUIRRE CERDA

FREIRE

①

③

SARGENTO ALDEA

LAUTARO

CRISTÓBAL COLÓN

IGNACIO SERRANO

⑰

SIMÓN BOLÍVAR

Vidriería Sur

EUSEBIO LILLO

PRESIDENTE ERRÁZURIZ

⑮

⑪

SIMÓN BOLÍVAR

AVENIDA ALMIRANTE SIMPSON

Huston Car Servicio
Automotriz & Motos

Bicicletas
Figon

Servicio
Automotriz
Pestana

LORD COCHRANE

Europcar

Lavandería
Monteaustral

EUSEBIO LILLO

LAUTARO

⑤

CHAURA

LOS COIGÜES

⑥

Naviera
Austral

⑲

HORN

⑳

Navimag

Suray Pesca

Bar West

FRANCISCO BILBAO

ABCDIN

FREIRE

Una
Velocidad

AVENIDA PRESIDENTE ERRÁZURIZ

ARTURO PRAT

Corona

Bigger
Supermarket

UniMarc

Parque
Ogana

Tehuelche Patagonia
Lodge (500m)

ANGOL
Plazoleta
Angol

18 DE SEPTIEMBRE

GABRIELA MISTRAL

FREIRE

LAUTARO

MAGALLANES

12 DE OCTUBRE

Central
bus station

⑱

㉔

AVENIDA OGANA

12 DE OCTUBRE

Sodimac
Home
Centre

Shell

CARRETERA AUSTRAL

Casa Tropera

169

dramatic cliffs in the background. At times the cliffs are not so distant, as the road weaves along the gorge, so take care particularly when the road is wet. There is a wind farm on the approach to Coyhaique.

Mañihuales to Coyhaique (*76km, under 2hrs; mostly gravel*) Aysén is a pleasant town, but purists may prefer to take the original Carretera Austral directly south to Coyhaique avoiding Puerto Aysén and Chacabuco. The road is paved from Mañihuales until the junction 12km south of the town, but Ruta 7 is gravel from this point onwards (approximately 54km) until the final 10km into Coyhaique. The route passes through some lovely valleys resplendent with colours that seem almost unnaturally bright (in summer, when sunny). There is a modest amount of traffic along this route, so take care, particularly at night. The road initially tracks the Río Emperador, with stunning views over the valley. This is also an agricultural and farming region, and it is not inconceivable to find cattle or sheep on the road. The gravel quality is generally fine, but there are some steep ascents and descents which might challenge a tired cyclist. Some heavy trucks servicing the farms use this road, adding to the degradation of the gravel surface and creating occasional ruts, particularly if wet. Villa Ortega is a miniscule village with a shop, but was recently connected to the cellphone network, so this is an opportunity to confirm a hotel reservation in Coyhaique. For the various detours east, see pages 154–6.

BY BUS Informal buses leave from the UniMarc supermarket, but with unscheduled times and routes liable to change. Buses departing from the central bus station are marginally more reliable, although it may be wise to confirm times and book tickets in advance, particularly in January and February. It is possible to take direct buses from Coyhaique to most destinations, including as far north as Osorno and Puerto Montt, and to Argentina.

Direct buses from Coyhaique do not generally go further **north** along the Carretera Austral beyond La Junta, at the northern edge of the Aysén region, but La Junta is a hub for buses further north into the region of Los Lagos (Futaleufú, Chaitén, etc). An exception to this is the weekly **Queilén Bus** services (*www. queilenbus.cl*) to Puerto Montt, Ancud and Castro (via Argentina), but passengers should note that they cannot leave the bus in Argentina.

Southbound buses from Coyhaique generally go no further than Cochrane, but likewise, connecting buses to Caleta Tortel and Villa O'Higgins depart from Cochrane. There are occasional direct buses to Puerto Cisnes, but failing that, take any northbound bus to the Cisnes junction and then take a local bus. There are direct buses to Chile Chico (via Puerto Ibáñez and crossing the lake), and Buses Transaustral Patagonia offer a twice-weekly service to Comodoro Rivadavia (Argentina).

Despite Coyhaique serving as a natural hub for public transport along the Carretera Austral, many destinations off the main road are not served and must be arranged locally. Given the broader unreliability of buses in the region, such connections incur an element of risk, thus building time into your itinerary is essential.

BY AIR Balmaceda airport is 55km to the southeast (page 186). **Sky Airlines** (*Arturo Prat 203; www.skyairline.cl*) and **LAN** (*Moraleda 402; www.lan.com*) offer flights on to Puerto Montt, Santiago and Punta Arenas. Two other airlines offer **local scheduled flights and charter flights** to Cochrane, Chile Chico, Melinka, Chaitén, Laguna San Rafael, Puyuhuapi, Palena, Futaleufú, La Tapera, Puerto Montt, etc. They are **Aerocord** (*(67) 2246300, contact: Graciela Cardenas;* e *gcardenas@aerocord.cl; www.aerocord.cl*) who offer a scheduled flight to Villa O'Higgins for $36,000 per person one-way on Monday and Thursday. Note this is subsidised by the State and non-residents can only fly (at this same price) if there is a spare seat available. Charter flights elsewhere are available. Aero Taxis Del Sur (*(9) 95838374, (9) 92562293, contact: Ernesto Hein;* e *e.hein.b@hotmail.cl, info@ aerotaxisdelsur.cl; www.aerotaxisdelsur.cl*) offers only charter flights.

TOUR OPERATORS

Coyhaique is littered with people and agencies claiming to be tour guides. In fact they're usually just agents representing operators situated local to the sights themselves. Hotels earn a small commission for recommending particular operators. For those traversing the Carretera Austral, many of whom will have their own vehicle, many of these activities do not require additional transport and are as easily, and often more cheaply, arranged local to the sight you're hoping to visit. Also, there are very few travel agencies with their own offices, meaning that everything is done by phone which adds an extra element of complication. One agency that does have a physical presence, and is able to offer impartial advice as well as tours off the beaten track is listed below.

The 'standard' tours offered by most agencies generally consist of the following: **marble caves** (easily arranged in Puerto Río Tranquilo through a variety of operators); **Ventisquero Queulat** (accessible from the main Carretera, small entrance fee); **Ventisquero San Rafael** (requires a tour operator); **Caleta Tortel glaciers** (can be arranged locally, but less hassle and more reliable through an agent); and **viewing the Andean condors** waking up in the morning from their nests on cliff edges (guide required).

The Mountain Training School km14, Camino Balmaceda, Lote B, Sector El Salto; (63) 2191833, (9) 8857 6322; e info@mountaintrainingschool. com; www.mountaintrainingschool.com. Offer a winter expedition mountaineering course on the Northern Patagonian Ice Field, & summer rock climbing courses in various locations across the Aysén region & Cochamó. For more than adventurous visitors only, willing to commit to an intensive 6-week course (approximately US$8,000). The school also provides expedition logistics services for independent mountaineers & kayakers, inc rental equipment, obtaining permits, & acting as emergency contacts. English & Spanish spoken.

Chile needs energy, and lots of it. Sustained economic development over two decades and a huge mining sector have increased energy consumption dramatically. Despite being one of the most prosperous countries in Latin America, it is energy-poor: it produces virtually no oil or gas of its own, and neither Argentina nor Bolivia will sell their gas to Chile.

Chile's mining industry is expected to nearly double its electricity consumption within a decade. It produces about a third of the world's copper (with China as a major consumer), and approximately 27% of the cost of copper production is attributed to energy costs. In 2014 the industry's regulator published a report warning that the copper-mining sector needs to increase its power capacity by 18,000 gigawatts in order to meet future demand.

In 2004, Endesa Chile, the largest private electric utility company in Chile, commenced a plan to develop five hydro-electric dams on the Río Baker (near Cochrane) and the Río Pascua (near Villa O'Higgins). It estimated the annual energy production from such dams to be 18,430 gigawatts.

And so began the 'HidroAysén' project.

Endesa (a subsidiary of the Italian conglomerate ENEL) holds a 51% share in the project. The remaining 49% is owned by Colbun, a Chilean private electricity supplier. HidroAysén's proposal was to deliver energy to Chile, and development to the region of Aysén. This development would come largely in the form of jobs, 20% of which would be employed locally, and promises of even more local employees once HidroAysén started local training initiatives. This in an area of comparatively low wages compared with the cost of living, and relatively high unemployment.

As well as jobs, HidroAysén offered to improve 187km of the Carretera Austral; construct a 100m jetty in Puerto Yungay; build a meat processing plant and a waste disposal dump in Cochrane; install cultural and tourist information centres in Cochrane, Caleta Tortel, Villa O'Higgins, and Puerto Bertrand; and to donate hospital equipment to Cochrane's hospital and the health centres of Caleta Tortel and Villa O'Higgins. They would provide VHF radio coverage for 95% of the project's area, various scholarships, training courses, school equipment, teacher training, charitable donations and construction of community spaces, and develop 14km of trekking trails in a conservation area for tourists. This led to accusations of trying to win favours by 'taking the place of the state', as many suspected that the company proposed engaging in functions that are usually performed by government.

Naturally HidroAysén also expressed its utmost commitment to environmental conservation. Their Environmental Impact Survey included a host of measures to mitigate the impact of the project on the local environment, and to preserve the local forests, water supplies, flora and fauna, despite flooding nearly 6,000ha of pristine wilderness, and constructing 2,300km of electricity transmission cables up to Santiago.

Not everyone was convinced by HidroAysén's environmental claims. Local and international environmentalists began to challenge the project, and in 2007 the Patagonia Chilena Sin Represas (Chilean Patagonia Without Dams) campaign was born. The Foundation for Deep Ecology, Pumalín Foundation and Conservación Patagónica, all established by US conservationist Doug Tompkins (see box, pages 104–5), supported the campaign.

Using one of Chile's most emblematic landmarks, the campaign began with an image of Torres del Paine being crossed by electricity pylons. However, since the project was located hundreds of kilometres further north, they were criticised of misinforming the public and so they countered with a clever campaign showing the famous stone figures of Easter Island being criss-crossed by pylons, with the slogan: 'It wouldn't be acceptable here. Neither in Aysén.'

Patagonia Sin Represas gained national attention. Polls suggested that 58% of Chileans were hostile to the project. Some 14 national services, among them the Forestry Service, the Ministry of Public Works, and the National Geology and Mining Service, also opposed the project.

An open letter was written to the then president Michelle Bachelet, requesting her not to approve the HidroAysén project. Fearing a nationwide movement against them, HidroAysén contracted three different PR companies to improve their national image and stress the positive impact the project would bring to the country and to the region of Aysén. One of these PR companies was Burson-Marstellar, who had previously represented some rather dubious companies, including Babcock and Wilcox, the owners of the Three-Mile Island nuclear reactor, which caused the world's second biggest nuclear disaster after Chernobyl, and Union Carbide, after 2,000 people were killed by a gas leak in Bhopal, India. MSNBC's anchor woman Rachel Maddow quipped: 'when evil needs public relations, evil has Burson-Marsteller on speed dial.'

However, in May 2011, the Chilean government (now under Sebastian Piñera) approved the HidroAysén project with 11 votes in favour and one abstention, sparking demonstrations in Puerto Aysén and Coyhaique. In June 200,000 people protested in Santiago, partly about the approval of the project, but also about the growing inequalities between private and public education. Teachers, students and unions joined the protests. Polls suggested 78% of Chileans were against the HidroAysén project.

In January 2012, Chile's Human Rights Commission of the House of Representatives presented a 416-page report showing irregularities and illegalities in the approval process of 2011. Among the other issues, one of the ministers who had approved the project was found to have owned 109,804 shares in Endesa.

Other grievances, both regional and national, had merged into the growing opposition to the project, and this came to a head in Aysén in February 2012, when a group of 20 organisations including Patagonia Sin Represas, students, workers' unions and fishermen all came together under the banner of the 'Social Movement of Aysén'.

Their list of demands was extensive: subsidies for gas, petrol, paraffin, wood, electricity and water; healthcare improvements; increasing the minimum wage; a university based in Aysén; regionalisation of water and mining resources; increased rights and benefits for fishermen; increased pensions for senior citizens and the disabled; and perhaps least surprisingly, greater decision-making in the construction of hydro-electric dams.

This joint movement channelled the anger and frustration in the region into protests focused mainly in Puerto Aysén and Coyhaique, which in turn led into riots in March, when the Chilean police used tear gas, batons and water cannon to control the protesters. The protests continued for more than a month. Transport in and out of the region was paralysed for two weeks. Many protestors were injured – including one shot by the police, and Coyhaique made it to the international news.

After the worst of the protests had died down, on 4 April, the report which had questioned HidroAysén's approval process in 2011 was rejected by the Supreme Court of Chile. On 2 January 2013 the Senate's Mining and Energy Commission legalised the project's Electrical Transmission Highway, slipping through the legislation just as most Chileans were starting their national holidays. Chile's president Sebastian Piñera had been an advocate of the HidroAysén project, but on 11 March 2014, Michelle Bachelet won the presidency for a second time. Within a month her Environment Minister Pablo Badenier led a committee to review 35 legal cases brought against the project, mainly by local communities which would be affected. According to Badenier, there were insufficient plans for relocating communities displaced by the proposed flooding caused by the dams.

On 10 June 2014, the government officially repealed the approval of the HidroAysén dam project, causing celebration among environmentalists and opposers of the project, and concern among its supporters. Endesa and Colbun had pointed out that just 0.05% of Aysen's surface area would be flooded – a small sacrifice for the vast amount of power it would supply – up to 20% of the country's energy needs within a decade. Bachelet's own Energy Minister, Maximo Pacheco, who voted against the project, expressed his concern about Chile's growing energy requirements, insufficient infrastructure, and rising costs.

Endesa's website states in a notice dated 29 January 2015:

There is uncertainty about the recovery of the investment, due to the fact that it depends on both judicial decisions and the Energy Agenda's definitions that the company is currently unable to predict. At the same time, HidroAysén is not in the company's immediate projects portfolio.

The case is currently under appeal. The project is paused, but not entirely cancelled, and Patagonia Sin Represas are still visible across southern Chile.

Pura Patagonia [168 D3] General Parra 202; ☎(67) 2246000, (9) 79589551; e info@ purapatagonia.com; www.purapatagonia.com In addition to offering a wide range of tours, & brokering other tours across almost any region of southern Chile, the company is able to offer tailored support to specific expeditions in the region & has its own vans. They rent bicycles (for local use) & have a range of bilingual guides. Conveniently the 2 owners are also general manager & president of the Cámara de Turismo de Coyhaique (*Tourism Association of Coyhaique; www.aysenpatagonia.cl*), & their knowledge extends beyond the immediate vicinity of Coyhaique to much of the region of Aysén.

WHERE TO STAY

Hotel Dreams Patagonia [168 B4] (38 rooms, 2 suites) Magallanes 131; ☎(67) 2264700; e reservas@mundodreams.com; www. mundodreams.com. The only 5-star chain hotel in Coyhaique, complete with casino, frequent live music, heated swimming pool, sauna, gym, conference hall & 2 restaurants. A characterless & rather generic chain hotel. Takes credit cards. **$$$$$**

Nómades Hotel Boutique [168 E1] (6 rooms, 1 apt) Baquedano 84; (67) 2237777, (9) 71080070; e info@nomadeshotel.com; www. nomadeshotel.com. The leading boutique hotel in Coyhaique & one of the finest on the entire Carretera Austral. If you feel like treating yourself to 1 truly decadent treat, this is a contender. Rooms face the mountains & the only sound audible is the rushing river below, & yet the hotel is a mere 5min walk to the central plaza. The rooms are spacious & bright thanks to large windows overlooking the gorge, have a balcony or chimney, large TV, room service, safety deposit box, Wi-Fi, etc. The restaurant is only open to guests for b/fast, & caters to almost any imaginable b/fast wish. Although not open for lunch or dinner, the hotel is 200m from Ruibarbo (page 177) – probably the finest restaurant in Coyhaique, & close to the city centre. The bar stays open until midnight. The interior is of wood & stone with a gaucho feel – rustic, quality materials, ample animal hides & antlers, etc, creating a certain Patagonian lodge ambience despite being in a city. English spoken. Wise to reserve in advance as popular & only 7 rooms. A spare bed can be added to any room, & the apt is approximately double the size of the regular rooms & sleeps 4, complete with a full kitchen – ideal for families staying for a few days. In peak season prices range from US$180 to US$300, in low season they are approximately US$60 cheaper, but also have special offers when prices can fall further. The managers will go to lengths to ensure a pleasant stay, & also can arrange tours in the region. Accepts credit cards (also used to guarantee a reservation). $$$$$

Tehuelche Patagonia Lodge [169 B8] (11 rooms) Camino del Bosque 1170; (67) 2210723, (9) 78145854; e contacto@tehuelchepatagoniatour.cl; www. tehuelchepatagonialodge.cl. A fantastic lodge ideally suited for those with private transport, as it is slightly out of town in a forest. The building is a restored wooden & rambling farmhouse oozing charm & tastefully decorated inside. The rooms are very spacious, some with a fantastic view over the forest to the mountains, very comfortable beds & excellent en-suite bathrooms. Wood-stoves, Wi-Fi, secure parking, etc. The restaurant is one of the best in town, although certainly not one of the cheapest, & the (included) b/fast is excellent, unlimited & contains every conceivable item,

including eggs to order. Not great value for money compared with other options in this price category – you can get better service/rooms for the same price elsewhere – & internet access is patchy. Staff speak English & Spanish. $$$$$

Coyhaique Suites Apart Home [168 E1] (3 apts) Diego Portales 61; (9) 79240658; e coyhaiqueapart@gmail.com; www. coyhaiqueaparthotel.com. Large family apts for 7 people fitted to a high standard with no expense spared. All windows are double-glazed thermo-panel for added insulation & noise control. There is a touch screen smart TV in all the bedrooms & common rooms with digital TV, games, Netflix, Skype & internet access. Central heating throughout the apt & a daily housekeeping service. Each apt has 2 bathrooms, a sgl bedroom below & 2 twin bedrooms & a matrimonial bedroom on the 1st floor. Meals can be arranged through the reception (⊕ 08.30–21.00 daily with a break for lunch). Laundry available. Excellent off-street parking. English & Spanish spoken. No pets & no smoking. A conference facility is also available. Accepts credit cards. $$$$

Hotel Austral [169 F5] (14 rooms) Colon 203; (67) 2232522; e hotelaustralchile@gmail. com. An excellent low to mid-range hotel with decent food, a little overpriced. Simple, en-suite rooms with double glazing offering protection from traffic noise & cold. 10min walk from town. $$$$

Pasarela Lodge [168 A1] (6 rooms, 5 cabins) km2, Camino a Puerto Aysén; (9) 98187390, (9) 98187444; e lapasarela@ patagoniachile.cl; www.lapasarela.cl; ⊕ Nov–May only. A riverside oasis within 2km of the relative chaos of Coyhaique. When approaching Coyhaique from Aysén, it is signposted from the main road to the right. Access is via a rickety suspension bridge crossing the Río Simpson, & the lodge is immediately to the left after the bridge. From the northern Carretera Austral, turn towards Aysén prior to entering Coyhaique & it is on the left. There are sgl, dbl, trpl & quadruple rooms, as well as cabins for up to 7 people. The main building of the lodge is spectacular, where the reception, sitting area, bar & restaurant are located. The rooms are housed in a separate building by the river, & are spacious & well decorated, with full central heating. The largest of the cabins consists of a main room with a dbl bed, sitting area, kitchen

& bathroom, & a separate room with 5 additional beds. The other cabins are more basic A-frame buildings, & a little cramped. All rooms & cabins enjoy the sound of the river. The lodge is owned & run by Albert & Mirtha, of German/Italian descent, & they also speak fluent English & Spanish. Albert is a keen fly-fisherman & fishing guide, & offers a range of fishing activities including courses for beginners. The lodge boasts a restaurant & bar for the exclusive use of guests, & a spectacular b/fast consists of homemade breads, jams & other locally sourced items (b/fast included with the rooms, at an additional cost for those in the cabins). For groups they can also prepare a parrilla. This is an upper-end, rustic, friendly place to stay slightly beyond the confines of the town. Accepts credit cards. **$$$$**

Cabañas y Departamentos Mirador [168 G4] (7 rooms) Baquedano 848; (67) 2233191; e miradorbaquedano@gmail.com. Close to the centre of town but facing the river & mountain – a peaceful setting ensuring a good night's sleep. Cabins or rooms. Wi-Fi, decent bathrooms, friendly owner, secure off-street parking. No b/fast. The bay window in the end cabin has truly spectacular views. **$$$**

Hostal Español [169 F6] (10 rooms, 6 cabins) Sargento Aldea 343; (67) 2242580; e reservas@hostalcoyhaique.cl; www. hostalcoyhaique.cl. A good mid-range family-run hostel about 10mins' walk from the centre in a quiet neighbourhood. Clean & friendly, with a Spanish theme throughout. All rooms have central heating, Wi-Fi, cable TV, private bathroom & are sgl or dbl. The rooms are large & tastefully decorated with great attention to detail to give a homely Spanish feel, down to the tiled bathrooms. There is a shared TV/lounge & a 24hr reception. A hearty continental b/fast includes cereals, fruit, yoghurt, ham, cheese & eggs. There is lockable off-street parking. The cabins on the opposite side of the road are fully equipped with microwave & wood-fired heater, etc, & are very spacious for 4 people. Bookings can be made online. **$$$**

Hostal Gladys [168 E3] (15 rooms) General Parra 65; (67) 2245288, (9) 99187649; e patagoniagladys@hotmail.com; www. hostalgladys.cl. Professional, well-run hostel in a great location. A stellar b/fast consisting of freshly brewed coffee, eggs to order, homemade jams, dried fruit, yoghurts, etc, all included in the price &

served to your table – in this price range could be the best b/fast in town. The rooms are somewhat unusual in that they have skylights rather than traditional windows, & are a little cramped with 2 people & bags. This is a good place to meet other travellers, reasonable value for money & excellent service. Wi-Fi & computers available, & covered secure parking for a few cars. **$$$**

Hostal Patagonia Live [169 C8] (4 rooms) Lillo 826; (67) 2230892, (9) 98867982; e contacto@hostalpatagonialive.cl; www. hostalpatagonialive.cl. A new hostel in town. Well run, clean, 1 block from Hostal Monica (see below). Reasonable-sized rooms, well-equipped bathrooms, decent b/fast, limited off-road parking, cable TV, central heating. Accepts credit cards. **$$$**

Turismo Ayelen Patagonia [168 E1] (camping for approx 20 people, 6 cabins) Av Baquedano 75; (67) 2574182, (9) 90893794; e turismoayelen71@gmail.com; www. turismoayelenpatagonia.cl; ⊕ campground: Nov–May, cabins: all year. A basic campground by the river including a simple outhouse with 2 shared bathrooms, kitchen & communal seating area. Outdoor & indoor BBQ facilities. No fridge. This is the closest campsite to Coyhaique, a 15min walk from the central square. The cabins are surprisingly pleasant, new, spacious & with views over the river. All have satellite TV, full kitchen, Wi-Fi & a seating/dining area. Sizes range from 3 to 7 people, & the 2 largest cabins have washing machines. No English spoken, ample parking. Good value. Reservations by email. *Campground* **$**, *cabins* **$$$**

Patagonia Hostel [169 D7] (2 dbls, dorm with 6 beds) Lautaro 667; (9) 62406974; e info@ patagonia-hostel.com; www.patagonia-hostel. com; ⓢ Patagonia-hostel. German-run, clean, professionally run hostel. Good location near the supermarkets & bus terminal, 5mins from the central plaza. Fluent Spanish, English & German spoken. The German owners, Sandra & Thomas, are a font of knowledge on the region & offer tours to Puerto Río Tranquilo & horseriding around Coyhaique. This is a popular hostel & fills up quickly, so book in advance. Dorms are $14,000pp, rooms are $34,000. Informative website that allows online reservations but payment is by cash only. **$$–$$$**

Hostal Monica [169 C7] (10 rooms) Lillo 664; (67) 2234302; e isolinayanez@gmail.com.

Lovingly run by an elderly couple for decades. Good value for money for the budget traveller, but could do with some maintenance & cleanliness is no more than adequate. All rooms en suite with reliable hot water & less reliable Wi-Fi access.

About 10mins from the centre, but convenient for the bus terminal & the main supermarkets. B/fast included, but very basic (coffee, bread, cheese & ham). Limited off-road parking. **$$**

✕ WHERE TO EAT AND DRINK

✕ **Restaurant Ruibarbo** [168 E1] Baquedano 208; ☎(67) 2211826; ⊕ 12.45–15.00 & 19.45–23.00 Mon–Sat. Considered one of the best in town, rightly so. Excellent selection of steak/lamb dishes, seafood & vegetarian. Good-sized portions, intimate atmosphere & produce is mostly organic & local. The daily fixed price lunch menu is very good value, also have a reasonable wine list. Owner speaks English & is very passionate about his food – always delighted to chat with his customers. Reservation required. *Lunch* **$$**, *dinner* **$$$$$**

✕ **Lito's Restaurant** [169 B6] Lautaro 147; ☎(67) 2254528; ⊕ noon–15.00 & 19.30–midnight Mon–Sat. Another favourite amongst locals, rumoured to have fantastic seafood but it had run out during our 3 visits. The meat dishes are excellent & plentiful. Good, buzzing atmosphere & a wide range of local boutique beers & a reasonable wine list. Friendly staff & positively good service. **$$$**

✕ **Restaurant Arisca** [168 F3] Baquedano 400; ☎(9) 75381668; ⊕ 13.00–02.00 Tue–Sat, 13.00–17.00 Sun & Mon. A quieter option for those looking for a more adult crowd in a pub attached to a brewery setting. They bring up Arisca beer made in Puerto Río Tranquilo to the Coyhaique market. Pub food in a Patagonia-style setting, with outdoor seating available when the weather is nice. Also serve seafood & vegetarian. **$$$**

✕ **Restaurante Histórico Ricer** [169 D5] Horn 40; ☎(67) 2232920, (67) 2216709. Great location by the plaza on the main pedestrian street, seating outside in the rare cases of sunshine, & always busy. On Fri & Sun the BBQ lamb dish is worth checking out (cordero al palo), but get there early. Not the best value for money in general, & perhaps best visited for an evening drink to watch Coyhaique life walk by. Good bar with decent range of beers on tap & in bottles. Also has a small shop & library. **$$$**

✕ **Tamango Restobar** [168 C4] Arturo Prat 176; ☎(67) 2242588, (9) 96400688; e info@tamango.cl; ⊕ 12.30–15.00 & 19.00–23.00 Mon–Sat. Great Peruvian restaurant with excellent-value

lunch menu (*$6,000*). Ceviche, meat & seafood dishes available. Regional boutique beers. Small, good vibe, semi-formal but avoid the table by the speaker. A welcome change from the standard fare. Centrally located. *Lunch* **$$**, *dinner* **$$$**

✕ **Casino de Bomberos** [168 C3] General Parra 365; ☎(67) 2231437. Something of a classic in Coyhaique, popular with the locals for both lunch & dinner. Very good value for money & large portions. Wide range of Chilean dishes. The restaurant is hard to find – it is at the back of the fire station & poorly signposted. Ask a local if in doubt. **$$**

✕ **Lado B** [169 E6] Bilbao 715; ☎(67) 2242173, (67) 2674473; ⊕ 11.00–23.00 Mon–Sat, 11.00–18.00 Sun. Decent new Chinese restaurant also serving Chilean fare. Good value, excellent service. Lunch, dinner & take-away. Good option for those wishing to broaden their diet from the standard Chilean cuisine. **$$**

✕ **Restaurant Delivery Sabor** [169 C5] Cochrane 345; ☎(67) 2583216, (9) 68485049; ⊕ noon–15.00 & 18.00–22.00 Mon–Thu, until 23.30 Fri & Sat. Good-quality sushi restaurant offering delivery service, limited range depending on fish available, no local beers, but pleasant change to standard fare found elsewhere on the Carretera. Accepts credit cards. **$$**

✕ **Restaurant Mama Gaucha** [168 C4] Horn 47; ☎(9) 2210721; ⊕ all day Mon–Sat. The best pizza in town, & former home of the local La Tropera beer. Good value, decent quality food – the artichoke starter is delicious. Great atmosphere, popular with foreigners & locals alike. Doubles as a sports-bar during important football games. It may be cliché to recommend this restaurant, so well known in the city, but this reputation has been earned for valid reasons. Conveniently located 50m from the central plaza & very close to the Navimag & Naviera Austral offices. Extensive range of pizzas. Fills up fast so get there early or reserve. **$$**

✕ **Rosselot Sur Delivery** [169 B6] Lautaro 143, local 2; ☎(67) 2210378, (67) 2211593; www.rosselotsurdelivery.cl; ⊕ 09.00–23.00 Mon–Thu,

09.00–midnight Fri, 11.00–midnight Sat, 13.00–22.00 Sun. Good for a quick lunch while waiting for a bus or a quick dinner after a long day. Burgers, sandwiches, fries & pizzas. Good value, large portions, & has its own range of beer. Accepts credit cards. $$

✗ **Club Sandwich Patagonia** [168 E3] Moraleda 437; 📞(67) 2244664; ⊕ noon–07.00 daily. Possibly the only place in town to stay open until 07.00, this is a great option for those arriving late at night. The set lunch menu is very good value for a filling portion. Service is fine, & dishes include decent hamburgers & take-away sandwiches downstairs for a reasonable price. Eat-in at the tables upstairs or take-away. Credit cards accepted. $–$$

✗ **Govinda Vegetarian Restaurant** [169 D7] Lautaro 650; 📞(9) 76224679; 🇫 Govinda Comida Vegetariana Coyhaique. A rare chance to eat at a vegetarian restaurant on the Carretera Austral. The daily menu consists of veggie-burgers, samosa, vegetarian lasagne, soups, salads & homemade bread. The vegetarian wrap is one of the most popular dishes & is only $1,900. A vegan menu is also offered. Credit cards accepted. $

💻 **Café Montana** [168 E4] 21 de Mayo 417; 📞(67) 2273073, (9) 66461430. Decent coffee, decent Wi-Fi.

💻 **Te Quiero Café** [168 C4] Dussen 360; 📞(67) 2210050. Located just off the main plaza with variety of good coffee, hot chocolate, tea, juices, cakes, sandwiches, & ice cream. Patchy Wi-Fi & a nice atmosphere with friendly staff. Good place to catch up with emails.

ENTERTAINMENT AND NIGHTLIFE

Coyhaique is the Carretera Austral's nightlife capital, although perhaps that's not saying much. Some restaurants double as bars once everyone has finished eating, Mama Gaucha (page 177) being a fine example. Coyhaique actually has a few dedicated bars, particularly around the Central Plaza and on General Parra, or the bar/brewery Casa Tropera (se below). Nightclubs seem to come and go so it's worth asking at the tourist information office on the central plaza.

☆ **Akelarre** [168 E3] General Parra 26. Large bar next to Pepe Le Pub that is the best place in the city to see live music. If there's not a band playing, join in for karaoke. Stays open late on w/ends.

☆ **Bar West** [169 B5] Bilbao 110, cnr Magallanes; 📞(9) 82196434; 🇫 viejobarwest. An old western-themed bar that claims to be the longest-running bar in Coyhaique. Large selection of beer & spirits, with karaoke on Thu & live music some nights. Popular with locals, good atmosphere.

☆ **Casa Tropera** [169 A8] Camino Aerodromo Teniente Vidal, km 1.5; 📞(9) 65970585; ⊕ noon for lunch, 19.30 until late for dinner Mon–Sat. A medium-sized pub with a brewery located just outside of town across the Río Simpson. Fantastic craft beer & the best hamburgers in town. Large, finely ground all-beef burgers topped with real cheese, bacon, or other delicious options. They also sell their beer in the more central Mama Gaucha pizzeria (page 177) if you want to try this highly recommended beer, but can't make it out to the brewery. Occasional live music.

☆ **Pepe Le Pub** [168 E3] General Parra No 72; 📞(67) 2246474; ⊕ 20.00 but doesn't get going until midnight. A louder, younger scene that has karaoke most nights of the week. Large selection of drinks & friendly staff.

☆ **Piel Roja Pub & Dance** [168 E4] Pub: Jose de Moraleda 495, dance club: Condell 117; 📞(67) 2236635. One of the few places in Coyhaique where you can dance all night long. Well-decorated bar is on the 1st floor & upstairs is the dance floor, although they are independent. A great place to mingle. Get to the pub early for food including pizzas, enchiladas & pastas. Happy hour every day from 19.00 to 21.00.

SHOPPING

Coyhaique is the main supply hub for the Carretera Austral outside of Puerto Montt. The range of products available is constantly increasing as Coyhaique catches up with the rest of Chile. There are boutique climbing/outdoor stores, electronic shops and most main banks. This is the first and possibly last chance to stock up on supplies at a reasonable price. Condell is home to most banks, with ATMs, and it is worth stocking up on cash here as there are few ATMs north or south.

CAMPING AND OTHER EQUIPMENT

ABCDIN [169 C5] Arturo Prat 380; www. abcdin.cl; ⊕ daily. A department store with a full range of computers, electronics & telephones.

Airsoft En Patagonia [168 B4] General Parra 554; \(67) 2245410. Outdoor equipment, including some rock climbing gear, & paintball equipment.

Condor Explorer [168 D4] Dussen 357; \(67) 2573634, (67) 2670349. Mountaineering & camping equipment, maps, Patagonia & Black Diamond rep in Coyhaique, & expedition arrangements.

Corona [168 C6] Arturo Prat 429; www.corona.cl; ⊕ daily. Probably the largest range of low- to mid-quality clothing at the cheapest prices. For high-end sporting & climbing clothes, go to one of the specialist camping & climbing stores.

North Face [168 D4] Horn 47; \(67) 2252096; ⊕ closed Sun. Clothing & camping gear.

Sodimac Home Centre [169 B8] Av Ogana 869; www.sodimac.cl; ⊕ daily. A large chain hardware store. Ideal for stocking up on tools or any other hardware items. They have a camping section &

also sell low- to mid-range boots & rainwear. Also useful for buying white gasoline for camp stoves (*bencina blanca*).

Suray [169 C5] Pesca Prat 265–269; \(67) 2234088; www.surayflyshop.com; ⊕ 09.00–21.00 Mon–Sat. Fishing supplies & some camping gear.

FOOD

Bigger Supermarket [169 C7] Lord Cochrane 646; www.bigger.cl; ⊕ daily. Another large supermarket chain competing with UniMarc. Both supermarkets are within a block of each other.

UniMarc Supermarket [169 B/C7] Lautaro 331; www.unimarc.cl; ⊕ daily. A large supermarket chain.

HANDICRAFTS

Artisan market Central Plaza; ⊕ daily, but more limited on Sun. Last chance to stock up on knitted gloves & local handmade trinkets, as well as the usual 'artisan' supplies found in most markets in South America all apparently made locally but appearing remarkable similar.

OTHER PRACTICALITIES

REPAIRS

Coyhaique is, for all practical purposes, the last opportunity on the Carretera Austral to make any repairs. All major car makes can be serviced in town, & parts are generally available or can be found quite quickly. Bicycle & motorbike mechanics are few & far between beyond the confines of the city.

Bicicletas Figon [169 E8] Simpson 805; \(67) 2234616; e figon_bici@hotmail.com; www. bicicletasfigon.com; ⊕ 10.00–19.00 Mon–Sat. Bicycle rental, repairs, spare parts including tyres, helmets & riding gear.

COPEC petrol station [168 C4] Balmaceda 455, off central plaza. Chipped windscreens are a common problem on gravel roads, surprisingly hard to repair, & if not repaired promptly a small chip will spread & require a full windscreen replacement. This petrol station in the centre of town has a quasi-employee who has the kit to repair such chips. The only such person

known along the entire Carretera Austral. Costs approximately US$50/chip – far cheaper than replacing a windscreen.

Huston Car Servicio Automotriz & Motos [169 E8] Simpson 768; \(9) 92147944; e hustonprimero@hotmail.com. Nelson Ego-Aguirre is well equipped to service most motorbikes, although he refuses to work with Chinese makes. He has a scanner for computerised bikes. Also services cars.

Salcedo Talleres [169 G5] Baquedano 807; \(67) 2234073, (9) 98623248. Full-service car mechanic, no motorbikes.

Servicio Automotriz Pestana [169 D5] Bilbao 457; \(67) 2214546; ⊕ 09.00–13.00 & 15.00–19.00 Mon–Fri, 09.00–13.00 Sat. Service & parts for Honda, Yamaha, Suzuki, Keewa, Euromot, SYM, Kymco & Zongshen, although will help with other manufacturers if possible. Also has a reasonable range of accessories.

NOT ANOTHER VOLCANO

It is almost impossible to visit Chile without seeing a volcano, and seeing one erupt is not as hard as one might imagine. Depending on the precise definition used, there are approximately 500 volcanoes in Chile, of which a little over 100 are active. **Chaitén** is possibly the best known within the region of the Carretera Austral, erupting in both 2008 and 2011 – the damage is still very visible. **Villarrica** made it to the international headlines in 2015 with some spectacular photos of night-time lava fireworks by the lake. **Puyehue**, just north of the Carretera Austral, closed airports as far afield as Australia in 2011. However, the **Volcán Hudson** is possibly the most feared – the 1991 eruption was one of the largest of the 20th century, and it is not far from Coyhaique.

Hudson is, fortunately, extremely remote. For this reason no-one actually died in the 1991 eruption. It is approximately 80km southwest of Coyhaique, or 65km south of Puerto Aysén, but can only readily be seen by air. Where the road to Lago Caro ends, Hudson is a mere 40km away, but not visible from this vantage point. The 4750BC eruption may have been responsible for wiping out what limited human population existed in this region at that time. The volcano was barely known until 1971, when a minor eruption caused lahars (mudflows) that killed five people. However, the 1991 eruption was big news in the region. Some 4.3km³ of ash was ejected from the volcano covering an area of approximately 150,000km² and reaching as far as the Falklands. At the time news of the eruption was overshadowed by the double-whammy of the eruption of Mount Pinatubo and Typhoon Yunya striking the Philippines at the same time, killing 847 people. The combination of these two eruptions led to global cooling over the following years and the Antarctic ozone hole grew to its largest level ever recorded. Hudson was placed on red alert in October 2011, but the subsequent eruption was minor.

The **Volcán Lautaro** is notable for being sub-glacial. Despite an altitude of nearly 3.5km, only the final 1km is visible above the ice of the Southern Ice Field. The only practical means to see the volcano is by plane from Villa O'Higgins (90km). From the airfield near Candelario Mancilla it is only 50km.

The following list focuses mainly on those both within reach from the Carretera Austral and easy to climb, or at least visit (altitude and any recent eruption in parentheses):

Puerto Montt Calbuco (2,015m, 2015) & Osorno (2,652m, 1869)
Hornopirén Yates (2,187m), Hornopirén (1,572m) & Apagando (1,210m)
Parque Pumalín Chaitén (1,122m, 2008 & 2011) & Michinmahuida (2,404m, 1835)
Raúl Marín Balmaceda Melimoyu (2,440m)
Villa O'Higgins Lautaro (3,623m, 1979)

Una Velocidad [169 C6] Cochrane 495; ⏰ 10.30–20.00 Mon–Fri, 10.30–19.00 Sat. Bicycle mechanic, sells accessories, familiar with cycle tourism along the Carretera. Brands include Shimano, Sram, Microshift, Knog, Orlieb, Kross, various tyres, etc.

Vidrieria Sur [169 E5] Simon Bolivar 180, beside the telephone tower; ☎ (67) 2219029; e colosltda@yahoo.com. Reasonable stock of the most common car windscreens that are replaced in the city. Other windscreens are ordered in.

LAUNDRY

Lavanderia Monteaustral [169 D7] Lillo 555, 1 block above Bigger supermarket; \(67) 2247009; e lavanderia@monteaustral.cl; www. monteaustral.cl. Laundry & dry-cleaning service. Laundry service is $1,500/kg for 1-day service. Express service is $2,500/kg.

Lavaseco All Clean [168 E3] General Parra 55; \(67) 2219635. Laundry & dry-cleaning service. Price/kg. Credit cards accepted.

LANGUAGE SCHOOL

Baquedano Language School [168 E1] Av Baquedano 20; \(67) 2232520, (9) 62464218; e pguzmanm@123.cl; www.balasch.cl; ⊕ all year. Currently the only language school along the Carretera Austral, & thus a unique opportunity to combine a journey with Spanish classes. There's acccommodation on site, arranged independently, or the school can arrange homestays. Prices vary according to selected accommodation & food option, & the intensity of the course taken

& number of students, but as a benchmark, a self-catering apartment within the school with 6 days of Spanish classes costs US$600 pp/week (laundry inc). The head teacher, Patricio Molina, is a qualified, experienced bilingual English/Spanish teacher with over 20 years' experience, & has lived & worked in Europe & the USA. They cater to all levels, from absolute beginners to advanced Spanish speakers wishing to perfect their language skills.

MONEY EXCHANGE

The following places will exchange euros, US dollars & possibly Argentine pesos:

Casa de Cambio Austral [168 D4] Horn 40
Casa de Cambio Emperador [169 B5] Freire 171
Casa de Cambio Prado [168 A3] 21 de Mayo 417

CAR HIRE

See page 187; all Balmaceda car-rental agencies have offices in Coyhaique.

SIGHTSEEING AND EXCURSIONS

Coyhaique serves mainly as a hub for transport and tour operators, but it's worth pausing here, if only to recharge one's batteries from the relative isolation of the Carretera. The region around the town also has a number of attractions, including one of the finest condor-spotting locations in all of Patagonia, accessible parks, a language school and a modest ski resort.

MIRADOR RÍO SIMPSON (RÍO SIMPSON LOOKOUT) This lookout is located on the bypass behind the casino, an easy, 15-minute walk from the central plaza. Walk west on the street Jose M Carrera until you reach the bypass, where there are spectacular views over the Río Simpson, the Río Claro and the greater Valle Río Simpson. Below the viewing point are the remaining buildings of the first milk plant of Coyhaique. In the distance are large wind turbines harnessing the power of the perpetual Patagonian wind. An eroded rock formation vaguely resembles the profile of a human head reportedly that of an Indian, thus the name Cabeza del Indio.

RESERVA NACIONAL COYHAIQUE (*www.conaf.cl/parques/reserva-nacional-coyhaique; entry Chileans/foreigners $1,500/3,000*) This national reserve covers 2,676ha and is conveniently located only 5km north of Coyhaique, making it an accessible detour and a chance to explore the native forests and birds of the region. It is also a good option with children and older people because of its accessibility by car and relatively easy, well-marked circuits within the reserve.

Take the paved road from Coyhaique to Puerto Aysén. Cross the first bridge and then turn right onto the gravel road which is signposted to the reserve. This access road and the roads inside the park are open to cars in the summer, but 4x4s are needed in the winter. The **CONAF staff** are helpful and provide a good **map** of the park with distances and altitudes. All trails are well marked. Take food, suntan lotion and water – especially if you are planning on trekking. The 7-hour trek up **Cerro Cinchao** (1,361m) is desert-like at the summit. The climate of the reserve is relatively dry and hot in summer, while rain and snow are frequent in winter. There is a 9km circuit which you can **drive** round. Sheltered barbecue areas (*fogons*) overlook Laguna Verde and the hills in the background. There is also a sealed path suitable for **wheelchairs** to a lookout over Coyhaique. A well-maintained **campsite** set amongst the trees at Casa Bruja is the only campsite in the reserve. There are 5km of tracks dedicated to **mountain bikers**.

The **two main treks** are the 10km (approximately) half-day, medium difficulty circuit and the 15km full-day, medium difficulty circuit leading to the top of Cerro Cinchao (1,361m) – an extension of the half-day circuit.

The first 3.5km of the walk to Laguna Verde has two main highlights. **Casa Bruja**, at km2 (the witch's house) is an early settlers' house in the area which provides an insight into living conditions in the region. The **viewpoint** just before Laguna Verde offers spectacular views of the farmland in the valley and Coyhaique city with the mountain backdrop behind the city. Besides these two notable highlights, however, the walk is disappointing due to the abundance of artificially planted pines. The slash-and-burn agricultural practices of the 1950s resulted in deforestation in this area and so, in an effort to minimise erosion, CONAF developed a strategy to plant fast-growing species. It is worth pushing on to **Laguna Verde** – the clear waters, abundant fish and birdlife and beautiful views across the forest and mountains that soar up to the high peaks behind the lagoon are worth the effort.

From here on this circuit is full of mature native bush, plentiful birdlife and another three lagoons. Some 500m past Laguna Verde on the right-hand side is the 6.7km **detour to Cerro Cinchao**. This is a 600m ascent of medium difficulty, rewarded with spectacular views of the reserve and panoramic views of the city. A good sunhat, sunblock, sunglasses and plenty of water are recommended for this section.

The trail descends to the forest to rejoin the half-day 10km circuit. From here, there is a gradual descent through the native bush and then a further 4km to return to the start point at the reserve entrance.

FRAILE SKI RESORT Situated 29km southeast of Coyhaique, Fraile is one of the more modest ski resorts in Latin America: it barely opened in 2015 due to the lack of snow. In theory it operates from May to September and has five pistes. However, you would be better advised to stick to the ski resorts around Bariloche, Las Leñas in Argentina, the resorts around Santiago or even Cerro Castor in Ushuaia.

CONDOR'S AWAKING (*Punta del Monte Estancia;* \ *(67) 2231601;* **e** *condores@ puntadelmonte.cl; www.puntadelmonte.cl*) This is a truly unique opportunity to observe the legendary Andean condor up close, as they awake in the morning, stretch their wings and finally launch themselves from their nests on the cliff edges into the thermal updrafts. Condors are large beasts, reaching up to 15kg and with a wingspan of up to 3m. They can weigh as much as a three-to-four-year-old child, and reach 1m in height. They take advantage of up-currents of warm air to launch off the cliffs, and rely on thermal currents to remain aloft with the minimum effort possible.

This Punta del Monte Estancia is a functioning farm, with 9,000 sheep, 200 Hereford cows, and 200 alpacas, but it is also uniquely located at a natural nesting area for the condors, with access from above. It is possible to observe their awaking, morning preparations and eventual launch from a matter of metres away. Alejandro

Galilea, one of the owners of the estancia, provides a fascinating explanation of the lives of condors.

Tours can be arranged from Coyhaique through an operator (see *Pura Patagonia*, page 174) including all transport, but for those with private transport it is possible to book directly with the estancia itself (see details on page 182). Either way, arrive at the entrance to the estancia by 06.30, approximately an hour's drive from Coyhaique towards the Argentine border (*43km to Coyhaique Alto, a further 6km to Paso Coyhaique; mostly gravel*). From here a 4x4 takes you the final 17km to the lookout point. The standard tour includes a roast lamb lunch, and returns to Coyhaique at 16.00. Prices depend on the number of visitors, ranging from US$134 per person for groups over ten people, to US$268 per person for two to four people. There is also the possibility to **stay overnight** in the estancia (avoiding such an early start) but for an additional cost (*US$356pp for a couple, up to US$229pp for 6 people*). Multi-day packages include horseriding tours and fishing trips amongst other activities as well as the celebrated condor-watching excursion.

⊕ AS THE CONDOR FLIES

Coyhaique is 460km from Puerto Montt and 380km from the border south of Villa O'Higgins to El Chaltén.

FOLLOW BRADT

For the latest news, special offers and competitions, subscribe to the Bradt newsletter via the website www.bradtguides.com and follow Bradt on:

- ⨍ www.facebook.com/BradtTravelGuides
- 🐦 @BradtGuides
- 📷 @bradtguides
- ⓟ www.pinterest.com/bradtguides

9

South of Coyhaique: to Cruce El Maitén via Lago General Carrera

The region south of Coyhaique perhaps contains the highest density of spectacular sights, glaciers and trekking opportunities along the entire Carretera Austral.

Lago General Carrera is gigantic, beautiful, and possesses some of the finest views of the Carretera Austral, with various adventures departing from this section of the road. The lake straddles Chile and Argentina (where it is known as Lago Buenos Aires), and is the second largest in South America. Strictly speaking the southern coastal road is not part of the Carretera Austral, but it is important for two reasons: it is truly spectacular, and is a common entry/exit point for visitors to the Carretera. As a branch off the Carretera, this section invariably involves doubling back on oneself if wishing to continue on the Carretera north or south. It is not an easy section to traverse, mainly for logistical regions, but is worth the effort.

A principal destination for those heading south is the tourist hub of **Puerto Río Tranquilo**, from where you can catch a boat to the marble caves and tours to the **Ventisquero San Rafael** – if you visit only one glacier in the region, this should be your choice. For those wishing to combine a trip to a glacier with a moderate hike, albeit with marginally more planning required, the **Ventisquero Leones** is highly recommended. *En route*, **Cerro Castillo** offers some of the best, and most accessible, hiking along the Carretera Austral, varying from leisurely strolls requiring no prior

ENTERING/EXITING THE CARRETERA AUSTRAL SOUTH OF CRUCE EL MAITÉN

The 120km-long 265-CH road along the south of Lago General Carrera from the Cruce El Maitén leads to **Chile Chico**, which is often the entry or exit point for those travelling along the Carretera Austral. In part this is understandable given the painful logistics of the connecting road back to the Carretera itself, as well as the smooth logistics on the Argentine side of the border. However, the Carretera south of Chile Chico, or more precisely, south of the Cruce El Maitén, offers some of the most wonderful scenery and adventures along the entire Carretera, and it is a pity to miss this. Beyond Chile Chico, there are two further border crossings: at **Parque Patagonia** (Paso Roballos, see page 234; possible with vehicle), and the legendary **Villa O'Higgins** crossing via the Ventisquero O'Higgins directly to El Chaltén in Argentina (pedestrians and cyclists only). To skip this section in favour of the comparatively drab terrain on the Argentine side of the border would be a pity.

experience, to some challenging technical climbs. The weather is volatile, at times turning an apparently easy hike into a dangerous adventure – an Israeli trekker died on this mountain in 2014.

The only commercial airport along the Carretera Austral is just south of Coyhaique in Balmaceda (not to be confused with the village Raúl Marín Balmaceda further north). South of the airport lie the fantastic roads around **Puerto Ibáñez**, including the little-known Levicán Peninsula. From Puerto Ibáñez it is possible to take a ferry directly to **Chile Chico** and enjoy the southern side of the lake, but this involves either missing Puerto Río Tranquilo and the surrounding glaciers, or doubling back later. Ideally visitors should visit both sides of the lake.

The **marble caves** are worth checking out, but if possible visit those around Puerto Sánchez rather than around Puerto Río Tranquilo – they are closer to the village, cheaper and deeper. However, there is no public transport to Puerto Sánchez and the road, although utterly spectacular, is one of the most dangerous in the region, with cliff edges merely centimetres from the road.

Cruce El Maitén is both the southern limit of the 'classic route', and the beginning of the more remote southern Carretera Austral. The dramatic scenery and abundance of activities covered in this chapter is a mere introduction to what lies in store further south.

LAKES SOUTH OF COYHAIQUE

There is no need to travel far from Coyhaique to discover stunning beauty. The village of **El Blanco** lies 34km south of Coyhaique on the Carretera Austral, 6km before the only fork in the road for approximately 200km. The road heads southeast towards **Balmaceda** (town and airport) and on to the **Paso Huemules** to Argentina, or southwest towards **Cerro Castillo** on the Carretera Austral. Although this stretch to El Blanco is not particularly interesting, paved and suffers relative traffic congestion (by Aysén standards), a number of small detours to the lakes are worth the effort.

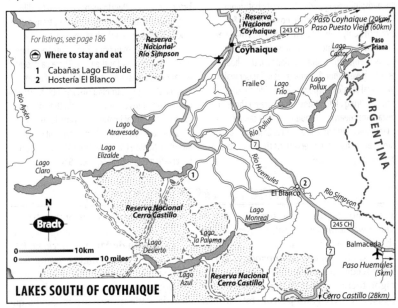

For listings, see page 186

Where to stay and eat
1 Cabañas Lago Elizalde
2 Hostería El Blanco

LAKES SOUTH OF COYHAIQUE

To the east lie three main **lakes**: Frío, Castor and Pollux. To the west, lie lakes Atravesado, Elizalde, Desierto, La Paloma and Montreal. The road to Atravesado actually continues all the way to Lago Portales, close to Puerto Aysén, but there is currently no means to reach Puerto Aysén itself. The largest and most visited lake in this region is **Elizalde**, where accommodation is available. The road to Elizalde continues to **Lago Caro** – a stunning drive, but without any services or accommodation. Some of the lakes to the southwest of Coyhaique border, or are within, the **Reserva Nacional Cerro Castillo**.

The **roads** in this region are generally gravel, but of reasonable quality. The road extending towards Lago Caro deteriorates and is perhaps best suited to a high-clearance vehicle or a 4x4. However, between Villa Frei and Coyhaique the road is now paved. The roads extending east towards Lago Pollux and Lago Castor actually connect to the main road from Coyhaique to the border (Paso Triana crossing), so for those wishing to enter or leave Chile without passing Coyhaique this is a short-cut between Argentina and the southern Carretera. Signposting in this region is good.

Public transport only traverses the main road, heading to and from Balmaceda airport, Puerto Ibáñez, Cerro Castillo and further south. This section is relatively well travelled, so hitching is easy. See pages 170–1 for information about public transport. To visit the lakes in this region, a private vehicle is required.

WHERE TO STAY AND EAT   *Map, page 185*

Cabañas Lago Elizalde (10 cabins) 33km from Coyhaique, next to Lago Elizalde; m (2) 2311902, (67) 2351112, (9) 97052914; e info@ catamaranesdelsur.cl; www.lagoelizalde.cl. An excellent & peaceful option close to Coyhaique, these cabins overlook the lake & have beach access. All cabins for up to 4 people with a mix of twin & dbl beds; fully equipped with private bathroom, kitchen, & balcony. No Wi-Fi, no restaurant, & electricity only from 20.00 to midnight. When not fishing, the surrounding forest is ideal for short walks to enjoy the beauty & silence in the shade of the native coihue & lenga trees or longer walks to several scenic viewpoints. Horseriding is also popular. Bring all food since there are no shops or restaurants nearby, although the staff can arrange a lamb roast with advance notice. Cash only, but cards can be used for reservations through Loberías del Sur, page 161. **$$$**

Hostería El Blanco (9 rooms & camping) El Blanco, 34km south of Coyhaique; (9) 79696027; all year. The only place to stay along this stretch of the Carretera Austral, at one of the main access points to the lakes southwest of Coyhaique, this is a surprisingly pleasant hostel & the best option relatively close to Balmaceda airport before arriving at Puerto Ibáñez or Cerro Castillo. Originally constructed in 1950 entirely from native woods & recently refurbished, the building is a monument in its own right. The rooms are of fine quality, particularly for the price. There's a decent restaurant (**$$**) serving typical Chilean fare at reasonable prices. Camping costs $4,000 & includes use of bathrooms & showers within the hostel. All rooms with central heating & private bathroom (shower, some with bath & shower). Full b/fast included. No Wi-Fi, but ample parking & laundry. Reservation required in Jan/Feb. **$$**

BALMACEDA – EXITING THE CARRETERA AUSTRAL

There's no real reason to spend any time here other than to make use of the **airport**. There was a museum, but it has closed; it boasts a fast-food restaurant, a couple of shops, and one reasonable place to eat/sleep – **El Rincon de Mirna** (*Mackena 832;* *(9) 83413528;* e *mirnanivia@gmail.com;* **$$**), but given that flights to and from Balmaceda do not generally leave or depart very early in the morning or very late at night, there is no obvious reason why a tourist would ever need to stay in the town. Note that there is **no petrol station** in Balmaceda – the nearest are in Coyhaique

(55km north), Puerto Río Tranquilo (193km southwest), or Chile Chico (93km south followed by a ferry across the lake). There is alo no ATM.

GETTING THERE
About the route
Coyhaique to Balmaceda (*55km; 1hr; paved*) The road between Coyhaique and Balmaceda is paved, and the first half of this stretch south of Coyhaique can be quite busy at times. Unless taking the detour to the lakes (pages 185–6), there is little to see or do along this section. At 6km southeast of El Blanco, the road (becoming the 245-CH) forks towards Balmaceda airport (a further 15km) or along the main Carretera Austral towards Villa Cerro Castillo (a further 53km). Regular shuttle buses synchronise with flight arrivals and departures from the airport to Coyhaique.

Balmaceda to Paso Huemules (*5km; 5mins; paved*) A further 5km east of Balmaceda and the airport is the Paso Huemules border crossing. Paperwork is done at the southern exit of Balmaceda. The road in Argentina is gravel. For those travelling north in Argentina, or coming from more northern Argentina, it is probably easier to use one of the Coyhaique border crossings (page 155). For those travelling south in Argentina, or coming from southern Argentina, it is probably easier to use the Chile Chico border crossing and take the ferry across the lake (page 218).

By bus Buses Suray operate a service between Coyhaique and Balmaceda airport, which coincides with arrivals/departures.

Car-hire companies The following companies are represented at the airport; each has a main office in Coyhaique. Most of the companies below include a full range of vehicles.

🚗 **Econorent** ☎(56) 2272220; e reservas@ econorent.cl; www.econorent.cl. Daily & weekly rentals.
🚗 **Europcar** ☎(67) 2255171, (9) 78063025; e Javier.rodriguez@tattersall.cl; www.europcar.cl
🚗 **Hertz** ☎(67) 2245780, (9) 77493315; e counter_coyhaique@autorentas.cl; www. hertz.cl
🚗 **Recasur** ☎(67) 2238990, (9) 90158550;

e info@recasur-rac.com; www.recasur-rac.com. Min 24hrs' rental.
🚗 **Traeger** ☎(67) 2231648, (9) 96406412; e contacto@traeger.cl; www.traeger.cl. A local company with 28 years' experience in the region. Daily, weekly & monthly rentals, with the option to rent a car with driver.
🚗 **Varona** ☎(67) 2216674, (9) 9291802; e rentacar@varona.cl; www.varona.cl

By air There are two Sky Airlines flights a day (*14.05 to Punta Arenas & 10.30 to Puerto Montt*) and three LAN flights (*10.50 to Puerto Montt, 13.30 to Santiago & 17.30 to Santiago via Puerto Montt*). Balmaceda airport has no internet, no ATM, and no tourist information. There is a small kiosk and a basic cafeteria upstairs. There are currently no international flights to/from Balmaceda.

Airport transfers As well as the standard bus companies working this route, private transfers to and from the airport can be organised with three companies. Prices in a shared van are approximately $5,000 per person, while a private taxi service is more expensive. It is wise to arrange both with 24 hours' notice.

Transfer T & T Balmaceda airport, by car-hire stands; ☎(67) 2256000, (9) 3123939; e tranytur@

gmail.com; www.tranytur.cl
Transfer Valencia Lautaro 828, Coyhaique;

(67) 223 3030; e transfervalencia@hotmail.com; **Transfers Velasquez** (67) 2250413, (9)
www.transfervalencia.cl   85050886; e transfer.velasquez@gmail.com;
                                                     www.transfervelasquez.cl

PUERTO IBÁÑEZ – A DETOUR

South of the Carretera Austral, at the junction 6km before Cerro Castillo, Puerto
Ibáñez is a modest town visited principally *en route* to/from Argentina or for the
Chile Chico ferry. The traditional pottery of the region is the cultural highlight,
utilising a reddish clay partially covered with stretched leather, often painted with
images from the archaeological cave paintings in the region. Around the town is
some beautiful countryside, but it is rare for visitors to spend more than a day in
the town itself. The central square is disproportionately large for a town this size,
but in proportion to the looming mountains in the background. Wide avenues and
long roads create the impression that Puerto Ibáñez is larger than it really is. It does
not even have a petrol station, and the few restaurants seem to open randomly, if at
all. However, it is logistically important as a main ferry route to Chile Chico, which
may necessitate spending a night here.

HISTORY The commune of Río Ibáñez was founded in 1921, but the town was not
founded until 1924. Both are named after a Chilean miner, Cornelio Ibáñez. The
commune also includes the localities of Cerro Castillo to the north, Chile Chico
to the south, Bahía Murta, Puerto Río Tranquilo and Puerto Sánchez to the west.
The commune is part of the province of General Carrera, and, of course, within the
region of Aysén.

Various **cave paintings** demonstrate clearly that this region was inhabited at
least 6,000 to 7,000 years ago. The main murals can be found in the Valle Ibáñez
and consist of handprints which, archaeologists assume, represent the people that
lived in the area during this period. There are also basic paintings of guanacos
and ñandú being hunted which shows how this population lived. In the winter
months, these animals would seek shelter and food from the snow-capped
mountains and bitterly cold windswept estepa (arid native grassland) in this
valley, making them an easy target for the hunters as they could be easily hunted
within the confinements of the valley. The most famous of these archaeological
sites open to the public is the 'Parédon de los Manos' ('Hands Mural'), with
paintings thought to be 3,000 years old. It can be accessed from the School
Museum in Cerro Castillo (page 197). Other samples of this art can be found on
the northern shores of Lago General Carrera and in the cave of the Río Pedregoso
close to Chile Chico.

The region was inhabited by the Aónikek (also referred to as Tehuleches, or
Patagones), who arrived in the deep southern region of Chile approximately 12,000
years ago. They were nomadic hunter-gatherers, and the first documented encounter
with Europeans was in 1520 with Hernando de Magallanes, one of South America's
key explorers. They lived in patriarchal societies, where wives were purchased with
guanaco skins, ñandú feathers (a small native ostrich) or by offering the family a
certain amount of hunting days. Guanacos were the main source of food and the
skins were used as clothing and to make boots. Despite the abundance of water in
the region, they barely ate fish, and needless to say fruit and vegetables were scarce
at these latitudes.

Today the town has a population of approximately 800, and survives mainly
from agriculture and tourism.

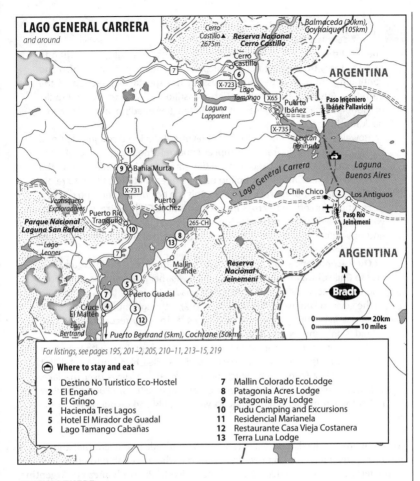

LAGO GENERAL CARRERA
and around

Balmaceda (30km),
Coyhaique (105km)

Cerro
Castillo▲ **Reserva Nacional**
2675m   **Cerro Castillo**

Cerro
Castillo

ARGENTINA

7

6

X-723

*Lago
Tamango* X65

*Laguna
Lapparent*

Puerto
Ibáñez

**Paso Ingeniero
Ibáñez Pallavicini**

X-735

*Levicán
Península*

11

9 ○Bahía Murta

*Laguna
Buenos Aires*

X-731

Lago General Carrera

Chile Chico 2 ○Los Antiguos

*Ventisquero
Exploradores*

Puerto Río
Tranquilo

Puerto
Sánchez

265-CH

**Paso Río
Jeinemeni**

**Parque Nacional
Laguna San Rafael**

10

8

*Lago
Leones*

13

7

ARGENTINA

N

*Mallín
Grande*

**Reserva
Nacional
Jeinemeni**

Bradt

1

5 ○Puerto Guadal

7

4

3

Cruce
El Maitén

12

0 ———————— 20km
0 ———————— 10 miles

*Lago
Bertrand*   Puerto Bertrand (5km), Cochrane (50km)

For listings, see pages 195, 201–2, 205, 210–11, 213–15, 219

🛌 **Where to stay and eat**

1	Destino No Turístico Eco-Hostel	**7**	Mallín Colorado EcoLodge
2	El Engaño	**8**	Patagonia Acres Lodge
3	El Gringo	**9**	Patagonia Bay Lodge
4	Hacienda Tres Lagos	**10**	Pudu Camping and Excursions
5	Hotel El Mirador de Guadal	**11**	Residencial Marianela
6	Lago Tamango Cabañas	**12**	Restaurante Casa Vieja Costanera
		13	Terra Luna Lodge

GETTING THERE
About the route

Balmaceda junction to Puerto Ibáñez (*78km; 1hr; paved*) South of El Blanco and the junction to Balmaceda, the Carretera Austral continues southwest on a fine paved road for 47km to a second junction. It continues west a further 6km to Cerro Castillo, or detours 31km south to Puerto Ibáñez. There are impressive views of the Lago General Carrera at the approach to Puerto Ibáñez.

Puerto Ibáñez to the Argentine border (*20km; 30mins; gravel*) Some 20km east of Puerto Ibáñez lies the border with Argentina (Paso Ingeniero Ibáñez Pallavicini). Paperwork is completed at the eastern exit of Puerto Ibáñez. The road quality towards the border is reasonable gravel, and even in winter the road is passable without the use of chains. However, reports are mixed as to the road quality on the Argentine side of the border, and it is approximately 100km further to Perito Moreno in Argentina, on gravel. This is not a common border crossing, and for those heading north (or arriving from the north), it may be wiser to use Paso Huemules (Balmaceda; page 187) or one of the various Coyhaique borders (page 155). For those heading south (or arriving from the south), the Chile Chico/

CHOOSING THE BEST ROUTE

There is little reason to visit Puerto Ibáñez in its own right, other than to take the **ferry** from here to Chile Chico. Taking the ferry to Chile Chico and continuing south involves either missing the spectacular section of the Carretera Austral between Villa Cerro Castillo and Puerto Río Tranquilo, or doubling back on oneself at El Maitén (ie: heading north to come back south).

However, skipping Puerto Ibáñez in favour of driving through Villa Cerro Castillo and Puerto Río Tranquilo implies either missing the stunning lakeside road along the south of Lago General Carrera east of Cruce El Maitén in the direction of Chile Chico, or doubling back on oneself at Chile Chico to rejoin the Carretera Austral at Cruce El Maitén. This can be done as one long day trip.

For those intending to **cross into Argentina at Chile Chico**, it is perhaps wisest to avoid the ferry and take the longer terrestrial route north of the lake and drive along the south of the lake to the border. Both these routes are worth doing if time allows it.

Our recommendation, for those with sufficient time, is to do a round-trip visit to Chile Chico in one or two days if the weather is acceptable. We would also highly recommend taking the back road from (close to) Cerro Castillo to the Levicán Peninsula (see box, page 192), although this cannot be done in reverse in anything other than a sturdy 4x4. Thus our recommended tour excludes only one section in this region: the ferry.

If time constraints are an issue, a good alternative for those with their own vehicle is to miss the southern coastal road to Chile Chico, and instead visit Puerto Sánchez (page 200), which offers comparable views over the lake. This would allow a visit to the marble caves (page 202) from Puerto Sánchez rather than from Puerto Río Tranquilo, which would also be our preference.

Los Antiguos border is far easier (page 218). Indeed, it appears that the Ibáñez border is principally used by people in a hurry who are unable to obtain a ticket on the ferry and prefer to drive from Chile Chico to Puerto Ibáñez via Argentina, which is quicker than going around the entire Lago General Carrera.

By bus Various shuttle vans operate between Coyhaique and Puerto Ibáñez to synchronise with the Sotramin ferries to Chile Chico (page 46). This is a well-transited route, and hitchhiking is also possible. There are no other public transport options in or out of Puerto Ibáñez. For those wishing to go towards Cerro Castillo or further down the Carretera Austral, take any shuttle up to the Carretera Austral and await a southbound bus or hitchhike.

Two shuttle buses operating between Coyhaique and Puerto Ibáñez are: **Buses Carolina** (♦ *(9) 89521529*) and **Transportes Lukas** (♦ *(9) 83541503*).

By ferry Puerto Ibáñez is the northern terminal for ferries across Lago General Carrera – see page 46 for details. Ferries permit bicycles as well as foot passengers, and have limited space for cars and motorbikes.

 WHERE TO STAY

🛖 **Patagonia Bordelago** (5 cabins) Luis Risopatron 55; ♦ *(67) 2423284, (9) 68472273*; e info@patagoniabordelago.cl; www. patagoniabordelago.cl. High-quality cabin complex with a well-maintained garden & parking. A good option for a larger family or group. Some staff speak German & English. 2 cabins have dbl or twin beds & 3 cabins have a dbl bedroom & a 2nd bedroom with 2 bunk beds. The cabins are fully equipped with satellite TV, microwave, refrigerator, Wi-Fi & wood-fired heaters. Native wood is used extensively for the furniture. Other services include a quincho, a kids play room, table tennis, board games in each cabin, a laundry service & mountain bike rental. Home-cooked local meals & b/fast can be arranged. They offer horseriding, fishing trips & 4x4 tours of the region. Reservations via their website. **$$$**

⌂ **Hostel and Camping Don Omar** (3 rooms & camping) Av General Carrera 365; \(67) 2423293; e omarpapp@gmail.com. No frills hostel with b/fast included. 3 twins with Wi-Fi. Small campground with good shelter & shade in the summer. Outside hot showers & toilets with BBQ areas. The hostel is not good value at $12,000/night but could be a good option when accommodation elsewhere is full;

camping $3,000pp. Reservations by phone or email with no deposit required. **$–$$**

⌂ **Hospedaje Don Francisco** (5 rooms) San Salvador 593; \(67) 2423234, (9) 85033626; e hospedajefrancisco@yahoo.com; ⊕ all year. This hostel feels like an old stately mansion that retains some of its original charm, at times resembling a museum. The rooms consist of 1 sgl, 1 twin, 1 trpl, 1 dbl & 1 dbl with a sgl bed, all with shared bathrooms, b/fast (included) with yoghurt & avocados, laundry & Wi-Fi. Patricia, the owner, prepares a good hearty home-cooked lunch or dinner for $6,000 (**$$**). One of the best-value hostels in this region. Credit cards accepted. **$**

⌂ **Hospedaje and Restaurant El Cata** (7 rooms) Av Padre Antonio Ronchi 30; \(67) 2423283, (9) 88521986; e lethi.cq@hotmail. com. A backpacker option with small rooms & shared bathrooms, Wi-Fi, & a basic b/fast is $3,000 extra. However, this hostel runs a reasonably sized restaurant, serving milanesa, chicken & chips/salad (**$**). **$**

✗ **WHERE TO EAT AND DRINK** Most restaurants are located in the hostels listed above, but there are some alternatives.

✗ **Restaurante Vabu** Av Padre Antonio Ronchi 192; \(67) 2423341. Both a restaurant & simple bar serving a menu of the day that sometimes runs out in the evening, consisting of homemade regional fare. After the food runs out, a few locals may gather over cans of Cristal & Escudo or a glass of their limited stock of spirits. **$$**

✗ **Servicio de Comida Ximena** Av Padre Antonio Ronchi 401 & cnr of Carlos Soza. A

small café that stays open until past midnight on w/ends. Simple food & drinks with vibrant Chilean dance music, the décor is *hauso* (the Chilean gaucho) themed. The only real late-night option in town, & the dancing starts well after midnight. **$$**

🍴 **Bakery Muffy** Av Antonio Ronchi 257; \(9) 95133550, (9) 87472174. Freshly baked bread daily except Sun.

OTHER PRACTICALITIES There is **no petrol station** in Puerto Ibáñez – be sure to fill up in Coyhaique (93km north of here), Chile Chico (across the lake), or Puerto Río Tranquilo (162km southwest). It is usually possible to buy petrol from unofficial vendors at elevated prices, but it's best not to rely on this (also in Villa Cerro Castillo). The **tourist information centre** is on the lake side of Parque Costanera – head to the end of Av Padre Ronchi where it meets the lake and it's in front of the new wharf.

Repairs
Vulcanización Amadeo Carlos Soza 157; \(9) 56420484, (9) 89924423. Quick & effective

puncture repair, based out of the back of Amadeo's house so outside ill-defined working hours he is not hard to find.

SIGHTSEEING AND EXCURSIONS If you're in Puerto Ibáñez, make time to visit a pottery workshop. While there is little else to see and do within the town itself, it makes a good base for excursions in the area, including trips to Chile Chico or into Argentina.

Pottery workshops The characteristic pottery of the region is made from the clay from the Río Ibáñez and is, broadly speaking, terracotta-coloured. Most workshops are on the plaza or a block away. The painting of the pottery is based around local prehistoric paintings found in the region. The classic symbol is of a long-necked guanaco (that to the untrained eye might appear like a giraffe) feeding its baby (*guanaca con cría*), taken from one of the prehistoric cave paintings.

Pottery is a relatively new arrival in Puerto Ibáñez. Father Antonio Ronchi (see box, page 125) launched training programmes in 1967 and into the 1970s for the female residents to develop an income-generating skill. A subsequent modification was to stretch thin sheets of leather around parts of the pottery, hand-stitched, typically around the bases of jugs. There are a variety of objects available for sale (cups, plates, bowls, jugs for example), and also two standard sets consisting of six or seven items, and available in different sizes. A tour of a workshop is interesting for Spanish-speakers, and generally free if you buy something. The pots are one of the few truly distinctive souvenirs of the entire Carretera Austral region and, while quality ranges widely, they are unique items not found elsewhere in Latin America. Many items are sturdy and not overly ornate, so can be fairly safely packed into a rucksack. Opening hours are informal.

The **Taller Artesanal Marina workshop** (*Carlos Soza 246;* \ *(9) 81728708;* e *artesanias_eva61@yahoo.es*) is owned by Eva Carrillo who was one of Ronchi's first students. Her workshop is on the north of the central plaza, and she offers a

THE LEVICÁN PENINSULA – A SCENIC DETOUR

Head 3km north out of Puerto Ibáñez on the main road and take the simple detour west towards the **Ibáñez waterfall**. This is worth a quick stop, but thereafter continue for approximately 1km across two bridges and up a very steep gravel road to a junction. To the left lies the Levicán Peninsula; to the right the road continues up to the Carretera Austral close to Cerro Castillo. It is possible that a high-clearance non-4x4 can reach Levicán, but do not attempt the *northward* section of this road towards the Cerro Castillo in a regular vehicle, due to a brutal gravel incline (for more on this road, see page 193).

Quite why there is a road to Levicán is unclear. It is barely inhabited. There are no services. At the thin stretch of land connecting Levicán to the mainland there are a few houses and small farms, and reportedly a campsite and a micro-brewery, but without signposts. The road continues onto the peninsula and ends abruptly at a beach on the west. The sole purpose of traversing this section is to admire the stunning beauty of the region, particularly on the return journey north, with incredible views of Cerro Castillo in the distance. Along this section, depending on the weather, views of Puerto Ibáñez, with the mountains in the background, reveal the true scale of the southeastern extreme of the Reserva Nacional Cerro Castillo. Periodic views of Cerro Castillo in the distance emerge through lesser mountains in the foreground. It is 23km from the dead-end of this road to the junction. Continue straight to return to Puerto Ibáñez, or veer left (in a 4x4 only) on the 'back route' to Cerro Castillo (page 193). With good weather the roads immediately to the north and south of the lake are some of the most beautiful in the entire of Aysén, and the road to the Levicán Peninsula is a fine example.

quick tour explaining the process, from preparing the clay and the moulds to the firing process, polishing and painting the finished product, and the use of leather.

CERRO CASTILLO

The dramatic approach to the village of Cerro Castillo offers vast panoramic vistas of the entire valley, with the snow-capped mountain range of the same name glistening to the west. A few dozen hair-pin bends later, the village itself is fairly drab, serving as a mere springboard to the mountain that deservedly features on most itineraries along the Carretera Austral. Besides the beauty of the valley, Cerro Castillo offers some of the most accessible trekking and horseriding opportunities along the Carretera. The jagged basalt peaks are the crown jewel of the national reserve, named for the resemblance to the battlements of medieval castles, and reach an altitude of 2,675m. The reserve covers 180,000ha of rugged mountains and roaring trout-filled rivers, waterfalls, hanging glaciers, lagoons and native bush. Indeed, Cerro Castillo, along with Parque Pumalín to the north and Parque Patagonia further south, are fast becoming as iconic a Patagonian trekking destination as the more established treks around Torres del Paine and El Chaltén.

GETTING THERE Note that the nearest petrol station is Coyhaique or Puerto Río Tranquilo, but see also the mini market, page 196.

About the route
Puerto Ibáñez to Cerro Castillo (*37km; under 1hr; paved*) The quickest and easiest route between Puerto Ibáñez and Cerro Castillo is on the paved X-65. The road is of modest interest until the junction (31km) with the main Carretera Austral. Cerro Castillo lies 6km west of this junction and 87km southwest of Coyhaique. However, the final section of road to Cerro Castillo is spectacular. The road ascends through a series of hairpin bends to a **viewpoint** over the entire valley, where the mountain range of Cerro Castillo is visible in all its splendour, with the minscule town of Cerro Castillo beneath. There is a parking area where budding photographers can safely snap one of the definitive shots of the entire Carretera Austral. A dozen hairpin bends later, to the valley, and you will arrive in Cerro Castillo.

The 'back road' from Puerto Ibáñez (*36km; 1hr; gravel)* This spectacular stretch of gravel road of 36km (connects the Carretera Austral, 5km west of Cerro Castillo, and the X-65 3km north of Puerto Ibáñez) is a true highlight of the region, but it is of very poor quality – steep, gravel, and even when dry this is barely passable in anything other than a 4x4. If done from north to south it is possible in a high-clearance car, but the hill towards the junction down through a gorge is so steep that it is not possible to do this route from south to north in anything other than a 4x4. Even motorbikes may struggle here. The road weaves through stunning forest, with views of Cerro Castillo and the panoramic horizon of the Reserva Nacional Cerro Castillo. In the foreground are a series of lakes, approximately eight, some of which are unnamed. This single section of road competes seriously as one of the most picturesque sections in the entire region of Aysén. There are no services along this relatively isolated stretch, and the only available accommodation is at Lago Tamango (page 195). If travelling along this route, it is worth taking the short 23km detour to the Lévican Peninsula before heading to Ibáñez (see box, page 192).

By public transport No official buses begin or terminate in Cerro Castillo, but almost all buses heading south from Coyhaique, or north from Cochrane,

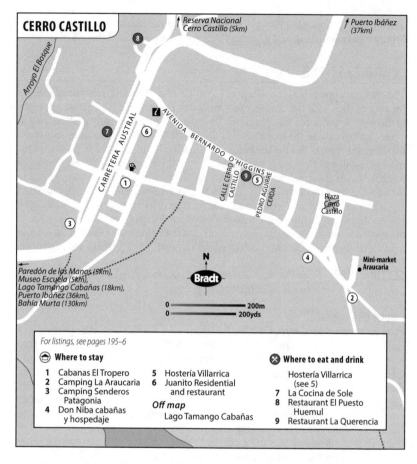

CERRO CASTILLO

↑ Reserva Nacional
Cerro Castillo (5km)

↑ Puerto Ibáñez
(37km)

Arroyo El Bosque

CARRETERA AUSTRAL

AVENIDA BERNARDO O'HIGGINS

CALLE CERRO CASTILLO

PEDRO AGUIRRE CERDA

Plaza
Cerro
Castillo

Mini-market
Araucaria

← Paredón de los Manos (5km),
Museo Escuela (5km),
Lago Tamango Cabañas (18km),
Puerto Ibáñez (36km),
Bahía Murta (130km)

N

Bradt

0 ———————— 200m
0 ———————— 200yds

For listings, see pages 195–6

🛏 **Where to stay**

1	Cabanas El Tropero	5	Hostería Villarrica
2	Camping La Araucaria	6	Juanito Residencial
3	Camping Senderos		and restaurant
	Patagonia		
4	Don Niba cabañas		**Off map**
	y hospedaje		Lago Tamango Cabañas

✕ **Where to eat and drink**

Hostería Villarrica
(see 5)
7 La Cocina de Sole
8 Restaurant El Puesto
    Huemul
9 Restaurant La Querencia

pass through the town. As a popular tourist destination, **hitchhiking** round here involves some fierce competition. The paved road from Coyhaique terminates at the southern end of the town, where glorious gravel begins. From Cerro Castillo, with a couple of stretches currently under construction, the Carretera Austral is paved all the way to La Junta. From Cerro Castillo south it is almost entirely unpaved, all the way to Villa O'Higgins.

Several private drivers offer a direct morning (*around 07.30, return around 17.00; $5,000 one-way*) trip to Coyhaique; ask the receptionist at any hotel to call and arrange since they don't have a bus stop. In Coyhaique they leave from in front of the UniMarc supermarket (*Lautaro 331*). Look for the white vans that have 'Villa Cerro Castillo' written on them. There is no public transport to Puerto Ibáñez either on the main road or the back road, nor to the Levicán Peninsula.

TOUR OPERATOR

Senderos Patagonia Southern exit of town on Carretera Austral; ☎ (9) 62244725; e senderospatagonia@gmail.com; www. aysensenderospatagonia.com. Offer a wide range of horse treks in the region, including some more off-the-beaten-track options, ranging from short day treks to multi-day adventures. The owner, Christian Vidal, is a recognised horse trainer, & practises 'Natural Horsemanship' – think of the horse whisperer. It is possible to observe him training wild Patagonian horses, which are very strong & sure footed in this rough terrain where they were born & raised – riders will be amazed where these Patagonian-bred horses will go. Senderos Patagonia also run a campsite/hostel (page 196).

WHERE TO STAY *Map, page 146, unless otherwise stated*

Cabañas El Tropero (2 cabins) Carretera Austral 305; (9) 77595766; e mirandatellez@ hotmail.com; www.eltropero.cl. Relatively new cabins, clean & comfortable, sleep up to 6 people, complete kitchen, cable TV, wood-stove heating, secure parking. A pleasant change from most of the other older low-quality cabins in the area. Central location on the Carretera Austral. The friendly owner, Eliana, offers a hearty b/fast for an additional $4,000pp consisting of lemon pie or apple cake, scrambled eggs, home-baked bread with cheese & homemade jam, plus tea or coffee. **$$$**

Juanito Residential and restaurant (10 rooms) Carretera Austral; (9) 73773110; e margaritamartelh@gmail.com. No-frills accommodation & food conveniently located beside the bus stop. The upstairs private rooms range in size from a sgl to a quadruple. There is 1 dbl room & a trpl room each with their own bathrooms; the rest have shared bathrooms. Kitchen, large dining room & sitting area with cable TV downstairs, Wi-Fi & laundry. A basic buffet b/fast consists of bread, cheese, ham & jams along with coffee or tea. The restaurant offers reasonably priced ($–$$) lunches & dinners as well as large sandwiches (also open to non-residents). Credit cards accepted. **$$$**

Lago Tamango Cabañas [map, page 189] (3 cabins) Back road towards Levicán, 18km from Cerro Castillo; (9) 99193708, (9) 98136634, (9) 93195627; e info@lagotamango.com; www.lagotamango.com; mid-Sep to mid-Apr. Lovely cabins with views over Lago Tamango & Cerro Castillo. Some 6km south of Cerro Castillo, take the turning to the south & continue for 12km. This detour is highly recommended as one of the most beautiful stretches of road in the entire region, & these cabins are the only accommodation along this section. They are set back slightly from the lake & have a small balcony from which to enjoy the view. Wood-stove heaters & electricity from a generator & solar panels. No cellphone coverage, internet, laundry, or TV. Instead the property has 200m of coast with a small beach. With advance warning, the staff here can arrange tours in the region, including to lesser-known archaeological paintings. The owners stumbled across the region years before there was a road here & have spent 2 decades slowly constructing their home & cabins by the lake. B/fast not included, but can be arranged for a small fee, otherwise be entirely self-sufficient for food – the nearest shop is in Cerro Castillo. Highly recommended. **$$$**

Don Niba cabañas y hospedaje (4 rooms, 1 cabin) Los Pioneros 872; (9) 94740408; e donniba19@gmail.com. A popular, clean & comfortable hostel with a reputation for serving a decent b/fast (included). 2 rooms with private bathroom, 2 shared, all dbl. The owner has an interesting collection of photos taken from the nearby archaeological site, the Paredón de los Manos. **$$**

Hostería Villarrica (5 rooms) Av Bernardo O'Higgins 592; (9) 66560173; e hospedaje. villarrica@gmail.com; www.hosteriavillarrica. wix.com/cerrocastillo. Excellent hostel with good restaurant. Large & spacious rooms with comfortable beds; 1 with 3 sgl beds, 2 with twin beds & a 4th en-suite room with a dbl & sgl. The large shared bathroom may be inadequate when the hostel is full. The upstairs wood-fired heater is ideal for drying wet clothes & boots, but may be insufficient to heat the hostel in winter. Access to the upstairs bedrooms is via a steep wooden staircase that could be challenging for some. B/fast is included & consists of fresh bread, homemade jams, cheese, ham, tea or coffee. The restaurant (page 196) includes large sandwiches & prepared dishes for lunch & dinner. The bar serves a selection of micro-brewed beers along with the standard beers & a small selection of wines. There is also a small minimarket located next door. Clean & represents good value for money. **$$**

Camping La Araucaria (3 large dome tents) Los Pioneros 962; (9) 73754574; e cabalgatacastillo@gmail.coml. A family rural tourism company that specialises in horseriding excursions, camping & parrillas. The campground is at the end of a no-exit street with good tree shelterbelts to give protection from the winds that lash this area. The dome tents have electricity & 4 bunk beds to sleep up to 8 people. The large flat camping area has some covered tables & benches, hot water & a large quincho. The owner, Felidor, organises a popular 3hr-horse trek to the School Museum (page 197) for $20,000pp. **$**

⚑ Camping Senderos Patagonia (2 cabins) Southern exit of town on Carretera Austral; \(9) 62244725; e senderospatagonia@gmail.com; www.aysensenderospatagonia.com. A small family-run campground with good shelter from trees & spectacular views of Cerro Castillo. The campsites are neatly terraced out of the side of a bush-clad hill providing privacy between sites. A small hostel is currently being built & should be completed in 2015 (see www.bradtupdates.com/schile for updates). There is hot water & Wi-Fi. Besides the stunning views, the owners, Cristian & Mary, are professional mountain guides & also offer horse trekking. Their company, Senderos Patagonia (page 194), specialises in small-group travel in Patagonia. **$**

✕ WHERE TO EAT AND DRINK *Map, page 194*

As well as the restaurants in the accommodation listed above, there are further options:

✕ Restaurant El Puesto Huemul Camino Estero del Bosque; \(9) 69021632; e contacto@puestohuemul.com; www.puestohuemul.com; ⏱ 14.00–22.00 daily. A gem of a restaurant run by an Argentine couple, this restaurant is located at the entrance to Cerro Castillo on the right-hand side as you enter the town from the north. The view from the large restaurant windows is a picture postcard, with trees in the foreground & the snow-capped peaks of the towering pinnacles of Cerro Castillo behind. The quality & service of the food & wine complements the view. All the food is prepared on site using organic regional ingredients wherever possible. Some of the most popular dishes are barbecued lamb, smoked salmon, homemade pasta, pizzas, guava pie, lemon pie, mixed salad & freshly baked bread. There is also a large wine selection & excellent advice to help you choose the most appropriate tipple for the occasion. Inside is a small shop selling regional products, boutique beers, marmalades, bottled fruits & hand-knitted articles from locally spun sheep wool. Excellent value for money. **$$$**

✕ Hostería Villarrica The restaurant of this hostel offers a wide range of *churascos* (sandwiches that resemble a large hamburger), including vegetarian options. The main plates are steak meals with a selection of fries, eggs or salad. There is beer on tap as well as a small selection of wines & regional beers. Friendly staff & good service in a relaxed family atmosphere. Good choice. **$$**

✕ Restaurant La Querencia O'Higgins 522; \(9) 95030746; ⏱ for b/fast, lunch & dinner. A favourite with locals. Tour buses use this restaurant as their lunch stop. Good-value set-menu lunches for around $5,000; the churasco is possibly large enough for 2. Limited selection of beers & wines. Good service. *Lunch* **$**, *dinner* **$$**

✕ La Cocina de Sole Carretera Austral 7; \(9) 87267082. An excellent place for a quick sandwich or a simple meal with drinks, located in 2 decommissioned Coyhaique buses joined together & converted into a roadside diner at the base of Cerro Castillo. The owner, Soledad, started this business in the back of a van which survives to this day as a drinks stall. These buses have nostalgic significance for the people of the region, particularly those who met their partners while riding on them! This is a late-night roadside diner & a great place to meet other travellers while sitting outside on the small deck watching the stars on a warm summer's evening. Great value for a quick, simple meal & drink ($5,000 for meal & drink). Great with kids. **$**

OTHER PRACTICALITIES The **tourist office** is located beside the radio masts as you enter town from the north (*cnr Av Bernado O'Higgins & Carretera Austral*), and is worth visiting if planning to hike in the region. There are very few shops in Cerro Castillo, and no laundry, petrol station, ATM, or dedicated car mechanic. The small **mini market** (*Araucaria Herminio Vargas 297*) has a wide assortment of essentials such as meat, fruit, dry foods, and possibly fuel for your car in five-litre bottles. The hardware store on Los Antiguos might be able to help with mechanical problems.

SIGHTSEEING AND EXCURSIONS Those who stop in Cerro Castillo for anything other than a sandwich generally come for one thing: the **trekking**. The paved road from the north ends at the town limit, and many simply push on south towards Puerto Río Tranquilo. Yet the climbing and trekking on Cerro Castillo are probably the most accessible along the entire Carretera Austral, and there are also excellent horse-trekking opportunities being developed around the village.

Horseriding This is a wonderful area for horseriding with many breathtaking views of snow-capped mountains, roaring rivers and picturesque lakes and it is a lot easier (and quicker) to ride a horse along this steep, bush-clad, mountainous terrain than it is to attempt it on foot. Cerro Castillo has a strong gaucho history as the horse was the main form of transport until recent times when the road was fully developed. Many of the old cattle trails used by the farmers to transport their cattle to market are now being rediscovered through horse trekking in the region, and tourists can now get off the beaten track and experience the true gaucho culture – Senderos Patagonia (page 194) offer treks, including one to the lagoon at the top of Cerro Castillo. The owner of Camping La Araucaria (page 195), Felidor, organises a popular 3-hour horse trek to the School Museum (see below) for $20,000 per person.

Museo Escuela (*School Museum; www.museoescuela-cerrocastillo.cl;* ⊕ *08.00–13.00 & 15.00–18.00 Mon–Fri, 08.00–13.00 Sat; entry $1,000/500 adult/child*) Follow the Carretera Austral south for approximately 4km and then take the first left turn after the bridge over the Río Ibáñez. Drive or walk for approximately 1km to the site of Villa Cerro Castillo's first school.

After years of neglect, the old Cerro Castillo School was recently restored – it was recognised as a National Monument in 2008 and inaugurated in January 2014 as a museum. This impressive two-storey building was built by settlers in 1955 and operated for 16 years. Its original construction used traditional materials and building techniques. Its outer walls are brick, the floor and rafters were hand-cut from enormous tree trunks, and the spectacular roof was constructed with hand-carved *tejuela* wood shingles. This beautiful building now serves to educate visitors about the settlers of Valle Ibáñez and the first inhabitants of the area. These were groups of hunter-gatherers who occupied these lands more than 5,000 years ago.

There is a large viewing platform to admire the landscape of the Río Ibáñez and Cerro Castillo. Below is a central investigation centre where archaeologists investigate more than 80 recorded sites of the original inhabitants of the area. Geologists and volcanologists also use the on-site laboratory to study the active and sometimes destructive nearby Volcán Hudson (page 180).

Sendero de Chile (*31km from junction with Carretera Austral; 2 days; easy*) This section of the Sendero de Chile (see box, page 121) extends along the beautiful back road towards the Levicán Peninsula, past a series of trout-filled, crystal-clear mountain lakes, surrounded by native bush – the view towards the Cerro Castillo peak is simply superb. It's a photographer's paradise. The view from the top of the hill on the eastern side of Lago Tamango, with the lake in the foreground and Cerro Castillo in the background, is one of the most spectacular sights in the region. The trek then descends into the southern beech forest of Valle Río Ibáñez and winds its way along the valley floor to finish in Villa Cerro Castillo.

Paredón de los Manos archaeological site This site is located only 200m before the School Museum and is an excellent opportunity to explore ancient Patagonian culture and see the traces left by the Tehuelches. The Valle Ibáñez is one of the most important archaeological regions in central Patagonia. The Paredón de los Manos is a rock wall protected under an overhang with hand prints of adults and children dating back approximately 3,000 years. The Tehuelche artistic style was constantly evolving with some of the earlier paintings depicting hunting scenes of guanacos. Later they began to portray hands as positive and negative images. They painted with a mixture of dyes, including blood and mineral oxides blown through a hollowed-out guanaco bone. Fortunately most of these paintings are protected from the elements. The guides are informative and give a brief description of the hunting that took place in the valley below. Some speak basic English.

Reserva Nacional Cerro Castillo (*www.conaf.cl/parques/reserva-nacional-cerro-castillo; $2,000/1,000/500 foreigner/Chilean national/child*) This 18,000ha national reserve is located 75km south of Coyhaique, and its main attraction is the impressive south face of Cerro Castillo (2,675m). The basalt spires are the crowning centrepiece and from a distance this mountain looks like a medieval castle. The upper slopes are covered with large névés and hanging glaciers, and below the formidable mountain peaks are beautiful valleys with roaring rivers and southern beech forests. The reserve headquarters are located at the southern point of Laguna Chiguay on the Carretera Austral, 60km south of Coyhaique and 35km north of Cerro Castillo.

TREKKING CERRO CASTILLO (*43–62km, depending on detours; 4 days, but can be shortened to 3 days; medium to demanding – requires a high level of fitness; highest pass is 1,600m*) The best time to trek Cerro Castillo is between mid-November and late March, subject to weather conditions – be aware that extreme weather and snow storms with gale-force winds can occur even in January – in 2014 a trekker died of hypothermia on this mountain. There are no refuges and mountain guides recommend a four-season tent, a three-season sleeping bag, layered thermal clothing and rainwear to cover all possible weather conditions. Trekking poles are recommended, especially to assist with river crossings and steeper descents. A mountain stove and food for an extra couple of days are prudent accessories in case you have to wait out a storm. Do not forget a brimmed hat, woollen hat, sunglasses and sunscreen. Be prepared for strong winds on the higher mountain passes.

It is not obligatory to register at the Reserva Nacional Cerro Castillo headquarters, but it is highly advisable, for safety reasons, to obtain up-to-date information (about the trek, the status of the river crossings, weather forecasts, etc), and also to pick up a free map. Ask (in basic Spanish) the park ranger to clearly mark on the map where the 'emergency exit' is, as it is not marked on the standard CONAF map. There is a CONAF **campsite** directly in front of the reserve headquarters which allows trekkers to get an early start the next day. For those starting at the reserve headquarters, the first stage of the trek is to walk or hitchhike 7.5km south along the paved Carretera Austral section to the trailhead at **Las Horquetas Grandes** (68km south of Coyhaique and 27km north of Villa Cerro Castillo). Those starting from Villa Cerro Castillo will need to arrange transport to this point (the tourist information centre or a hostel can arrange this, hitchhike or take a northbound bus). Las Horquetas Grandes is no more than a sharp bend in the road where two streams meet. If arriving from Coyhaique, take any bus to Cochrane or Puerto Ibáñez; the drivers are familiar with this drop-off point.

This four-day trek can be shortened to three days either by exiting at the 'emergency exit' on day three, or by combining days three and four into one 18km, 8–10-hour day.

Day one: Las Horquetas to the Río Turbio campsite (18km; 5–7hrs)

The trek starts on an old logging road that is now used by local gauchos to herd cattle into the valleys for summer grazing. The road veers left past an old house and continues through vibrant lenga forest and farmed pastures. It follows a beautiful clear stream that must be crossed three times – take care particularly after heavy snow melt or rain. Water levels are usually higher in spring and can be chest-high. Consider wearing sandals for river crossings in order to keep trekking boots dry, and trekking poles will assist with balance. The increasingly rough 4x4 track skirts around a reed-covered lagoon with black-necked swans. The trek continues for 14km to the **CONAF hut** where the entry fee is paid at registration (this is the entrance to the actual reserve; the trek starts on private land). There is a small **campsite** with toilet, fireplace, table and benches. After another 30 minutes, trekkers arrive at Río Turbio roaring through a huge alpine valley. The track then follows the gravel riverbed south, with spectacular views of glacier-fed waterfalls over huge vertical cliffs, until it re-enters the lenga forest. Some 40–50 minutes later the trail reaches the **Río Turbio campsite** at the head of the Valle Río Turbio, where there are simple tables and a dry toilet. The rare huemul deer sometimes grazes in this section.

Day two: Río Turbio campsite to Bosque campsite (9.5km; 4–5hrs) The

trail continues upstream along the Río Turbio, which is fed by the **Ventisquero Peñon** (not visible from the main trek). The glacier and lagoon can be accessed via a **small detour** that starts 1km west of the Río Turbio campsite. For this, follow the river's south bank for about half an hour until you arrive at the muddy meltwater pool below the glacier. Back on the main trail, continue uphill through the forest and along a steep scree section to cross the El Peñon saddle (1,460m). This scree section is treacherous and may be covered in snow in spring, further complicating the pass. However, the views from the pass are spectacular, particularly for the relative proximity to a glacier emerging from Cerro Peñon and a full view of Cerro Castillo. Andean condors are often spotted here gracefully gliding between the mountain peaks with their huge wingspans. Once trekkers have descended from the El Peñon Pass on the steep and unstable scree-covered slopes, the trail borders a small stream fed from the icy outcrops that hang off Cerro Peñon stream. This is where the jagged peaks of the Cerro Castillo become visible. The track continues downstream until it arrives at the **Estero del Bosque junction** with the somewhat larger western branch of the stream descending from the Estero. The track veers right into the Valle Estero del Bosque and ascends moderately to the El Bosque campsite set within a sheltered in a valley amongst the thick lenga forest. There is a toilet, a fireplace, table and benches. In the event of bad weather this is a safe refuge to pause before the high pass the next day.

Day three: Bosque campsite to Porteadores campsite (8.2km; 5–6hrs) An

early start is recommended as winds on the pass tend to pick up around midday. The trail begins with a steep initial **climb** along the banks of the stream cascading down from the Cerro Castillo glacier lagoon, until the track reaches a small plateau at the base of the Castillo. The view from the plateau is worthy of a short break and photograph opportunity. The track then ascends the moraine surrounding the lagoon until a vantage point overlooking the turquoise lagoon and the Valle Ibáñez. This is arguably the most spectacular vista in the entire reserve. On a fine day the view extends to Lago General Carrera and beyond to Argentina. To the other side, the mountain and glacier provides a stark contrast to the turquoise lake, interrupted with the sound of ice cracking and tumbling into the lagoon below. Despite the scenic location this could equally be one of the most dangerous places on the mountain if the weather takes a turn for the worse – gale-force winds are not uncommon here. In the event of a storm lie low as there is no shelter in this section, and advance between gusts. This ridge has a clearly marked **emergency exit** (*salida de emergencia*) following the tragic death of a hiker in 2014. The track then crosses the Cerro Castillo saddle (1,600m) before descending to the forest and on to the **Porteadores campsite**. There are impressive views of Cerro Palo from here.

Day four: Porteadores campsite to Villa Cerro Castillo (*10km; 3–4hrs*) This
is potentially the shortest day of trekking due to the flat nature of the landscape – a far cry from the mountainous terrain of previous days. For those yearning for more exercise there is an optional 4–6-hour round-trip detour up the **Valle Estero Parada** and onto the **Campo Neozelandés campsite**. Otherwise the trail descends through the **Parada Canyon** to Villa Cerro Castillo, with views towards the Río Ibáñez. The trek leaves the reserve through a traditional Patagonian sheep and beef ranch, from where it is an 8km trek to Cerro Castillo, 6km of which is along a country road.

BAHÍA MURTA AND PUERTO SÁNCHEZ – A DETOUR

Bahía Murta has relatively little of interest to the typical tourist: accommodation is sparse, food even sparser, it is not close to the marble caves of either Puerto Sánchez or Puerto Río Tranquilo, and it is a 4km detour from the Carretera Austral. However, the road to Murta continues 25km on to **Puerto Sánchez**, which is a delightful little village. Apparently public transport is available from Puerto Sánchez, but we have seen no evidence of this. The road to Puerto Sánchez is both one of the most spectacular and dangerous along the entire Carretera Austral. It is rarely traversed, but worth the effort, and visiting the marble caves from Puerto Sánchez is arguably more pleasant than from Puerto Río Tranquilo.

GETTING THERE
About the route
From Cerro Castillo to Bahía Murta and Puerto Sanchez (*130km; 4hrs; gravel*) The Carretera Austral continues for 101km west and then south from Cerro Castillo. The road quality is acceptable but the paved road ends at Cerro Castillo, and from this point onwards a high-clearance vehicle is essential. There are no villages, towns or services along this section, possibly due to being comparatively close to Volcán Hudson (page 180) – dead trees and ash along the way serve as reminders of previous eruptions. The road passes some small lakes and weaves along two rivers (Río Ibáñez and then Río Murta), but while scenic, there is little reason to pause until the road finally reaches Lago General Carrera.

Bahía Murta is a minor (4km) detour from the Carretera Austral, some 24km north of Puerto Río Tranquilo. The road to Puerto Sánchez from Bahía Murta was completed in 2000, until which point access was exclusively by boat, usually from Puerto Río Tranquilo. Traversing the road is an adventure in itself:

it's hard to imagine how anyone could cram in more hairpin bends into so short a road. Take extreme caution. One sign warns of 'danger for 12km' – this is no understatement. There are no safety barriers; the road winds around some perilously high cliffs with landslides both above and below, and in many places there is barely sufficient room for even a single vehicle to pass, let alone two. Although only 25km, allow for an hour for this section. The ascent from Bahía Murta is simply brutal; cyclists beware. Over the pass, the road meanders less steeply down to Puerto Sánchez. Views over the lake are stunning – this is one of the only locations from which to enjoy a bird's-eye view of the turquoise Lago General Carrera. The road further south towards Chile Chico also offers stunning views of the lake, but from a lower altitude. Attempting this road when wet is unwise.

By public transport Bahía Murta is 4km from the Carretera Austral, but by far the easiest option is to take any bus travelling between Cerro Castillo and Puerto Río Tranquilo and ask to get off at the junction to Bahía Murta and walk or hitchhike to or from the village. Given the proximity and popularity of Puerto Río Tranquilo, getting a space on a bus might be difficult, particularly in peak season. However, the Chile Chico bus offered by **Transportes Costa Carrera** departs from Bahía Murta on Wednesday and Sunday at 13.00, so catching this bus from its departure point is easier. When travelling from Chile Chico to Bahía Murta (departs Tuesday and Friday at 13.00), many passengers leave from Puerto Río Tranquilo and thus there is often space towards Bahía Murta.

Travelling the final 25km to **Puerto Sánchez** is even harder. There *might* be public transport, *occasionally*, but we've never seen it, but for a village with possibly 100 inhabitants and only one public telephone, this is perhaps not so surprising. Even residents of Bahía Murta rarely go there. For those without private transport hitchhiking might be the only option. It's a long, steep walk.

WHERE TO STAY AND EAT *Map, page 189*
Puerto Sánchez (population 100) offers no formal accommodation, but you can **camp** for free (with no facilities other than tables) at the entrance to the village. A river behind the campsite at least has fresh, clean water. There are two small **shops** and, perhaps surprisingly for a village without a single guesthouse, two **laundries**. Around town there are three main activities: a drive up to an old abandoned mine, fishing, and boat trips to some marble caves.

Patagonia Bay Lodge (8 rooms) Murta Vieja camino a Capilla Santa Rosa; ✆ (32) 2996911, (9) 66408112; e gerencia@patagoniabay.cl; www.patagoniabay.cl; ⏱ Sep–Mar. The best accommodation in the region, situated 25km north of Puerto Río Tranquilo. On the northern side of the river & bridge 'El Engaño', at the head of this arm of Lago General Carrera, take the small road southeast (signposted). The building is extraordinary, built around the cardinal points of the compass, it blends modern Cubist architecture with traditional materials from the region. The main living area of the hotel is a huge cavernous space, entirely made of wood with a large stone chimney. The rooms are located in wings accessed by a number of wooden staircases, some of which appear to be floating mid air. The rooms are all dbl or twin, but a 3rd bed is available if required, all with well-equipped private bathroom & views over the forest or to the lake in the distance. Full b/fast included; dinner available if booked in advance for $16,500 (trout, vegetarian options, lamb, risotto $$$$$). Lunch can be arranged. The property is 40ha with 800m of beach on the lake, kayaks available, & they can arrange tours (fishing, horseriding, the marble caves in Tranquilo or Sánchez, etc). Wi-Fi, but no laundry. Certainly preferable to hotels in Puerto Río Tranquilo at this price level. Reservations essential in high season, deposit required. Credit cards accepted. **$$$$**

🏠 **Residencial Marianela** (6 rooms, 1 cabin) Av 18 de Septiembre 476, Bahía Murta (opposite church by plaza); ☎ (9) 82282782; e angelica1373@gmail.com. A basic but clean option for backpackers consisting of 6 twin rooms all with shared bathroom, a basic b/fast, Wi-Fi,

satellite TV, ample off-street parking & laundry service. Also runs a restaurant ($) with a menu of the day for $6,000. There is a basic cabin at the back for 5 people. Reservations are taken by phone or email. This hostel is often full in Jan & Feb so book in advance. Rooms are $10,000pp & the cabin is $50,000. **$**

EXCURSIONS AND SIGHTSEEING For many, a trip to the **marble caves** at Puerto Sánchez is preferable to the more touristy caves in Puerto Río Tranquilo. Firstly, they are far closer to the town – with a decent pair of binoculars the caves are visible from the shore. The boat trips are therefore shorter, and thus cheaper (*$30,000 per boat, up to 6 people*), and less exposed to the prevailing winds. Secondly, the caves are not heaving with hundreds of camera-toting tourists – it is quite likely there will be no more than a couple of boats per day. Finally, the caves are at least as spectacular as those at Puerto Río Tranquilo. Although there is not the famous Marble Cathedral of Tranquilo (page 207), the caves are deeper and more abundant. It is also possible to swim in the caves without the worry of endless boats zipping around. Take a wetsuit (7mm minimum), mask and snorkel, fins and weights, as these are unavailable locally. Diving in the caves is great fun, and it is possible to enter the caves far further than by boat. Water transparency is not great – this is a glacial lake. However, deep cracks within the caves offer free divers some fun exploring. Some caves are sufficiently deep to warrant taking a waterproof torch. **Turismo Puerto Sánchez** (*look for the blue & white boat at wharf;* ☎ *(9) 73752280;* e *lalarcon@manquehue.net*) is run by Luis Alarcon Osorio who offers several **boat tours**, principally to the marble caves close to the village, but also to see historical wrecks of the boats that the early settlers arrived in. He can also arrange guided trips through the **old mine shafts** above the village.

For a **spectacular panoramic view** of the village, the Lago General Carrera and the rugged Andean mountain backdrop, walk for 10 minutes or drive up the hill behind the old mine to a viewing platform.

PUERTO RÍO TRANQUILO

Thanks to some extensive marketing Puerto Río Tranquilo has emerged as a tourist hub. The town is not particularly attractive, but is located close to some **marble caves** which draw tourists by the thousand meaning that, during peak times, finding accommodation and transport can be problematic; be sure to make advance reservations. The sheer volume of tourists also makes hitchhiking tricky – in fact, Tranquilo and the road to Chile Chico are possibly the worst sections for hitchhiking on the whole route – and public transport is relatively limited. However, while the town itself may be underwhelming, it is well located. Just across the lake (or, more likely, 49km driving) is the lovely village of **Puerto Sánchez**, with caves at least as impressive as those of Puerto Río Tranquilo. Approximately 30km south is the entry point to the **Ventisquero Leones**. From Puerto Río Tranquilo, it is only 49km to the junction at **Cruce El Maitén**, where the Carretera Austral continues south towards Cochrane and east on one of the most important subsidiary roads along the spectacular south side of Lago General Carrera towards Chile Chico and into Argentina (page 211).

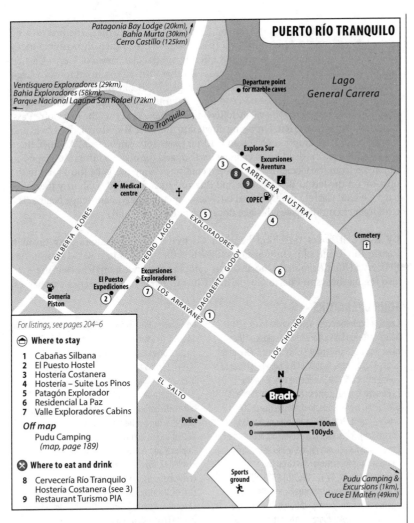

Patagonia Bay Lodge (20km),
Bahía Murta (30km)
Cerro Castillo (125km)

Ventisquero Exploradores (29km),
Bahía Exploradores (58km),
Parque Nacional Laguna San Rafael (72km)

Río Tranquilo

Lago
General Carrera

Departure point
for marble caves

Explora Sur

Excursiones
Aventura

③

⑧

⑨

CARRETERA AUSTRAL

COPEC

ℹ

+ Medical
centre

†

⑤

EXPLORADORES

④

Cemetery
†

GILBERTA FLORES

PEDRO LAGOS

Excursiones
Exploradores

⑥

DAGOBERTO GODOY

⑦

El Puesto
Expediciones

②

LOS ARRAYANES

①

Gomería
Piston

LOS CHOCHOS

For listings, see pages 204–6

🛏 **Where to stay**

1 Cabañas Silbana
2 El Puesto Hostel
3 Hostería Costanera
4 Hostería – Suite Los Pinos
5 Patagón Explorador
6 Residencial La Paz
7 Valle Exploradores Cabins

Off map
Pudu Camping
  (map, page 189)

❌ **Where to eat and drink**

8 Cervecería Río Tranquilo
   Hostería Costanera (see 3)
9 Restaurant Turismo PIA

EL SALTO

N

Bradt

0 ———— 100m
0 ———— 100yds

Police

Sports
ground
⚐

Pudu Camping &
Excursiones (1km),
Cruce El Maitén (49km)

Perhaps the biggest draw to Tranquilo is the recently constructed road to **Bahía Exploradores**, and on to the embarcation point for boats towards **Ventisquero San Rafael**. Although this is a stunning glacier, the lesser-known Ventisquero Leones (28km south of Tranquilo) is a cheaper alternative involving a healthy trek through a forest rather than the relatively sedentary trip to San Rafael.

GETTING THERE
About the route
Cerro Castillo to Puerto Río Tranquilo *(125km; 2–3hrs; gravel)* A diverse section of the Carretera Austral with reasonable quality gravel passable in any vehicle, but be aware that dust clouds when passing other vehicles reduce visibility considerably. There are corrugations on steeper sections and pot-holes on flatter sections, especially around valleys with swampy ground. There are no imminent plans to pave this section so get used to gravel from this point onwards.

The road initially follows the canyon formed by the Río Ibáñez. The first turning to the left leads to the **Museo Escuela** (page 197). The road then zigzags up a rocky outcrop devoid of any vegetation, but offering spectacular views of Cerro Castillo and the Valle Ibáñez below. At km7 there is another turn-off to the left towards **Lago Tamango** (the 'back road' to Puerto Ibáñez, page 193, ideally by 4x4). The Carretera continues along a ridge before descending to **Laguna Verde** on the left at km18, and then winds its way along the valley following Río Ibáñez to cross the low Cofré Pass. Laguna Cofré is on the left. Dropping down into the **Valle Río Murta**, dead trees and ash from the 1991 eruption of Volcán Hudson (page 180) can be seen. At km70 there is a lookout over the dead forest (*bosque muerta*) and the opaque turquoise-green Río Cajon fed from the glacier melt. The road continues along the Valle Río Murta to the turn-off on the left to Bahía Murta and Puerto Sánchez (km100). Shortly thereafter Lago General Carrera finally comes into view, and the Patagonian steppe begins. The road then circumnavigates the lake until Puerto Río Tranquilo.

By bus All buses travelling between Cochrane and Coyhaique pass through Puerto Río Tranquilo. Only one company is actually based in town – Transportes Bellavista (*Río Chrifo s/n*), who also offer camping and have a small hostel. There are also regular buses to Puerto Guadal and Chile Chico with a number of companies.

TOUR OPERATORS

Canopy Exploradores Valle Exploradores, 52km from Puerto Río Tranquilo, with sales kiosk on the main street. $15.000pp for 1½hrs. Treetop adventures across 10 platforms, 9 zip lines & 2 rappels. Similar to GoApe in the UK. Suitable for the whole family.

El Puesto Expediciones Pedro Lagos 258; (9) 62073794; www.elpuesto.cl. Hostel (page 205) & travel agent. Activities include boats, kayaks, horseriding, hikes, rock & ice climbing, & can arrange trips to San Rafael, rafting in the Río Baker, & fishing.

Excursiones Aventura Kiosk on the main street; (9) 87451486, (9) 93838523; e excursionesaventura@gmail.com. A small agency that runs the expedition to walk on the Ventisquero Exploradores with certified guides. The tour lasts between 6 & 8hrs, of which 2–4hrs are actually on the ice. They provide all equipment (crampons, helmet, etc), park entrance fee, & a light snack. If the weather is nice a windbreaker & fleece should be enough, making this an easy way for anybody with a moderate fitness level to walk

on a glacier. Price is $35,000 with own transport or $40,000 in a van to & from the trailhead.

Excursiones Exploradores Los Arrayanes 205; (9) 82528854; e reservas@valleexploradores.cl; http://excursionesexploradores.cl. Trips to the Ventisquero San Rafael on a larger, comfortable boat with bathroom on board seating up to 22 people & run by the same company that offer decent cabins in town (page 205). Recommended.

Explora Sur Kiosk on the main street; (9) 76499047, (9) 87688906; e contact@explorasur.cl; www.explorasur.cl. Trips to the marble caves & chapel, Ventisquero Exploradores, the marble caves near Puerto Sánchez, the abandoned mine at Puerto Cristal, & fishing.

Río Exploradores (9) 62050534; e reservas@ exploradores-sanrafael.cl; www.exploradores-sanrafael.cl. 2 small boats, 1 covered (10 people) & 1 open (12 people). Offer a broader range of tours on & around the Ventisquero San Rafael, including to the Isthmus of Ofqui & Valle Exploradores.

 WHERE TO STAY *Map, page 203, unless otherwise stated*

Despite being the de facto hub of the region, and bursting at the seams in peak season with visitors to the caves and glacier, Puerto Río Tranquilo is a drab town that serves simply as a launch pad to the surrounding region. The range of hostels, hotels and campgrounds expands each season, but they fill up fast and simply arriving in mid-January and hoping to find a place to sleep can be a grave disappointment – book in advance. If you're looking for decent accommodation and distance isn't an issue, then try the **Patagonia Bay Lodge** (page 201), just 25km north of the town.

El Puesto Hostel (10 rooms) Pedro Lagos 258; 📞 (9) 62073794; e contacto@ elpuesto.cl; www.elpuesto.cl. Touted as the premier accommodation in Puerto Río Tranquilo, but more likely the best of a mediocre bunch. Typical of the new breed of 'boutique' hostels – pleasantly designed but overpriced. Includes a decent b/fast & sketchy internet, but no laundry service. The design of the building is great (Francisco, the co-owner, is an architect), & guests must remove shoes & wear the slippers provided indoors. The rooms themselves are certainly a cut above the typical hostel, with comfortable beds, a cosy atmosphere, large windows, fully equipped bathrooms & a fine wooden finish. There is a decent restaurant (for guests only, vegetarian options, all local produce, river-caught salmon & trout, ethical treatment of animals), a lovely spacious sitting area, & ample parking. They arrange tours in the region (page 204), & own the main access point to the Ventisquero Exploradores, although free public access might be imminent. Popular with tour operators so reservations essential. A good-quality hostel, but not necessarily the best value for money. **$$$$**

Valle Exploradores Cabins (6 cabins) Los Arrayanes 205; 📞 (9) 82528854; e reservas@ valleexploradores.cl; www.valleexploradores.cl. Refreshingly nice cabins in a town historically known for limited accommodation. Each cabin has 2 rooms, either twin or dbl, each with its own private bathroom. A simple kitchen is adequate, particularly considering that few will spend more than a couple of days in town. Reliable hot water supply, & the internet connection was surprisingly high speed. Decent sitting area, although the tables are a little small for a full dinner. Cable TV, & a dedicated parking spot next to each cabin to avoid lugging bags far. The same company also operates one of the boats to the Ventisquero San Rafael (page 204). **$$$$**

Hostería Costanera (12 rooms & 1 cabin) Cnr of Pedro Lagos & Carretera Austral; 📞 (9) 57432175; e ipinuerhostal@gmail.com; www. hosteriacostanera.com; ⏱ all year. The largest & most upscale hotel in town, with all front rooms having great views overlooking the lake. 5 dbls, 5 twins, 1 trpl, 1 quintuple & a cabin for up to 6 people. Includes a basic b/fast, free internet in the dining area, & parking. The on-site restaurant

(page 206) serves lunch & dinner & is one of the more expensive places to eat in Puerto Río Tranquilo. The owner is the daughter of some of the original settlers in town, who arrived in 1937. Accepts all major credit cards & major currencies (US$, euro, & Argentine pesos). **$$$**

Patagón Explorador (4 cabins) Exploradores 238; 📞 (9) 99118124, (9) 66490508; e toya_jara@yahoo.es; ⏱ all year. Rustic, spacious cabañas close to the centre of town. The owners have a store just next to the cabins where travellers can stock up on supplies. The cabañas have Wi-Fi, cable TV, wood-stoves, refrigerators, kitchens & hot water. Laundry available for $3,000/load. 50% reservation policy. **$$$**

Pudu Camping and Excursions [map, page 189] (camping, 1 cabin) Carretera Austral, 1km south of Puerto Río Tranquilo; 📞 (67) 2573003, (9) 89205085; e campingpudu@gmail. com. An upmarket campground on the shore of Lago General Carrera. The campsite is set in a valley with good natural shelter & a rock cliff face to the west. The 14 pitches have a rustic table & benches, with BBQ areas & wind breaks (but no electricity). New bathrooms with hot water. A new quality cabin with double-glazed windows, for 5–6 people set on the hillside with amazing views of the lake is also now available year-round, with a dbl bedroom & a 2nd room with bunk beds & a trolley bed under. There is a couch in the lounge that can sleep an extra person if needed. The beautiful pebbled beach, with spectacular lake & mountain views, is suitable for swimming. A laundry service, massage bed & sauna are also offered. The access road is suitable for all types of vehicles including buses & trucks. Excursions can be booked from the campsite including fishing trips, horseriding, glacier treks & the (almost obligatory) marble caves. Reservations can be made online or by phone; confirm 3 days before arriving. *Camping* **$**, *cabin* **$$$**

Hostería – Suite Los Pinos (8 rooms, 1 cabin) Dagoberto Godoy 51 (in front of COPEC petrol station); 📞 (67) 2411572, (9) 73990240; e lospinos-hosteriasuite@hotmail.com; ⏱ all year. All rooms with private bathroom & thick mattresses, central heating, cable TV, Wi-Fi & basic b/fast included, making this hostel very popular with motorcyclists. 1 twin, 3 dbls & 4 sgls. The cabin has 1 en-suite dbl bedroom, a dbl bed & 2 sgl beds with a shared bathroom. Laundry service available. There's a café/restaurant (⏰ 08.00–22.00; $$). B/fast, lunch & dinner available ($7,000; $3,500 for non-guests). Better quality than many alternatives, for a slightly higher price. A 50% deposit is required to make a reservation. Credit cards accepted. **$$**

🏠 **Cabañas Silbana** (4 rooms, 3 cabins & camping) Dagoberto Godoy 197; 📞 (9) 94138195; e silbanitapinuers@gmail.com. A basic, clean backpackers' hostel. B/fast is $3,000. extra The hostel has a lounge with a large wood-fired stove that guests can use for cooking; 1 room with 3 sgl beds, 2 rooms with twin beds & 1 room with a dbl bed. The wooden cabins are very basic, all with sgl beds (1 cabin is for 10 people, the other 2 are for 6). The small camping area has toilets & showers & a place to cook with a table & chairs. Reservation by phone. Wi-Fi is available. **$**

🏠 **Residencial La Paz** (5 rooms) Exploradores 336; 📞 (9) 66488061; e lapazenpatagonia@hotmail.cl; ⏰ all year. A large hostel with bare-bones rooms, comfortable beds, cable TV, Wi-Fi, & a communal large kitchen. There is no reservation policy, & the laundry service is $6,000/load. The owners have a shop connected to the hostel for any travellers who need to stock up on supplies. They also do guided excursions to walk on the Ventisquero Exploradores for $45,000. **$**

✖ WHERE TO EAT AND DRINK *Map, page 203*

✖ **Cervecería Río Tranquilo (Arisca)** Carretera Austral s/n; 📞 (9) 98955577; 🅵 Cervecería Río Tranquilo; ⏰ lunch & dinner until midnight. Excellent & popular brewpub directly on the Carretera Austral. Great food, albeit a bit pricey, with 3 quality beers that are brewed next door. Menu includes selection of meats & sandwiches, river salmon ceviche & sashimi when available. Friendly service & a full bar for non-beer drinkers. **$$$**

✖ **Hostería Costanera** Cnr of Pedro Lagos & Carretera Austral; 📞 (9) 57432175; e ipinuerhostal@gmail.com; www. hosteriacostanera.com. Not the best-value food in town but decent quality & views over the lake, generally have 1 special for both lunch & dinner, or à la carte which lists traditional regional foods like salmon, beef, & pork. Standard fare. **$$$**

✖ **Restaurant Turismo PIA** Carretera Austral 257; 📞 (9) 66096573, (9) 52399212; e mmooch2012@hotmail.com; ⏰ 11.00–midnight daily. A popular fast-food restaurant that serves sandwiches & soft drinks, with a midday menu. One of the few late-night options. Credit cards accepted. *Take-away* **$**, *sit-down* **$$**

OTHER PRACTICALITIES There are two **petrol stations** in Puerto Río Tranquilo, but no ATM or dedicated laundry, although hostels or hotels may offer a laundry service to residents. **Shopping** is limited to a couple of small supermarkets, and the reception at Valle Exploradores Cabins (page 205) has a limited range of clothes for sale, but for all practical purposes.

Mechanic
Gomería Piston El Salto 283; 📞 (9) 57707814. Tyres & basic mechanical repairs. Possibly your only chance of getting your vehicle or motorbike repaired in town.

EXCURSIONS AND SIGHTSEEING The main reason people find themselves in Puerto Río Tranquilo is to visit the Ventisquero San Rafael and the marble caves. Other activities in or around town include rock climbing, fishing and horseriding, all of which can be organised through the tour operators listed on page 204.

The **Ventisquero Leones** some 28km south of Puerto Río Tranquilo also deserves a mention (see page 214 for a full description). The main guide offering this service is based out of Puerto Guadal but offers transport to and from the trailhead, including with pickup or drop-off at Guadal, Puerto Río Tranquilo or Cochrane, for an additional fee. Leones has the advantage of fewer tourists and a lower cost than the better-established tours to San Rafael, although accessing the glacier does involve a bit of trekking and, with no village close by, it also requires marginally more organisation to arrange a trip. In terms of sheer size, the snout of Leones is certainly smaller than that of San Rafael, but is still an impressive sight.

Marble caves The original attraction in Puerto Río Tranquilo is the network of marble caves. The glacial waters of Lago General Carrera have eroded the limestone walls surrounding this section of the lake over centuries to form unusual, Salvador Dali-esque caves. These structures appear almost to have melted into the water, supported by frozen-in-time lava-like columns which disappear into the watery base of the caves. Some of the caves are large enough for small boats to sail into them and, on a sunny day, the light reflects off the cave walls and from the relatively shallow pools at the bottom of the caves creating surreal ripple-like patterns along the walls while the water itself reflects in myriad shades of turquoise.

Countless operators offer trips to the caves and there is no need to book in advance. The journey typically takes around 2 hours including the ride to and from the caves, and boats leave from the shore of the lake next to the Carretera in the middle of the town; it can be rough and cold so be sure to take a windproof jacket. It is possible to **kayak** to the caves (the same vendors of the boat trips also rent kayaks), but do consider the strength of the wind, particularly when attempting to return in the evening. The standard boats take approximately five to seven people and cost $45,000, but negotiating for a group price is a possibility. The more luxurious method to reach the caves is via the ultra-modern **Karut boat** (*www.karut.cl; $18,000pp*), which resembles a floating spaceship. This is certainly more comfortable, but is less able than the regular boats to actually enter the caves. Being covered is an advantage, and might be more suitable for those travelling with young children. Karut also offer trips directly to Puerto Sánchez and Puerto Cristal.

For those with their own boat or kayak, there is no need to use a tour operator as the caves are not privately owned. The best way to visit the caves is actually by **swimming**, as it is then possible to enter into the deepest sections. However, this has to be arranged privately, and is more easily done in Puerto Sánchez, where the tours are more flexible. Note that the water is extremely cold all year: a wetsuit is essential, and not available for hire.

The marble caves are certainly worth a visit, but in peak season the sheer number of tourists can be off-putting. Some prefer a trip to the caves in Puerto Sánchez (page 200).

Ventisquero Exploradores The second key attraction around Puerto Río Tranquilo is the relatively accessible glacier approximately halfway along the 58km road to Bahía Exploradores. A short trek up to a viewing platform permits views over the Ventisquero Exploradores, and tours are available to hike down to, and onto, the glacier itself. The hike to the viewing platform is well marked and not technical. However, people with limited mobility and young children may find it exhausting, and slippery. There is no public transport along this road, and few people live along it so hitchhiking is difficult. However, it is a standard tour offered by various operators (page 204), including transport. For those with a vehicle the road is poor-quality gravel, meaning that a high-clearance vehicle is essential but 4x4 is not necessary. Although only 58km, budget for 2 hours one-way to reach the end of the road at Bahía Exploradores, or 1 hour if only going to the glacier itself. The road connects with the Carretera Austral at the northern exit of the town.

The glacier emerges from the Northern Ice Field, and as such is part of the Parque Nacional Laguna San Rafael, and thus accessible to all. Currently a nominal fee is charged to those wishing to traverse the private property that leads to the viewing platform (belonging to the owners of the El Puesto hostel). However, in March 2015 Victor Osorio, the Minister of Bienes Nacionales, announced that they had restored free public access to the glacier. 'We have realised an act of justice, to re-establish public access to an asset that belongs to all Chileans.' Thus the entry fee may soon be dropped!

The view of the glacier from the viewing platform is not to be compared to trips to glaciers in the region such as Montt, Steffen, San Rafael, O'Higgins, Leones or Queulat. However, for those with limited time, this is one of the most accessible glaciers in the region, and also one of the cheapest to visit. All the main tour operators offer this trip, and it is also possible to arrive by private vehicle, pay the entry fee and do the trek independently. However, a guide is highly recommended if trekking onto the actual glacier.

Parque Nacional Laguna San Rafael (*www.conaf.cl/parques/parque-nacional-laguna-san-rafael; $3,000/1,000/4,000/1,500 Chilean national adult/child/foreign adult/child*) This park is fast becoming a key tourist attraction for the entire Carretera Austral region, facilitated in part by the recent opening of a road connection from Puerto Río Tranquilo. Previously access was possible only from Puerto Chacabuco or Puerto Montt on more expensive boats travelling far greater distances or by charter plane (which is still an impressive means to view the glacier!). The national park extends as far south as Caleta Tortel but in practice the main access points are to Ventisquero San Rafael (by boat), Ventisquero Leones (trekking and boat), or Ventisquero Steffen near Caleta Tortel (trekking and boat). Experienced trekkers can enter the park independently at other locations, and guides are available in Puerto Bertrand and Cochrane for multi-day hikes towards the ice field, but these are non-standard treks for experienced hikers and mountaineers. There are no formal, marked trails in the park authorised by CONAF.

The park itself is approximately 17,400km² and encompasses the entire Northern Ice Field. Within the park are a number of mountains, including San Valentin (4,058m) and Nyades (3,078m). A number of glaciers emerging from the ice field are accessible without huge effort: San Rafael; Leones, just south of Puerto Río Tranquilo; Soler, reached from Puerto Bertrand; Steffen to the south, accessed from Caleta Tortel; and with some additional effort the Ventisquero San Quintin (hiking beyond San Rafael). However, San Rafael, and the lake named after it, are the main attraction, with a number of companies offering tours to the glacier's snout.

Laguna San Rafael is incorrectly named, as it is connected to the open ocean to the north and is therefore not a lake at all, but due to the formation of mountains around the lake it appears to be an enclosed body of water. Indeed, the southern edge of the lake borders the Isthmus of Ofqui. In 1937 the Chilean government embarked on a project to connect the Laguna San Rafael to the Río Negro, enabling a direct channel to the Golfo San Esteban to the south of the isthmus. The project was abandoned in 1943 due to lack of funding. This would have enabled boats to traverse through the inner passages of the region from Puerto Montt to Puerto Natales without having to pass the dreaded Golfo de Penas. The Navimag route between these two cities passes through the Messier Canal, but at approximately the same latitude as Caleta Tortel the boats must circumnavigate the Taitao Peninsula into open ocean, causing many a Navimag passenger to suffer sea-sickness.

Ventisquero San Rafael The most common reason to enter the park is to visit the Ventisquero San Rafael, and this is only possible with a guided tour as a boat is required (see page 204 for operators), and the park fee is included in the tour price. Flights over the glacier can be arranged (at a cost!) by charter or with Aires del Sur (page 255).

The first documented visits to the glacier date back to 1675. Darwin visited the glacier on the *Beagle* in 1834. John Byron, grandfather of Lord Byron, was shipwrecked on Wager Island in 1742, and has an island named after him at the southern side of the gulf. He was eventually rescued by members of the Kaweskar tribe who lived in this region at the time. It is not clear if Byron actually visited the Ventisquero San Rafael.

The Ventisquero San Rafael is in retreat. Historical accounts clearly record the extent to which the glacier protruded into the lake – early witnesses claimed that most of the lake was covered by the glacier. This protrusion has now vanished and the glacier is firmly confined to the valley. It is estimated to have retreated 12km over the last 150 years. Although this may seem dramatic, the Ventisquero Jorge Montt is perhaps the fastest retreating glacier in the region, shrinking almost 1km from February 2010 to January 2011.

Intriguing history and worrying evidence of global warming aside, the glacier is an impressive sight by any standards. Only three boats regularly visit the glacier (those owned by the tour operators in Puerto Río Tranquilo, and the catamaran from Los Loberías in Puerto Aysén; pages 204 and 161) and, during a visit, it is quite possible to see no other people or boats. Occasional airplanes and helicopters may interrupt the silence momentarily as they fly overhead, providing an astonishing point of reference to the sheer size of the glacier. At places it looms over 60m high from the water level, and is over two miles wide. Boats keep a suitable distance from the face of the glacier for fear of icebergs (*témpanos*) breaking off and generating waves large enough to overturn a boat.

The boats travel down the Elefantes Canal and then through a relatively narrow channel into the laguna itself, at which point the glacier become visible. Initially it appears to be of modest size, until you realise the size of the laguna; from this distance it is possible to see up onto the ice field behind the glacier and appreciate the sheer magnitude of ice. The Northern Ice Field is the smaller of the two, covering 4,200km² and extending 120km from north to south. As the boat approaches the snout of the glacier the icebergs become larger, and it is probable that you will see chunks of ice calving off the glacier. The pressure caused by the sheer volume of ice squeezes the air bubbles out of the snow as it is subsumed into the glacier, and because compacted ice better absorbs light at the red end of the spectrum, the light reflected from the glacier appears surprisingly blue. Particularly on a sunny day the contrast of the bluish glacier, the ice field behind, the lake, icebergs and sky are simply mesmerising. The only sounds are the occasional bird and the groaning of the glacier as it inches forward, sometimes interrupted by the thunderous roar of chunks breaking off.

A trip to the Carretera Austral is incomplete without a visit to a glacier, where you can watch in real time the mechanism that shaped much of our planet, and the Ventisquero San Rafael is one of the more accessible glaciers in the region. Well worth a visit.

There is little here except an important junction towards Chile Chico, invariably packed with hopeful hitchhikers, and a couple of very decent lodges. Note that the nearest shops or restaurants are Puerto Guadal (10km to the east), Puerto Río Tranquilo (49km to the north), or Puerto Bertrand (15km to the south). The only food options are the restaurants in the only two hotels.

GETTING THERE
About the route
Puerto Río Tranquilo to Cruce El Maitén (*49km; 1hr; gravel*) This section includes some of the most spectacular vantage points of Lago General Carrera – there are some great photo opportunities, particularly in the morning and evening. The road quality is reasonable quality gravel with a number of steep hills and tight curves, passable in any vehicle.

At km5 on the left is the entrance to **Puerto Mármol**. The road then ascends to the top of a hill offering one of the best panoramic views of the lake. At km32 the road crosses the **Río Leones** (the entry point to the Ventisquero Leones trek) – with views of the snow-capped peaks of the Northern Ice Field. Lago General Carrera drains into **Lago Bertrand** under the bridge at km43. **Lago Negro** is on the right at km49 and the **Cruce El Maitén** is at km50.

WHERE TO STAY AND EAT *Map, page 189*

Hacienda Tres Lagos (12 dbl/twins, 2 suites, 4 bungalows) 1km north of Cruce El Maitén; \(67) 4111323; **m** (2) 23334122; **e** ventas@ haciendatreslagos.cl; www.haciendatreslagos.cl; ⊕ Sep–Apr. More comparable to a resort than a hotel or lodge, this upmarket complex is perched on the northern shore of Lago Negro, not far from the road to Chile Chico, 50km south of Puerto Río Tranquilo, & close to Puerto Bertrand. This ideal location permits the hacienda to offer just about every conceivable tour in the region from the Ventisquero San Rafael & the marble caves in the north to fishing on the Río Baker to the south, trekking & horseriding in the region & some excursions towards Guadal. The Ventisquero Leones is the only obvious current omission, but may be added to the roster soon. The main building is built in the style of a lodge, rustic with plenty of wooden finish, where the principal restaurant & suites are located. The bungalows are ideal for families, sleeping up to 4, & are located to the south of the main building facing the lake. 4 dbl/twin rooms are each housed in 3 separate buildings to the other side of the main lodge. All standard features included, including access to a games room, hot tubs & sauna; laundry, massage & transfers from almost anywhere are available for a (fairly hefty) fee. B/fast included, dinner/lunch is available (**$$$$**). There is also a full quincho for lamb roasts, a cinema, an art gallery & a cafeteria. Every room overlooks the lake & has a

---

A CRUCIAL JUNCTION

The Cruce El Maitén is one of the most important junctions on the entire Carretera Austral. Those doing the 'classic' route north to south will depart the Carretera Austral here and head east along Lago General Carrera towards Chile Chico and then Argentina. Those planning the 'classic' route from south to north, entering from Chile Chico, will head north at the Cruce El Maitén. For those not wishing to leave Chile and continue either north or south along the Carretera, the Cruce El Maitén raises a difficult question: go to Chile Chico along the spectacular coastal road, or leave this section out? See page 190 for more on this.

balcony. Private beach with kayaks, & a 10-person covered boat for tours on lakes General Carrera & Bertrand. The tours are somewhat overpriced compared with arranging them independently, but this lodge is about relaxing & not having to deal with such administration – ideal for families, & probably for multiple-day stays. Full-board multi-day packages are also available including transfers & excursion – see their (decent) website. This was the first officially certified luxury hacienda in Patagonia. A decent one-stop shop, accommodation is approximately US$300/couple, a little higher in the suites, lower in the bungalows. Credit cards accepted. **$$$$$**

⌂ **Mallin Colorado EcoLodge** (4 cabins) Carretera Austral Sur, km273; ☎ (9) 71376242; m (2) 5718632; e paulach@mallincolorado.cl; www.mallincolorado.cl; ⏲ Nov–Apr. Rustic cabins with superb interiors overlooking Lago General Carrera set in a 500ha estate. One of the best established upper-end lodges in the region, along one of the most picturesque sections of the entire Carretera Austral. 4 independent cabins sleep between 2 & 7 people, with viewing points & trails connecting the rest of the complex, including trails over the back of the ridge with views over the glaciers at the edge of the Northern Ice Field. Excellent bathrooms in all cabins depending on the size of the cabin – the 6-person cabin has 3 bathrooms. All cabins have a sitting area overlooking the lake with comfortable armchairs & plenty of space & light, & quality beds with duvets. Full b/fast included. Only the largest cabin has a full kitchen, otherwise guests use the restaurant (**$$$$**). Laundry service, no cellphone coverage, & Wi-Fi only in the restaurant. Most people choose to spend 3 or 4 nights here enjoying the range of activities on offer. Treks within the property access the Laguna Mallin & a waterfall. Also offer tours through subcontracted, trusted guides to the marble caves, fishing trips, treks to the glaciers & rafting on the Río Baker, as well as horseriding on their private land. The owners are Danish–Chilean, & the décor reflects the European–Latin influence. The restaurant is something of a fusion of Danish & Patagonian cuisine. Prices are comparatively high depending on the number of guests & choice of cabin, ranging from US$140/night to US$210/couple. Cheaper & comparatively comfortable accommodation is available elsewhere, but Mallin Colorado is a well-established, fully fledged luxury lodge in a truly unique region, & offers a viable alternative to the limited accommodation options in Puerto Río Tranquilo. An excellent option for those travelling with a family. Accepts credit cards. **$$$$$**

⊕ **AS THE CONDOR FLIES**

Cruce El Maitén is 600km from Puerto Montt and 230km from the final end point of the Carretera Austral at the border crossing to El Chaltén.

CHILE CHICO – A DETOUR

Chile Chico is the start or end point for those doing the 'classic' route along the Carretera Austral. Across the border lies Los Antiguos and Perito Moreno, with transport to the rest of Argentina and the road between Chile Chico and Cruce El Maitén offering some of the most stunning scenery of Lago General Carrera. For those wishing to complete the entire Carretera Austral this may involve doubling back on oneself, but on a sunny day it is a mild hardship to have to repeat such a stunning 115km road. The more pressing decision for those with a vehicle is whether to do the three-day hike between Chile Chico and Parque Patagonia (pages 221–3) – who gets the car?

THE ROAD SOUTH OF LAGO GENERAL CARRERA From the Cruce El Maitén, a 115km gravel road connects the Carretera Austral to Chile Chico and Argentina, passing through the villages of Puerto Guadal and Mallin Grande. On a sunny day the views of the lake are breathtaking, as the coastal road winds around headlands and through sections of forest until the Patagonian steppe emerges closer to the border. Without stopping it is possible to reach the Argentine border in under 3 hours.

Puerto Guadal appears at first sight to be little more than a sleepy village, population approximately 600, *en route* to elsewhere, but it is a hub for adventure activities, and Terra Luna Lodge (pages 213–14) is an excellent base from which to explore the region.

The first settler arrived here in 1926 on the boat *Andes* – the only form of transport in the region before any roads were built. Some of the early settlers were of Lebanese or Arab decent, and set up the first trading companies focused on wool and leather. In the 1950s zinc and lead were mined from the La Escondida site, 12km from the village. French investors wishing to exploit the mineral reserves in the region boosted the local economy in the 1970s precisely when agricultural prices were in decline. Following the construction of the Carretera Austral and the subsequent road connecting the Carretera to Guadal which was completed in 1986, the village has increasingly focused on tourism – to the extent that the cellphone companies installed an antenna in the town in 2012.

Mallin Grande, some 28km from Puerto Guadal, is extremely small (despite its name). The central plaza is home to a number of chickens and turkeys. The church and medical post are the only buildings of note. A small footbridge unites the main village with the back of the gardens of three houses perched on the other side of a creek.

Getting there
About the route
Cruce El Maitén to Mallin Grande (via Puerto Guadal) *(44km; 1hr; rough gravel)*
The road suddenly opens up here with towering mountains in front and dramatic 180° vistas over glaciers. The lake is only periodically visible. More hairpin bends and precipices are encountered, but west of the El Maitén Bridge the road flattens.

The initial 10km is smooth, relatively flat gravel until Puerto Guadal. The next 34km is rough gravel with frequent inclines, hairpin bends and precipices, and caution is required. There are occasional cars and buses, often in the centre of the road and travelling fast.

Tour operator
Kalem Patagonia Los Alerces 557; \(67) 2431289, (9) 88112535; e turismokalempatagonia@gmail.com; **f** Turismo Kalem Patagonia. Born in Mallin Grande & based in Guadal, Pascual Diaz is an excellent guide & his tours are some of the most interesting in the region. The quality of service & attention to detail are impeccable: picnics include a tablecloth, decent cups, a freshly prepared meat & cheese platter, a small bottle of wine (& the traditional whisky with glacial ice when visiting a glacier), fresh fruit, etc. His 'off-the-shelf' tours include trekking to the Ventisquero Leones (*$60,000pp, min 4 people*); horseriding around Mallin Grande (*½- to multiple-day treks; priced accordingly*); a fossil trail (*$25,000/35,000pp ½/full day*); a 12-day horseride from Cochrane to Villa O'Higgins (the *ruta los pioneros*); & the 10-day trek between Villa O'Higgins & El Chaltén via the Southern Ice Field. This last trip goes initially to Candelario Mancilla (as with the 'standard' route), but then heads up towards the Ventisquero Chico & up to the Garcia Soto refuge on the Southern Ice Field & then down to Chaltén. The optimal number of trekkers is 4, in sufficiently good physical condition for over a week of trekking without horses. Pascual is also able to offer tailor-made tours, including far off the beaten track to both ice fields, & alternative routes through the Reserva Nacional Jeinemeni. He has his own 4x4 van, a satellite phone for emergencies in remote regions, & for a reasonable additional fee can offer transfers. For example, he can pick passengers up at Puerto Río Tranquilo, take them to the Ventisquero Leones (1 complete day) & drop-off at Cochrane.

Service-oriented, experienced, punctual & returns phone calls – highly recommended. Pascual speaks basic English, but other guides in the company speak English & French.

Where to stay and eat   *Map, page 216*

Most visitors may prefer to push on to Chile Chico, but there are some accommodation options should you become stranded. As well as the options listed below, **Claudio Hermosilla** (*cnr of Volcán Hudson & Los Pioneros, Mallín Grande*) offers a room for $10,000, including breakfast and a hot shower. A simple dinner increases this by a further $4,000, but given the absence of a restaurant Mallín Grande, and only miniscule and informal shops invariably closed, this is a decent option within the village. Of the hotels in and around Puerto Guadal, **El Gringo, El Mirador de Guadal** and **Terra Luna** all have good restaurants.

Patagonia Acres Lodge (3 cabins, 2 rooms) 5km east of Mallín Grande; ✆(9) 62245873; m (2) 19624525; e jcharrison@ patagoniaacres.com; www.patagoniaacres. com. Without a doubt the finest place to stay along the entire southern shore of Lago General Carrera. Fully equipped, comfortable cabins with spectacular views over the lake & small decks to enjoy the sunset, access to a beach below & kayak rental possible. The property has its own jetty for launching boats. Games room with table tennis & a number of hiking trails within the 160ha property. Gym, jacuzzi & hot tub available, & even includes a rustic 9-hole golf course (clubs available without charge). Owned by an Arizonan family who also sell parcels of land on the property. All services provided, including laundry, Wi-Fi, etc. Can also arrange off-site activities & airport transfers. While for some the distance from Guadal (40km) & Chile Chico (70km) might be a disadvantage, the benefits include utter privacy & the tranquillity of the lake. Accommodation prices are reasonable for this calibre of lodge, at US$200 for a 2-person room in the lodge or US$350 for the 4-person cabin. However, this price includes b/fast & dinners, fishing equipment & mountain bikes. Also offer 3-, 4- & 5-night packages including accommodation, food, various activities, guides, & all transport. Accepts credit cards & PayPal. **$$$$$**

Hotel El Mirador de Guadal (8 cabins) 2km east of Puerto Guadal on the road to Chile Chico; ✆(9) 92349130; m (2) 28137920; e sveringa@elmiradordeguadal.com; www. elmiradordeguadal.com; ⏰ Oct–Apr. The finest accommodation in Guadal, owned by a Dutch/ Chilean couple. Extremely nice stand alone rooms in wood-cabin style (without kitchens) each with a deck & stunning views over the lake.

Large comfortable beds & wood-fired stoves for heating. The finish is top-notch & the complex has lake access, but no kayak/boat rental. Full b/fast included, & the restaurant also serves dinner in a delightful building, also with views over the lake. The centre of town is a short drive or stroll. Wi-Fi in the restaurant only, ample parking & laundry. TVs are notable for their absence, deliberately to encourage a total disconnection from the outside world. The hotel can arrange various activities in the area, including trips to the marble caves, glaciers, horseriding, boat trips on the lake including to the Ventisquero Leones (page 214, via jet boat rather than the longer hike) & more. Dutch, English, German & Spanish spoken. Reservations required, with deposit. Accepts credit cards & can receive bank transfers to Chilean or European accounts. **$$$$**

Terra Luna Lodge (cabins, rooms, a house & a treehouse – 54 people max) 1km east of Puerto Guadal; ✆(9) 84491092, (9) 98863903; e info@ terra-luna.cl; www.terraluna.cl. A bewildering range of accommodation options, this lodge will appeal to most tastes: from simple, rustic cabins to surprisingly nice hotel-style rooms, a fantastic treehouse accessed by ladder, & a luxurious jacuzzi cabin overlooking the entire lodge & lake. The rooms themselves are cosy with fully equipped bathrooms, lovely views over the lake, & a positively homely. Ideal for families as well as solo travellers, & because the rooms/cabins are relatively dispersed they also offer a degree of privacy despite the relatively large nature of the complex. There's also a restaurant (**$$$$**), lake access & endless activities – there is little reason to leave the premises at all. Prices are also surprisingly reasonable, ranging from approximately US$80/night for a couple, up to US$200 for the house which sleeps 6. The treehouse

VISITING VENTISQUERO LEONES

One of the various glaciers protruding from the Northern Ice Field, or more precisely, from the San Valentín Ice Field, is the Ventisquero Leones. This flows into the Lago Leones, which flows in turn into the Río Leones. The entry point to the trek to the glacier is 28km south of Puerto Río Tranquilo (shortly after the bridge, somewhat unimaginatively named the Leones Bridge). The journey begins with a 4x4 drive of approximately an hour, at which point it is no longer possible to proceed in a vehicle. Although not technically challenging, reaching the Ventisquero Leones involves some modest effort – perhaps 3 or 4 hours of trekking, as opposed to sitting on a boat most of the day (as at the Ventisquero San Rafael). In part as a result of this, the cost of reaching the Ventisquero Leones is currently about half that of a trip to the Ventisquero San Rafael.

The public and well-marked trail passes through two private properties for approximately 9km on mostly flat ground to the edge of the lake. At this point the glacier is clearly visible, but is some 11km away on the other side of the lake. There are two boats servicing the route across the lake: that of Pascual Diaz (page 212), and that of Terra Luna Hotel (page 213). It's worth keeping in mind that some operators offering this trip, go no further than the lake's edge, but it's really worth crossing the lake to the snout of the glacier.

The glacier appears initially to be deceptively close, perhaps in part because there is no point of reference from which to gauge distance. Only as the boat chugs towards the glacier does the true distance gradually emerge, as the glacier slowly grows larger and larger.

This glacier is so remote and relatively unknown that encountering another person is highly unlikely. The boats are able to approach the glacier safely (unlike at the more popular Ventisquero San Rafael; see page 209) – so close, in fact, that it is possible to view the subtleties of the ice wall in detail without a zoom lens. The picnic spots, too, are so close to the edge of the glacier that in the utter silence, you can hear the cracking and groaning of the ice.

is US$150/night & sleeps 2. The lodge boasts a sauna & hot tub, a projector, a bar/restaurant (with disco lights upstairs if absolutely necessary), laundry & Wi-Fi. The menu of the day is $14,000. However, most interesting are the tours on offer. They can arrange the standard tours in the region (marble caves, horseriding, various treks, mountain biking, fishing, fossil tour, rafting on the Río Baker), including transfers, but also have their own jet boat able to explore the lake & go up the Río Leones towards the glacier (see above). This does involve some mild trekking, & the lodge has a zodiac on the Lago Leones able to approach the glacier directly – this is a far quicker & less arduous means to arrive at the spectacular Ventisquero Leones compared with the slower route involving a longer trek (page 212). English, Spanish & French spoken. Particularly good

option if travelling with kids. Accepts credit cards. All-inclusive packages available. **$$$**

🏠 **Destino No Turistico Eco-Hostel**
(6-person dorm, 1 dbl) Camino Laguna La Manga km1.5; e info@destino-noturistico.com; www. destino-noturistico.com; ⏲ Nov–Apr. The term 'eco' is often abused, but this is a truly ecological destination. Some may find it a little extreme, but one has to admire the efforts Rocio & Marcelo have gone to in order to minimise the carbon footprint of this hostel. Located about 1.5km to the east of town up a hill, the hostel then then requires walking a few hundred metres with luggage – not ideal for wheelie bags, & more convenient for those with a car, perhaps ironically. Set back a little from the lake the views are not as impressive as some of the hotels in town, but for those with an

interest in conservation this is a gem. The hostel doubles as an educational centre, with posters explaining how to minimise environmental impact. Every measure to save energy is exploited, from solar-powered lamps, outdoor cool boxes (in lieu of a fridge), a solar oven, & the building is designed for optimal natural temperature control. Water management is likewise considered carefully, with solar-powered hot water, minimal water usage & composting toilets (surprisingly hygienic & odour-free). The gardens contain a range of wild plants & flowers (stick to the trails). Needless to say recycling is taken pretty seriously. B/fast is not included, but they sell local fair-trade products on site, & guests have use of a kitchen. No Wi-Fi or TV. Parking on the trail up to the hostel – for those wishing to park on the premises, a 10% surcharge is made to the room rate. They can arrange local tours, & the website contains up-to-date bus information (they are fans of public transport). The rooms themselves are comfortable, with good bedding. The owners love to share information about their vision; a stay in this hostel is certainly informative, & it is hard to imagine how they could reduce their carbon footprint further. Telephones do not work reliably so reservations by email only, & be sure to read the reservations & cancellation policies carefully. Perhaps marginally overpriced given that b/fast isn't included, but fair given the cost of establishing such a self-sufficient infrastructure. **$$–$$$**

El Gringo (2 dorms) Los Lirios 510, Puerto Guadal; (9) 73940396. Great location on the central square & cheap accommodation. No Wi-Fi, but has laundry service. Food options include pizza, sandwiches, churascos & excellent smoothies. B/fast extra, all shared bathrooms. Wide range of teas. Decent warm beds. Good budget option. **$$**

Restaurante Casa Vieja Costanera Los Guindos 333, Puerto Guadal; (67) 2431291, (9) 78007333; 10.00–02.00 daily. Simple restaurant opposite the ECA store which doubles as a bar, serving fries, a daily menu, pizza, *pichangas* & sandwiches. Limited range of local ales & regional wines. Wi-Fi. **$$**

CHILE CHICO After Coyhaique and Puerto Aysén, Chile Chico is probably the next largest town in the region. It has a pleasant micro climate, receiving less rain than elsewhere, and is slightly warmer. However, besides pottering around the pleasant town, doing a little shopping and withdrawing money from the ATM (shops and ATMs are rare in this region), filling up with petrol and grabbing a bite to eat, there is relatively little in town to entertain visitors for long. Most either head towards Argentina, or into the Reserva Nacional Jeinemeni (page 220).

History Some 10,000 years before modern day settlers started occupying the land around Chile Chico, indigenous groups such as the Tehuelches inhabited this region. In 1902, after the 1881 treaty between Argentina and Chile which defined the borders, Chilean migrants who had been living on the Argentine side of the border started to arrive, settling in several regions of Aysén including Chile Chico. In 1909 a group of migrants set up home on the southern shore of Lago General Carrera attracted by the peculiar microclimate of the region which they found similar to the central region of Chile, allowing for the cultivation of grains and fruit and raising of livestock. This was their new homeland, their small country which henceforth became known as Chile Chico ('little Chile'). Despite the isolation the settlers built their houses with the intention to put down firm roots. In 1914 they officially requested permission to occupy the land and developed a small village.

Owing to the relative prosperity of the region farmers were drawn to the area with the intention of establishing cattle ranches. In 1917 an advertisement appeared in a national Chilean newspaper announcing the sale of public lands by the Chilean state. In a dubious auction the land around Chile Chico was awarded to Carlos von Flank who represented the powerful and wealthy landowning consortium Braun & Menendez. At first they tried to negotiate with the settlers to sell their land and livestock. The price they offered, however, was very low and no deal was reached. It

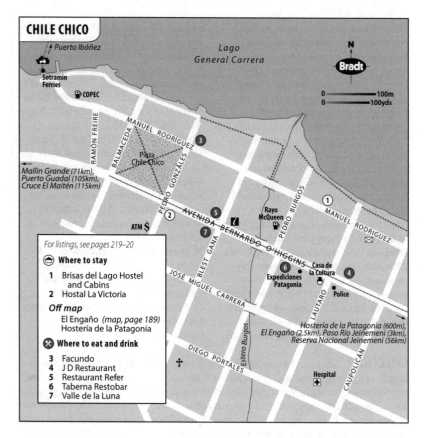

CHILE CHICO

Puerto Ibáñez

Sotramin Ferries

COPEC

Lago General Carrera

N

Bradt

0 ———— 100m
0 ———— 100yds

RAMÓN FREIRE

MANUEL RODRÍGUEZ

BALMACEDA

Plaza Chile Chico

Mallin Grande (71km),
Puerto Guadal (105km),
Cruce El Maitén (115km)

PEDRO GONZALES

3

AVENIDA BERNARDO O'HIGGINS

ATM $

2

5

i

7

Rayo McQueen

PEDRO BURGOS

1

MANUEL RODRÍGUEZ

BLEST GANA

JOSÉ MIGUEL CARRERA

6

Expediciones Patagonia

Casa de la Cultura

4

LAUTARO

Police

DIEGO PORTALES

Estero Burgos

†

CAUPOLICAN

Hospital

Hostería de la Patagonia (600m),
El Engaño (2.5km), Paso Río Jeinemeni (3km),
Reserva Nacional Jeinemeni (56km)

For listings, see pages 219–20

Where to stay

1 Brisas del Lago Hostel
   and Cabins
2 Hostal La Victoria
   Off map
   El Engaño *(map, page 189)*
   Hostería de la Patagonia

Where to eat and drink

3 Facundo
4 J D Restaurant
5 Restaurant Refer
6 Taberna Restobar
7 Valle de la Luna

was then decided to evict the settlers. The settlers organised to stop their eviction led by a man called Antolin Silva Ormeño, known as 'the general'. The first encounter between settlers and police was amicable. The settlers were determined to defend the land they had fought so hard for and a group of only ten surrounded the police camp at sunset to give the impression there were many of them. Frightened, the licencees and police officers left and sent word to Santiago that numerous bandits had threatened them and forced them to evacuate.

Another police contingent of 30 was sent to the area led by a young lieutenant. Meanwhile the settlers prepared their defence and sent a delegation to Santiago to plead for their rights to the territory they had been granted. A group of 40 settlers took up arms to face the police in the disputed zone. The police withdrew, claiming it was impossible to attack their fellow Chilean citizens who had done nothing wrong, had made their humble homes there and were flying Chilean flags made of clothing and rags. The lieutenant was sacked and a new police force was sent, leading to violence and the burning of houses of the settlers, some of whom were imprisoned. The first clashes occurred after one settler was killed. A group of 50 settlers opened fire and killed three police officers, wounding another and taking 12 hostage. As a result the police, von Flank and his partners, fled to Argentina on foot.

Von Flank upped the political stakes by falsely claiming that the settlers were invading Argentine territory, prompting the Argentine government to send 122 men and three officials towards Chile Chico to put an end to the supposed invasion.

The settlers, meanwhile, travelled to Buenos Aires and on to Santiago where they spoke with the Minister of the Interior who ordered the immediate end of all official activities against the settlers and withdrawal of all armed forces from the area. He decided to expire the lease of the land that had been awarded to von Flank, finally recognising the rights of the settlers. The Argentine troops had arrived at the border but were recalled. The settlers were finally able to celebrate their victory. These events were later called 'The War of Chile Chico'.

On 21 May 1929 the official foundation of Chile Chico took place.

Initially the inhabitants raised livestock, but commerce and transportation developed due to the proximity to the lake and roads leading to the Atlantic. Chile Chico became the centre of distribution of wool produced around Lago General Carrera as well as an access point to the Río Baker. The first railroads in the region were made by settlers, including routes through Paso de las Llaves (now the highway along the south of Lago General Carrera) and later from Puerto Ibáñez and the Levicán Peninsula, providing access to the markets of Coyhaique. However, the biggest contribution to the development of the area was Chile Chico's acquisition of iron boats that moved goods on several routes on the binational Lago General Carrera. At first it was mainly products for import and export that were transported, subsequently passengers too.

Owing to the abundance of lead and zinc in the soil, in 1940 Chile Chico became the major intermediary for mining and mineral exports and experienced its first true boom. Many restaurants, hotels, theatres and other establishments emerged. Sadly this 'golden age' didn't last as trails in the region north of Chile Chico were widened and a road connected Puerto Ibáñez with Puerto Aysén, the main maritime port of the entire Aysén region. Chile Chico's role as a transportation hub abated. The situation was worsened by the subsequent closure of the mines.

More recently Chile Chico has found another 'goldmine'. Because of its favourable climate it now grows and exports cherries. The difference in timing of the cherry season between the central area of Chile and that of Lago General Carrera enables growers to extend the productive season and gives them an important advantage to buyers in Europe and Asia. Tourism is another sector that is seeing continued growth as a result of the increased popularity of the Carretera Austral.

Following World War II, approximately 30 Belgians emigrated to Chile Chico, some descendants of which still live in the town, and the European influence is visible in the architectural styles of some of the older houses. For those interested in history it is worth staying either at El Engaño, where the historian Danka Ivanoff lives; or the Hostería de la Patagonia, run by one of the daughters of the original Belgian settlers (both page 219). Danka Ivanoff has written ten books covering various aspects of the history of the region. The book *Cuando éramos niños en la Patagonia* (*When we were children in Patagonia*) is available in the Hostería de la Patagonia, recounting the lives of the Belgian children growing up in Chile Chico.

Getting there Chile Chico is notorious for poor logistics. Buses to and from the town are small, few and infrequent. The boat to Puerto Ibáñez (page 46) is often full, particularly for those wishing to travel with a vehicle in high season. Shuttles over the border run more frequently, stopping at to Los Antiguos (Argentina), which is well connected with Perito Moreno, from where a wide range of buses travel north towards Esquel and Bariloche, south towards El Chaltén and Calafate, and east across the steppe towards the Atlantic and Comodoro Rivadavia. Hitchhikers and those attempting to connect with the Carretera Austral to/from Chile Chico via public transport routinely moan about logistical problems along this section.

About the route

Mallin Grande to Chile Chico (*71km; 2hrs; rough gravel*) This is a treacherous road; unsuspecting drivers may be tempted to risk higher speeds along decent compact gravel, only to be met with vicious sections of loose gravel, major corrugations and violent pot-holes. There are some extremely steep inclines and descents, often along cliff edges without protective railings – this is not a good section to drift off the road.

The road initially passes through dense forest, but gradually transforms into drier, sparsely vegetated steppe as the arid Argentine Patagonia approaches. Be aware that this road is extremely bendy and be ready for oncoming vehicles; take care as the precipices are very close to the road, tumbling hundreds of metres into the lake. Occasional landslides may mean there are rocks scattered across the road, which also passes through a number of dynamited rock sections where it is not clear whether two cars could pass each other. Cerro Castillo is periodically visible in the distance across the turquoise lake. Even in mid summer there may be snow along the upper sections of the route. It is worth driving slowly, not only to avoid an accident, but to absorb the vistas. There are countless photo opportunities, but few places to park a car safely: however tempting, do not stop on a bend.

Shortly before Chile Chico the road passes **Lago Verde** (not to be confused with the town and lake also called Lago Verde further north), with stunning views over the lake and towards the snow-capped mountains, spoiled somewhat by an open mine.

The landscapes approaching Chile Chico are positively lunar: rocks jut out in bizarre formations and poplar trees are twisted into awkward angles by the relentless wind. Beyond Lago Verde the road veers straight east, losing sight of the lake for perhaps 20km and passing some minor marshlands before arriving at Chile Chico on the lakeshore.

Chile Chico to the Argentine border (*3km; 5mins; paved*) This stretch is passable in any vehicle. The border is open all year from 08.00 to 20.00, extended to 22.00 from December to April. The paved road continues 2km to the first Argentine town of Los Antiguos and a further 65km to Perito Moreno.

By public transport This stretch of southern Chile is notoriously difficult for both hitchhiking and public transport. There are a few **buses** a week both north to Coyhaique and Puerto Río Tranquilo (via Guadal and Cerro Castillo) and south to Cochrane. However, all routes are subject to change, and buses do not take credit cards – tickets must be bought in the local offices in cash. In high season it is easy to become stranded in a location for hours, if not days, particularly between Chile Chico–Mallin Grande–Puerto Guadal–Puerto Río Tranquilo. For up-to-date bus times, see **Destino No Turistico Eco Hotel's** website (page 214, although the degree to which this website can keep up with the frequent changes to bus schedules is questionable). For details of getting here by **ferry**, see page 46.

Tour operators

Expediciones Patagonia Bernardo O'Higgins 416; \(9) 84641067, (9) 57093935; e turismobaker@gmail.com, fgiorgia5@gmail.com. Chile Chico is short on tour operators. Fortunately the main company is professional & helpful. Run by Ferdinando Giorgia, they focus on tours between Coyhaique & Cochrane. They have excellent knowledge of the Reserva Nacional Jeinemeni & arrange tours on the standard hiking trips as well as the lesser-known treks to the interior glaciers; visits to the archaeological sites & lakes within the park; trips to the fossil trail along the south side of the lake towards Mallin Grande; & trips to the marble caves in Puerto Río Tranquilo. They can also advise, or guide, the trek right through the park, into Parque Patagonia, & ending in Casa Piedra (*3 days*). They have 3 vehicles, so can arrange tailor-made trips, logistics & offer transfers.

🏠 Where to stay *Map, page 216, unless otherwise stated*

🏠 **El Engaño** [map, page 189] (6 cabins) 2km east on coastal road from Chile Chico; ☎(9) 91348162, (9) 78894007; e elengano.spa@gmail. com; www.turismoelengano.com. Fully equipped modern cabins very close to the lake & with views across to Cerro Castillo, but with trees protecting the cabins from the often ferocious wind. The term 'spa' does not refer to massage/sauna but is the legal structure of the company (as in 'ltd' or 'inc'). Facilities include 2 hot tubs, ample parking, laundry service & a quincho. Can also arrange tours in the region including fishing trips, & pre-booking Sotramin ferry crossings to Puerto Ibáñez. However, the highlight of this hostel is that the mother of the owner is none other than Danka Ivanoff Wellmann, a well-known historian in the region, who also gives short talks to guests, & is a wonderful source of fact as well as the myths of the entire southern section of the Carretera Austral (see page 270 for more on her book about the mysterious cemetery in Caleta Tortel). Good value & a truly golden opportunity for those interested in the history of the region, but best with private transport. **$$$$**

🏠 **Brisas del Lago Hostel and Cabins** (7 rooms, 3 cabins) Manuel Rodriguez 433; ☎(67) 2411204; e brisasdellago@gmail.com. Basic accommodation 1 block north of main street; 1 sgl, 5 dbls/twins, 1 trpl, with & without private bathroom. Basic b/fast included, Wi-Fi & parking available, but no laundry. Functional but lacking in character. The cabins are better, with 2 offering partial views over the lake. Fully equipped, including cable TV (only in the restaurant in the main hostel). A short walk to the centre. **$$$**

🏠 **Hostal La Victoria** (10 rooms) O'Higgins 210; ☎(67) 2411344, (9) 91323826; e lavictoria@ outlook.com. A reasonable & centrally located option, perhaps a little overpriced for the rather thin walls & ceilings, but modern & comfortable. All rooms with private bathroom. Decent b/fast included, communal sitting area, free use of kitchen, & able to arrange transport in the region. **$$$**

🏠 **Hostería de la Patagonia** (6 rooms, camping) Chacra 3A Camino International; ☎(67) 2411337, (9) 81592146, e hdelapatagonia@gmail. com; www.hosteriadelapatagonia.cl. A beautiful, tranquil setting with views over a pleasant garden. Located slightly outside of town on the lakeside of the road towards the border. Spacious rooms for between 1 & 5 people, with comfortable beds, wide windows & decent bathrooms (both shared & private). Also offers camping for a modest $4,000pp including bathrooms, hot water & electricity outlets. The truly unique feature of this farm-stay option is a large boat in the garden, which has been converted to a fantastic cabin complete with bathroom & a small kitchen. The house is one of the original settler homes, partly resembling a museum, originally built in 1953. The owner is a direct descendant of the Belgian settlers (page 217) & speaks French. Basic b/fast included, with yoghurt, cereals & homemade bread & jams. Can arrange dinner upon request. Garden has a pizza oven & parrilla, as well as a hot tub. Great dining/communal room, Wi-Fi & laundry. Good option for bikers as has large private off-road parking. A short stroll into town. Very fine accommodation for a reasonable price. Deposit usually required. Takes credit cards. **$–$$$**

🍴 Where to eat and drink *Map, page 216*

As well as the places listed below, other options include **Restaurant Refer** (*Blest Gana 22*; **$–$$**), specialising in meat dishes, and **J D Restaurant** (*O'Higgins 501*; ⊕ *08.30– midnight; accepts credit cards*; **$–$$**) offering quick snacks and standard Chilean fare as well as local beers.

🍴 **Facundo** Manuel Rodriguez 243; ☎(67) 2411452, (9) 99173453; e (turismofacundo@gmail. com; ⊕ 12.00–16.30 & 19.00–midnight daily (closed Sat lunch). Probably the best restaurant in town, with a couple of tables offering a view over the lake. Reservations required in high season as this is a popular place with locals, travellers & government employees. Good vibe, friendly service

& attentive owner. Menu of the day is great value. Specialities include mechada (shredded meat) & salmon, & between Dec & Feb lamb is available. Also has 2 cabins for rent: $45,000 for 4 people, $55,000 for 6 people. *Lunch $, dinner $$$*

✗ Valle de la Luna Northwest cnr of O'Higgins & Blest Gana; ☏ (9) 91285824; ⏰ 13.00–15.30 & 19.00–22.30 Wed–Mon. Mid-range family restaurant popular with locals & with space for 40 people. Serves decent *lomo a lo pobre*, positively good salmon but meat dishes are nothing special. A range of wines is available; no-frills décor. Offer a menu of the day for $5,000; à la carte is notably

more expensive & not such good value. *Lunch $, dinner $$*

✗ Taberna Restobar O'Higgins 416; ☏ (9) 69011314; e taberna.restobar@gmail.com; ⏰ noon–15.00 & 18.00 to late daily. A fun bar located underneath tour operator Expediciones Patagonia (page 218). Good range of local beers & Crystal on tap, blaring music & occasional karaoke, good vibe. Homemade food, salads, milanesas, soups & a menu of the day; vegetarian options available. Evening fare is light snacks, pizzas, chips, etc. Serves a reasonable cup of coffee during the day. Accepts credit cards. $

Other practicalities There is an **ATM** (Banco Estado) on Pedro Gonzalez 112 just north of the central plaza, and a COPEC **petrol station** by the harbour. The **tourist information centre** is barely worth visiting for the lack of information available, while the Casa de la Cultura occasionally has some local artwork or cultural events (on O'Higgins), and boasts a rather unusual boat parked on the road as a historic relic from the golden era when Chile Chico was an important transport hub. The boat, *Andes*, was bought from England in 1922 and remained in operation until the early 1990s. It was the principal means of transport for those living around the lake, particularly prior to the construction of the road.

Mechanic
Rayo McQueen Pedro Burgos 20; ☏ (9) 54113845; ⏰ 09.00–13.00 & 15.00–19.00 Mon–Fri, 09.00–14.00 Sat. Able to do most car & motorbike repairs, but note that he doesn't do welding, & doesn't have a scanner for motorbikes.

Spare parts available, & those that need to be ordered from Coyhaique can arrive within 24hrs. Has experience with KTM, BMW, Kawasaki & Honda. The only bike mechanic in town. Also works with 'Bruno', another car mechanic who also has a tow truck. Has a limited range of tyres for sale.

RESERVA NACIONAL JEINEMENI (*www.conaf.cl/parques/reserva-nacional-lago-jeinimeni; $2,000/$1,000 foreign adult/child, $1,000/500 Chilean adult/child; $10,000 per campsite in addition to entry fee*) This national reserve is up there with the finest parks in the region, with a stunning trek through the reserve and into Parque Patagonia and onto the road connecting the border with Argentina (Roballos) and Cochrane. Established in 1967, the park extends for 161,100ha and is the third-largest reserve in the Aysén region, and the fifth largest in Chile. Flora and fauna abound – expect to see a variety of woodpecker species, condors and black-chested buzzard-eagles, as well as huemul and abundant guanacos. Only the very fortunate will spot the elusive puma.

Getting there Access to the park is from the main road connecting Chile Chico to the Argentine border. Approximately 1km east of Chile Chico, the X-753 heads 55km south to the park entrance. The road is gravel, rough, and involves some minor river crossings. Public transport is not available along this stretch so most people come with private vehicles, although this presents its own difficulties for those intending to do the one-way trek to Parque Patagonia. Taxis are expensive and, as this road is rarely transited, hitchhiking is difficult. Tour operators charge for this transit, but those staying the night in Chile Chico might be able to plead with the hotel owner for a lift.

THE SENDERO PIEDRA CLAVADA   (9km; 3hrs; easy)

En route to Reserva Nacional Jeinemeni, just 25km south of Chile Chico (ie: approximately halfway to the main park entrance) is the Sendero Piedra Clavada **hiking trail**. Parking is available off the main road at the trailhead. The trail forms a loop, and easily can be completed in under 3 hours. Although technically within the national reserve there is no park ranger here. This trail serves as a decent warm-up for the trek through the reserve, and it is possible to do in a single day from Chile Chico for those not continuing on to the park proper.

The route first passes an unusual 42m-high rock pillar formed by millennia of wind erosion (the 'nailed stone') before coming to a 1,145m-high panoramic viewpoint towards Lago General Carrera (the 'portezuelo'). Next, you reach the 'Cueva de los Manos' where prehistoric hand paintings and images of guanacos can be seen, estimated to be between 8,000 and 10,000 years old, before finally reaching the Valley of the Moon (an arid landscape) some 2.5km from the trailhead.

The main road continues 20km past the trailhead for the Sendero Piedra Clavada to the main park entrance, where the entry fee is paid.

Where to stay The only formal **campsite** in the park is less than 1km from the main park entrance, at the northern edge of Lago Jeinemeni. Facilities include a table and benches with a roof, fire pit, wood and new, clean bathrooms. The crystal-clear, lake-fed stream by the campground is full of trout (bigger ones can be caught in February). The ranger lives in the park, but if he's not around it is possible to park outside the office, pitch your tent in the clearly marked camping sites and pay later or the next day.

Hiking in the reserve (and beyond) The **maps** provided by CONAF include only the sections of the trail within the park boundary, not the sections within Parque Patagonia to the south. However, the park ranger knows the entire trail and the southern section is very well marked.

All trailheads and detours are well signed, and although they are adequately maintained, it is not to the higher standard of the privately owned Parque Patagonia.

From the campsite, the **Sendero Mirador trek** (*1.6km round-trip; 15–30mins; easy*) heads west on a well-maintained trail through the lenga forest to a viewpoint above the lake. Here, trekkers are rewarded with a southerly panoramic view of the beautiful, dark blue Lago Jeinemeni set against the rugged, multi-coloured mountain range (the rocks are made up of different minerals).

There are **two other hikes** along this stretch, the first of which leads to another viewpoint on the south side of the lake (*1.8km round-trip; 15–30mins; easy*), showing a similar perspective to the first viewing platform but this time with a northerly view of the lake. The second goes to Lago Verde (*5.2km round-trip; 1hr; easy*) – not to be confused with the Lago Verde just west of Chile Chico, or the Lago Verde near La Junta. It passes Laguna Esmeralda after 400m and crosses the Río Desagui, before continuing for a further 2.2km to the southeastern extreme of Lago Verde. The views over the lake are superb – this is an excellent place to pause and appreciate Mother Nature at her best, or do a spot of trout fishing.

Hiking from Jeinemeni to Parque Patagonia (*47km; 23hrs over 3 days; medium*) This is a highly recommended trek with stunning alpine mountain scenery, passing glaciers, lakes and pristine native forest. There are no dangerous high mountain passes and most of the trek is sheltered from the Patagonian wind with deep canyons scoured out by glaciers and huge, almost-vertical rock faces towering up to the sky. A high level of fitness is required to trek the 8–10-hour days with a backpack, tent, food and gear suitable for this environment. The trail entry and exit access points make this an ideal trek to do one-way to save doubling back and covering the same ground again.

Day 1: Park entrance to Valle Hermoso campsite (*15km; 8hrs; medium*) The
trailhead starts from the campground beside the CONAF office at the reserve entrance. Cross the bridge over the Río Jeinemeni next to the campground and walk along the southern shore of Lago Jeinemeni. This is a flat lenga-forested section with views of the lake and the surrounding mountains. After 3km is a **detour** to a wonderful view over the lake, which is worth the effort. A **second well-marked detour** to the southern shore of Lago Verde via Laguna Esmeralda lies at the western end of **Lago Jeinemeni** shortly before Laguna Esmeralda. After **Laguna Esmeralda** is the first knee-deep river crossing – walking poles or a stick will come in handy. The trail continues up a stony river bed with numerous stream crossings but most can be negotiated without having to remove trekking boots. A **third detour** leads to the eastern shore of Lago Verde. The trail continues for a tough section along the riverbed with no visible trail markers. Look for a low point in the mountain range to the left that is covered in trees: a small red arrow on the riverbank points to where the trail leaves the riverbed towards a short but steep pass, from which there is an amazing view of Lago Verde. A stick or trekking poles will assist in the steep descent to Lago Verde, particularly at the deeper river crossing over to the northern shore (14km from the starting point). From this point, the trail continues for an hour along the riverbed and through the lenga forest to the **campsite**, with a basic toilet and small hut for cooking and eating.

Day 2: Valle Hermoso campsite to Valle Aviles second campsite (*10km; 6hrs; medium*) Shortly after the campground, hikers can head right (northwest) for a 90-minute **detour** to the **Ventisquero Estero**. This is a walk up a stony riverbed to the glacier-fed lagoon. On a sunny day, the views over the lagoon towards the glacier might be worth the effort for those with spare time. The main trail continues along an uncomfortable boulder-laden section of riverbed with multiple stream crossings until it veers left and joins the **Valle Aviles**, which leads to Parque Patagonia through snow-capped mountains and glaciers. There is a slight climb up over a low valley pass followed by a descent into the Valle Aviles with amazing mountain scenery in all directions. This is where Parque Patagonia begins (*no entry fee*). After 1½ hours' trekking through a bush-clad valley, there is a bridge where the Lago Escondido overflow meets the Valle Aviles watershed, across which you'll find the first, very basic, **campsite** in the new park. From this point, it is 24km to the end of the trail at Casa Piedra in the Valle Chacabuco, so it is worth stopping here. Alternatively, it is possible to push on to a **second basic campsite** 1 hour further down the Valle Aviles.

Day 3: Valle Aviles second campsite to Casa Piedra campsite (*22km; 9–10hrs; medium*) From the second campsite, the trail continues along the eastern side of the **Valle Aviles** through lenga forests with broad views of the valley. After an hour's walk, there is a swift-flowing river crossing over to the western side of the valley, shortly after which you'll come to a small hut that can be used as an emergency

shelter if required. From this point the landscape changes from lenga forests to the drier, windswept native pasture lands of the steppe – keep an eye out for guanacos and Andean condors. Some 30 minutes past the hut you'll come to the deepest river crossing: between knee- and waist-deep for the average person (subject to climatic conditions). The trail continues for several hours until a spectacular swing bridge that spans 30m over a 34m-deep canyon. This is also the northernmost point of the Aviles loop which starts and finishes at Casa Piedra, with excellent views of the glaciated landscape. The trail then heads a long way down towards a second swing bridge across the Río Chacabuco and 30 minutes later ends at the **Casa Piedra campground**, 25km from the park headquarters along the main border road between Argentina and the Carretera Austral. Traffic is limited – you can try hitching, but be prepared to walk. It is flat and beautiful, passing large lagoons full of birds including ducks, white-necked swans, flamingos and other wildlife. The regenerating grasslands are now home to many guanacos.

A future trek to Cochrane through Reserva Nacional Tamango The southern edge of the Lagunas Altas Trail in Parque Patagonia is very close to the northern boundary of Reserva Nacional Tamango. It is possible to walk from the trail to the northernmost trails in Tamango which connect to Cochrane itself; however, the trail connecting the two parks is unmarked and not yet officially open. Seek advice from the staff at Parque Patagonia before attempting this.

⊕ AS THE CONDOR FLIES

Chile Chico is 570km south of Puerto Montt, and 280km north of the border to El Chaltén south of Villa O'Higgins. The southbound condor flying via Chile Chico is thus two-thirds of the way to the end of the Carretera Austral.

THE CARRETERA AUSTRAL ONLINE

For additional online content, articles, photos and more on the Carretera Austral, why not visit www.bradtguides.com/schile.

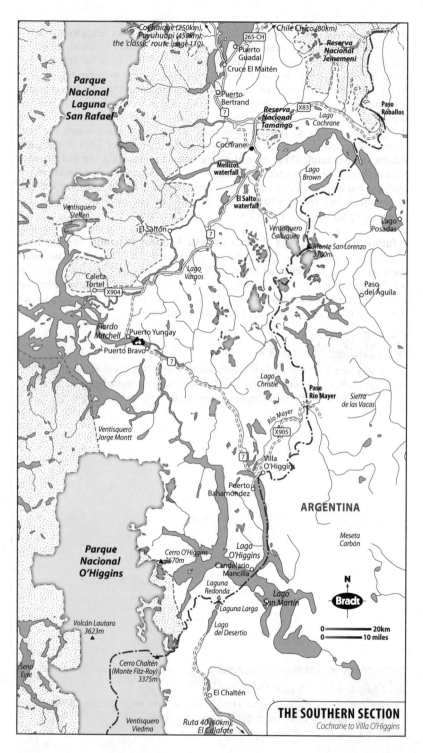

Cochrane (250km),
Puyuhuapi (450km),
the 'classic' route page 110)

Chile Chico (80km)

265-CH

Reserva
Nacional
Jeinemeni

Puerto
Guadal

Cruce El Maitén

Parque
Nacional
Laguna
San Rafael

Puerto
Bertrand

7

Reserva
Nacional
Tamango

X83

Lago
Cochrane

Paso
Roballos

Cochrane

Mellizos
waterfall

Lago
Brown

El Salto
waterfall

Ventisquero
Steffen

El Saltón

7

Ventisquero
Calluqueo

Lago
Posadas

Monte San Lorenzo
3700m

Lago
Vargos

Caleta
Tortel

X904

Paso
del Águila

Fiordo
Mitchell

Puerto Yungay

Puerto Bravo

7

Ventisquero
Jorge Montt

Lago
Christie

Paso
Río Mayer

Sierra
de las Vacas

Río Mayer

X905

7

Villa
O'Higgins

Puerto
Bahamóndez

ARGENTINA

Parque
Nacional
O'Higgins

Cerro O'Higgins
2670m

Lago
O'Higgins

Candelario
Mancilla

Meseta
Carbón

N

Laguna
Redonda

Lago
San Martín

Laguna Larga

Bradt

Volcán Lautaro
3623m

Lago
del Desertio

0   20km
0   10 miles

Seno
Eyre

Cerro Chaltén
(Monte Fitz-Roy)
3375m

El Chaltén

Ventisquero
Viedma

Ruta 40 (60km),
El Calafate

THE SOUTHERN SECTION
Cochrane to Villa O'Higgins

Part Four

THE SOUTHERN CARRETERA AUSTRAL

10

The Deep South: Cruce El Maitén to Caleta Tortel

For those doing the 'classic' route along the Carretera Austral, the Cruce El Maitén is the southernmost point of the journey. For those hardy souls continuing further south, the first village after the Cruce El Maitén junction is **Puerto Bertrand**, source of the thundering Río Baker, and launch pad for a number of more adventurous treks towards the ice field. To the east is the magnificent **Parque Patagonia**, one of the most ambitious private conservation projects on the continent, which will soon merge with Jeinemeni and Tamango national reserves to form a park to rival even Torres del Paine further south.

Next comes **Cochrane** – an up-and-coming town in southern Chile. Previously little more than a backwater, before being touted as the proposed epicentre of the controversial hydro-electric plans on the rivers Baker and Pascua (see box, pages 172–4), Cochrane is now finding its feet as a hub for tourists, with a superb array of activities on its doorstep. Continuing 126km further south, **Caleta Tortel** is an atmospheric village with a slightly spooky history and is unique for having been constructed entirely on wooden boardwalks. It also serves as a good base to visit two glaciers as well as a mysterious graveyard.

While the Carretera Austral can hardly be described as 'the beaten track', the section north of Cochrane, and certainly the section north of the Cruce El Maitén, is *relatively* discovered. From this point south, traffic thins, road quality worsens, and distances between inhabited locations grow larger.

PUERTO BERTRAND

Blink and you may miss Puerto Bertrand, a small village of around 300 inhabitants. Located at the dramatic southern extreme of the lake of the same name with the looming Cordon Contreras mountains for a backdrop, this is the origin of the Río Baker, Chile's largest river in terms of volume of water. Lago General Carrera flows into Lago Bertrand, and the Carretera Austral follows the Río Baker south to Cochrane and to the eventual delta at Caleta Tortel. Thus Puerto Bertrand arguably deserves a slice of the fame that the Río Baker receives.

The village is famous as a trout fisherman's paradise, with excursions either on Lago Bertrand itself, or on the Río Baker. It is also a base for horseriding, and rafting on the river as well as trekking towards (and even on to) the Northern Ice Field, and kayaking on the lake.

The Río Baker narrowly escaped becoming Chile's largest hydro-electric project in history, as fierce resistance from the local community finally persuaded the Chilean

For those **without a private vehicle** it is possible to cross the border into Argentina at El Chaltén further south (pages 261–5), thus allowing exploration of the deep south before leaving the Carretera Austral. This is our recommended route. However, for those **with a private vehicle**, the options are more complex. The southernmost border crossing passable in a vehicle is **Paso Roballos** in Parque Patagonia (page 234), but exiting the Carretera here potentially means skipping superb scenery further south, including Caleta Tortel and Villa O'Higgins. If time allows, consider making the trip south at least to Caleta Tortel and then doubling back to the Paso Roballos border.

government not to dam the river (see box, pages 172–4). The river discharges an average of 870m³/s – to put this into perspective, the River Thames in London discharges under 70m³/s, so for a river of only 170km in length, it is astonishing.

HISTORY The first settlers of Puerto Bertrand arrived in the 1920s and dedicated themselves to sheep farming, but the village was not formed until the 1940s. According to the village's records, the village itself was formed when two families of original settlers, the Sansana and Esparza families, donated part of their lands so that the Río Baker Estancia (now known as Valle Chacabuco and owned by the Tompkins family) could have access to the water for loading their sheep. The actual limits of the donated land fell into dispute, a subject which still hasn't been fully resolved to this day. The settlers of Puerto Bertrand lived off livestock farming and forestry. The Río Baker Estancia also employed a large number of settlers as farm hands. This vast estancia was owned and run – to various degrees of financial success – by Lucas Bridges, an Englishman born in 1874 in Ushuaia, Argentina, the son of an English missionary.

In its heyday, the estancia had 85,000 sheep over 500,000ha, until 1964, when the Chilean government under the new President Eduardo Frei Montalva re-appropriated the land instead of renewing its lease, distributing it among local families. This process of land appropriation was reversed from 1973 onwards under the regime of Augusto Pinochet.

In the 1980s, Puerto Bertrand made several important advances. In 1982 the first village council was made official, which allowed them to approach the state for financial assistance, much needed due to the drop in wool prices which was severely affecting the local economy and forcing several landowners to sell their land.

The village came together as a community to build a health centre, under the guidance and motivation of Father Antonio Ronchi (see box, page 125). Running water and electricity also reached Puerto Bertrand around this time. The Foundation for the Development of Aysén (an NGO dedicated to promoting economic and social change in the region) also intervened with assistance in education, business management and technical training, specifically related to farming and other needs of the local community. In 1986 The Carretera Austral reached Puerto Bertrand, connecting it with Chile Chico.

Puerto Bertrand has two organisations in charge of its tourism sector: the government-run Comité de Desarrollo Turístico (Tourism Committee), and the privately run Red de Turismo Rural Río Baker (River Baker Tourism Network). While the former claims to have greater interests in the local community, the latter has greater resources and infrastructure, and the two organisations have had several disagreements over who should run the village's local tourism industry. Today, the peace and tranquillity of Puerto Bertrand, surrounded by nature at its most pristine, show little sign of the struggles and conflicts that its hardy settlers have lived through over the years.

GETTING THERE There is **no public transport** specifically to or from the village, but buses between Cochrane and either Chile Chico or Puerto Río Tranquilo and up towards Coyhaique will stop at the junction to Puerto Bertrand, which is approximately 100m from the village.

About the route
Cruce El Maitén to Puerto Bertrand (*14km; 25mins; gravel*) Some 14km of consolidated gravel road connects Puerto Bertrand with the Cruce El Maitén. Shortly after the junction, the road climbs along the eastern shore of the small but picturesque Lago Negro. The **viewing platform** on the right is one of the iconic views of the Carretera Austral.

TOUR OPERATORS For a good local guide, Arcadio Soto and his son offer fishing excursions and guided treks in the region ((9) 87232288; e *arcadsoto@gmail. com*). They have a 6m, 40HP fibreglass boat.

Rafting Buena Vista On the beach in village; (9) 95183300, (9) 78814999. Class III rafting trips on the Río Baker with a snack at the end. Provide all equipment (wetsuits, helmets, life jackets) & offer warm showers afterwards. Approximately 1½ hours on the river, & the total trip is around 2½ hours. Also have 3 fully equipped cabins for 3, 5, or 7 people ($35,000, $60,000 & $75,000 respectively). Can organise boat trips to Lago Plomo or the Ventisquero Soler for up to 7 passengers & have several small kayaks they rent by the hour.

WHERE TO STAY The 10km of the Carretera Austral south of Puerto Bertrand is home to a number of lodges and cabins along the river's edge catering to most budgets and offering excellent fishing options. Options within Bertrand itself are more limited.

Borde Baker Lodge (7 cabins) 8km south of Puerto Bertrand; (9) 92345315; m (2) 25858464; e contacto@bordebaker.cl; www.bordebaker.cl. Superior dbl cabins overlooking the Río Baker, appear rustic on the outside but modern & comfortable on the inside. All cabins have great views of the river & mountains, & are oriented such that other cabins are invisible, maintaining an intimate environment. Top-quality private bathrooms, goose feather duvets, LED lighting, & both firewood & gas heating. The wooden, elevated pathways that connect the cabins with the main building & dining area are reminiscent of Caleta Tortel. Excellent b/fast included. Wi-Fi. The fine on-site restaurant offers an excellent wine list & the open kitchen allows guests to watch the chef prepare gourmet delicacies ($$$$). A great place for quiet & solitude with exceptional service. Credit cards accepted. All-inclusive packages available. $$$$$

Rápidos del Río Baker (5 cabins) 3km south of Puerto Bertrand; (9) 78866722, (9) 92181140; e info@rapidosdelriobaker.com; www.rapidosdelriobaker.com; ⊙ Oct–Mar. One of the more economical cabins along this stretch of the Río Baker, these are simple, slightly dated & in need of minor maintenance, but are utterly peaceful & with access to the river. Sleep 4 or 6 people. Set amongst trees & built with brick & wood, the main criticism is that they do not face the river. The kitchen is adequate, hot water is fine, they offer laundry, & there is patchy internet in the restaurant (which has sketchy opening hours). They have a boat & offer guided fishing trips on the

Baker. Heating via wood-stoves. If the restaurant is closed there are shops or restaurants in Bertrand, which *may* be open. Stock up in advance – more suitable for self-catering. **$$$$**

🏠 **Green Baker Lodge** (5 rooms, 7 cabins) 3km south of Puerto Bertrand; ☏ (9) 91597757, (9) 75162510; e info@greenbakerlodge.cl; www.greenbakerlodge.cl. A well-established adventure lodge where guests often stay for multiple days to enjoy a multitude of outdoor activities on offer, including fly-fishing, trekking, horseriding, rafting on the Río Baker (grades 3 & 4), glacier walks, ice trekking, mountain biking & a canopy across the river. 7 comfortable new cabins for 2 to 7 people, each with balconies & views of the river, living/dining room & a fully equipped kitchen. The furniture is made of *rauli*, a native red Chilean wood. The hotel has 5 lovely, spacious en-suite rooms. 4 rooms have 3 sgl beds, 1 has a dbl bed & 3 sgls. The cabins are hidden among large coigües and notros trees beside the river. There is a beach for fishing or launching a boat, & a hot tub on the banks of the river offering a view of the Northern Ice Field. The restaurant & BBQ area were recently remodelled & are located by the river. The menu of the day (lunch & dinner) is $15,000 without drinks. B/fast is $5,000 but is free with accommodation paid in dollars. Laundry service & Wi-Fi. Reservations require a 50% deposit. Accepts credit cards. **$$$–$$$$**

🏠 **Residencial Los Coihues** (5 rooms) Amador Esperanza 265 (on the plaza beside the church); ☏ (9) 82308953; e f_bustamante@hotmail.cl; ⊕ all year. A basic but clean backpacker hostel. Shared bathroom, laundry service & ample parking. Lunch & dinner can be organised (**$$**) – home-cooked beef, chicken, pork or salmon with potatoes. A decent b/fast is included with eggs. No internet. Good value. **$**

❌ **WHERE TO EAT AND DRINK** There are no formal restaurants in Puerto Bertrand. However, Arcadio Soto's family (page 228) have an informal restaurant which also doubles as a shop (*Amador Esparza;* ☏ *(9) 84260993;* ⊕ *Oct–Mar noon–15.00 & 19.00–21.00).* Traditional local food including salads, steaks, pork, chicken and lamb – a set menu costs $8,000. Wine, juices and soft drinks available. The house across the street also offers dinners.

SIGHTSEEING AND EXCURSIONS Activities in Bertrand revolve around the mountains or the lake and river. In addition to fishing, rafting on the Río Baker is popular, with tour operators in Bertrand or based in the lodges further south. Any accommodation in this region can arrange a local guide for water-based activities. Hiking towards the ice shelf is possible, but generally less formal than in other areas, without formal marked trails maintained by CONAF. It is essential to obtain local information (and ideally a guide), and is more suited to experienced trekkers and mountaineers.

There are two **river confluences** between Puerto Bertrand and Cochrane. The first, where the rivers **Nef and Baker** meet, is particularly spectacular – a ferocious waterfall metres before the differing colours of the two rivers swirl together dramatically as the Baker heads further south. It is clearly signposted with parking facilities (free entry) on the west of the Carretera Austral 20km south of Puerto Bertrand or 30km north of Cochrane; a small trail leads down to a viewing platform. The second, lesser-known confluence is the union of the rivers **Chacabuco and Baker**, accessible from the Carretera Austral via a short walk west where the road towards Paso Roballos and Parque Patagonia heads east from the Carretera Austral.

PARQUE PATAGONIA

(*www.patagoniapark.org;* ⊕ *park all year, lodge & campgrounds Oct–Apr; free*) Currently the land (over 200,000 acres) between Reserva Nacional Jeinemeni (south of Chile Chico) and Reserva Nacional Tamango (north of Cochrane) is referred to as the Valle Chacabuco, and was acquired by Conservación Patagónica (CP), the foundation established by Kris Tompkins in 2000. The Río Chacabuco and the main road connecting the Carretera Austral to Argentina at Paso Roballos (page 234) run through the valley. CP is in the process of merging Valle Chacabuco with the two national reserves to form the Parque Patagonia, creating 2,400km² of national park stretching from Cochrane to Chile Chico, encompassing most of the land east of the Carretera Austral up to the Argentine border. This park will challenge even Torres del Paine further south as one of the primary tourist destinations in Patagonia, and is already undoubtedly one of the highlights of the entire Carretera Austral. For more on the work of Kris and Doug Tompkins, see box, pages 104–5.

CP has developed important infrastructure within the park and the plan is that, once complete, Parque Patagonia will be donated to the Chilean government (as a national park). The main headquarters include a hotel, accommodation for staff and management, a school, roads, offices, and scientific facilities. The board of CP includes a number of leading scientists who advise on the best means to restore the land to its original state. All materials used in construction are sourced locally and recycled where possible. Food is organic and also sourced locally. Six bridges were constructed to facilitate the trekking trails.

Parque Patagonia is located in one of the few east–west valleys in Chilean Patagonia, and while to date there are only three marked trails, more are planned. This is a park in its infancy, but the early signs are very encouraging. The park offers unspoiled wilderness, extensive wildlife, excellent trekking, and luxury accommodation for those with decent travel budgets. For the rest of us, the campground is more than adequate. Note that it is not permitted to light fires in the park, or indeed any park in Patagonia (Argentine or Chilean), due to the ease with which forest fires can begin. Camp stoves are essential.

HISTORY The Valle Chacabuco had been used by Tehuelches for centuries, if not millennia. A number of archaeological sites discovered in the region, and the various cave paintings on both sides of the border, are testimony to ancient civilisations living in these regions. In 1906 William Norris reached the Río Baker from Argentina via the Valle Chacabuco on his fateful journey to Caleta Tortel (pages 246–7).

In 1908 the Compañia Explotadora del Bakerleased the land around Valle Chacabuco from the Chilean government to set up a large-scale sheep farm, managed by Lucas Bridges. From the outset the estancia struggled to make a profit, forcing Bridges to increase the density of sheep. Over-grazing further reduced profitability, and pushed the estancia into debt. Shareholders of the Sociedad, including Bridge's own family, began selling their shares. The lease expired in 1964 and the government did not renew it. Under the agrarian reform of President Eduardo Frei the Sociedad was liquidated. The land was appropriated by the government and given to local families. In 1967 both Tamango and Jeinemeni national reserves were formed, but the Valle Chacabuco, the land between the two, was still privately owned.

In 1980 Pinochet claimed the entire Valle Chacabuco from these families and sold it at auction to a Belgian landowner, Francisco de Smet, for US$0.5 million. The over-grazing was so severe – with parts of the valley so arid and windswept that they resembled desert – that de Smet was once again unable to turn a profit from livestock. Cheaper Australian wool further lowered the international price of wool, and many estancias across Patagonia were unable to compete. Large-scale sheep farming was simply not viable. De Smet sold the 173,000-acre estancia to CP, the foundation established by Kris Tompkins (see box, pages 104–5), in 2004, for US$10 million.

CP gradually bought up neighbouring (and equally unviable) estancias. Their first course of action to restore the land to its original fertile nature was to remove all fences and livestock, so that native animals could roam freely. Livestock were sold gradually so as not to depress prices and thus harm the livelihood of other farmers in the region. Invasive plants were removed by an army of volunteers, and native grassland was replanted. Gradually native species, pushed to the brink of extinction, began to bounce back. It is now estimated that Valle Chacabuco is home to 10% of the world population of huemules. Pumas, previously hunted by ranchers (illegally – the puma is a protected species), were also allowed to roam freely, and fears that they would multiply in number and devastate the native huemul population have proved unfounded. CP embarked on an ambitious project to tag and monitor pumas in order to study their behaviour and discovered that the greatest enemy to the endangered huemul was in fact dogs from the nearby town of Cochrane.

As the grasslands began to show signs of recovery, so too did the guanaco population, which in turn attracted more pumas. Puma remained the vilified enemy of local ranchers, and allowing pumas to roam freely was disliked by many. Evidence from the tagging project dispelled such myths: the puma population within the park was stable, and individuals were territorial. Local ranchers were quick to blame Valle Chacabuco for their sheep lost to pumas, but were slow to produce evidence supporting their claims (such as sheep carcases), and even slower to admit hunting pumas themselves (illegal under Chilean law).

Doubtless pumas did occasionally eat sheep and CP sought a solution to this problem. They began breeding guard dogs (great Pyrenées) that had demonstrated for centuries an uncanny ability to protect herds from predators. When the puppies are only 20 days old they are integrated into the herd, drinking sheep milk and sleeping on sheepskins. A rigorous training programme takes approximately a year, and the dogs successfully guard their herd with almost 100% success. Parque Patagonia has a corral that has suffered not a single loss of sheep to puma since the guard dogs were introduced. The dogs are now provided to local ranchers, and puma kills have declined dramatically.

Recognising that livestock was the foundation of the local economy, as well as the main source of employment to many people in and around Cochrane, CP offered all former employees of the estancia ongoing employment as park rangers or conservation workers, some of whom still work in the park today.

GETTING THERE Parque Patagonia is most easily visited with a private vehicle or bicycle, as the trails are far apart from one another and the park headquarters, lodge and campground are 11km east from the main junction with the Carretera Austral. There is no public transport to the park headquarters, although all buses along the Carretera Austral must pass by the main junction. However, park rangers and employees travelling along the main road will generally offer a ride to the park headquarters where the Lagunas Altas trail is located, as well as the campsite.

If making a reservation at the lodge, they can help with arranging a taxi from Cochrane if required.

About the route
Puerto Bertrand to Parque Patagonia (*43km; 1hr; gravel*) The gravel road from Puerto Bertrand to the junction leading to Parque Patagonia, and onto Cochrane, is mostly good quality. There are no services along this section, but two

points of interest: the lookout over the confluence of the Baker and Nef rivers (page 229), and the alternative route to Cochrane (which bypasses the park altogether; see page 237). The main road through Parque Patagonia and onto the Paso Roballos border crossing is the X-83, which joins the Carretera Austral 16km north of Cochrane or 32km south of Puerto Bertrand. It is a further 11km to the main park buildings, or 72km to the border.

The Carretera runs parallel to the Río Baker, which is visible for large sections of the journey until turning off to Parque Patagonia. Be aware of guanacos on the road.

WHERE TO STAY AND EAT There is only one **hotel** in Parque Patagonia, and one formal campground. Camping is possible only in designated areas. The lodge and restaurant are expensive, considering the minor logistical inconvenience of bringing food from Cochrane (the nearest town with any shops for stocking up on supplies). For those on even a reasonable daily budget the camping and cooking combination will save a lot of money. Given the array of activities in the park, this is perhaps not the best location to splash out on expensive accommodation, only to spend most of the day up a mountain. However, budget constraints aside, this is superb accommodation in a unique setting, with a reasonable restaurant.

There is also a handicraft **shop** in the main park building selling a range of products from the region, including knitwear, honey, wooden bowls, baskets, linen products, etc, as well as books and maps. However, for camping equipment and basic food supplies, stock up in Cochrane.

The Lodge at Chacabuco Valley
(6 rooms) Parque Patagonia headquarters; e reservas@vallechacabuco.cl; ⏺ Oct–Apr. This is a splendid building made entirely from recycled wood & stone from the quarry within the park. Rooms accommodate 2, 3 or 4 people, & it is essential to reserve in advance. Each room is unique, finished to a high standard, with decent hot water, comfortable beds & a desk. The views from the rooms are generally toward the southern side of the valley, so you can watch wildlife from your bed. The main sitting area, where an excellent b/fast is served (included – every conceivable item available including eggs to order, in apparent unlimited supply) has a small bar, huge windows facing the valley & large comfortable sofas. There is a wide range of coffee-table books, mainly published by the Tompkins & focused on nature & conservation. The internet connection is a tad slow. Remove shoes at the door, as the wood & tiled floors scratch easily – there is underfloor heating to prevent cold feet! In summary, this is without a doubt one of the finest accommodations along the entire Carretera Austral, & an ideal launch pad for trails in the region. The downside? All this comes at a high

price: rooms range from US$150pp (quadruple occupancy) up to US$350 (sgl occupancy). A very pleasant treat, but an extravagant one if planning to spend most of the day hiking mountains.
$$$$–$$$$$

Stone House Campground (Camping Casa de Piedra) (7 covered, various uncovered, rarely fills up) 25km east of Parque Patagonia HQ; ⏺ Oct–Apr. No reservations, operates on a first-come-first-served basis. Basic facilities, due to be completed by 2015/16 season. **$**

West Winds Campground (60 sites)
Parque Patagonia headquarters; ⏺ Oct–Apr. No reservations – operates on a first-come-first-served basis, but rarely fills up. Complete bathrooms, decent sinks for washing dishes, & facilities to wash clothes, but the water is tepid at best. However, given the lack of alternative accommodation in the park, & the modest price ($5,000, paid in the headquarters), this is a small gripe. Sites around the edge have covered tables & benches. The main campground is verdant lush grass, sufficient to lure guanacos for a quick bite. It can get surprisingly cold in the campground at night so be sure to have a decent tent & warm sleeping bag, even in Jan. No electricity. **$**

✖ Bar and Restaurant El Rincón Gaucho

Parque Patagonia headquarters; ⊕ Nov–Apr 13.00–14.00 & 20.00–22.00 daily. This place has somewhat of a monopoly within the park &, as such, while this is a lovely restaurant in a delightful setting, it's perhaps not the best value for money. The building was constructed to the same high quality as the lodge, with hypnotising huge black-&-white photographs of animals & Mount San Lorenzo along the interior walls, & a view towards the east of the valley through the main windows, where there will invariably be a few-dozen guanacos grazing. Picnics can be ordered in advance, consisting of a sandwich, fruit & cookies; or a simple set lunch (*US$20*). Dinner is again a set menu varying daily, generally consisting of a salad, main course & dessert (*US$35*). Wine is overpriced. Budget-conscious visitors may be better off in the campground eating pasta! Nonetheless very good quality food & service. English spoken. **$$$$**

THE MAIN TRAILS There are currently three main trails in the park extending 113km in total, with more scheduled to open in 2015 onwards. From the junction with the Carretera Austral to the Argentine border, the road is 72km passing through many areas worth exploring as well as the trailheads of the Aviles and Lago Chico trails. Maps are available in the park headquarters and are worth obtaining. The trails are generally well marked with the exception of the Lago Chico trail (as of early 2015).

The **Aviles trail** (*47km; 23hrs over 3 days; medium*) currently connects Valle Chacabuco with Reserva Nacional Jeinemeni. Until the two are merged under Parque Patagonia, the only difference is that the markers are better in Valle Chacabuco. The full trail is described in detail on pages 221–3. The southern portion of this trail can also be visited as a day trek (*15km loop; easy*), and forms a loop travelling on both sides of the Río Aviles, thus no need to backtrack on the same path. Note that the trailhead is 25km west of the park headquarters. This trail ends at the reserve entrance, which is 55km south of Chile Chico.

The **Lagunas Altas trail** (*23km loop; 1 day; medium*) begins at the West Winds campground close to the park headquarters, and takes a full day. It winds through forests and passes a number of lakes, with views across the Valle Chacabuco. This is probably the most accessible trail for those without private transport, as it begins and ends close to the park headquarters. It ascends the southern side of the valley and reaches the border of Reserva Nacional Tamango. Keep eyes peeled for Andean condors. Eventually this trail will extend further south to the shore of Lago Cochrane and then head southwest to the Río Cochrane and onto Cochrane. Currently, however, this is an unmarked trail. Confident and well-equipped mountaineers may be able to complete this alone, or hiring a guide in Parque Patagonia may be possible (ask in the reception, or email the park in advance). A shorter trail, **La Vega** (*3km; easy*) connects the West Winds campsite with the park headquarters.

The **Lago Chico trail** (*26km from main road, 14km with 4x4 to trailhead; ½–full day; medium*) is not well marked, but is fairly straightforward. The trail begins 40km west of the park headquarters and is thus easier for those with a private vehicle. From the trailhead at La Juanina do not attempt to drive up the path in anything other than a decent 4x4. As with the Lagunas Altas trail, the trek begins by ascending the southern side of the valley, initially on a gravel road through a forest (*7km one-way, easy*). Over the ridge the view is stunning, looking out towards Lago Cochrane with Monte San Lorenzo behind. From this point, there are no further trail marks (as of early 2015) so take care – there is no cellphone coverage. However, the lake provides an obvious point of reference as long as you remember how to return to the ridge at the correct location for the return descent. Expect to see large herds of guanaco, and the forested sections provide ample birdwatching opportunities. The loop trail is apparently 12km, but we got entirely lost and never found the trail, instead we used the lake as a reference. It is possible to bushwhack to the shore of Lago Cochrane. If in a decent 4x4 and able to ascend the initial gravel road, this may be a half-day trek. However, for those walking the gravel road, and particularly those intending to approach Lago Cochrane, this is a full day. Unless you're intending to camp, be sure to return to the ridge before dusk. The trail is not technically demanding, but the lack of markers may mean this trek is more suitable for those with some mountaineering experience or those with a guide.

THE SCENIC ROAD THROUGH THE PARK TOWARDS THE BORDER The road through the park connects the Carretera Austral with Paso Roballos to Argentina. Even if you've no plans to cross the border, it's worth driving this road, as it passes a number of important sights as well as numerous lakes and opportunities to observe wildlife. This route follows the Valle Chacabuco, with towering mountains on both sides, verdant vegetation following decades of over-grazing, and abundant animals and birds. This was a historical entry point to the region used by the early pioneers. As with the trails, it is worth picking up a map at the park headquarters or downloading one from the website (page 229).

> **NOTE**
>
> This is currently the southern-most border crossing by car or motorbike.

The entire route is 72km one-way from the junction with the Carretera to the Argentine border, on gravel. Beware of animals on the road. Traffic is sparse. The road can flood later in the season, and while a 4x4 is not strictly necessary, a high-clearance car is advisable, particularly if crossing into Argentina. From the park headquarters, 11km east of the junction, this would be a 122km round-trip, possible in a day; if you're combining this with either of the trails along this section (Aviles or Lago Chico) it will be a long day. From Cochrane, 16km south of the junction, this would be a 168km round-trip. Also consider that the nearest petrol station is in Cochrane.

At the park entrance is the confluence of the rivers Baker and Chacabuco (page 229). As soon as you enter the park, guanacos are abundant. The initial 8km are of limited interest, until Valle Chacabuco becomes visible. Shortly thereafter lies the park headquarters offering the only formal accommodation in the entire park, and the only restaurant.

Continuing east towards Argentina the road passes **Lago Cisnes** and **Laguna de los Flamencos** (meaning 'swans' and 'flamingos' respectively). Both lakes are of interest to ornithologists, and indeed, the entire park is a birdwatcher's paradise. Again, guanacos are abundant in this region. Some 25km further east of the park entrance is the **Puesto Casa de Piedra**, the trailhead north along the Aviles trail towards Jeinemeni. A campground is under construction here, to be completed by the 2015/16 peak season. A further 15km east is La Juanina – a small gathering of houses, formerly part of an old estancia, now used by park employees. This is the trailhead for the **Lago Chico trail**. Within walking distance of La Juanina is the original house used by Lucas Bridges.

The landscape begins to transform at this point, with the first signs of arid steppe. Vegetation becomes scarcer, with fewer to no trees, just shrubs. Approximately 10km east of La Juanina is the **Chilean border control**, although it is a further 10km to the Argentine border.

In addition to the abundant grasslands that bear no resemblance to the former arid over-grazed estancia purchased in 2004, native species are once again flourishing here. Lakes along the main road through the park are teeming with birds, including flamingos. Black-faced ibis are also common (*Theristicus melanopis, bandurria* in Spanish), and relatively unafraid of humans. Their distinctive long beaks enable them to eat worms and insects, and they are often seen wandering around grassy sections probing for their dinner. Another bird often seen in the lakes is the black-necked swan. The park is also frequented by one of the smallest owls in the world – the Patagonian pygmy owl; but this is not strictly nocturnal and thus easier to spot. However, they are small and well camouflaged. Also, perhaps surprisingly, Austral parakeets are quite common, but seem brightly coloured and tropical for such a region – this is the most southerly parrot in the Americas.

Guanacos are so abundant as to border on becoming a nuisance! Do not be surprised to wake up in West Winds campsite and find a nosey guanaco sniffing around your tent, and take care driving along the main road. Andean condors are making a return to the park. As carrion-eaters, they lack talons for hunting, and the increasing guanaco population is an integral part of their diet. The park does not use pesticides – such chemicals previously hampered the development of condor chicks. Vizcachas (*Lagidum viscacia*) are also common. Previously hunted for their meat and fur, they are now flourishing. Their greatest natural predators are foxes and pumas, but having made their homes in inaccessible cracks in rocks, their dexterity and loud warning calls, they are able to survive.

Other fauna include culpeo foxes and the hairy armadillo. Somewhat like a small ostrich, the lesser rhea is also relatively common and can often be seen running in a state of seeming panic with no particular destination in mind. The park is also home to approximately 30 pumas, but sightings are rare.

The park suffered some wild fires in 2014, but damage was relatively mild, particularly when compared with the damage caused by fires in Torres del Paine.

COCHRANE

The province of Capitán Prat covers 37,242km², has a population of approximately 4,000 inhabitants and consists of three communes: Cochrane (the provincial capital), O'Higgins and Tortel. It is the southernmost province in Aysén, and the extreme southeastern corner of it penetrates south of the 49th parallel. Cochrane itself is sleepy, but has a delightful plaza, and a smattering of shops and restaurants, as well as a petrol station and the last ATM before Argentina for those continuing south.

HISTORY The Valle Chacabuco and the region surrounding what is now Cochrane was discovered in 1899 by the explorer Hans Steffens as he traversed the Río Baker for the first time. In 1908, the Sociedad Explotadora del Baker, owned by Magellanic cattle farmers under management of Lucas Bridges, acquired the land within the valley in order to construct a large-scale sheep farm (Estancia Chacabuco).

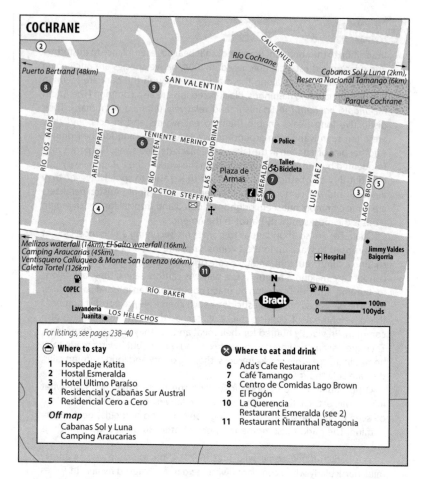

COCHRANE

Puerto Bertrand (48km)

Río Cochrane

CAUCAHUES

Cabanas Sol y Luna (2km),
Reserva Nacional Tamango (6km)

Parque Cochrane

SAN VALENTIN

RÍO LOS NADIS

ARTURO PRAT

TENIENTE MERINO

RÍO MAITÉN

LAS GOLONDRINAS

ESMERALDA

LUIS BAEZ

LAGO BROWN

• Police

Taller
Bicicleta

Plaza de
Armas

DOCTOR STEFFENS

Mellizos waterfall (14km), El Salto waterfall (16km),
Camping Araucarias (45km),
Ventisquero Calluqueo & Monte San Lorenzo (60km),
Caleta Tortel (126km)

COPEC

RÍO BAKER

Lavandería
Juanita

LOS HELECHOS

Hospital

Jimmy Valdes
Baigorria

N

Alfa

Bradt

0   100m
0   100yds

For listings, see pages 238–40

🛏 **Where to stay**

1   Hospedaje Katita
2   Hostal Esmeralda
3   Hotel Ultimo Paraíso
4   Residencial y Cabañas Sur Austral
5   Residencial Cero a Cero

Off map
    Cabanas Sol y Luna
    Camping Araucarias

✕ **Where to eat and drink**

6   Ada's Cafe Restaurant
7   Café Tamango
8   Centro de Comidas Lago Brown
9   El Fogón
10 La Querencia
    Restaurant Esmeralda (see 2)
11 Restaurant Ñirranthal Patagonia

The town of Cochrane originated in 1929 as a small settlement to house farm employees. It was originally called 'Las Latas', and located within the estancia, 8km east of the junction with the Carretera Austral heading towards Argentina, in what is now Parque Patagonia. However, the shareholders of Estancia Chacabuco disliked the proximity of the village, and decided to move its inhabitants claiming that a lack of water was the principal reason. The new village was called 'Pueblo Nuevo' (New Town) and it was from here that the present town grew. It was formed in 1930 by government order.

The town was later renamed Cochrane to honour Thomas Cochrane, 10th Earl of Dundonald, a British naval captain and radical politician who made great contributions to Chilean independence (see box, page 237).

The town of Cochrane was officially inaugurated on 17 March 1954, with ten houses in total. The streets and sites of Cochrane were finally laid out in 1955 by three land surveyors: Carlos Pizarro Araneda, Germán Pozo and Fernando Malagueño. On 26 October 1970 the municipality of Cochrane, which then belonged to the Department of Chile Chico, became part of the Baker Department together with the villages of Villa O'Higgins and Caleta Tortel. Esteban Ramírez Sepúlveda became its first governor. In 1975 a new province was created, Capitán Prat, and Cochrane became its capital.

Following a career in the British Royal Navy, Cochrane was elected to the House of Commons in 1806. He campaigned for parliamentary reform and his outspoken criticism of the war and corruption in the navy made him powerful enemies. After being convicted in the Great Stock Exchange Fraud he was expelled from parliament in July 1814, stripped of his knighthood, fined £1,000 and humiliated in a pillory.

His naval career, however, was far from over. Cochrane arrived in Valparaiso, Chile in 1818 when the country was preparing for its battle for independence. On 11 December 1818, upon request of Chilean leader Bernardo O'Higgins, Cochrane became a Chilean citizen. He was appointed Vice Admiral and took charge of the Chilean navy in Chile's war of independence from Spain.

Cochrane developed a taste for battles for independence, and in 1823 took command of the Brazilian navy in their quest for independence from Portugal. In 1827 he helped Greece's independence from the Ottoman Empire. In 1831 his father died, and Cochrane inherited the earldom. He returned to the British navy the following year. His knighthood was finally restored in 1847 by Queen Victoria. He died in 1860, and is buried in Westminster Abbey. The Chilean navy hold a wreath-laying ceremony at his grave in his honour each year in May. In 2006, the Chilean navy acquired a Type 23 frigate from the British navy (formerly the HMS *Norfolk*) and named her *Almirante Cochrane*.

GETTING THERE
About the route
Puerto Bertrand to Cochrane (*48km; 1hr; gravel*) This section is gravel, mostly of good quality. The road has recently been widened as far as the detour to Parque Patagonia. However, there are steep inclines along the entire section between Bertrand and Cochrane, so cyclists may struggle. South of the detour to Parque Patagonia and Argentina the road narrows as it winds along the Río Baker beneath. Be aware that guanacos may stray into the road. The view down to the valley is wonderful, with the rich autumnal colours of grasslands and other vegetation.

Approximately 20km south of Puerto Bertrand, just past the confluence of the rivers Nef and Baker when travelling south, is a detour to the right (south) – **El Manzano Pasarela**. This is an alternative, and very scenic route to Cochrane suitable only for those in a 4x4. However, this bypasses the turning to Parque Patagonia and on to Paso Roballos, thus is not ideal for those wishing to visit either.

This detour initially passes a rickety suspension bridge over the Río Baker, and then continues on the south/west of the river through farmland. There are no services, no restaurants and no hotels along this stretch. The road is very poor quality, with steep inclines, bare rocks, occasional horses and other animals in the road, and is not suitable for most vehicles. Perhaps because of the altitude reached, the views are more impressive than those from the Carretera Austral, taking in mountains not visible from the main route. A novelty river crossing over the Río Baker concludes this detour some 7km north of Cochrane. The 'boat' is called 'Balseo Baker', and is an ingenious pulley system that transports up to two cars at a time across the river using entirely the force of the river. It runs from 08.30 to 18.00 with a break for lunch, and is free.

By bus   Several buses go north to **Coyhaique**, including Buses Don Carlos (*inside the Residencial y Cabanas Sur Austral;* \ *(67) 2522150, (67) 2232987; daily*), and there are a few services a week to Chile Chico (via Puerto Guadal) with Buses Marfer (\ *(9) 77568234*) and Buses Turismo Baker (\ *(9) 84641067, (9) 76555644*). Numerous companies ply the route to **Caleta Tortel**, and Buses Aldea (\ *(67) 2638291, (9) 81801962, (9) 56412361*) has a daily service in high season. Buses Katalina (\ *(9) 79613358*) offers a twice-weekly bus all the way to **Villa O'Higgins**. Buses Marcial Moya (\ *(9) 87464743*) is the only company serving San Lorenzo, twice weekly.

TOUR OPERATORS

Jimmy Valdes Baigorria   Lago Brown 388; \ (9) 82678115, (9) 84252419; e lordpatagonia@gmail. com; www.lordpatagonia.cl. Highly recommended guide focused on 2 main routes – the multi-day trek from Cochrane to Villa O'Higgins, & treks around San Lorenzo & the Ventisquero Calluqueo. He has a boat able to cross to the glacier. Various tours offered for all skill levels.

Katenke   Café Tamango, Esmeralda 464; \ (9) 82094957; e katenke@outlook.com. A hidden gem run by veterinarian Cristian Restrepo, out the back of Café Tamango. Cristian is a certified PADI Open Water instructor & a licensed operator of water activities. He offers full scuba-diving courses in Lago Cochrane, as well as recreational dives in the lake. He also speaks English. The water in the lake & river is unbelievably transparent – unlike many of the glacial lakes of marvellous colours but limited visibility – he even offers a snorkelling trip down the Río Cochrane. It begins walking distance from the café, & while the swim is 3.5km it ends walking distance from the café again. The price, $30,000pp, includes all equipment hire with decent 7mm wetsuits suitable for the temperature of the water, which ranges from 10 to 12°C. It also includes all safety training, & is available to people without any prior experience (as long as they can

swim!). Floating down the river with the absolute minimum of effort is as much a meditation as a swim. At times the river narrows & the forest encroaches sufficiently to create an almost tunnel-like effect. The depth ranges from 50cm to 10m, with some fun opportunities for apnea. The riverbed varies from rocks to a clay base, a variety of reeds, minor cases of didymo, occasional tree trunks, endless trout, & a range of colours (on a bright day). The tour is best done in the morning, and takes a total of 3hrs door-to-door including training, with about half of this spent in the water. Although drifting along a river might not be the most obvious tour in the region, for those fancying a change from treks, lakes, horses & glaciers – this is a surprisingly fun, relaxing adventure, well executed by a competent guide. Christian is also active in maintaining the cleanliness of the river & periodically arranges days of manual refuse collection with children from the local schools. A highly recommended tour.

Ultimo Paraíso   (See below for contact details) Fishing with Carlos from the hotel along the Río Cochrane. US$300/day for 1–2 people including lunch. Destinations further afield are priced at US$400/day. 1 of the 2 best guides in town.

WHERE TO STAY   *Map, page 236*

Hotel Ultimo Paraíso   (6 rooms) Lago Brown 455; \ (67) 2522361; e hotelultimoparaisochile@hotmail.es; www. hotelultimoparaiso.cl; ⊕ all year. Delightful accommodation run by an English-speaking Spanish couple, Carlos & Nela, who have lived in Cochrane for nearly 2 decades. Wi-Fi, a slightly overpriced laundry service & an abundant b/fast. Quiet, spacious rooms which are warm in winter, cool in summer. The rooms can be adapted to sgl, dbl or trpl occupancy, & are made mostly of

cypress, all with a well-equipped bathrooms. Wood-stoves in each room for the winter, & tasteful pictures of the region adorn the walls. Wonderfully comfortable beds to rest weary bones after hundreds of kilometres on bumpy gravel. Carlos is a dedicated fisherman & can advise on the top spots to hook a fish, as well as the usual tours in the region. They are not formal operators (although Carlos can easily be persuaded to offer a fishing trip), but know the reliable guides, & are happy to help. The full b/fast includes homemade Spanish delicacies. Parking on site is only available for motorbikes, but parking on the street is not risky in Cochrane. Also has a pleasant but small garden, & a cosy bar/sitting area. Prices may be high by Cochrane standards, but this is the only truly quality place to stay in town. Strict reservations policy; essential in peak season. Credit cards accepted. **$$$$**

🏠 **Cabañas Sol y Luna** (2 cabins) 2km towards Reserva Nacional Tamango; 📞(9) 81579602; e contacto@turismosolyluna.cl; turismosolyluna.cl; ⏰ all year. Good-value, high-quality 4-person fully equipped cabins. Slightly out of town (15mins' walk) but offering utter peace & quiet, sauna & outdoor hot-tub under the Patagonian stars to relax weary bones (additional cost). This is also the home of Baker Beer, & Jimena is happy to show people around the small brewery (150 bottle capacity; supplies some of the restaurants in town, & Sabores Locales (page 250) in Caleta Tortel). No restaurant, so stock up in town. Wood-stoves for heating, no laundry. Can help arrange local tours. Head north on Luis Baez (past mate-shaped building), over bridge, & then veer right towards Reserva Nacional Tamango. Recommended. Also unusually sells face masks. **$$$–$$$$**

🏠 **Residencial y Cabañas Sur Austral** (17 rooms & 2 cabins) Arturo Prat 334; 📞(67) 2522150, (9) 88277003; e ssalazarquiroz@yahoo.es. One of the oldest accommodations in Cochrane, centrally located only 2 blocks west of the plaza. A good option for larger groups. 11 en-suite rooms & 6 with shared bathrooms, sgls, twins & dbls. Spacious rooms with good mattresses. The cabins have a dbl bedroom & 3 or 4 sgl beds. Ample off-street parking, Wi-Fi. Confirm reservation 2 days before arrival. The bus company Don Carlos (page 238) offers transport between Cochrane & Coyhaique & operates from this hostel. No deposit required. Price includes basic b/fast. **$$$**

🏠 **Hospedaje Katita** (12 rooms) Arturo Prat 536; 📞(67) 2522061, (9) 78810631; e gonzalezvasquezanamaria@gmail.com. One of the better budget options in Cochrane. Simple, clean, adequate bathrooms, basic b/fast included.

No laundry, communal area with TV downstairs, very friendly & chatty owner. Will remind visitors of grandma's house, & the owner, Alicia, fits the profile perfectly, having lived in the house for 47 years. Located 2 blocks from the central plaza just around the corner of Ada's restaurant (see below). Lavatory paper occasionally in short supply but frequent reminders to Alicia can rectify this. Wi-Fi available but may require tinkering with router. **$$**

🏠 **Hostal Esmeralda** (7 rooms) San Valentin 141; 📞(9) 97186805. Basic accommodation in 6 sgls & 1 dbl above the rather good restaurant downstairs (page 240). Credit card, Wi-Fi, no laundry. **$$**

🏠 **Residencial Cero a Cero** (13 rooms) Lago Brown 464; 📞(67) 2522158; e ceroacero@gmail.com. A clean, well-run hostel. The thick new mattresses ensure a good night's sleep & are a pleasant change from the thinner & narrower mattresses that most hostels offer. The carpeted rooms are spacious with good natural light. 6 rooms have private bathrooms (4 twins, 2 dbls), the rest have shared bathrooms (twin, dbl & sgl). Decent b/fast is included, laundry service available. **$$**

⛺ **Camping Araucarias** 45km south of Cochrane. This campsite is situated 3.5km from the Carretera Austral on a gravel trail at the northern end of the Barrancoso Bridge – a minor detour for cyclists or trekkers, which isn't excessively hilly & is definitely worthwhile. It is a fantastic campsite with spectacular views towards snow-capped mountains. Also has a small refuge with a bed, but a viable option for those with a sleeping bag & mat in the event of a downpour. The owner, Marisol, grows her own vegetables for sale to visitors, & can also prepare an asado. No cellphone coverage, but contact can be made from the Municipality in Cochrane (radio frequency HF4580). 1 trail on the grounds, but ample opportunities to explore the region. This is an original pioneer ranch. Offers horse treks in the region. A bargain at $3,000pp, ample room, cold showers, simple kitchen available, & simply stunning views. **$**

🍴 **WHERE TO EAT AND DRINK** *Map, page 236*

🍴 **Ada's Cafe Restaurant** Teniente Merino 374; 📞(9) 83995889, (9)88274673; e adascaferestaurant@gmail.com; ⏰ 11.30–

15.30 & 19.30–midnight daily. One of the biggest restaurants in Cochrane with a large menu covering lamb, fish, chicken, pizza, & more. Good selection of wine, beer, & cocktails. Excellent service, clean, & popular with both locals & tourists. Bustling atmosphere when busy in this otherwise sleepy town. **$$$**

✗ El Fogón San Valentin 653; ☏(9) 76447914; ⏰ 10.00–midnight daily. Good food, menu of the day, help yourself to a range of beers from the fridge, decent service & popular with locals. Food is good quality & reasonable value. Not to be compared with the hostel housed in the same building – this is a place to eat, not sleep. **$$$**

✗ Restaurant Esmeralda San Valentin 141; ☏(9) 97186805; ⏰ 11.00–16.00 & 19.00–23.00 daily. One of the better options in a town with a few options. Menu includes meat, chicken, salads, fish & other standard Chilean fare. Decent wine & beer. The *lomo fogón* is the speciality of the house, a steak with spicy sauce of chili, peppers & garlic, highly recommended ($7,800). Budget hostel upstairs (page 239). **$$$**

✗ Café Tamango Esmeralda 464; ☏(67) 91584521; ⏰ 09.00–20.00 Mon–Sat. An upmarket café on the eastern side of the plaza 200m from the information centre. A great option for those looking for wholesome natural organic food or vegetarian options. Try the delicious cakes made from local fruits & berries, or the organic vegetable soup. This café also offers large sandwiches, salads, pizzas, quiches, pancakes, natural juices & ice creams. Even the meat patties for the sandwiches are made on site with no preservatives. They serve a decent coffee too. There is inside & outside seating options. Prices range from $2,300 for a cappuccino, cakes $2,800, sandwiches $4,000–5,000. Not the cheapest place in town but the quality & service is excellent. Accepts credit cards. **$$**

✗ Restaurant Ñirranthal Patagonia Av Bernardo O'Higgins 650; ☏(9) 78782621; e terecata_cu@hotmail.com; ⏰ 10.00–23.00 daily. A bustling little place located a block off the plaza. The menu has all the classics: beef, chicken, pork, lamb, conger eel, merluza, & salmon. What distinguishes Ñirranthal is its surprising variety of sauces compared with elsewhere. Diners can choose their dish a lo pobre, with *merquen* (chili pepper), pepper sauce, mushroom sauce, caper sauce & shrimp sauce. Omar, who is co-owner with his wife Teresa, insists that if you're arriving late in the day & call ahead, they'll stay open for you. Cash only, but does accept US$. **$$**

✗ Centro de Comidas Lago Brown Los Ñadis 164; ☏(9) 88274507; e rinacarmen@gmail.com; ⏰ 10.00–midnight. Sandwiches, pichangas, pizzas, empanadas, steak, milanesa. Limited beer & wine selection. Clean & modern, but lacking in character. Food is reasonable, standard Chilean fare with sizeable portions. Lunchtime menu is a good value at $4,000. **$**

☆ La Querencia bar/nightclub Teniente Merino 430; ⏰ 23.00 w/ends. Sleazy late-night dive located in a converted barn serving cheap standard beer. Interesting, certainly not a high-class joint, but about the only option in town at the time of writing. This is the place to let your hair down & meet some locals.

OTHER PRACTICALITIES The **ATM** (Banco Estado) on the plaza is a vital visit as there are none further south, and the next ATM to the north is in Coyhaique or Chile Chico. Be sure to fill up with **petrol** while in Cochrane at COPEC (*cnr of Arturo Prat & O'Higgins*): the next petrol station to the south is in Villa O'Higgins, at least 224km, or in Puerto Río Tranquilo to the north, 111km. There is another service station 1km out of town as you enter from the north. There are **shops** in Cochrane, but only for common supplies.

Repairs

Alfa Bernardo O'Higgins s/n, opposite the hospital; ☏(9) 92127663; e marvinarriagada@yahoo.com. ar. Basic mechanical repairs & service including light fabricating & soldering. Has a small supply of spare parts for common brands. No motorbikes (there is no motorcycle mechanic in town). Tyres, batteries, soldering job has car scanner.

Taller Bicicleta Esmeralda 464; ☏(9) 91584521; e contacto@mejorenbici.cl; www.mejorenbici.cl. Located behind Café Tamango on the eastern side of the plaza, offers bicycle repairs, guided tours & bicycle rentals, including helmets, etc, & speaks English.

Laundry

Lavandería Juanita Los Helechos 336; ☏(9) 90130567, (9) 79839031; ⏰ closed Sun. One block south of the COPEC station.

SIGHTSEEING AND EXCURSIONS Cochrane offers a surprising range of activities, growing each year. The snorkel trip down the Río Cochrane is simply sublime and a relaxing way to spend a couple of hours (page 238). Fishing trips can be arranged through Hotel Ultimo Paraíso (page 238).

Reserva Nacional Tamango (*www.conaf.cl/parques/reserva-nacional-lago-cochrane-o-tamango; $4,000/1,500 foreign adult/child, $2,000/500 Chilean adult/child*) This national reserve is nearly 7,000ha and located 6km northeast of Cochrane. The reserve is bordered by the Tamango, Tamangito and Hungaro mountains on three sides and the Río Cochrane and lake to the southeast, and has a dry temperate climate in the summer but snow in the winter. Principal flora includes lenga and coihue trees, Ñirre (*Nothofagus antarctica*), calafate, mata verde and chaura shrubs. The large Andean condor is sometimes spotted here, as well as the southern lapwing, great grebes, black-crowned night herons and kingfishers, plus various migratory birds. Foxes and guanaco are common, and it is also possible to spot the elusive huemul. The park also has a resident population of pumas, and it is possible to observe the Patagonian skunk and the hairy armadillo.

There is a basic CONAF **campsite** at the park entrance beside the crystal-clear waters of the Río Cochrane. A small map is available from the park entrance where you pay the entrance fee.

There are **two main treks**. The first, **El Hungaro** (*16km round-trip; 7–9hrs; medium*), goes to Bahía Paleta along the shores of Lago Cochrane. This is a full-day excursion and offers the best chance to see the huemul in the wild as they are relatively protected in the park. The second trek, **Las Correntadas** (*7km round-trip; 3–4 hrs; easy/medium*), runs along the northern bank of the Río Cochrane to a viewing point where the river enters Lago Cochrane. There are numerous viewing points over the crystal-clear river, reportedly one of the most transparent in the world. It is possible to take a small boat trip up the Río Cochrane to the lake (ask in headquarters for details). For the more adventurous, there is also a trail directly to the Valle Chacabuco and on to the Parque Patagonia headquarters. Ask at the Reserva Nacional Tamango headquarters for details and a map. Eventually the three parks/reserves will be joined (Valle Chacabuco, Jeinemeni and Tamango). Trekkers can arrange a guide from the park entrance. The trails are well marked and maintained, but a guide can give an interesting insight into the huemul deer and how they are trying to protect them, as well as helping to identify birds and trees within the reserve.

Ventisquero Calluqueo and Monte San Lorenzo At 3,706m, the ice-covered Monte San Lorenzo is the second-highest mountain in the region and straddles the Argentina–Chile border roughly 60km south of Cochrane. Major work is being put in to the access road, which was previously only suitable for 4x4s. There are two approaches, one that leads to the attractive Ventisquero Calluqueo which itself touches the small Lago Calluqueo, and the other to the Fundo San Lorenzo and on to the Refuge Toni Rohrer that serves as the basecamp for ascents of Monte San Lorenzo. To get to the refuge, it is best to arrange a horse in Cochrane or directly from the Soto family. Luis Soto lives on a small farm at the base of the mountain and getting in contact with him is no easy task – ask at the tourist information booth on the central plaza.

To get there from Cochrane, head south approximately 6km and turn left on a gravel road just before Laguna Esmeralda. The scenic drive borders Laguna Esmeralda to the east and follows the Río El Salto until reaching a fork in the road after about 25km. To the right is the road to the Ventisquero Calluqueo, which is a further 20km along a mostly single-lane gravel road until the trail to the lake starts. To the left is the road to the Soto farm where the trail starts up the valley to the Refuge Toni Rohrer. Until the new road is finished, this road is a rough 4x4-only track that slowly deteriorates. Buses Marcial Moya traverses this route once a week (page 238).

The drive to the **Ventisquero Calluqueo** takes under 2 hours, but crossing the small lake requires the services of Jimmy Valdes Baigorria who keeps a small boat on the lake (page 238). Finding the start of the trail is not particularly easy. Once the glacier is visible the road starts uphill and the condition deteriorates rapidly. There is just enough room to turn a car around. The trail itself is a short 20 minutes to the lake. The boat ride across is about 1 hour one-way, where there is a pleasant area for a picnic and taking pictures.

The hike up **San Lorenzo** is technical, requiring ice gear and skis, and takes at least three days. Once at the Soto farm, the refuge is another 3 hours' walk and has enough space for around 20 people. From there it's at least 8 hours up to another campsite near the Ventisquero Agostini, and then another 12 hours on ice and over crevices to the summit. This is a challenging climb for professional mountaineers.

Mellizos waterfall A dramatic 10-minute detour, the impressive Mellizos waterfall is 14km south of Cochrane on the Carretera Austral heading towards Caleta Tortel. Park at the bridge over the Río El Salto and walk 100m to the west, along the river. Take extreme caution as there are no guard rails: the rocks are slippery, it's a vertical drop into fast-moving water tumbling over a rock-filled waterfall, pounding through a gulley.

El Salto (waterfall) in Valle Castillo From Cochrane it's 16km southwest to El Salto – a majestic waterfall on the Río El Salto. Head south on the Carretera and turn right just past the rodeo after the bridge over the Río Cochrane onto a well-maintained gravel road (X-892). Wind through a picturesque valley until reaching a suspension bridge that is unsuitable for vehicles – it is possible to leave your car on the side of the road. Cross the bridge on foot and find the path off to the left that leads to several viewing areas to appreciate the voluminous cascades. The round trip can also be walked in around 6 hours from town or cycled in about 4 hours.

> ⊕ **AS THE CONDOR FLIES**
>
> Cochrane is 645km south of Puerto Montt, and 190km from the border to El Chaltén south of Villa O'Higgins.

CALETA TORTEL – A DETOUR

A true highlight of the southern region, Caleta Tortel is a magical place, and a gateway to the northern and southern ice fields. While a day trip isn't really enough to do the village or the sights justice, it is perhaps the most expensive village along the entire route and so an overnight stay might not be an option for the budget-conscious. The logistics of even getting to a hotel with a suitcase can be a challenge. There is no petrol station or ATM, and the nearest decent shop is in Cochrane, so it should come as little surprise that the village appears overpriced. Trips to the glaciers require not only a substantial boat journey, but fuel is brought in from

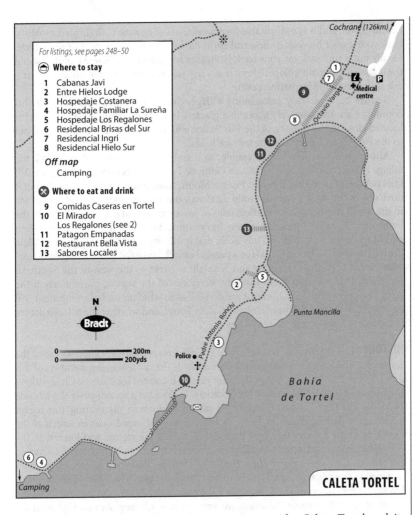

For listings, see pages 248–50

Where to stay
1   Cabanas Javi
2   Entre Hielos Lodge
3   Hospedaje Costanera
4   Hospedaje Familiar La Sureña
5   Hospedaje Los Regalones
6   Residencial Brisas del Sur
7   Residencial Ingri
8   Residencial Hielo Sur

Off map
    Camping

Where to eat and drink
9   Comidas Caseras en Tortel
10 El Mirador
    Los Regalones (see 2)
11 Patagon Empanadas
12 Restaurant Bella Vista
13 Sabores Locales

Cochrane (126km)

Medical centre

Octavio Vargas

Punta Mancilla

Padre Antonio Ronchi

Police

N

Bradt

0 ————————— 200m
0 ————————— 200yds

Bahía de Tortel

Camping

CALETA TORTEL

Cochrane and thus expensive. Budget restrictions aside, Caleta Tortel and its spooky legends are a true highlight.

The 'commune' of Tortel, within the province of Capitán Prat, covers an area of approximately 21,000km² and has only two populations: Caleta Tortel and Puerto Yungay. The total population is a little over 500 people, and vast parts of the commune are protected. To the south lies the Parque Nacional O'Higgins containing a large part of the Southern Ice Field; to the north lies the southern extreme of the Parque Nacional Laguna San Rafael and the limit of the Northern Ice Field; and to the west lies the remote Reserva Nacional Katalalixar, accessible only by boat.

Caleta Tortel is built almost entirely on boardwalks at the base of the mountain around a series of small bays. The sea is visible through the planks beneath your feet, and the boardwalks extend for kilometres. Houses were gradually built above the first houses, up the side of the mountain, involving a series of steep stairs weaving chaotically between houses and trees. Even small plazas with playgrounds have been built on these boardwalks. Thanks to this architectural design, every house has a view over the bay, and out to the Baker Canal. There are no cars or horses in

Caleta Tortel, and it is not suitable for wheelchairs of anyone with limited mobility. Park your car or bicycle, or descend from the bus, at the upper part of the village, ideally put a rucksack on your back (suitcases are not so convenient), and descend the stairs to the main village. There is a water taxi service available upon request – ask at the tourist information centre.

Besides being a truly astonishing village, the main points of interest in this commune are the relatively accessible glaciers in both ice fields – Caleta Tortel is located close to the estuary of the Río Baker, which feeds into the Baker Canal out to the Pacific, and separates the two ice fields.

Although not visible (or accessible, to a great extent) from Caleta Tortel, the village is not far from the (in)famous Golfo de Penas. The Navimag ferry (page 27) sails between Puerto Natales and Puerto Montt, mostly along interior canals, but it does sail in the open ocean at Golfo de Penas, one of the roughest stretches of sea in the world responsible for endless tales of sea-sickness and prolonged visits to the bathroom! If, as is rumoured, a new ferry connection between the Aysén region and Magallanes is established, it is likely that it will begin at either Yungay or Caleta Tortel, traverse the Baker Canal (or a parallel canal), and head south along the Canal Messier between the O'Higgins and Katalalixar parks to the west of the Southern Ice Field. This will transform the local economy of the region, particularly if the ferry also takes vehicles. Opinions are divided as to whether such development will be beneficial for the charm of isolated Caleta Tortel, and whether the infrastructure is capable of supporting more visitors.

HISTORY This region was first inhabited by indigenous nomadic canoeists called the Kawesqar, who have since almost entirely vanished. The last remaining members of this group live in Puerto Eden, one of the most remote inhabited locations in Chile – along the Messier Canal to the west of the Southern Ice Field at approximately the latitude of Monte Fitz Roy. The first documented case of a European 'discovering' this region is Hernando de Magallanes in 1520. Various subsequent expeditions in search of the Lost City of the Césares (see box, pages 92–3) visited the region, and interest in the Río Baker Estuary attracted a number of explorers in the late 19th century, including the famous German explorer Hans Steffen in 1898. In 1901 the Chilean government awarded a concession to Juan Tornero to populate the region with 1,000 families, which led to the formation of the Compañia Explotadora del Baker, and eventually to the mysterious death of some 70 Chilote workers, some of whose graves are visible on the famous Island of the Dead (see box, pages 246–7) – one of the greatest mysteries of all of the Carretera Austral, and a major tourist attraction in Caleta Tortel.

Various companies remained in the region attempting to exploit the abundant timber resources until the early 1940s, when a series of fires largely rendered the region uninhabitable. The Chilean Armada established an outpost in what became Caleta Tortel in 1955, and development continued at a leisurely pace, including a small landing strip, until the village was formally founded in 1981, with under 300 inhabitants. Development continued, with a renewed municipal building and school, construction of additional boardwalks, drinking water, sewage works, a small hydro-electric plant, a library, a covered central plaza (it rains extensively in Caleta Tortel), and various piers for boats. In 1999 work began on the 23km road connection to the Carretera Austral, completed in 2003.

Famous priest Father Ronchi (see box, page 125) built the church, FM radio station and set up several productive projects in Caleta Tortel. Testimony of this is the hull of the boat, which he brought to improve the transfer of passengers and stimulate activities of timber production. Although the boat is no longer in use today and its condition has deteriorated, its shell is still intact. Outside one of the well-known chapels is a life-size wooden statue of Father Ronchi in honour of his memory.

In 2000 Prince William spent ten weeks in Caleta Tortel on an Operation Raleigh trip – the inaccessibility of the village largely kept the media at bay and the locals, though aware of who the prince was, treated him no differently to anyone else. He received no special favours on the project: chopping logs, lighting fires at 06.15 and making porridge for the team of 16, all of whom slept on the floor in sleeping bags in a communal room – a far cry from the prince's usual accommodation. Details as to his actual activities are scarce, but included working in the community, painting schools as well as trying his hand as a DJ for Radio Tortel. Kate Middleton did a similar trip the following year.

Besides hosting future kings, the main economic activities of the region are the extraction of cypress, tourism and a limited amount of agriculture.

GETTING THERE
About the route
Cochrane to Caleta Tortel (*126km; 2½hrs; gravel*) From Cochrane the road heads south approximately 103km on gravel to the junction for Caleta Tortel. From here it is approximately 23km further to Caleta Tortel to the west, or on to Puerto Yungay, where the boat crosses the Fiordo Mitchell to Río Bravo for the final stretch of the Carretera Austral, to Villa O'Higgins (another 100km). To the initial junction the road is fairly decent gravel with occasional steep descents and ascents, often along vertical cliff edges. Although the road is not as well travelled as more northerly sections of the Carretera, occasional oncoming vehicles may be in the centre of the road and travelling at speed. Long sections of this road are raised, thus take extra precaution to avoid a wheel going over the edge – it is often better to stop entirely until oncoming vehicles pass. The road is spectacular, with high snow-capped mountains above and the thundering Río Bravo below. One particularly photogenic moment is the confluence of the rivers Bravo and Colorado, although take care pausing on the blind corners to take a photo. When the road grader has recently traversed it can be particularly treacherous. There are no imminent plans to pave this section.

By bus See page 238 for details on how to get here from Cochrane.

TOUR OPERATORS As well as the operators below, an alternative guide with a decent boat and good reputation is **Juan Ruiz** (*(9) 82477140*).

Borde Rio Tortel Expeditions (9) 99408265; e borderiotortel@gmail.com; ﬁ Borderio Tortel Expediciones. Guided kayak tours around Caleta Tortel run by Enrique Fernández, with capacity for up to 6 people. Includes all kit, wetsuit, snacks & hot drinks, & has a vehicle to transport passengers & kayaks to more remote regions. 3 main tours offered: to the Isla de los Muertos (via a waterfall & boats abandoned by the first settlers), navigating along the lesser tributaries of the Río Baker Delta (*6hrs, $35,000pp*). The 2nd tour involves a longer descent of the Río Baker starting at Vagabundo

(near where the Carretera Austral splits either towards Puerto Yungay or Caleta Tortel) – 28km in total and a full-day trip (*$60,000pp*). The 3rd tour is also a full day, on Lago Vargas a further 10km north from Vagabundo (*$80,000pp*). Enrique lives in Tortel, so tours are possible all year, but Sep–Apr are the most common months. Can also arrange tailor-made trips.

Claudio or Paulo Landeros Playa Ancha; (9) 82386781; e paulolanderos800@gmail. com, Claudio.landeros@live.cl; ﬁ Expediciones Patagonia Landeros C. These brothers offer boat

THE TRAGIC, OR SINISTER, HISTORY OF TORTEL

A mere 20 minutes by boat from Caleta Tortel, in the Río Baker Estuary, lies the mysterious **Isla de los Muertos (Island of the Dead)**. Prior to the formation of the village of Caleta Tortel, the only inhabited spot in this region was on the northern shore of the estuary, called Puerto Bajo Pisagua, a few hundred metres from the graveyard. The intrigue surrounding this small graveyard has become one of the most enduring legends in the region, and there is still no definitive explanation of why nearly 70 people died on the island in the winter of 1906, 28 of whom were buried in anonymous graves marked only with a cross.

The following summary is taken from a superb book entitled *Caleta Tortel y su Isla de los Muertos*, written by the well-known historian Danka Ivanoff Wellmann – see pages 219 and 270 for more details.

The Chilean government had awarded 13 concessions in the region of what is now the commune of Tortel as early as 1893, despite the lack of even a basic map, let alone a population. A wealthy businessman named Mauricio Braun was interested in the region for possible exploitation of timber, and acquired the rights from one of the concession holders, Juan Tornero. The first investigative sorties were not overly optimistic regarding the possibilities, but Braun did not despair. Bringing other partners into the venture, they stumbled across a young, adventurous British explorer called William Norris in Buenos Aires. He was promptly hired by the Compañia Explotadora del Baker to investigate the region, establish a cattle ranch, and to find a direct route from Argentina to this isolated region on the other side of the Andes. On the first trip, in early 1905, armed with an ill-defined number of co-explorers, some horses and a substandard map, Norris managed to find Puerto Bajo Pisagua by following the Río Chacabuco (through the future Parque Patagonia), and travelling down the Río Baker. Braun had sent a number of men to Bajo Pisagua to meet Norris. These men, and others soon to arrive, were to work on improving the route from Argentina until Norris's return in April the following year, when he would bring the animals. In Norris's 1939 account of events is a wonderful description of the contrast between the arid Argentine side of the border and the Chilean side, and his optimism for the region:

> There are no words to describe the contrast between the east and west. The east is a torrid, rocky and windswept desert. The west is a territory with water, covered with forests and meadows, with an excellent climate and very little wind in the valleys. Very near the coast, within reach of the river [Baker], are millions of cypresses in very good condition… I think the Baker Valley, when the outside world eventually discovers it, will be the best place in South America. The central valleys and higher regions are the best for raising sheep and cattle. There is grass, water and trees everywhere, sufficient to build many cities. In the lowlands good vegetation is unlimited.

With a sufficiently persuasive story for Braun, Norris returned to Argentina to buy the animals required to establish a local industry, which would also exploit the local timber. He had assured those who remained in Bajo Pisagua, under the interim control of Florencio Tornero (brother of the former concession-holder), that he would return by April 1906. Accompanied by thousands of cattle and horses, the second journey was a little more complex and delayed for bad weather. Norris eventually arrived on 15 May that year to La Colonia, further upriver, where he installed the animals. Tornero was under strict instructions to return the employees to Chiloé before the winter, but when Norris travelled down to Bajo Pisagua he was surprised to find the entire team awaiting him, hungry and tired. What subsequently occurred that winter of 1906 is the subject of much debate.

Some have suggested the men were poisoned by the company in order to avoid paying them. Others say they were accidentally poisoned by a toxic liquid required to wash sheep that had contaminated the food on the rough journey by sea to Bajo Pisagua. But neither story holds up to reason. Why would the company kill its staff, only to have to replace them thereafter? And why would they have brought such toxic liquids if there were not yet any sheep in the region? And yet the 'poison story' remains the dominant account of what happened to this day. So why did so many people die at Bajo Pisagua that winter?

In June 1906 Tornero had waited for a passing boat on an island for 12 days, surviving on shellfish alone. He finally caught a boat to Punta Arenas and immediately arranged for a northbound boat to pick up the group, but the boat sunk in the Magallanes Strait with five crew and vital cargo destined for Bajo Pisagua. He then arranged for a second boat from Talcahuano to rescue the group, but a devastating earthquake struck Valparaíso on 16 August and the boat was requisitioned and sent to Valparaíso to assist with the rescue effort. But this does not explain why he had not made greater efforts to get the men off the island before the winter. The men were seafaring Chilotes, and Norris mentioned in his memoirs a relative abundance of animals in the region (including guanaco and ostrich). How is it these men had not decided to fish and hunt for food as supplies dwindled? And perhaps the greatest tragedy of all – Norris had begged some men to help him row upstream to where the cattle were located in order to obtain food, but for fear of missing the boat they so eagerly awaited to take them off this dreaded island, none agreed to help. And if the men were murdered, why were they buried in individual graves? But if exhaustion, starvation and scurvy were the culprits, who built the coffins, dug the graves and made the crosses? Why did Norris not detail the events in his memoirs of 1939, but only in a private letter to his uncle written in 1906? And yet, even in this private account, he failed to mention that he was nearly lynched in Chiloé when he finally managed to rescue some of the Chilotes to their island, as described in an account written by a friend of his. Or was her account flawed? And why is one of the crosses inscribed 'Here lie the bodies of Margarita Gallardo and her son Anselmo' dated 1915, some nine years after the fateful winter in question?

In late September 1906 the surviving members were able to return to Chiloé, although 12 died on the journey. The following year many of these survivors returned to work in Bajo Pisagua, with Norris, employed by the same company. Had these survivors believed the company had attempted to murder them, how likely is it that they would return the following year? The company never paid Norris for his work.

We may never know what truly happened in Bajo Pisagua in 1906. Stories of mass murder attract attention and sell boat trips to tourists, but starvation and scurvy are the most likely explanations for the events of that fateful winter. But they are not the *only* explanations.

trips to the Montt or Steffen glaciers (*$60,000pp; min 7 people, max 10*). As they were born near Ventisquero Montt they know it very well, & can note how it has retreated over their lifetimes. As licensed tour-boat operators, life vests are included, & their boat is sufficiently fast to do the round trip to either glacier in a day & still have time to explore. Conditions permitting it may be possible to climb onto an iceberg near the snout of Ventisquero Montt. The tour also includes a light trek on the mainland towards the Ventisquero Montt where huemules are fairly common. Includes the usual whisky with glacial ice, in abundance. The trip to Ventisquero Steffen includes the boat transport & the guided hike to the snout of the glacier. As they are in opposite directions, you cannot visit both glaciers in 1 day, although it is possible to combine either with a stop at the graveyard (*$60,000/trip, also up to 10 people*). They are somewhat chaotic, & while they suggest booking in advance, it can be hard to reach them

in practice. However, they have been doing the trip for a decade & know the region well. It is helpful to stay at their sister's hostel, Brisas del Sur (page 249), as she acts as something of a co-ordinator for the brothers, who are often out of contact.

Entre Hielos Lodge Sector Central; ☏ (9) 95793779, (9) 95995730; e contacto@ entrehielostortel.cl; www.entrehielostortel.cl. Offering 3 main tours, principally to residents of the hotel (see below), operated by the lodge itself, ie: not subcontracted. The boat holds up to 8 passengers, & prices are per boat regardless of the number of passengers. The Isla de los Muertos & the estuary of the Río Baker is US$130. A 1-day trip to Ventisquero Steffen (with trekking) is US$510, or a 2-day option with camping is US$220pp (min 4), but they do not charge this night in the hotel in addition. The 3rd tour is to the Katalalixar archipelago and Isla Harper including trekking to a lake (*US$510/boat, 1 full day*).

WHERE TO STAY   *Map, page 243*

For those on a tight budget camping is possible in Caleta Tortel, but far from optimal. There are no facilities and the campsite is wet, cold and windy, and located at the extreme end of the boardwalks, perhaps a 30- to 45-minute walk from the car park. It's free though.

Entre Hielos Lodge (6 rooms) Sector Central; ☏ (9) 95793779, (9) 95995730; e contacto@entrehielostortel.cl; www.entrehielostortel.cl. Simply put, the finest place to stay in Caleta Tortel, & is reasonably priced by Tortel standards although might stretch the budget for some travellers. It is located approximately 5mins along the main boardwalk after the descent from the car park, & is signposted to the right up a few steep sets of stairs – not at all suitable with large suitcases – keep an eye open for the signposts on the way up. The lodge does not actually offer much of a view over the ocean, but towards the forest. Rooms are impeccable, clean & comfortable, with fully equipped bathrooms (shower only). Great beds, decent walls for soundproofing (lacking in most other places to stay), & utterly peaceful. The owners, Maria Paz & Noel Vidal, have excellent knowledge of the region (Noel is from Caleta Tortel), & they have their own boat to offer tours (see above). Complete b/fast included (fresh ground coffee, fruit juice, eggs to order), Wi-Fi, laundry, comfortable sitting area with a range of

books. Dinners are offered on request & the lodge has its own chef, thus qualifying as possibly the best restaurant in town, but with a price to match (**$$$$**) – open to the public by prior reservation. The restaurant has featured in *Gastonomia Gourmet Patagonia*. Speak English. Reservations obligatory all year, & a 30% deposit is required. Min 2-night stay. Takes credit cards. **$$$$**

Cabañas Javi (2 cabins) Sector Rincon alto; ☏ (9) 56952351; e javicabana@gmail.com. New cabins of a reasonable quality conveniently located only a min's walk from the information centre beside the car park. The cabins are on the right-hand side just before descending to the main village, complete with cable TV, microwave oven, fridge, Wi-Fi & laundry facilities. 1 cabin sleeps 6 with 1 dbl & 4 sgls, the other sleeps 4 with 1 dbl bed & 2 sgls. Reservations can be made with no deposit required. A great option for a family or older people due to the proximity of the car park, avoiding the need to negotiate the steep stairs to the main boardwalk with luggage. Good value. **$$$**

⌂ Hospedaje Los Regalones (5 rooms) Sector Rincon Bajo; ☎ (9) 88982594; e los_regalones@ hotmail.com; ⊕ all year. An improvement over cheaper options, but still with thin walls. The rooms, all dbl or twin with private bathroom & basic b/fast included, are spacious & comfortable, with carpet & decent finishing. Views of ocean from the dbl rooms. Laundry offered, but no internet. TV in the communal areas & in the restaurant beneath the hostel (same owners, where b/fast is served here). The restaurant (⊕ 07.00–midnight; $$$ with wine) offers standard fare – salmon, seafood & meat dishes, but in generous portions. It is centrally located in the village, watch out for a sign pointing to the right at the end of the boardwalk of the central section. A unique feature is that the entire building appears to sway slightly each time someone climbs the stairs, not enough to make one dizzy, but simulates the effect of being at sea – perhaps deliberately for a village built almost in the ocean itself. Although the price is slightly over most competitors at $40,000/room, the marginal benefit is obvious. Deposit required, & fills up in Jan & Feb. **$$$**

⌂ Hospedaje Costanera (7 rooms) Zona Municipalidad; ☎ (9) 66770236; e h.costanera@ gmail.com; ⊕ year-round. This was the first hostel in Caleta Tortel, operating for over 15 years. Clean & tidy, built of solid wood. 2 dbls & 5 trpls, but some of the trpls are dark & lack natural light – try to get one with windows, often with amazing views of the bay. All rooms with shared bathrooms, basic b/fast, no Wi-Fi or laundry service. The location is a short hike from the car park & is just before the large municipal building & the church. Not so recommended for older people for the relative distance to walk, with luggage, & the steep steps. The owner, Luisa Escobar, is friendly & can help book excursions. **$$**

⌂ Hospedaje Familiar La Sureña (6 rooms) Sector Playa Ancha; ☎ (9) 92149807; e la.surena@ live.cl; ⊕ all year. Basic accommodation with a view out to sea from some rooms. 1 sgl, 3 trpls, 1 twin & 1 dbl (which has a private bathroom, otherwise shared). Wooden construction & thin walls, basic b/fast included, no Wi-Fi but does offer laundry, which is rare in Caleta Tortel. Guests can use kitchen. Basic but cheap. Deposit required to make a reservation. **$$**

⌂ Residencial Brisas del Sur (7 rooms) Sector Playa Ancha; ☎ (9) 96988244; e valerialanderos@hotmail.com, brisasdelsur@ gmail.com; ⊕ all year. Another budget option next door to La Sureña. The downstairs dbl is worth avoiding at all costs – the bathrooms are upstairs & involve walking outdoors, often in the rain, & the ceiling is so thin that those upstairs chatting may as well be in the room itself. The upstairs rooms, however, are positively pleasant & have a lovely view out to sea. There is a small communal sitting area where b/ast (basic but included) is served. Although a little far from 'downtown' Caleta Tortel, the major advantage of this hostel is that the owner, Valeria, has 2 brothers both with boats & offering tours to the glaciers & the graveyard (page 245). Because the brothers, Claudio & Paulo, are often out of cellphone coverage Valeria acts as a de facto tour operator for their trips. Valeria's husband, Ruben, also has a boat that can make it to the graveyard but not to the glaciers. No Wi-Fi or laundry, but guests can use the kitchen. **$$**

⌂ Residencial Hielo Sur (6 rooms) Rincon Bajo; ☎ (9) 56346080; e hielosur@hotmail. com. Reasonable option for budget travellers. Impressive ocean views from some of the upper bedrooms, & located on the stairs down from the carpark. 2 dbls & 4 sgls all with shared bathrooms & a basic cooking area for guests. Walls are extremely thin & can be noisy at night especially in rooms above the dining area. Very basic, rustic construction & the bathrooms are barely adequate. One of the few hostels with a licence to serve beer & wine, often until late. Guests can use kitchen to reduce costs further. B/fast $2,500 extra, other meals can be arranged upon request. No internet or laundry service. **$**

⌂ Residencial Ingri (3 rooms) Sector Rincon alto; ☎ (9) 95903742, (9) 56634576; e herminia@gmail.com; ⊕ Nov–Mar. This hostel is conveniently located only a couple of mins' walk from the information centre by the car park. It is on the right-hand side of the main boardwalk just before descending to the main village. 1 room has 2 bunk beds & the other 2 rooms have a sgl bed & a bunk bed. Clean & tidy but no frills, no Wi-Fi, basic b/fast included. Exceptional value by Caleta Tortel standards. An ideal option for backpackers looking for economical bunk accommodation in a new building. **$**

✕ WHERE TO EAT AND DRINK *Map, page 243*

✕ **Sabores Locales** Sector Rincon; ☎(9) 90873064; e saboreslocales@yahoo.es; ⊕ Sep–Apr, thereafter by appointment only. Serious competitor for the 'best restaurant in town' award. Lovely view from an elevated wooden building, all ingredients sourced locally where possible, good service & friendly atmosphere. Located at the west end of the main bay in the village, close to the centre, up a flight of stairs from the main boardwalk. The owner, Maritza, is a true Caleta resident, & knows all the history, tours & the unusual places to visit. She has artisanal beers, when available, including the local brew from Tortel. Salmon is the speciality of the house, but the menu includes all standard fare from the region, with fruit & vegetables from her organic garden, including nalca & calafate. A couple will pay $40,000 for a decent meal with wine – not the cheapest restaurant in town, but worth a splurge. $$$$

✕ **El Mirador** Sector Centro. Decent salmon, excellent view, but small portions & not great value for money, even by Caleta Tortel's standards. Above the municipal plaza. Suffers periodic shortages of wine & beer. $$$

✕ **Los Regalones** Sector Rincon Bajo; ☎(9) 88982594; e los_regalones@hotmail.com. Decent restaurant, part of hotel (page 249). Located next to staircase to Entre Hielos, good option, wide range of seafood & barbecued meat, speciality of the house is crab au gratin. $$$

✕ **Comidas Caseras en Tortel** Rincon Alto; ☎(9) 95061909; ⊕ all year 12.30–15.00 & 17.30–22.30. As the name suggests, this is traditional Caleta food. Located on the Octavio Varga boardwalk coming down from the car park towards Tortel, this relatively new restaurant offers possibly the finest views in town. Specialities are salmon, gnocchi, cazuela, lamb & soups, served with local greens & homemade bread. The owners, Loida & Juan, provide great service, & the location is ideal. $$

✕ **Restaurant Bella Vista** Sector Rincon Bajo; ☎(9) 62117430; ⊕ noon–23.00. Great views, as the name suggests, & abundant servings at this family-owned restaurant just a short walk on the boardwalk from the main stairs that come down from the parking area. Regional cuisine, including salmon or steak a lo pobre at $8,000, or pastas & stews around $5,000. Also salads. Reasonable wine selection for the size of the restaurant, since it has only about 5 tables. $$

✕ **Patagon Empanadas** Next to the Bella Vista. Reasonable deep-fried empanadas with a view out to sea; fast food, less speedy service. Fine for a quick bite. $

SIGHTSEEING AND EXCURSIONS Merely pottering about in Caleta Tortel, particularly on a sunny day, is a worthy activity. Explore the upper boardwalks, some of which offer sweeping views over the village – walk to one of the few landing strips in the world accessed by a boardwalk! There is also loop track (*2hrs; medium*) to the **mirador** or **viewing platform** above the town, from which you will see spectacular 360° views of the village, Río Baker and the Baker Canal. For this, take the boardwalk to the landing strip and turn left onto a well-marked trail after 100m. This circuit trail enters the far end of the town again in Playa Ancha at the western end of town close to the campsite. Alternatively, trek up to the hydro-electric power plant for a view over the village (*45mins one-way; marked; the trail starts at the eastern edge of the village*). There are more ambitious treks close to Tortel, but these are neither marked nor offered as formal tours, but the more adventurous trekkers may wish to seek local advice and head off into the wilderness. The trekking potential in this region is huge, and trails will likely open up over the coming seasons.

The **glaciers** are a highlight, but might stretch the budget of some visitors – they are far from the village and fuel costs are high. The glaciers around Puerto Río Tranquilo (San Rafael and Leones, for example; pages 209 and 214) are more economical. However, if you can find a decent-sized group, the price may be reasonable. Glacier trips can be combined with trips to Caleta Tortel's mysterious **graveyard** situated on the Isla de los Muertos in the estuary of the Río Baker, although a visit to the graveyard alone is well worth the effort and reasonably priced.

Isla de los Muertos For those interested in the history of the entire region of the Carretera Austral, a boat trip to the graveyard is highly recommended. Before you go, read as much as possible about the events of 1906 (see box, pages 246–7) and then speak to some residents about their opinions – this will only serve to further increase the mystery, or mythology, of the graveyard. A pleasant alternative to taking one of the regular boats is to go by kayak (page 245).

Jorge Montt and Steffen glaciers The **Ventisquero Jorge Montt** is stunning, accessible, and rarely visited. A round trip from Caleta Tortel takes most of the day, but can be combined with a trip to the Isla de los Muertos (pages 246–7) on the way back. The journey itself is stunning, as the boat weaves through a seemingly endless series of islands and peninsulas. Eventually some small icebergs will come into view, and rounding the final curve the full splendour of the glacier emerges. This is the most northerly glacier of the Southern Ice Field, and its rapid retreat means that icebergs are abundant so it is not possible to approach the nose of the glacier. However, from the relative distance of the boat it is possible to appreciate the scale of the ice shelf above, which is not always the case with other glaciers. The size is awe-inspiring.

The Patagonian glaciers are retreating faster than in any other region on the planet. NASA estimate that the rate of ice-thinning more than doubled here between 1995 and 2000 compared with 1975 and 2000. A December 2011 study by glaciologist Andrés Rivera used time-lapse photography to measure the retreat from February 2010 to January 2011, and discovered the glacier was retreating at 13m per day. A historical map dating back to 1898 reveals the glacier has retreated nearly 20km.

Opinions differ regarding the extent to which mankind is responsible for the disappearance of such glaciers, but less so in the case of the Ventisquero Jorge Montt. In January 2012 a man was detained in Cochrane for stealing 5,000kg of ice from the glacier to use in cocktails in Santiago de Chile.

Despite the slightly depressing environmental implications, the glacier is truly spectacular, and it is possible to disembark from the boat and walk along the eastern side of the canal towards the glacier, where huemules are often spotted.

Caleta Tortel is sandwiched between the Northern and Southern ice fields, together comprising the third-largest ice field on the planet after Greenland and Antarctica. To the north of Caleta Tortel lies the most southern glacier of the Northern Ice Field – **Steffen**. It ends in a lagoon from which the Río Huemules is born. It is named after Hans Steffen, the German explorer of Aysén. A trip to the Ventisquero Steffen takes an entire day, and unlike the Ventisquero Montt to the south, involves a 14km round-trip hike. Steffen is also in retreat, but not to the extent of Montt (2.1km from 1987 to 2010). The journey from Caleta Tortel first passes the Río Baker Delta, and then heads north up the Fiordo Steffen. At the entrance to the fjord it is possible to see an **abandoned saw mill** – timber was the main driving force of the early settlers. The fjord veers east at which point the glacier becomes visible beyond the estuary of the Río Huemules. The boat will go upriver to the beginning of the trek. A guide is advised, and usually doubles as the boat owner. Neither of these glaciers is well visited, Steffen involves a little more effort, is even more isolated, and passes through more extensive vegetation. It is a longer day compared with Montt, and thus harder to combine with the trip to the Isla de Los Muertos on the way back.

⊕ **AS THE CONDOR FLIES**

Caleta Tortel is 705km south of Puerto Montt, and a mere 140km from the border to El Chaltén south of Villa O'Higgins.

10

11

Exiting/Entering the Carretera Austral: Villa O'Higgins and beyond

Few visitors venture this far south: there is no border crossing south of Cochrane suitable for private vehicles meaning that, for those with a car, there is no choice but to double back up to Cochrane. The road quality in the region is poor, with steep inclines and, while the **Ventisquero O'Higgins** is impressive, for those who have already visited the more northerly glaciers, perhaps the final section from Puerto Yungay to Villa O'Higgins can be skipped.

However, for cyclists, hitchhikers or travellers using public transport it is not only possible, but also highly recommended, to traverse this final section and push on through to Argentina. The 100km road from Puerto Bravo to Villa O'Higgins is dramatic, as it traverses some high mountains and runs alongside impressive rivers, but there is relatively little to do *en route* until arriving at Villa O'Higgins. For more adventurous, independent **mountaineers** there are some ambitious multi-day hikes skirting the Southern Ice Field. The truly dedicated hiker can actually trek from Cochrane to Villa O'Higgins without using either the Carretera Austral or the ferry, but this is a week-long, remote trek and not for the faint-hearted!

The **border crossing** itself is an undisputed highlight, being as it is one of the most exciting and unusual border crossings in the Americas – but be prepared for delays, and plan ahead.

Ultimately the Carretera Austral is not simply a region, but a bridge connecting northern and southern Patagonia and, at least for now, Villa O'Higgins is the end (or beginning!) of the Carretera Austral. Potentially by 2016 there will be a direct ferry from southern Aysén to Puerto Natales, on the doorstep of Parque Nacional Torres del Paine. This may fundamentally alter tourism in all of southern Patagonia, as travellers could connect directly with one of the trekking highlights of the Americas without having to pass through Argentina. It is not clear as of May 2015 if this will be a pedestrian-only ferry or allow vehicles, nor is the precise route known. Check www.bradtupdates.com/schile for the latest information.

VILLA O'HIGGINS AND AROUND

The picturesque region around Villa O'Higgins is rugged – dominated as it is by dramatic rivers and glaciers, but it is also relatively inaccessible. As such, despite the ample trekking options in this area, most visitors spend their time here planning their onward journey north or south. Villa O'Higgins is the last **border crossing** into Argentina along the Carretera Austral, for those without a vehicle. The border crossing is only open in the summer (November–March inclusive) and can only be used by pedestrians and cyclists. Information relating to this crossing is scarce and many believe it's not actually possible to get into Argentina from here, thus pages 261–5 describe in detail the precise means to cross this important border to El Chaltén (Argentina). For those with patience and budget available, it is possible to take a short but spectacular flight over the ice field here, but the weather is volatile and the prices are punchy – see page 255.

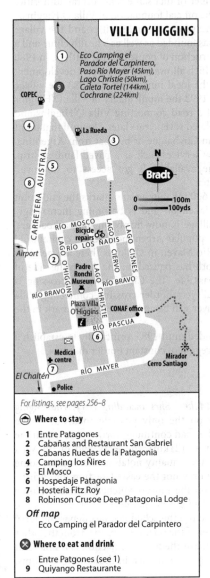

VILLA O'HIGGINS

1 Eco Camping el Parador del Carpintero, Paso Río Mayer (45km), Lago Christie (50km), Caleta Tortel (144km), Cochrane (224km)

COPEC 9

4

La Rueda 3

N

Bradt

0 ——————100m
0 ——————100yds

CARRETERA AUSTRAL

5
8

RÍO MOSCO
Bicycle repairs
LAGO NADIS
RÍO LOS ÑADIS
LAGO CIERVO
LAGO CISNES

Airport

2
LAGO O'HIGGINS
Padre Ronchi Museum
RÍO BRAVO
LAGO CHRISTIE
RÍO BRAVO

RÍO BRAVO

Plaza Villa O'Higgins
CONAF office
i
RÍO PASCUA
6

Medical centre
7
RÍO MAYER
Mirador Cerro Santiago

El Chaltén
Police

For listings, see pages 256–8

🛏 **Where to stay**
1 Entre Patagones
2 Cabañas and Restaurant San Gabriel
3 Cabanas Ruedas de la Patagonia
4 Camping los Ñires
5 El Mosco
6 Hospedaje Patagonia
7 Hosteria Fitz Roy
8 Robinson Crusoe Deep Patagonia Lodge

Off map
Eco Camping el Parador del Carpintero

✖ **Where to eat and drink**
Entre Patgones (see 1)
9 Quiyango Restaurante

HISTORY Long before the first explorers arrived, the region of Villa O'Higgins was inhabited by several indigenous groups, such as the Aónikenk who were also called Patagones (and later Tehuelches). They lived in small groups of about 20 people that were linked by blood relations and were expert hunters of Patagonian fauna. They were nomadic and had simple, easily movable homes, mostly made of animal skins. Nowadays these indigenous groups have completely disappeared due to several factors: persecution by landowners of various nationalities; diseases such as syphilis, measles and tuberculosis; and alcoholism.

The first explorers travelled to the region for scientific and geopolitical reasons. In 1877 two Argentine explorers, Francisco Perito Moreno and Carlos Moyano, named the huge lake they stumbled across after the hero of Argentine independence, San Martin. The Chileans later changed the name to Lago O'Higgins, after their own independence hero, Bernardo O'Higgins, who commanded the fight that freed Chile from Spanish rule. The eastern arm of the lake lies within Argentine territory where the San Martin name persists to this day. In 1899 the river outlet was explored by Hans Steffen, a prominent German geographer who was carrying out border studies for the Chilean government. In 1902 a British mediator equally divided the lake between Chile and Argentina.

Once these remote territories were discovered it didn't take long for the

11

first settlers to arrive. The Chilean government accelerated the settlement process by granting farming concessions. In addition to the people attracted by these concessions, European settlers started to arrive on their own account.

Around 1965 an incident between the Chilean and Argentine police, fuelled by ongoing land and border disputes in which a Chilean officer died, encouraged the Chilean president to strengthen sovereignty in the region. That same year inhabitants of the river mouth of the Río Mayer set out to build a landing strip to enable them to receive supplies and support from the main urban areas in Chilean Patagonia, and to reduce dependency upon Argentina. The works were completed at the end of winter 1966. On 20 September of that same year several authorities arrived from Aysén and Magallanes for the official foundation of Villa O'Higgins.

In the years that followed settlers were given ownership titles and the village started taking shape. A primary school was founded as well as a health clinic and a gym. Subsidies were granted for the construction of houses for the settlers. In 1980 Villa O'Higgins became a municipality which allowed for the further development of the area and catered to the needs of the local inhabitants. In 1983 the village started to generate its own electricity. In 1992 the municipality of Villa O'Higgins had 337 inhabitants and construction of a road connecting Villa O'Higgins and Puerto Yungay began, being finally completed seven years later. Up until that point O'Higgins was accessible only by air from Coyhaique or by boat from Argentina. When the road was opened in 1999 new services such as a paved landing strip, internet and satellite telephone became available. It got access to improved electricity and better quality drinking water.

Currently Villa O'Higgins has around 600 inhabitants and marks the end point of the Carretera Austral. Tourism has taken off and is becoming increasingly important for the local economy. The village is now firmly on the backpackers' map due to its strategic location near the popular Argentine trekking capital of El Chaltén. A new road has been built to Río Mayer, in Chile, as there are pending plans to open a border crossing, but work has paused on the Argentine side of the border, rendering the crossing impassable. The Chaltén border crossing is only open in the summer months. An all-year border crossing connecting Villa O'Higgins with Argentina via the Río Mayer will be an important landmark in the history of the village.

El Chaltén, in Argentina, was not founded until 1985, principally to establish a permanent Argentine population in this region of constant border disputes.

GETTING THERE AND AWAY
About the route
Caleta Tortel to Villa O'Higgins (*144km; 5hrs including ferry; challenging gravel*) Head north from Caleta Tortel on the only possible road out of the village, towards Cochrane. After 23km the road continues northeast to Cochrane (103km), or south towards Puerto Yungay (21km), the ferry and on to Villa O'Higgins. From this junction south the road quality notably deteriorates. Some of the inclines are brutal, and this is certainly not the easiest section for cyclists. The road terminates at **Puerto Yungay** on the Fiordo Mitchell, where the only means to cross to **Puerto Bravo** is on the *Padre Antonio Ronchi* ferry. The crossing is free, and as long as passengers arrive before the scheduled last departing ferry of the day they are guaranteed to cross even if the boat must return from the other side – see page 46 for details. At either end of the ferry connection is a small hut that is open 24/7 and it is possible to sleep without cost in these waiting rooms.

At Puerto Yungay there is also a small cafeteria and one of only two monuments to Pinochet – the other is in La Junta.

It is 100km from Puerto Bravo to Villa O'Higgins, with few opportunities to sleep along the way, although wild camping is possible (of interest to cyclists in particular). The road begins on the south side of the Fiordo Mitchell, and is initially relatively flat. After 9km is a turning to the right (ie: south) signposted 'Río Pascua 25km' or 'Ventisquero Montt 64km'. Despite this apparently clear direction, the road ends at a precarious cliff and does not reach the glacier. The road is of modest interest (it is certainly beautiful, with some dramatic views of lakes and landslides), but it is not entirely clear why it was built, as almost no-one lives along this section. The road does reach the **Río Pascua**, but it is not clear how the road could ever reach Ventisquero Montt. It appears the signpost was completed long before the road itself. The main road then follows sections of the rivers Bravo and Colorado and passes a number of lakes. This is one of the more challenging sections of the entire Carretera Austral and all the quieter for it.

There are no detours until 6km prior to Villa O'Higgins, when a turning to the left signposted 'Estancia Las Margaritas' on the X-905 leads towards the **Paso Río Mayer** and on to **Lago Christie** (pages 259–60). The final stretch to O'Higgins is relatively uneventful, until greeted by the first houses and a petrol station at the edge of the town. Fill up – it's 224km to Cochrane.

By air Aerocord flies twice a week from Coyhaique. Although this is a spectacular flight and heavily subsidised by the state, priority goes to local residents and the flight is invariably full. In peak season it is nearly impossible for non-residents to get a seat on the nine-seater plane. The only means to buy a ticket is by visiting or calling their Coyhaique office (pages 100 and 171).

By bus There is no public transport along the Río Mayer detour towards the border, nor to Lago Christie. It is possible to cross the border to/from El Chaltén by public transport (buses and boats combined with some light trekking). Despite having a surprisingly impressive bus terminal, there are only two buses per week, which go to Cochrane – see Buses Katalina, page 238. However, ask around, as the community are very amenable to offering rides.

TOUR OPERATORS

Aires del Sur Adelaida Vargas 497; (9) 93578196; e airesdelsur14@gmail.com; http://transportesaereosdelsur.com. A new service, offering spectacular flights over the Southern Ice Field in a Cessna P206 (high wing for better views). Flights last 1hr & the principal pilot, Vincent Beasley, doubles as the tour guide. Spanish, English, French & German spoken. The price is US$250pp based on 5 passengers for trips purchased in Villa O'Higgins – tickets bought through agents will cost slightly more. The Southern Ice Field is only 8mins' flight from the landing strip in Villa O'Higgins, so very little time is spent in transit. This bird's-eye view allows passengers to see countless glaciers, including Jorge Montt & O'Higgins, as well as the lesser-known Pascua, Oriental, Bravo, Lucia, Mellizo Sur, Ambrosio, Rosa, Gaea, & Chico. Other options include flights over the legendary Monte Fitz Roy & Cerro Torre, & Volcán Lautaro. It is also possible to fly to the Northern Ice Field (longer transit), or to Monte San Lorenzo closer to Cochrane. At 3,706m San Lorenzo is the 2nd-highest peak in Patagonia (after San Valentin, 3,910m), itself boasting a number of glaciers. Depending on the desired flight path, & also to serve clients crossing from El Chaltén (Argentina), a 2nd landing strip south of Candelario Mancilla is also used, & is closer to Fitz Roy and Lautaro. The plane has a wing-mounted GoPro capable of filming the entire flight in HD for an additional fee. Weather is a major factor in this region – it is wise to have a day or 2 of flexibility, but it is not hard to find things to do around Villa O'Higgins! Clearly this is not a budget option, but when one considers the logistical difficulties of operating a plane in this region, the proximity to the spectacular scenery, & the uniqueness of witnessing sights usually only visible in Antarctica, this is well worth squeezing into a budget if at all possible. Accepts credit card.

Fly Fishing Villa O'Higgins (see *Entre Patagones*, page 257). Alfonso offers half-day & multi-day trips to rivers & lakes in the region, including lakes Tigre, Cisnes & Ciervo, the river that drains from Lago Cisnes & the Colorado Sector (near the Paso Río Mayer). Classes available for beginners, both in fly-fishing & recreational fishing, including use of a Cataraft (*3hr-trip $50,000, full day $150,000*).

Private Fishing Trips Antonio Ronchi L28, Cabanas Ruedas de la Patagonia; \(9) 76042400; e marc_campos11@hotmail.com; f Cabanas las ruedas Villa O'Higgins. Marcus Campos Olivares has a new boat that has built-in buoyancy for extra safety & is fully registered to take tourists. He offers tours to the beautiful Lago Cisnes either for a lake excursion or for sport fishing. All fishing gear is supplied if required. Prices for at least 3hrs are $16,000/hr (discount to $10,000/hr if staying in his cabins – page 257).

Tsonek Expeditiones 1km north of Villa O'Higgins; \(9) 78929695; e info@tsonek.cl;

www.tsonek.cl. English-speaking ornithologist Mauricio Melgarejo offers a birdwatching tour (*4hrs; $15,000pp; min 2, max 4*), in which the only sounds you'll hear will be from the birds. He also offers trekking trips to the Ventisquero Tigre (*8hrs; $35,000pp; min 2, max 6*), one of the most visited & most beautiful glaciers in the region, as well as fly-fishing excursions (*4hrs; $90,000pp; 1–2 people*) – being a local, he knows the best places to find trout. All tours include transport from the campsite (page 258), a packed lunch, & relevant equipment (binoculars, fishing rods, etc).

Villa O'Higgins Expeditions In front of the aerodrome at the northern entrance to town; \(67) 2431821, (9) 82103191; e info@ villaohiggins.com; www.villaohiggins.com. The most comprehensive tour operator & information source in town. The owner, Hans Silva, knows everything worth knowing about Villa O'Higgins & the surrounding region. They can help set up the entire crossing to/from Argentina or simply make reservations for the boats. Their website has updated information on accommodation & services in Villa O'Higgins including public transport, & works closely with the community to give them a web presence. Unfortunately they do not accept credit cards on their website so international visitors cannot make reservations without calling & possibly working something out with Hans.

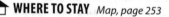

WHERE TO STAY *Map, page 253*

🏠 **Robinson Crusoe Deep Patagonia Lodge** (12 rooms) Carretera Austral km1, 240; \(2) 23341503/4 (Santiago office), (67) 2431909, (67) 2431811, (9) 93578196 (Villa O'Higgins); e info@robinsoncrusoe.com; www. robinsoncrusoe.com. Modern & elegant, this B&B lodge is the highest quality & most expensive accommodation in Villa O'Higgins. With fantastic mattresses & duvets, a full gourmet buffet b/fast, 2 wood-heated communal hot tubs, & wall-sized double-glazed windows overlooking the mountains in every room, refined travellers can find comfort here in this village at the end of the road. Built in 2012, all rooms have a full private bath & Wi-Fi. The clubhouse is a large cosy space that serves as the b/fast area & is a fine atmosphere for relaxing by the fire or chatting over a cup of coffee or glass of wine. The bilingual & friendly staff can help organise excursions, since

the hotel also runs a travel agency & operates the 'Quetru' boat excursion to Ventisquero O'Higgins & the Lago O'Higgins crossing to Candelario Mancilla. The manager, Daniel Muñoz, is a private pilot & a top fly-fishing guide who has offered his services to the likes of Prince William & Tom Selleck. English spoken. Reservations are recommended at least 30 days in advance & can be made through their Santiago office or on their website. US$190/225/292 sgl/dbl/trpl. Accepts credit cards. **$$$$$**

🏠 **Cabañas and Restaurant San Gabriel** (8 cabañas) Lago O'Higgins 310, just off the main plaza; \(67) 2431878, (9) 62102400; e L-2@ hotmail.com. Sleeps 2–10 people per cabin with kitchen (3 en suites) with shared kitchen & private bath, 3 sgls with shared bath. Run by a family with a long history in Villa O'Higgins who also run 2 mini markets, these cabins are scattered around

2 different blocks & range from new to rustic. They have 2 cabins about 2km out of the village for travellers interested in agro-tourism. With their wide selection, families or groups could find something suitable. The restaurant has a good lunch menu & serves as the ticket office for buses to Caleta Tortel & Cochrane. **$$$**

🏠 **Cabañas Ruedas de la Patagonia**
(3 cabins) Antonio Ronchi Lote 28; ☎ (9) 76042400; e marc_campos11@hotmail.com; f cabanas las ruedas de Villa O'Higgins. Higher-end cabins set on a quiet street backing on to the bush-clad mountain range. Located directly towards the hills from the COPEC service station. The smaller dbl-bedroom cabin resembles a honeymoon suite with elegant linen curtains & is suitable for wheelchairs. A wagon-wheel window from yesteryear is a unique feature for all these bungalows. The other 2 larger cabins sleep 5 & 6 people respectively. Satellite TV, a sauna & BBQ area are included. An American b/fast consisting of juice, yoghurt, cereals, cheese, ham & jams is available for an extra $2,500pp. The owner Marcus Campos Olivares has a fully licensed tourist & fishing boat for excursions & fishing trips on Lago Cisnes. Prices are $16,000/hr for a min of 3hrs or $10,000/hr if staying at the cabins. Wi-Fi & reservations with 50% deposit. Accepts credit cards. **$$$**

🏠 **Entre Patagones** (6 cabins)
Carretera Austral; ☎ (67) 2431810, (9) 66215046; e info@entrepatagones.cl; www.entrepatagones.cl. Reasonable cabins located at the northern entrance to Villa O'Higgins before the COPEC petrol station, run by master fisherman Alfonso Diaz. Also home to possibly the best restaurant in the village (page 258). The cabins sleep 2 or 4 people with a simple kitchen, decent bathroom with reliable hot water & comfortable beds. Ample off-road parking, not that crime in O'Higgins is a big concern. B/fast is not included & the internet connection is lousy – even worse than the rest of the village. 2 cabins have a TV. Deposits normally required, but call to negotiate if this is a problem, & be sure to confirm a reservation shortly before arrival. Alfonso also offers fishing trips, & is currently building 2 yurts to increase accommodation options. **$$$**

🏠 **El Mosco** (3 dorms, 6 dbl/twins, 2 trpl, camping) Carretera Austral s/n; ☎ (67) 2431819, (9) 976583017; e patagoniaelmosco@yahoo.es; www.patagoniaelmosco.blogspot.com. The most popular place in town for backpackers, cyclists & budget travellers. The owner (Orfelina Barriga) & staff are very well informed on the region & can provide ample, top-quality information about tours & access to/from O'Higgins. The dormitories sleep 6 people each & are perfectly comfortable (*$9,000pp*); a sgl is $18,000; 3 comfortable dbls with bathroom (*$45,000*) or with shared bathroom (*$35,000*); the 2 trpls cost $55,000 & have private bathrooms. For an additional fee a sauna & hot tub can be fired up. Camping is also available at $5,000. All guests have access to a well-equipped large kitchen. The location could not be better, in front of the Robinson Crusoe hotel where the bus from the El Chaltén crossing stops. Also doubles as an agent for local tour operators, including tours to Lago O'Higgins, Ventisquero O'Higgins & crossing into Argentina, treks to El Mosco refuge, the Submarino & El Tigre glaciers, & can advise on the longer treks into the glacier of the Southern Ice Field & the trek all the way to Cochrane (Ruta de los Pioneros). A lovely & popular hostel run by very helpful people. **$–$$$**

🏠 **Hospedaje Patagonia** (9 rooms) Cnr of Lago Christie & Río Pascua; ☎ (67) 2431818, (9) 73765288; e hospedaje_patagonia@hotmail.com. This is the oldest hostel in Villa O'Higgins & an excellent option for budget travellers. The building is 30 years old & has thin walls & a squeaky floor, but rooms are spacious, clean & have large windows. There is a large restaurant & dining room/lounge & basic b/fast is included; lunch & dinner can be purchased for $5,000. There is 1 sgl room with a private bathroom, & another sgl & 7 twin rooms with shared bathrooms. Satellite TV, Wi-Fi & laundry service are also provided. Reservations can be made without a deposit. **$$**

🏠 **Hosteria Fitz Roy** (4 rooms) cnr of Teniente Merino & Río Mayer; ☎ (67) 2431839; e hospedajefitzroy@gmail.com; www. villaohiggins.com/fitzroy/index.htm. Probably the best hospedaje in this price bracket in Villa O'Higgins. Run by a charming woman (who is also a teacher at the school) called Yaline, the hostel is homely, & at the southernmost point of the village, a 3min walk from the plaza. The rooms are cosy & warm, with comfortable beds & ample space, with a clean, shared bathroom & reliable hot water. The largest room is a trpl, & has a private bathroom with a large jacuzzi (use of which incurs an additional charge as it uses up most of the water of the hostel). This room has 1 dbl & 2 sgls, is ideal for a family, & costs $48,000, although it is slightly less if not fully occupied. The corner dbl room has great views over the mountains. Yaline will also prepare lunch or dinner upon request, & can prepare packed lunches. Basic b/fast is included, laundry, cable TV & Wi-Fi are available, guests are free to use the kitchen, & there is a large communal sitting area, & even a movie-projector & screen for rainy evenings. Importantly for those travelling from Argentina & potentially unable to find Chilean pesos (there is neither money-changer nor ATM in O'Higgins), Yaline accepts PayPal, & can even do cash advances for PayPal if asked nicely! **$$**

⚑ Camping los Ñires (approx 30 sites) Carretera Austral s/n beside COPEC petrol station; ☏(67) 2431212. A large centrally located campsite with shade from mature native trees. Kitchen & eating area, 6 toilets, hot water, & facilities for washing clothes. Horseriding can be arranged through the owner, Rodolfo, for $5,000/hr. No reservations. **$**

⚑ Eco Camping el Parador del Carpintero (Tsonek) (10 sites on wooden platforms, 10 sites in bush setting) 1km north of Villa O'Higgins; ☏(9) 78929695; e info@tsonek.cl;

www.tsonek.cl. This rustic eco-campsite is set in the bush & is a model for self-sustainability. All timber is from fallen trees within the bush. Tent sites are marked by wooden platforms that provide a clean level surface & don't damage the forest floor. The toilet is a dry composting toilet. Water comes directly from a mountain spring. The administration building is made from recycled plastic drink bottles filled with plastic bags to make 'eco-bricks', which are then covered with a mud & cement mix with occasional glass bottles to allow natural light to enter. There is a communal building for cooking on a large wooden stove, or for reading one of the many eco-building books from the library. 5hrs/day of electricity provided by a solar panel & an ingenious small electric generator powered by a modified bicycle. Wi-Fi available. Hot water for showers & washing dishes comes from the wood-fired stove. There is also a greenhouse where organic vegetables are grown. This eco-campground accepts volunteers & dogs. The friendly & informative owner, Mauricio Melgarejo, is an ornithologist, speaks English, & offers birdwatching, fly-fishing & trekking tours (page 256). Parking on the main road is limited. **$**

✗ WHERE TO EAT AND DRINK *Map, page 253*

✗ Entre Patagones Northern limits of town, on Carretera Austral; ☏(67) 2431810, (9) 66215046; e info@entrepatagones.cl; www. entrepatagones.cl. Of the same owner of the cabins & fishing outfit (page 256), this is a fair restaurant by Chilean standards & a positively decent restaurant by O'Higgins standards. The set menu is approximately $10,000pp including a starter, main course & pudding, changing daily. Typical dishes include trout, chicken, steak, cazuela, empanadas & cakes. Reasonable range of wines & beers. Popular. **$$$**

✗ Quiyango Restaurante Carretera Austral, entering village from north; ☏(9) 84594546. An excellent restaurant for meat lovers. The daily dish is lamb, beef or chicken with potatoes & a salad.

Portions are large & cooked to perfection. The lamb is cooked slowly over hot embers for 3hrs. The friendly owner is proud of Chilean culture & delighted to share the secrets of his cooking. There is a reasonable selection of beers & wines to choose from. The owner has a great sense of humour & is very flexible with his late-night closing hours. Wi-Fi is available. The daily set menu with wine is $12,000–15,000. This restaurant also doubles as a café. All cakes are baked on the premises using local ingredients where possible. There are also 3 basic (& slightly dark) cabins on site for 4, 6 or 8 people. Not the finest cabins in the village but could be an option if others are full (**$$$**). Accepts credit cards. **$$$**

OTHER PRACTICALITIES There is a **bicycle repair** shop on Río Los Nadis 143, which offers basic repairs with a limited stock of spare parts. The **CONAF** office (*Lago Cisnes 101;* ☏ *(67) 2431834*) can give up-to-date information about treks in the area and can also supply maps. There are two **petrol stations**, but **no ATM or bureau de change** in town.

Mechanic

La Rueda Also a petrol station, Lago Christie turn by COPEC. Claudio Sanchez offers basic repairs, simple welding, including tyres, cars, motorcycles & bikes.

SIGHTSEEING AND EXCURSIONS Within Villa O'Higgins there are relatively few highlights. Besides some basic shopping in small stores, or visiting the museum, most activities are outside the village. **Fly-fishing** and **birdwatching** are popular activities, possible both with and without a guide (see page 255 for tour operators). **Trekking** options relatively close to the town include to the **Mirador Cerro Santiago**, just 30 minutes (1km) from the Villa O'Higgins on a well-marked trail, which overlooks the village, the native bush and the mountains in the background. The trail continues for another 40 minutes to a second viewpoint with stunning views of the surrounding mountains, rivers, lakes, bush and glaciers.

The short detour (driving only, no public transport) to **Lago Christie**, northeast of town and approaching the Paso Río Mayer (not passable) is a pleasant day trip through stunning scenery, passing a delightful chapel built by Father Ronchi, before reaching the lake itself. For more advanced, multi-day treks towards, or onto the ice shelf, consult the CONAF office (page 258). These are not standardised tours, often involve quite some planning, and are suitable only for experienced mountaineers. Rescue services in this remote region are extremely limited.

The two key highlights around Villa O'Higgins, which are often combined into one trip, are **crossing the border** towards El Chaltén, and visiting **Ventisquero O'Higgins**. For those with a more generous budget, a **flight** over the ice field is a treat – the only other places in the world where such a spectacular perspective is possible are Greenland and Antarctica. By comparison, this flight will seem like excellent value for money! Aires del Sur are the only operator in town (page 255) offering this service. Otherwise, a (long – 12-hour) day trip from Villa O'Higgins costs $89,000 with Robinson Crusoe (page 256). Bring your own food and dress for cold, wet and windy weather. See page 262 for more on this trip.

Back in town, the **Padre Ronchi Museum** (*main plaza;* ⊕ *10.00–18.00 daily*) is a small, quaint museum located in a restored chapel that was originally built under Ronchi's supervision in 1977 (see box, page 125, for more on Father Ronchi). Most of the exhibits have signs in Spanish about the history of Father Ronchi and the early settlers around Villa O'Higgins. His bedroom with some artefacts are off the back. The museum is, however, of limited interest to those not yet familiar with the history of Ronchi and his legendary status in the Aysén region.

Paso Río Mayer and Lago Christie – a detour

This is a pleasant, scenic detour for those with a high-clearance vehicle, beginning 6km north of Villa O'Higgins and passing a number of glaciers *en route* to the lake. A gravel road of approximately 50km leads to the Argentine border at Río Mayer and on to Lago Christie. The road passes a small **chapel** built by Father Ronchi and still lovingly maintained – it incorporates an unusual roof-construction called *canogas* – interlocking hollowed-out tree trunks. The **border crossing** is technically open, and Chilean Carabineros will process formalities, but the border is impassable on the Argentine side in a vehicle although at least theoretically possible on foot, but this involves a number of dangerous river crossings and extensive swampland. It is advisable to seek the support of a local resident with horses. Argentine territory officially begins 20m behind the Chilean border post, but there is approximately 10km of treacherous terrain to reach the actual border post, and

11

in the intervening section it is not immediately obvious how a potential rescue could be arranged, as the Chilean authorities are not formally allowed to cross the border without permission from Argentina, and the lack of telephones in the region further complicates matters.

It's a shame this border crossing is not more practical: in the winter months, when the El Chaltén crossing is closed, this could be the obvious terrestrial alternative for residents of Villa O'Higgins. The Paso Río Mosco to the south of Villa O'Higgins is also impassable, but theoretically it is possible to reach Estancia Tucu Tucu. Again, not a practical option.

From the Chilean border post at Río Mayer the road continues north perhaps 5km to the shore of **Lago Christie**. This is a pleasant drive involving one minor river crossing. The road follows the river emerging from the lake passing some small **waterfalls**, with ample **wild camping** options along the way. Lago Christie is a beautiful, remote lake and a delightful place to wild camp and explore the area.

⊕ AS THE CONDOR FLIES

It is 57km from the centre of the plaza in Villa O'Higgins to the border crossing towards El Chaltén. Puerto Montt is 778km, almost perfectly north. The condor flying directly from Puerto Montt to this border crossing would face a daunting 833km journey!

From Villa O'Higgins there are only two ways out: north along the Carretera Austral, or south to El Chaltén in Argentina.

The border crossing between El Chaltén (Argentina) and Villa O'Higgins (Chile) is a great option for hikers and cyclists, and one of the legendary border crossings of the continent. Called the 'Portezuelo de la Divisoria' border in Argentina, it goes by the name 'Dos Lagos' in Chile. Infrequently travelled and without a road for vehicles, the border can only be crossed on foot or bicycle and takes a minimum of two days. Crossing the border here is the only way to traverse the Carretera Austral in its entirety without doubling back since the next closest border crossing is north of Cochrane (page 234). With proper planning it is possible to cross this border without having to camp. The border is open from November to mid-April.

Take extra food for the crossing (in case of delays) and cash in local currency as there is no bank, official exchange office, or ATM in Villa O'Higgins (in fact, there isn't one until Cochrane further north) and most establishments do not take credit cards or Argentine pesos.

For those coming from Argentina, plan on a bare minimum of US$50/day in cash, while for those entering Argentina from Chile, the first town with facilities (including an ATM) is El Chaltén.

TOUR AND TRANSPORT OPERATORS At least three companies offer this crossing as a package tour: Robinson Crusoe and Villa O'Higgins Expediciones (in Chile, page 256), and Zona Austral (in Argentina, see below). Keep things simple: if you're travelling from Chile into Argentina, book in Chile with a Chilean firm – and vice versa from Argentina.

While it is no doubt cheaper (and possible) to make this journey independently, booking ahead can mean less hassle, and fewer delays – there is no chance of being stranded if the Lago O'Higgins boat is full (there are only two to three per week and, in high season, there is a good chance the boat will be full). Independent travellers can pay for the crossing on the boat itself, but this is risky and might mean delays if there is no space. Booking with Robinson Crusoe in advance (the only operator currently to accept credit cards) means that your place on the boat is guaranteed.

Chaltén Travel El Calafate: Av Libertador 1174 & El Chaltén: bus terminal, Ventanilla 4; ☎ + 54 (0) 11 48659428, +54 (0) 2962 493392; e contacto@ chaltentravel.com; www.chaltentravel.com. El Chaltén to Lago del Desierto: 08.00, returning at 13.00 or 16.00 depending on whether it's a full-day or half-day excursion (*ARG$260 for either option*). Also transfers to/from downtown El Calafate & daily to Bariloche.

Transporte Las Lengas El Calafate: airport counter & El Chaltén: Viedma St 95 & bus terminal, window 6; ☎+54 (0) 2962 493023, +54 (0) 2962 493227; e laslengaselchalten@yahoo.com. ar; www.transportelaslengas.com. El Chaltén to Lago del Desierto: noon daily, returning at 17.00 (*ARG$200 one-way*). They also offer transfers between El Calafate airport & El Chaltén, synchronised with flight arrivals & departures.

Zona Austral Cmte El Calafate: Espora 65 Local 3 & El Chaltén: Av MM de Güemes 173; ☎+54 (0) 2902 489755, +54 (0) 2962 493155; e info@zonaaustralturismo.com; www. zonaaustralturismo.com. Run buses & boats & thus offer a package deal on the crossing. El Chaltén to Lago del Desierto: 08.00 daily, returns at 13.00 (*ARG$260/280 one-way*). It is also possible to book the boat trip across Lago O'Higgins with them, but only in US dollars. Accept credit cards, but fees in Argentina are prohibitive.

THE CROSSING The trip consists of four stages (listed here from Villa O'Higgins in Chile to El Chaltén in Argentina). The first is from Villa O'Higgins across Lago O'Higgins (potentially via the Ventisquero O'Higgins) to Candalario Mancilla; the second involves hiking into Argentina and reaching the northern shore of Lago del Desierto; the third section involves crossing, or hiking around, Lago del Desierto, to the southern shore of the lake; and the final stage extends from the southern shore of the lake to El Chaltén in Argentina. Note that the border is not open all year: this trip is only possible from November to Easter.

Stage 1: bus/boat from Villa O'Higgins to Candelario Mancilla across Lago O'Higgins (via the Ventisquero O'Higgins) From Villa O'Higgins, you'll need to
take a shuttle bus south to **Puerto Bahamóndez** (*7km; $2,500, one-way*), from where Robinson Crusoe (page 256) runs the main boat trip to **Candelario Mancilla** (*08.30 Mon, Wed, Thu, Sat in high season, once or twice a week in low season*). This can either go direct from one port to the other (*2½hrs one-way; $44,000 one-way, $70,000 round-trip*) or include the Ventisquero O'Higgins excursion (*9hrs; $70,000*). In the opposite direction, the boat stops at Candelario Mancilla around 10.00 for those joining the glacier tour and again at around 16.00 for those going direct to Villa O'Higgins.

While you can pay on the boat, it is highly advisable to book this route in advance, especially in January/February. Credit cards are accepted on board, reservations can be made online or via the Robinson Crusoe agency in Villa O'Higgins (page 256). Keep your eye out for the **'Fin de la Carretera Austral' sign** in Puerto Bahamóndez, marking the official end (or beginning!) of the Carretera Austral. The boat trip does not include food, so bring your own, but the detour to the glacier does include a glass of whisky with glacial ice. Dress for cold, windy, and wet-weather conditions, and be prepared for a bumpy ride. Robinson Crusoe can also arrange accommodation in Candelario Mancilla as part of their package. They also partner with some Argentine agencies to book the entire crossing with boats and an optional horseride for some sections of the trajectory.

There are at least **two other boats** crossing the lake that run with less precise frequency, and are mainly used by the people living in the area; they will take passengers but do not visit the Ventisquero O'Higgins. Ask either in Candelario Mancilla or O'Higgins if/when these other boats operate, although generally it's on the same days as Robinson Crusoe, but at slightly different times.

Ventisquero O'Higgins – a detour Ventisquero O'Higgins can be seen either via the boat ride or a several-day trek from Candelario Mancilla. Most of the boat trip is spent travelling to and from the glacier (*5hrs round-trip*), but travellers are rewarded with a magnificent, up-close view of one of Patagonia's largest glaciers. Upon approach, the boat passes floating icebergs, and the tongue of the glacier is seen spilling off the Southern Ice Field into the lake. The 100m-high jagged walls protrude out of the lake and the sounds of the 'calving' glacier resonate like thunder. The front face is about 3km wide, making it one of the biggest accessible glaciers in Patagonia, and the boat stays for almost 2 hours in the area for passengers to take plenty of pictures and experience it up close. Lago O'Higgins reaches depths of 836m (the deepest point is close to the glacier), making it the deepest lake in the Americas (General Carrera secures the #2 spot at 586m).

Stage 2: hiking from Candelario Mancilla (Chile) to the northern shore of Lago del Desierto (Argentina) (*23km; 5–7hrs with several sources of drinkable water; medium*) Candelario Mancilla is actually the name of the first settler in this

region, the founder of a small **estancia** (also of the same name) that is still run by his descendants and who mainly make a living from agriculture and logging. Basic accommodation and meals are available in the estancia, and camping is allowed on their land (sometimes for a small fee, around ARG$2,500). There are only a few indoor beds available on a first-come-first-served basis unless booked in advance through one of the agencies listed on page 256. They do not sell provisions, so those travelling north are advised to bring extra supplies in case you miss the boat across Lago O'Higgins or bad weather causes them to be cancelled completely, potentially for up to several days!

From Candelario Mancilla the hike towards Argentina starts off uphill and arrives at the Chilean Carabineros military post and border control after approximately 1km; it is clearly marked. This is where border formalities are processed (⊕ *Nov–early Apr 09.00–20.30*), and from here the trail continues steeply uphill with fantastic views of Lago O'Higgins. From Candelario Mancilla the trail gains altitude quickly, winding its way up a gravel road to a dense forest where it levels out.

The trail is initially passable by 4x4, and continues for approximately 17km passing **Laguna Redonda** and a small landing strip until reaching the formal border marker delineating the two countries.

From here, the trail to the Argentine Gendarmeria (where passports are stamped) is downhill for only 6km, but the quality of the trail deteriorates substantially. In fact, this 6km section within Argentina is the main bottleneck for vehicular access between the two countries, as it is only passable by foot, bicycle or horse. There is no public transport. The trail is well marked and suitable for anyone with reasonable fitness. The trail passes to the east side of **Laguna Larga** (do not follow the faint trail to the west of the lake).

This area was still in dispute between Argentina and Chile up until recently, and Chile would like to claim all the land between Lago O'Higgins and Monte Fitz Roy as theirs. Argentina has little motivation to relinquish this land or put in a road. There are several places to wild camp in this section, the most scenic being next to either of the two lakes. The track is passable by bicycle but is muddy in wet conditions and there are several short sections where bikes will need to be carried a few metres across a stream or over fallen trees.

Just 6km south of the border marker, located on a flat grassy meadow on the north coast of Lago del Desierto (Punta Norte), is the Gendarmeria. Knock on the door to secure a passport stamp. Hikers may camp for free, but no food or services are available. Several nice shady spots with good protection from the wind can be found if there are not too many other campers, which is generally the case. There is plenty of fresh water available. This border is open only during the warmer months of the year from November to early April, from 09.00 to 20.30, or whenever you can round up somebody to stamp your passport.

Stage 3: Crossing Lago del Desierto

By boat (*1½hrs*) This is a mildly chaotic and informal lake crossing, more easily arranged from south to north than vice versa, but inevitably requiring a degree of flexibility, and food to last a few days just in case. Most traffic to Lago del Desierto is day trippers from El Chaltén who do not intend to cross the border into Chile, hence it's easier to traverse from the south – those travelling from the north are essentially catching the return section of trips originating from the south side of the lake, which can only take on passengers if there is room on the boat.

Several independent captains traverse Lago del Desierto, all originating at the south end. For those **coming from El Chaltén** and wishing to traverse the entire lake, be sure to check if the boat goes all the way across to **Punta Norte** since some tours go only about 75% of the way across to show passengers the glaciers before returning to the south shore. This is a great tour, but it won't get you any closer to the Chilean border, nor is this of any use for travellers heading south from Chile. Prices for the full crossing range from ARG$250 to ARG$450 depending on the captain (and his mood), and must be paid in cash in Argentine pesos. The first boats leave around 10.00 (if they have enough passengers) and later boats leave when another bus shows up, up until about 16.30. For those coming from El Chaltén to catch a boat across the lake, you should ask the bus driver to continue to the pier for the best chance of securing a place on the boat. However, usually just talking to the bus drivers when you book your ticket will help you get a seat. No matter what the agent tells you, though, you may still have to wait until the captain has enough people before he leaves.

On a good day several glaciers, including the Vespigniani and the Huemul, are seen to the west in the Vespigniani mountain range, and the northern face of Fitz Roy sometimes pokes through the clouds when looking south.

Travelling **from the north** to the south side involves waiting until a boat arrives with enough space to take on additional passengers, and the last boat of the day is usually around 16.30. Independently pre-booking these boats is practically impossible, so a tour operator is required if you want to reserve.

On foot (*10km; 4–5hrs; difficult*) For experienced hikers, it is possible to trek around the lake, thus eliminating the need to take the boat. A roughly 4-hour trail on the east side of the lake follows a track that has some steep uphill scrambling and downhill sliding sections, and doesn't really follow the coastline due to some rugged cliffs. To the west looking over the lake, hikers can appreciate views of the Huemul and Vespigniani glaciers as they walk through lush forest with trees that date back hundreds of years, some measuring up to 15m in height. It is impossible with a bicycle and is poorly maintained, but well marked.

Practicalities Most people only stay overnight near the lake because of transportation issues, but the area does provide pleasant opportunities for additional short hikes, fishing, or simply relaxing. Most trails in this area, however, are not noteworthy other than as a means to get between Villa O'Higgins and Chaltén.

On the south side of Lago del Desierto there are some basic facilities. Located about 1km south of the pier, a small **hostel** (*Estancia Lago del Desierto;* \ +54 (0) 2962 493010; US$30–50/night) offers basic accommodation and limited food options. There is also a formal **campground** (*Camping Lago del Desierto;* \ +54 (0) 2962 493010; US$8pp). The mid-range **Aguas Arriba** lodge is located halfway down the east coast (*6 rooms; www.aguasarribalodge.com; US$40–80/night*). It offers all-inclusive packages in their eco-friendly establishment and makes a great basecamp for some exclusive fly-fishing or hiking in the area. The lodge is reached by boat or a 3-hour walk from the south coast of the lake (a little under 3 hours from the north side; medium difficulty).

Stage 4: southern shore of Lago del Desierto to El Chaltén (*40km; 1½–2hrs one-way; gravel to dirt track*) Lago del Desierto is approximately 40km from El Chaltén, and vans that shuttle this route all originate and have their offices in El Chaltén, which makes booking this leg difficult if coming from Chile. Travellers will have to try to catch a ride on one of the return trips (starting midday until early evening), which can be met at either the pier or the Estancia Lago del Desierto.

Ask boat captains and the staff at the estancia about availability, but space is usually limited. Hitchhiking is another option. Cyclists can plan on a 2–3-hour ride, mainly downhill. Desperate travellers can ask the estancia to call a taxi from El Chaltén, which will be expensive.

Leaving Lago del Desierto, the first 20km is a dirt track that would be difficult for small cars in wet conditions. The final 20km to El Chaltén is a decent-quality gravel road. The scenery along the way varies from lush forest to dry steppe, and almost all buses will make a short stop at the raging Saltos del Río de las Vueltas waterfall about 5km from the lake. This is a pleasant waterfall, but hardly a highlight of Patagonia.

MOVING ON FROM EL CHALTÉN

To El Calafate As well as being the closest village to Monte Fitz Roy, El Chaltén is also situated close to El Calafate – a useful transport hub with buses north, south and east, and an airport with flights to Ushuaia, Buenos Aires and Bariloche. Calafate is also the jumping-off point for visits to Ventisquero Perito Moreno, although this is not such an attraction for those heading to/from the spectacular glaciers along the Carretera Austral.

To Bariloche For those hoping to access the Carretera Austral further north (most likely via Chile Chico), the key route is on Argentina's Ruta 40 towards Bariloche. This is a main highway running broadly parallel to the Carretera Austral on the Argentine side of the Andes, and is *mostly* paved, but as with the Carretera Austral, a high-clearance sturdy car is recommended for the gravel sections. A good public transport option from El Chaltén is Chaltén Travel (page 261), and the trip between El Chaltén and Bariloche takes two days and makes some intermediate stops. The halfway point is the village of **Perito Moreno**, which is close to the Cueva de las Manos (Cave of the Hands, a UNESCO archaeological site). Some of the hand paintings found here date back more than 9,000 years.

From Perito Moreno various shuttles head west via Los Antiguos, Argentina (with Chaltén Travel or Taqsa bus: *www.taqsa.com.ar*), to **Chile Chico** in Chile – a main entry/exit point to the Carretera Austral (pages 217–18). This route is offered from mid-November until Easter and costs approximately US$100 per day (*12hrs*). Out of season the bus frequency reduces drastically, and in high season buses fill quickly so it is wise to reserve a seat in advance.

The **border crossing to Chile at Cochrane** (Paso Roballos, page 234) is not possible with public transport, and the road between Ruta 40 and the actual border is rarely transited, so this is not an ideal border crossing for those without a private vehicle (or bicycle). Consequently, many use the **Los Antiguos/Chile Chico border crossing** (pages 217–18), and not wishing to double back on themselves, skip the southern section of the Carretera Austral. For those without a car, the strong recommendation of this book is to cross directly into Chile from El Chaltén and to continue north along the entire Carretera Austral. For those wishing to cross back into northern Argentine Patagonia (Villa La Angostura, Bariloche and so on), the most convenient border crossing is Cardenal Samoré, northeast of Puerto Montt.

North of Perito Moreno, Ruta 40 continues on to **Esquel, El Bolson, and Bariloche**. Each of these cities also serves as an entrance or exit to the Carretera Austral.

Exiting/Entering the Carretera Austral: Villa O'Higgins and beyond   CROSSING INTO ARGENTINA

11

265

Appendix 1

LANGUAGE

BASIC VOCABULARY

hello	*hola*
good morning/afternoon/night	*buenos días/buenas tardes/buenas noches*
goodbye	*adios*
how are you?	*¿como está?*
very well	*muy bien*
well	*bien*
good, OK	*bueno*
yes/no	*sí/no*
of course	*claro*
please/thank you	*por favor/gracias*
excuse me (I need to pass)	*con permiso*
excuse me (sorry)	*disculpe*
you're welcome	*de nada*
a pleasure to meet you	*mucho gusto*
today/tomorrow	*hoy/mañana*
yesterday	*ayer*
sorry	*lo siento/perdón*
what?	*¿qué?*
when?	*¿cuando?*
why?	*¿por qué?*
how?	*¿cómo?*
a lot/much	*harto*
here/there	*aquí/ahí*
open/closed	*abierto/cerrado*
large/small	*grande/pequeño*

BASIC PHRASES

Where is…?	*¿Dónde está…?*
What's this street called?	*¿Cómo se llama esta calle?*
Where are you from (your country)?	*¿De dónde es?*
How far is it to…?	*¿A que distancia…?*
How much does it cost?	*¿Cuánto vale?*
May I…? Is it possible…?	*¿Se puede…?*
I am English/American	*Soy inglés/norteamericano*
I don't understand	*No entiendo*
Please write it down	*Por favor, escríbalo*

Do you speak English?	¿Habla inglés?
Is there a doctor nearby?	¿Hay un médico por acá?
I need to call an ambulance	Necesito llamar una ambulancia

DIRECTIONS

left/right	izquierda/derecha
north/south	norte/sur
east/west	este or oriente/oeste, occidente or poniente
northeast/northwest	noreste/noroeste
ATM	cajero automático
airport	aeropuerto
bus stop	parada
border crossing	paso/frontera
cove	caleta
fjord	fiordo
forest/woods	bosque
glacier	ventisquero
ice flow	témpano
jetty/pier	embarcadero
lake	lago/laguna
mountain	cerro/pico
mountain range	cordillera/sierra
next to	al lado de
national park	parque nacional
national reserve	reserva nacional
opposite	frente
path (trekking/horseriding)	sendero
pass (over mountain)	portezuelo
port	puerto
river	río
road/highway	camino/carretera
main highway	ruta
shelter	refugio
street/avenue	calle/avenida
viewpoint/lookout	mirador
Are there buses to…?	¿Hay buses a…?
A ticket to…?	¿Un boleto/pasaje a…?
How can I get to…?	¿Como puedo llegar a…?
When do buses return from…?	¿Cuando vienen los buses de…?
Where is the nearest place to buy petrol?	¿Donde está el lugar más cercano para comprar gasolina?
Where is the nearest telephone?	¿Donde puedo hacer una llamada?
Can you show me on the map?	¿Me lo puedes mostrar en el mapa?

ACCOMMODATION

single/twin/double	sencillo/doble/matrimonial
en suite/shared bathroom	con baño (privado)/con baño compartido (communal)
camping	camping
hotel	hotel
hostel	hostal/residencia/hostería/casa familiar
Do you have a room?	¿Hay un cuarto?

EQUIPMENT/SUPPLIES
Camping

camping fuel	*bencina blanca*
cooking stove	*estufa*
drinking water	*agua potable*
fire	*fogón*
fire wood	*leña*
tent	*carpa*
sleeping bag	*bolsa de dormir*
Can I camp here?	*¿Puedo acampar acá?*
Can I make a campfire here?	*¿Se puede hacer fuego acá?*

Driving

4x4	*cuatro por cuatro*
bicycle	*bicicleta*
car	*auto*
motorcycle	*motorcicleta*
petrol	*gasolina*
puncture repair	*gomería/vulcanizadora*
paved/gravel/dirt road	*pavimentado/ripio/tierra*
map	*mapa*
seat belt	*cinturón de seguridad*
pot-hole	*bache*
landslide	*derrumbe*
My car/motorbike/bicycle has broken down	*Se rompió mi auto/moto/bicicleta*
I have a puncture	*tengo un pinchazo*
How is the road?	*¿Como está la ruta?*

FOOD AND DRINK

beef	*vaca*	butter	*mantequilla*
beer	*cerveza*	cheese	*queso*
bread	*pan*	coffee	*café*
breakfast	*desayauno*	dinner	*cena*
burger	*churasco*	eel (ling)	*congrio*

268

hake	*merluza*	shellfish	*mariscos*	
lamb	*cordero*	steak	*churrasco*	
milk	*leche*	tea	*té*	
lunch	almuerzo	water	*agua*	
potatoes	*patatas/papas*	wine	*vino*	

Can I make a reservation?	*¿Podría hacer una reserva?*
When do you open/close?	*¿A qué hora se abre/cierre?*
A table for XX people	*¿Una mesa para XX personas?*
Do you take credit card?	*¿Se puede pagar con tarjeta de crédito?*
The bill, please	*¿La cuenta, por favor*
Do you have vegetarian food?	*¿Hay comida vegetariana?*

NUMBERS

0	*cero*	7	*siete*	14	*catorce*
1	*uno*	8	*ocho*	15	*quince*
2	*dos*	9	*nueve*	16	*dieciseis*
3	*tres*	10	*diez*	17	*diecisiete*
4	*cuatro*	11	*once*	18	*dieciocho*
5	*cinco*	12	*doce*	19	*diecinueve*
6	*seis*	13	*trece*	20	*veinte*

Appendix 2

FURTHER INFORMATION

BOOKS
History and culture

Chatwin, Bruce *In Patagonia* Vintage Books, 1998. The classic Patagonian read, arguably the first book to popularise Patagonia since its first publication in 1977.

Chenut, Jean *Cuando éramos niños en la Patagonia* Pehuén Editores, 2006. Account of the early Belgian settlers to the region around Lago General Carrera. Packed with extensive black-and-white photos.

Darwin, Charles *The Voyage of the Beagle*. Darwin's pathfinding account of his 1831–36 expedition on the HMS *Beagle*, covering regions along the Carretera Austral. Originally published in 1839.

Guevara, Che *The Motorcycle Diaries*. Che Guevara never made it south of Osorno, so the book does not encompass any region of the Carretera Austral, but is one of the definitive travel books of the entire South American continent.

Hudson, William Henry *Idle Days in Patagonia*. Early account of flora and fauna of the region.

Ivanoff, Danka *Caleta Tortel y su Isla de los Muertos* Fundación Río Baker, 2012. The finest account of the mystery surrounding the graveyard at Caleta Tortel and a good introduction to Lucas Bridges. Mrs Ivanoff has written a number of other books about southern Chile, including parts of the Carretera Austral. Indeed, those staying at the El Engaño cabins (page 219) in Chile Chico are afforded the privilege of meeting and chatting with Mrs Ivanoff. Her books are available in Chile Chico, Coyhaique and Perito Moreno (Argentina), and her book of the war of Chile Chico is available for free download on www.memoriachilena.cl.

Ludwig, Luisa *Puyuhuapi – Curanto y Kuchen* Kultrun, 2013. A 'book of histories' – a heart-warming account of the early pioneers of Puyuhuapi and the surrounding region, written by the daughter of one of the first pioneers. A wonderful insight into the early life of the first villages, intertwined with early 20th-century European history.

McEwan, Colin *Patagonia: Natural History, Prehistory and Ethnography* Princeton University Press, 2014. This book describes how the intrepid nomads of Tierra del Fuego Patagonia confronted a hostile climate and learned how to live there. It provides an overview of the history of the land and its people. A fascinating look into the people Darwin met while on the *Beagle*.

Moss, Chris *Patagonia – A Cultural History* Signal Books, 2008. An engaging overview of the literature, legends and history of Patagonia, with some sections relating to the region spanned by the Carretera Austral.

Murphy, Dallas *Rounding the Horn: Being the Story of Williwaws and Windjammers, Drake, Darwin, Murdered Missionaries and Naked Natives* Basic Books, 2005. Some overlap with the Carretera Austral, but possibly the most amusing, well-written account of deep Patagonia, combining maritime history, exploration, the first contact with the indigenous residents, and a thumping account of the exploration of the channels of the extreme south.

Pucci, Idanna *La Italiana de Patagonia – Homenaje a Eugenia Pirzio Biroli*. A fascinating account of the life and works of the long-serving mayor of Puerto Cisnes, including many first-hand accounts of her life. Written by her niece, in Spanish and Italian, available directly from the author (e *idannapucci@gmail.com*).

Guides and maps

COPEC *Chiletur Zona Sur* COPEC, 2015. Definitive road atlas of the region, best up-to-date maps available of the region. Limited additional information. Covers the entire southern region from Santiago to Tierra del Fuego.

Beccaceci, Marcello D *Natural Patagonia* Pangaea, 1998. This book takes readers on a panoramic journey through one of the world's most magnificent and varied landscapes, explaining its formation and the remarkable animals and flora that thrive in the rugged reaches of Patagonian Argentina and Chile.

Jaramillo, Alvaro *The Birds of Chile* Princeton Field Guides, 2003. Features concise identification-focused text positioned opposite the superb colour plates to allow quick and easy reference. There are over 470 species detailed, including all breeders, regular visitors and vagrants.

Pike, Neil and Harriet *The Adventure Cycle-Touring Handbook* Trailblazer, 2015. The definitive guide to planning for an extended cycling trip.

Pixmap Cartografía Digital *Chile's Lake District: Puerto Varas–Ensenada–Cochamó*. Double-sided map useful for trekking in the region; one side 1:100,000 map covers Lago Llanquihue with Puerto Varas and the area to the east, the other side 1:75,000 map further south, extending from the Reloncaví Estuary and Puelo eastwards to the El León border. Available from Stanfords (*www.stanfords.com*).

Zegers, Claudio Donoso *Arboles Nativos de Chile*. A useful tree identification guide for Chile's main native trees with commentary in English and Spanish. Produced for CONAF (Chile's national park administration) and available at their information office in Santiago.

Contemporary travel

Crouch, Gregory *Enduring Patagonia* Random House USA, 2003. Excellent mountain-climbing book covering some regions encompassed by the Carretera Austral.

Krull, Robert *Solitude: A Year Alone in the Patagonian Wilderness* New World Library, 2009. Although slightly south of the most southerly point of the Carretera Austral, this intriguing book describes a year living in total isolation on an uninhabited Chilean island. Survival and enlightenment in equal measure.

Reding, Nick *The Last Cowboys at the End of the World* Crown Publishing, 2001. A fascinating, insightful and witty account of living with Chilean gauchos in Cisnes Medio (near Villa Amengual).

Walker, Justin *The Dictator's Highway* Lulu.com, 2015. The only travelogue of the Carretera Austral, superbly written, eloquent, witty and accurate. Great read; the only criticism is that the author was predominantly hitching and thus does not manage to venture off the main Carretera Austral to some of the lesser-known regions.

Other

Orrego, Juan Pablo and Rodrigo, Patricio *Patagonia Chilean ¡Sin Represas!* Definitive text (in Spanish) of the struggle to prevent the damming of the Pascua and Baker rivers. Available from www.patagoniasinrepresas.cl.

NEWSPAPERS AND MAGAZINES The main newspaper in Coyhaique, with news of the region, is *El Divisadero*. A good magazine available in most large towns (ie: Coyhaique, Puerto Aysén, Puerto Montt or in Chiloé) is *Destinos*, with cultural/culinary/touristic information of the southern region of Chile. Also available online at www.revistadestinos.cl.

WEBSITES
Maps

www.pdf-maps.com A mobile map application that enables you to download maps for offline use on your Apple iOS or Android smartphone or tablet. You can then use your device's built-in GPS to track your location on the map. Excellent maps for the walking trails between Chile Chico and Cochrane, including the Reserva Nacional Jeinemeni and Parque Patagonia. The cheap, downloadable PDF maps include a base map, contour lines, points of interest, trail information, elevation profile, campgrounds, educational content, and photography.

www.maps.com The Chilean Patagonia map features city inserts, up-to-date road details, campsites, national parks, hiking paths and trails as well as places of interest.

www.rutas.bienes.cl/?p=1144 Online trail map for the Palena to Lago Verde trek (page 121).

www.wikiexplora.com/index.php/Lago_Verde_-_Lago_Palena Online trail map and route description for the trail from Lago Palena to Lago Verde (part of Sendero de Chile; see box, page 121).

http://es.wikiloc.com/wikiloc/view.do?id=353802 Online trail map from Lago Verde to La Tapera (page 153).

Weather

www.meteochile.gob.cl Weather forecast for all larger towns and cities in Chile. This website has satellite images and a very good link to the opening hours and current state of border crossings.

News

www.aysenenlinea.cl
www.diarioaysen.cl/regional
www.eldivisadero.cl/home
www.radiosantamaria.cl
www.redaysen.com

Conservation

www.conaf.cl This is Chile's national park administration website. It contains maps and information about all its parks and reserves. The website is in Spanish with only the rules and regulations section also in English.

www.deepecology.org Covers a range of issues, but closely associated to the work of Doug and Kris Tompkins, major conservationists in southern Chile, thus of great relevance for those traversing the Carretera Austral.

Other conservation NGOs in the region:

www.anihuereserve.com/index.html Reserve protecting flora and fauna around Raúl Marín Balmaceda.

www.aumen.cl/blog NGO focused on nature conservation, scientific investigation and awareness raising regarding Aysén Province.

www.ciep.cl Scientific research centre focused on sustainable development of Aysén.

www.codeff.cl/somos/sedes/Aysén One of the first conservation NGOs in the region, active in campaigning for the protection of flora and fauna.

www.conservacionpatagonica.org Foundation behind the formation of Parque Patagonia.

www.fundacionpatagoniasur.cl Conservation foundation across southern Chile, protecting fragile ecosystems, promoting education and facilitating sustainable development.

www.parquekatalapi.cl A small park close to Puerto Montt offering workshops and courses related to nature.

www.patagoniasinrepresas.cl News on developments in the ongoing challenge to protect rivers in the region.

www.reforestemospatagonia.cl Environmental foundation focused on Chilean native forests.

www.theconservationlandtrust.org and **www.tompkinsconservation.org** Dedicated to the creation of national or provincial parks, protection of wildlife, land restoration and local development.

Tourism
www.horizonsunlimited.com Motorbikers' hub, with local contacts, routes, etc.

www.sernatur.cl The Ministry of Tourism website, with all contact details for local offices where maps, etc, are usually available.

http://theglobelovers.com/worldbiketour/carretera-austral-cycling-guide One of a number of blogs dedicated to cycling the Carretera Austral.

Index

Page numbers in **bold** indicate major entries; those in *italics* indicate maps

INDEX OF ADVERTISERS